UNVEILED

UNVEILED

One Woman's Nightmare in Iran

Cherry Mosteshar

ST. MARTIN'S PRESS
NEW YORK

UNVEILED: ONE WOMAN'S NIGHTMARE IN IRAN. Copyright © 1995 by Cherry Mosteshar. All rights reserved. Printed in the United States of America. No part of this book may be used or reproduced in any manner whatsoever without written permission except in the case of brief quotations embodied in critical articles or reviews. For information, address St. Martin's Press, 175 Fifth Avenue, New York, N.Y. 10010.

Library of Congress Cataloging-in-Publication Data

Mosteshar, Cherry.
Unveiled : one woman's nightmare in Iran / Cherry Mosteshar.
p.   cm.
ISBN 0-312-14061-4
1. Mosteshar, Cherry.   2. Women—Iran—Biography.
3. Women—Iran Social conditions.   4. Journalists—Iran—
Biography.   I. Title.
HQ1735.2.Z75M666   1996
305.4'092—dc20   [B]   95-45131   CIP

First published in Great Britain by Hodder & Stoughton

First U.S. Edition: March 1996
10   9   8   7   6   5   4   3   2   1

To Mummy, Mahmonir Pessian Mosteshar-Gharai

Contents

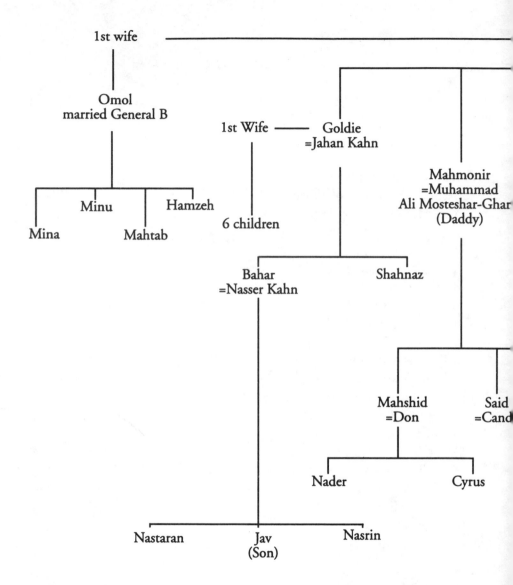

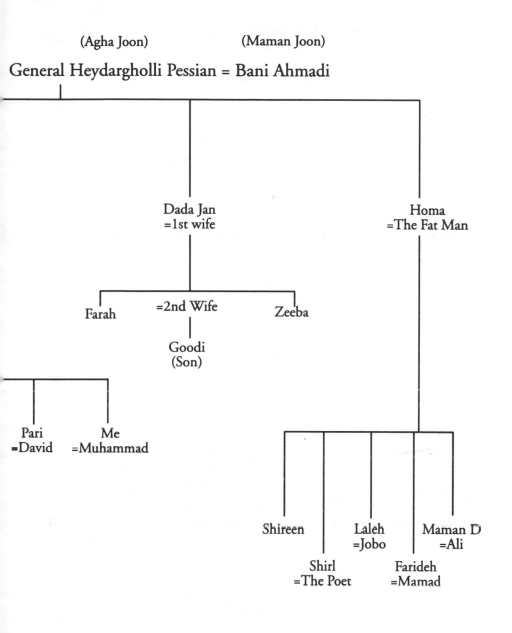

(Agha Joon)   (Maman Joon)

General Heydargholli Pessian = Bani Ahmadi

Dada Jan
=1st wife

Homa
=The Fat Man

Farah   =2nd Wife   Zeeba

Goodi
(Son)

Pari
=David

Me
=Muhammad

Shireen

Shirl
=The Poet

Laleh
=Jobo

Farideh
=Mamad

Maman D
=Ali

Acknowledgements

This book could not have been written without the support and encouragement of many wonderful people. Firstly, thanks to Sarah Bull and Julia Kaminski, two of the nicest women you could ever wish to count as friends, for the lunch and encouragement that set the ball rolling.

Thanks to my agent and friend, Cat Ledger, may Hugh Grant's thunderbolt never find its mark. A very special thanks to my editor, Humphrey Price, for treating my battered ego with such care and for understanding the heart of this book so fully.

Special thanks to Charles Spicer, my very charming U.S. editor, for working miracles and for his much appreciated confidence in me and this book. My warmest thanks to Katerina Christopoulos for her support, endless enthusiasm, and hard work.

Thanks to the long-suffering Linden Stafford who put up with all my trials and tribulations during the editing of the manuscript, and to Dawn Bates for all her hard work.

I would most particularly like to thank Ali Akbar Hashemi Rafsanjani, President of Iran and a wily old fox, for not putting me behind bars despite severe provocation. Thanks to Rupert Elvin for making me look glamorous, and to Nick Rawlinson, playwright and actor and far away more dishy than the aforementioned Grant, for giving me the the confidence to go out there and sell myself, and to all those who gave me support and encouragement through writing.

Thanks to my parents, Mahmonir and Muhammad Ali Mosteshar-Gharai, for teaching me that I had to be someone in my own right and for helping me through all the troubled times when I doubted that I could be. And to my sisters Mahshid and Pari, and my brother, Said, for their love and encouragement.

And last, but not least, my thanks and love to the Iranian people for whose suffering I weep.

The names, positions and my relationships with certain people in this book have been changed so that they cannot be identified. This is for the protection of the innocent and, more importantly, the guilty.

There is a place a mere five hours' flight from where I sit writing this book where I have a price, and that price is that of just half a man.

There is another world, a strange world where a man can kill me and escape execution unless my family pays to top up my worth to the price of a man.

If my father should die in this other world, I inherit one share to every two shares my brother gets. And if my husband dies I can expect only one-eighth of the life we built together.

There is a place, just five hours from here, where sons belong to their mother for only the first seven years of their lives.

There is a place where I am only half a witness in its courts.

There is a place where I need my father's permission to marry, no matter what my age.

There is a place where I need my husband's consent to get a passport and his agreement before I can travel.

There is a place, just five hours' flight from here, where I am but half a man.

Prelude

In Search of Paradise

All good Muslims go to heaven, of that there is no doubt. However, some get there more quickly than others. For most sinners there is a lengthy stopover in purgatory where they get a chance to cleanse themselves of those little transgressions that might block entry into God's garden. The length of the stay in purgatory depends on just how many Brownie points have been picked up in life or how swiftly surviving relatives can arrange for more plus points to be added to our score.

What constitutes cause for loss of points depends on exactly what arm of the Islamic Church you might be poised on. A bareheaded Bosnian woman may well expect her place in heaven if she upholds the pillars of the faith, while her nineties Iranian sister would be condemned to extra time in limbo for deliberately exhibiting a stray strand of hair.

For those who do not quite manage to perform all their daily prayers, a mullah or other holy person can be employed to say them instead of the deceased. Relatives can also pay someone to observe all those obligatory Ramadan fasts that might have slipped the deceased's mind or even to go to Mecca on the requisite pilgrimage on their behalf.

Martyrdom has grown in popularity over the centuries because of its properties as a get-out-of-purgatory-free card that qualifies the deceased and their close blood relatives to go straight to the golden gate; no stopover, no questions asked. Men who go to war for Islam are given a key – made in Taiwan – with which to unlock the gates should their maker take their lives. It is not unknown for mullahs to hold prayers on the front lines calling for the faithful who are about to fight to be blessed with the gift of martyrdom. Surviving the battle is considered to be the booby prize.

Martyrdom for the Islamic Republic of Iran can guarantee not only heavenly favours but terrestrial cash. Families are helped financially by the Martyrs' Foundation; they get free holidays to holy shrines in the Middle East, housing priority points, reserved places at university and company directorships; and widows even have the Marriage Foundation to find them a replacement husband.

Once gained, paradise is an enclosed garden where luxuriant trees and exotic fauna shelter the good and the pure from storm and tempest. For Muslim men here await unimaginable delights. Rivers flow through this Eden carrying milk, honey and wine – a delight to the drinkers – beside trees bearing the fruits of forgiveness. From these the saved can sip at their pleasure while they recline on silk-lined couches.

Abstinence during life is rewarded with excess of all the forbidden fruits for eternity.

Good Muslim men can look forward to having their every desire pandered to by seven wide-eyed houris – fairies – each and every one a spotless and perpetual virgin. These virgins are chastely amorous pearls whose one purpose is to compensate man for his labour on earth. Eternity is spent in dalliance with this 'perfectly formed' celestial harem.

A truly Islamic life should be spent in the pursuit of just one thing, a place in heaven. If Muslim men should gather earthly goods along the way, so much the better, for they have that much more to spend on gaining the treasures of the afterlife.

And what of the fate of all good Muslim women? While the menfolk sip of the pleasures of heaven from silver and crystal goblets, their women are given the privilege and pleasure of building the rest of heaven. There are no virginal boys to peel their grapes for them, nor are they encouraged to taste the pleasures of the rivers and the trees. However, the spotless virgins relieve the women of the arduous task of providing carnal satisfaction for the breadwinners.

Women's reward for a life of washing and cleaning and bearing children without fuss or complaint is to turn into builders, carpenters, painters and decorators. This is a privilege above that of their men, who just get to lounge about; women go on doing God's work beyond the grave.

Muslim scholars may dispute this view and apologists may claim that there is no reference to this in the Koran, but ask your average Muslim on the street and this is what he or she has been taught to expect for a life of virtue.

1

A Memory of Spring

I can still remember the day I first became an Iranian. This came as a bit of a shock after years of posing as a Persian. It was 1971 and I was in the lower fourth when Muhammad Reza Pahlavi, the Shah-an-Shah Aryamehr (the King of Kings and Light of the Aryans), decided to celebrate 2,500 years of the Persian monarchy. To do this he had chefs flown in from Maxime's, flowers brought in from greenhouses in the United States and designers summoned from Paris, Rome and Milan to dress the imperial ladies.

As world leaders gathered to mark the occasion at Persepolis, the capital of ancient Persia, the second Shah of the Pahlavi dynasty – considered by old families such as mine as upstarts – asked the world to call his nation by its native name, Iran.

Overnight he had turned wine into oil. The land of poets such as Hafiz and Saadi, who glorified wine, the rose and the enchanted nightingale, was transformed into the land of oil-wealthy jet-setters. An Iranian was a different creature altogether from the noble Persian. For one thing Iranians were forever being confused with Iraqis and other assorted Arabs. It is not a good idea to confuse the Aryan people of Iran with the Semitic Arabs. Make this mistake in front of your average Persian and you would have your shortcomings in the education department politely but ruthlessly pointed out. But an Iranian would be more likely to knock your head off.

As if this split between Iranian and Persian wasn't confusing enough for a simple Oxford girl such as myself, we were soon to be treated to yet another change: the Islamic revolution. Ayatollah

Ruhollah Khomeini again transformed us, but this time we became terrorists and murderers.

Perhaps it was the price we had to pay. Being Persian had been easy when few ordinary people in Britain knew exactly where it was – somewhere near Greece? Africa, isn't it? I was different and exotic and I loved it. Luckily I had been raised to think it desirable to be different and perhaps just a tad eccentric. I was in charge of the impression people had of me because I was their main source of information about Persia.

The Persia that I had grown up with – through stories told me by my parents – was a land where the women were strong and beautiful and the men were brave and honourable. People drove in grand carriages drawn by immaculate Arab steeds to magnificent balls, or they spent their time in defence of their kingdom in even grander wars. My Mother's roots in Georgia, Armenia and Azerbaijan, parts of the world that had belonged to the former Soviet Union, added to my conviction that I belonged on the pages of *War And Peace*.

There was a day, before the revolution in 1979, when I had been one of the richest young women on our street in wealthy North Tehran. With the coming of the Islamic state I was transformed into an evil Taghouti – the Koranic term for a rebel used as one of the names for Satan and later used by Ayatollah Khomeini to describe those who disobeyed his rule. I was marked as a traitor in my native Iran even before I had a chance to be anything other than my parents' rebellious youngest child. I say native, but I did little more than be born and almost die of worms there. Two years into my life I was whisked away to my new home in the land of the Little Satan. I have been trying, unsuccessfully, to return ever since.

In 1959 my Mother brought me to Britain with my sister Pari to join my Father, my brother Said and my eldest sister, Mahshid. Said was in hospital with a rotting gut and Mahshid was at boarding school where she had been sent to protect her from Iran's moral deterioration.

Fifteen years later, when my Father threw a young man out of the house for fondling my best friend at my birthday party, I imagined it was because we were Persians. Sitting at home while my friends did the pubs and clubs of Oxford, I imagined it was because I was an Iranian, as the world now insisted. Being a Persian in Oxford also meant no jewellery and no nylons until I was sixteen. It meant unplucked eyebrows and hairy legs until my eighteenth birthday and no heavy make-up until I was away from home at university. Because I am a Persian I have never smoked in front of my Father or my grandparents, I have never said no to orders from my much older siblings. Because I am a Persian I live at home when I am single or unemployed.

All this was because I am a Persian and a Muslim. So, believe me, it came as quite a shock to go back to Iran in 1970, at the age of thirteen, to discover cousins of the same age in make-up with plucked eyebrows and shaved legs and to find those just three years older than me going out with boyfriends and to parties alone.

But – and it's a big but – I had been taught to mix with men as if they were just women with more facial hair. I was made to drink in front of my parents so that I knew my limit and could not be led astray and taken advantage of. I was taken to the Moulin Rouge and to Las Vegas so that I could see the seedy side of life and never feel I was missing something or be vulnerable to being led astray. I was also taught that I had to work, because Work Maketh the Person, and it was something to do in order to improve your soul, not your bank balance. Mummy told me that I should feel sorry for my cousins in Iran who got married and never had to organise their own lives or earn their own living.

It struck me that being Iranian in Iran was a lot more fun than being Persian in Britain.

The only trouble with Iran, as far as I was concerned, was that they did insist on doing everything in Farsi, a language I was (and remain) particularly bad at. Now if they spoke English, French or even Arabic I would have had some chance of achieving my ambition to be Foreign Minister. But in Farsi it would take me the entire day just to read a simple memo about paper-clips. To my shame I had forgotten every last word of the classical Persian I read at Manchester University before I even sobered up from the post-finals party.

A ministerial post might have been out of my reach, but by the time I left school I had already decided to follow in the steps of my Aunt Goldie and my Mother's Uncle Naj, to change the world for the better by becoming a journalist. As luck would have it, there were some fine English-language newspapers in Tehran as well as an English service on the television. After much string-pulling I started my career in 1975 as a writer on the *Tehran Journal* and at the

National Iranian Radio and Television Service during a year off between school and university.

No matter what they chose to call themselves, the people of Iran are many things but never boring; we live on a canvas which is larger than life. A people of extremes, when we are down we are suicidal and when we are up we are euphoric. When we love we worship but when he hate we loathe with a passion. This duality is reflected in Iranian music, which can make you dance and cry at the same time. When we feel like a bit of exercise and a good cry, as one does, we just pop on the latest by singers such as Satar, Iran's answer to George Michael. But for getting really, really depressed Golpayagani, a sort of Leonard Cohen with a good voice, is the real McCoy. When, as a teenager, I was diagnosed as a manic-depressive I responded: 'No, I'm just Iranian.' Two years later there was a revolution and the world began to see my point.

Shia Islam is rich in tales of brave battle, glorious martyrdom and mystical revelation. My family reflected this tradition. My forefathers had exercised power over this land; they had fought and died for it. But they were also Sufis and philosophers and we were brought up to believe in the duty incurred by privilege. Surely it was in the land of my illustrious ancestors that I could make sense of who and what I was.

My first memory of defending my country's honour was at the tender age of seven. I was at St Philip and St James's School in Oxford, and a Greek boy a couple of years older than me, with particularly gungy ears (which I discovered after poking him in the ear after some offence against my nation only to find my finger covered with green slime), had claimed that the Persians were defeated by the Greeks because we were inferior warriors. Like an avenging angel I leapt upon him from my vantage point on the steps to the school chapel. I still remember with some pride that on this occasion history was reversed.

I have been defending Iran ever since. From childhood I was taught that family and country came before all else. My Mother's family had a long history of military leaders dying for their country. Colonel Muhammad Taghi Pessian, my grandfather's cousin, is a national hero. He had opposed the then Reza Khan, later to become the first Pahlavi Shah, when it was clear that he was to betray the ideals that had inspired the coup that removed the Qajars from the Peacock Throne. The colonel was beheaded after a failed uprising, and to this day he is worshipped in many areas of Iran. There were those who still say the colonel should, and could, have seized the throne for himself. But we Pessians are republicans.

I loved my Mother's stories of her childhood. There were parties in gold and mirror-lined ballrooms where the guests arrived in carriages that wound up a drive lit by crystal gas chandeliers. It was the Middle East but it came straight out of *War And Peace* – stories of beautiful ladies and dashing young officers. These people served Reza Shah and his ill-fated son, but they never accepted the new dynasty.

Iran, the land of the trader and the corrupt official, lacked the glamour of our parents' lives. I remembered very little of the world we had left behind, but my eldest cousin Bahar could still recall hiding to watch parties where women arrived iridescent in silks, furs and diamonds.

Looking back I now realise that the only Iranians I had ever really known were either people like myself, brought up in the West and too wealthy ever to feel the need to question the meaning of the universe, or our servants, who tended to tell us what we wanted to hear. Perhaps there had always been a sad and devout nation hidden away from the Imperial Country Club and the night clubs. The men and women who were my kin wore Valentino and Dior, had homes in Paris and Rome and Los Angeles, and spoke Persian mixed with more than the odd word of French and German. Those like my family spent their winters in massive homes in the best parts of Tehran and their summers in palatial villas in the north. They were brought up by nannies and received their early education from governesses flown in from Paris and Berlin. Their men were educated at military academies in Europe and Russia and later in the USA, before returning to govern.

General Hydargholi Pessian (Agha Joon), my maternal grandfather, and several of his six brothers had been trained at a German military academy, and he had fought in the German army during the First World War. They came back with Western ideas that had no place in a still very traditional society. When Agha Joon was shot and wounded on an inspection tour of the north, it was feared that Reza Shah was trying to remove this thorn in his side. The first Pahlavi Shah was afraid that my grandfather would follow his cousin and lead a rebellion among the army.

Agha Joon ('Grandfather Dear') had opposed the excesses of Reza Shah ever since Reza Khan declared himself as monarch rather than a democratically elected head of state. For some time the Shah had been looking for an excuse to put my grandfather in prison, and he finally found it when Agha Joon refused to hand over the family home – known as the Pessian Palace – to the Shah. Agha Joon had refused the Shah's offer to take over the house by writing a letter assuring the monarch that 'the day I find a better place to house my family, Your Majesty is welcome to everything I leave behind'.

Agha Joon would be considered progressive even today. He produced women with their sights far above the domestic. When Agha Joon went to prison in 1936, General Amir Ahmadi (Dayee Jan), his brother-in-law, had asked him to turn over control of the children to him. My grandfather had replied that he had no control over his wife or children, they were people in their own right, and he could not turn over something he did not have.

Agha Joon's refusal to give the charge of his family to Dayee Jan enraged Maman Joon, who worshipped her brother, now Interior Minister, and was eager to check the independent ways of the young girls. Maman Joon and her Mother, Khanoum Maman ('Lady Mother'), resolved to marry off the girls before they could go astray. Auntie Goldie defied all attempts to marry her off and found her own husband, Jahan Khan. Mummy fell in love with my father and refused all sorts of Middle Eastern princes and Iranian nobles. Finally she threatened suicide if her parents did not give their consent. She was married at sixteen. The two remaining sisters, Omol and Homa, were handed over to primitive men who wielded authority over them.

Mummy brought up her daughters to be strong and independent. As a child I would love to hear the sayings of Agha Joon, especially when he argued that society should be such that a girl could walk naked into a barracks of soldiers and come out with her virginity intact rather than be forced to cover herself. Maman Joon had been treated like a partner, not a dependant, by her husband. She continued her studies, she spoke French and German, had a personal fitness coach and was not expected to have anything to do with the running of the home. When a cook had made the mistake of asking her what to make for dinner, Agha Joon had chastised the woman, saying that if he had wanted his wife to worry about such things he wouldn't have employed a household staff.

The full-length veil called the *chador* and the segregation of the sexes were something lost in history, a magical world that Khanoum Maman had lived in but with little relevance to me several generations down the enlightened road. I did not realise that there was a school of thought that still believed that the only way to preserve a girl's virginity was to keep her under lock and key. Reza Shah, a foul-mouthed yob if my great-uncle is to be believed, had banned the veil in 1935 when my Mother was only twelve years old. Many still remember with fear the patrols that were sent to roam the streets, pulling off the *chadors* of those women who defied the law.

To mark the new law the Shah threw a grand ball where the Mothers, wives, sisters and daughters of the rich and powerful were to parade themselves without Islamic trappings. Many of those who attended had already abandoned the veil, considering it something for the uneducated and the elderly. Maman Joon remembers that ball with sly pleasure. Dayee Jan had come to check her appearance before they left. 'He said he had just one thing to tell me, and that was to keep away from General Z's son,' Maman Joon recalls. 'And he was right. He was the sort of man who would tell you that your powder smelt nice.'

She also remembers her male Swedish personal trainers whose sole job was to reduce her ample figure in readiness to go forth into the streets unveiled. Girls do not have to wear the veil until they are nine, so at twenty-eight Maman Joon had hardly worn it before it was banned.

My Mother was taught all the womanly skills of cooking, sewing and giving orders to the houseful of servants, but she had also been taught how to manage the household finances, spending many hours with the estate manager and his books. When she was fourteen Agha Joon had a little shop built into the wall of their summer home, known to all in the northern district of Shemiran as the Pessian Palace. Mummy was supplied with pencils and notebooks to sell to the children who passed by on their way to school, in case she would ever need the skills to earn a living. She and her sisters learned to ride, spoke four languages and mostly achieved high academic grades. They had tennis courts and swimming pools in the grounds of their home and were coached by the best teachers money could import.

Said, my brother, was to be the only son among the offspring of both my parents' siblings for many years and was thus precious beyond imagining. An infection from the instrument used to snip his umbilical cord left my brother's intestines and stomach weakened and rotting. When he was thirteen the frail innards finally gave in and his veins started popping. So in 1959 my father rushed the boy to a hospital in England while my Mother travelled to Mahshad, the capital of Khorasan province in north-eastern Iran, to pray at the shrine of Imam Reza.

This was the second holiest spot in Shia Islam, and one of my father's cousins was a trustee of the shrine. With such connections we were treated to a private meeting with the dead Imam after the riff-raff had been cleared out. I was only two years old but it is my most vivid memory of Iran. The place sparkled like Aladdin's cave as I waited in the courtyard at midnight. The shrine's golden dome glittered in the spotlights which were reflected in the fountains adorning the courtyards. I was fascinated by the glimmering shrine and as my Mother prayed I studied the reflection of the candles that lit the mausoleum as they twinkled off the mirror-lined walls. I was dumbfounded at the thought that beyond the silver-trellised tomb to which my Mother clung and prayed there was the body of a God – or so I imagined. Imam Reza was in fact a descendant of Hazrat Ali, the founder of the Shia faith.

The miracle was granted: the bleeding eased enough for the surgeons to operate on Said's stomach. That night I spoke to God, although I had no idea who he was, through the Imam. I just knew that he would always take care of me and my family if I was kind to others and never did anything that would hurt another human being or that was not honourable. I still turn to Imam Reza in moments of pain and worry, and he has never let me down.

Soon afterwards we were off to England, where we intended to stay for a few weeks. But we stayed for ever; Mummy never wanted to be that far away from a good hospital again. Once Said was out of hospital – some six months later – we moved to Oxford where my cousin Hamzeh was studying.

Father returned to Iran, and we started to learn to live without sunshine. England was a dose of reality compared to the life we had led in Iran. Instead of waking up to a choice of two pools behind the tall walls that kept the rest of the world out, we would be down at the municipal baths with real people. It wasn't until I went to university in Manchester that I realised how in North Oxford I was almost as far from real people as I'd been in Iran. In Iran I had been treated and lived like a princess, and in England I was still kept apart from real people by the chauffeur-driven Rolls-Royce that took me to school – and a public school at that. We had been 'old money' and after a short difficult spell in the sixties were again living the life of privilege.

At thirteen, sipping champagne in First Class next to the obligatory SAVAK agent, I was on the way 'home' to what I imagined would be a fairyland. I cried as I stepped out of the aircraft and felt the warm embrace of Iran, welcoming me home.

There followed many summer holidays with Iran's jet-set. But I came to despise a way of life that called for designer clothes and prestigious marriages. Admittedly I was not a great authority on Iran beyond court circles. By the time I returned to work in Iran for a year between school and university, in 1975, the only national dress I was aware of was the Chanel suit. I saw little of what ordinary people went through. Our chauffeur would drop me off outside the television centre at 5 a.m. At noon I would usually grab a rushed lunch of caviar and champagne at the Imperial Country Club, where I would pontificate on the agony of people I had glimpsed *en route*.

I arrived at interviews for my afternoon job in a car with court number-plates, a concession granted to my father by the Shah's stepmother. This was guaranteed to inspire something less than full honesty in the interviewee. Once the article was written my father's secretary would type it up and the house boy would deliver it. On the occasions I got the urge to actually go to the paper I would hide in the owners' office. My masterpieces exposing corruption and greed would appear the next day full of praise for George – as we called the Shah in conversation for fear of being overheard and beheaded.

Despite falling out with the censors at the paper, or perhaps because of it, I was offered a job as a television producer. Before I could take it I had to go back to England and get my degree. As I left the station on my last day I jokingly said to my mentor: 'Behave yourself while I am away. If you fall out with the Shah

I'll be jobless.' He was one of the first against the wall when the revolution came.

The 1980s brought Mrs Thatcher's Little England mentality, while a new ingredient was added to this schizophrenic hotchpotch of identities: militant Islam.

We had always taken our Muslimness for granted. Islam was a culture before it was a theology. But the Islam I served in 1979 – progressive, socialist, liberating and above all compassionate – was, it turned out, only a figment of my imagination. The more people in England came to know about the Middle East, the more I began to feel an alien. As the eighties progressed, I was turning into a terrorist stereotype.

*   *   *

I grew to know my family mainly through stories and brief summer visits. Of all the relatives who came to stay with us in Oxford over the years, my cousin Bahar was my favourite.

I first met Bahar – whose name meant spring – when I was nine. Into my childhood world walked this ray of sunshine, carrying her crippled son lovingly in her arms. Even then I realised that there was something of a mismatch between this vivacious girl and her elderly, terminally serious husband.

Bahar was everything her name implied: she was spring, she was renewal and she was desire. She struggled her entire life to hold on to joy despite the pain and tragedy that came her way. Her flawed heart had laboured since birth to fuel the spirit that thrilled at beauty and refused to be defeated. Her adult life was spent in planning her escape from a life that was smothering her.

She loved to shop, and I still covet those wonderful, thigh-high patent-leather boots she bought on the King's Road in London in the sixties. I remember her skipping around our house singing, 'There are a thousand men in my life, and all eat Shredded Wheat', improving the words of a television advertisement of the time that had settled for a mere two men.

I know she loved her two daughters, but she hid it well. The girls were dragged around Europe with her every summer, the elder one clearing up after her disorderly Mother, constantly reminding Bahar that they were about to miss a train or run out of money or time.

'Who cares?' Bahar would laugh as she threw back her russet hair and went back to concentrating on applying her false eyelashes and painting bright-red lips.

We had just visited our tenth boutique after a morning tour of London's art galleries when suddenly Bahar turned a purple-blue colour. Her veins were bulging as if they were going to break through her delicate, marble-white skin.

Bahar flopped on the pavement, struggling for breath. 'Ho, ha, ha, ha,' she said, desperately trying to make happy noises so as not to alarm those around her. We knew she could die at any moment, but somehow she always survived, the strength of her spirit overcoming the frailty of her body.

Bahar's Mother, my Aunt Goldie, had been a liberated woman before the term had been invented. When as a child Goldie had been asked to help the maid clear the table – ladies must learn to do what they instruct their staff to perform – she had dropped the lot in full view of her father and the entire family. Later that night my Mother went to comfort her sister. 'I'm not upset; I did it on purpose,' Goldie told her shocked sister. 'If I had done it right they might have asked me to do it again, and I have more important things to do than housework.' She was never asked to clear the table again.

At twelve she had already written her first novel, and at sixteen she had it published in Iran and in Europe. By her twenties she had made her name as a journalist – under a male pseudonym. Her work was spotted by another novelist and newspaper editor, Jahan Khan, who asked to meet the talented young man whose outspoken articles had set intellectual Iran talking. He had intended to offer the man a job, but he fell in love with the golden blonde who presented herself at his office, and he offered her a wedding ring instead.

Jahan Khan, a writer whose romantic novels had outraged polite Tehran society, had fallen deeply and madly in love. There was just one tiny problem: he had another wife and five children. He hounded Goldie until she agreed to marry him, but only on one condition – that he did not divorce his first wife. So Auntie became a second wife and produced two daughters, Bahar and Shahnaz. As their parents pursued their careers the two sisters were brought up by their maternal grandmother, Maman Joon. The marriage lasted fifteen years; Auntie Goldie gave birth to two stillborn sons and finally gave up the struggle of being Muslim wife and career woman at the same time.

After their parents divorced, the girls went to live with their father and step-family, as is the norm in Iran. This turned Bahar's life upside-down, for in her grandmother's home she had been the little princess, the apple of Maman Joon's eye. Now she was a stranger in someone else's home and found that she could no longer get her own way. Shahnaz had mostly been ignored in her grandmother's home, and remained ignored in her new home.

The spoilt child grew into a truly feminine woman. A flutter of the false eyelashes would reduce the toughest male to jelly. Like her Mother, Bahar was talented and headstrong. Unlike her Mother, who was blessed with a progressive father, Bahar was not allowed to go her own way. Before she could grow and discover her true self, her prince was found to keep her in line.

The prince, Nasser Khan, was twenty years her senior and represented everything that Bahar was not. He was grossly serious and painfully orthodox. But he was a prince and thus a highly suitable husband – never mind that they did not have a single thing in common. Nasser Khan was seen as the perfect antidote to her flighty spirit. Bahar was given to a man who could tie the dreamer to the earth, who could tame the wild heart and dampen the reckless spirit. He was solemn where she was animated, pious where she was mystical and wooden where she was bewitching.

Having won a bride who was lovely beyond his wildest dreams, the prince without an empire set about the task of breaking her. His young wife's breasts were too small, her hips were too boyish, her cooking was bad, and so on. When she gave birth to a brain-damaged son, it was of course her fault. Wasn't she, after all, the one with a bad heart?

Little Jav became the centre of his Mother's life. A lesser woman would have taken refuge in depression, the route chosen by our Aunt Homa in her flight from a bleak marriage, but she chose to fight back. She almost dared life to destroy her, knowing that she was on borrowed time. In her late twenties she had assured my Mother in that devil-may-care way of hers that she would never live to see fifty. Two weeks before that deadline she would follow her son to the grave. Bahar had never looked at Jav's death, when he was twelve, as a tragedy. Instead she rejoiced that he was free of the stiff body that had trapped him in life. Yet was something missing from her smile?

She was a gypsy, constantly craving new stimulus and adventure. Denied fulfilment inside her marriage she looked for it outside. Somewhere along the way she had fallen in love with one of the intellectuals she had come to admire while growing up. She gave her heart to a poet, to ease the strain of being told constantly that she had failed as a wife and as a woman.

The last straw in her relationship with her husband came as she lay in hospital half dead from the pressure of giving birth to their first child. The couple had a maid who lived in a basement room with her ten-year-old son. While Bahar was away the woman had committed suicide by eating rat poison. Soon the scandal-mongers spread the word that the woman was the prince's mistress and the boy his son. They claimed that the prince had had a row with the woman that day and had returned to find her in a coma on the floor, and that he had left her to die. The boy never recovered from the shock of finding his dead Mother nor the sexual abuse he suffered in the orphanage he was sent to after the suicide.

I doubt very much that the prince had it in him to have a mistress or to stand by while she died. But the scandal was damaging, and Bahar lost all hope in her life with him and finally gave in to the poet's advances. The poet courted her relentlessly and Bahar played the game with exquisite delicacy, giving enough to tantalise but not enough to quench his thirst. He was also old enough to be her father but talented enough not to need to compete with or resent her potential. The trapped bird talked of a day when her daughters would leave to live their own lives and she could be free to follow the example of her own Mother.

Goldie, after her divorce, communicated with the rest of us through endless telephone calls or hilarious letters. I adored her and can still hear her voice with its slight quiver as she called me her 'Little Sunshine'. Once Shahnaz had been accepted at university, Goldie had her back to live with her for a few years. The girl picked up her Mother's reclusive ways but also learnt that women can live on intellect and career alone. The two women lived happily and privately and uproariously, as was illustrated by the incident of the night caller.

Auntie Goldie lived in a massive house on a road named after her father. The thieves who chose to try their hand in her home that night must have thought they had it easy – a house crammed with goodies and with no men to protect it. The two-man team crept in during the early hours and as one started to clear the downstairs the other went to the second floor in search of jewels.

Auntie loved her food and often took a nice little snack to bed with her. That night she had left the remains of a small feast of bread, cheese and jam on the table in her dressing-room. The hapless burglar stopped to fill his stomach. As he was munching away a great mass leapt upon his shoulders and sank its teeth into his neck. It was my aunt. The thief fought back for dear life as Shahnaz watched, shouting: 'Shall I get the scissors, Mummy, shall I give you the scissors so that you can dig his eyes out?'

The struggle went on for more than half an hour. Now the man got the upper hand, then Auntie pinned him down again. Finally Goldie picked the exhausted man up in her arms and flung him from the window. The next day the impression of his body could still be seen in the earth under the window.

Women such as Goldie and Shahnaz, who went on to be a political analyst at Tehran University, brought about change in a society that was at least moving forward under the last Persian monarch. Before the revolution there had been at least the illusion of change, and these women believed that they were on a one-way road to becoming liberated people rather than chattels.

As for Bahar, no matter how painful life was within her home, known to us as the House of Gloom, she never lost hope of better days around the corner. We would sit on the step that separated her sitting-room from her dining-room and try to get the ancient gramophone working, while Bahar fantasised about the life she could have had if she had married one of Iran's playboy millionaires. 'If you are going to sleep around you should be sure to do it with class,' she would giggle.

The smell of rose-water still reminds me of Bahar. I can still see her huddled on her bed surrounded with balls of cotton wool, dabbing away the day's accumulated make-up and planning a life on the Riviera.

2

End of the Old Order

When Woody Allen wrote that comedy was 'tragedy plus time' he could have been talking about my numerous attempts to return to my homeland. Some of the most devastating events now seem hilariously funny – with a little help from the certain knowledge that I have survived.

As Khomeini's Children rose to remove the Shah, Grandmother's cousin, Field Marshal Reza Khan, occupied the top job at the War Ministry. Unlike Dayee Jan Amir Ahmadi, Maman Joon's brother, who had earned himself a reputation as a ruthless commander, Field Marshal Reza had urged the Shah not to open fire on the demonstrators.

I had longed for the revolution, but when it came it brought repulsion at the horror of the executions that followed it. I watched from the safety of my flat during my final year at Manchester, as people I had known from childhood were displayed in the morgue. The dream of freedom had turned into a nightmare. My Father was condemned as a CIA agent, and my personal fortune was confiscated. Members of my extended family went into hiding, and some went to the notorious Evin prison.

As it seemed that I was losing my homeland, the urge increased to go and become a part of its future. There were, however, a couple of problems. My inability to fully master the language has had Iranians falling about with hysterical laughter every time I open my mouth. Add to this a strong English accent and slightly Armenian features and you can see that the odds are stacked against me.

The arrival of the mullahs and Mrs Thatcher in the same year rocked both my worlds. Iran seemed to be becoming a satellite of the Arab world while Britain was in danger of becoming the newest state of the union soon to be presided over by Ronald Reagan. Both countries were rebuilt in the image of their new leaders. The mullahs murdered one world while Thatcher mutilated the other. Then the mullahs went too far: they had the audacity to seize my extensive property in Iran. I had been richer as a teenager than anyone who has not done a good day's work in their life had a right to be. And of course I had been sensitive enough to feel frightfully guilty about it all. Now I found myself under attack.

It was very hard for me to believe that my Persia was changing so radically, despite the images of the revolution on television. Was it really possible that anything, even the mullahs, could break the Persian spirit? Surviving a history of aggression and subjugation, the Persians had emerged from their ancient history with their identity and spirit intact. The coming of Islam had forced the Zoroastrian Persians into a dual world of paying lip-service to the Arab faith in public and revering their fire-god in private. When Islam split, however, Persians embraced the Shia branch and became its leaders. As Khomeini took control of my country I was still convinced that the Persian love of wine, women and song would triumph over the new-found enchantment with the pulpit.

I was anything but enchanted, especially as the condemnation of my Father led to my becoming one of the nouveaux poor. My cut of the family cash had been invested in property shared with Baba, my Father. It was this that was now taken into the care of the Islamic Republic. My parents had separated three years before the revolution, and Baba disappeared from our lives. By the time Khomeini had his day in Iran I felt completely adrift, my family and my two countries having changed suddenly and dramatically.

The first glimpse I got of the land of Cyrus and Darius after it seemed to have been overrun yet again by a new wave of Muslim hordes, led by Khomeini, was early in 1980. Despite the coming of the Ayatollahs, floozies such as I could still roam the streets unveiled, if we had skins hard enough to protect us against the occasional 'Die, slut' from a passing Sister of Zahra, the women fighters of Islam who covered themselves with the *chador* which has come to symbolise Iranian womanhood.

Iran was first converted to Islam in the seventh century, but it wasn't until the sixteenth century, under the Safavids, that Islam became the official state religion. Since then Shia Islam had remained the state religion and subsequent monarchs ruled in varying forms of partnership with the mullahs. But Reza Shah had started the move towards a secular state with all power resting in the hands of the crown rather than shared with the turban.

The once Marxist-Islamic revolution had been hijacked by the extreme right and any hope of real democracy was fading fast. Khomeini had promised to retire to Qom, a holy city, but he didn't appear to be in a great hurry to do so. Yet there were still those who hoped the country would sort itself out. Many believed that, once the people had worked through their anger, the summary executions would stop and the mullahs would retire to mosques, leaving intellectuals and democrats to build a free, secular state. But Khomeini's Children started to turn on each other as they competed for control. The university campuses became the front line where the war between the fundamentalists and the intellectuals was being fought out.

Our home had been raided and every last piece of underwear taken for the oppressed. A minister slept in my parents' bed and his children swam in our pool. So the return was strange, with Mummy and me having to live in another person's house for the first time. This was the first of three very unhappy stays in the House of Gloom.

Bahar's home life was in as much turmoil as was our nation. She had finally decided to separate her bedroom from that of her colourless prince. Nasser Khan took the opportunity of having two of her aunts captive in his house – Auntie Homa had come up from Shiraz – to complain about his wife's refusal to fulfil her sexual duties. It was all very embarrassing for a still fairly naïve twenty-three-year-old. I could not understand how Bahar could find sex with her husband so repulsive after so many years of marriage and three children.

Many years later I was to learn that husbands can rape their wives and that a man who gets up to perform his ritual cleansing every time he touches you can make you feel like a dirty whore. Islam as Iranians practise it dictates that any sexual arousal or intercourse must be followed immediately by a washing and prayer ritual.

The saga of the piano teacher's lover changed the balance of life in Bahar's household. The revolution was just one year old. Living in God's Republic had already challenged our grip on reality but the story of the lover plunged us into an episode of *Dallas*.

Broken by the collapse of the system that had given him power and position, Nasser Kahn, who had been a senior security official under the Shah, had retreated to wait for the CIA to restore the old order. Nasser Khan was tall, with striking features, light-green eyes and sandy-coloured hair. But there was something woolly about him, something that made you think he would topple over if you blew in his direction. Nasser Khan's body, although fit, was twenty years older than his wife, while his mind was a century behind. He lived by the clock, waking at the same time each day, going through all his religious duties, eating by the clock, napping by the clock and having sex by the clock, unable to vary his schedule no matter what crisis was going on around him. As he became enfeebled by his fall from power, Bahar gained the upper hand for the first time in their tortured marriage.

At first Bahar was invigorated by the upheavals of the revolution. The man who had ruled over her was now putty in her hands. With her daughters Nastaran and Nasrin increasingly able to run the house, Bahar was taking more time for herself. She was a talented artist and had started to concentrate on developing her skills as an artist and piano player. By the 1980s she was getting more and more commissions for her portraits, and we saw less of her than ever as she escaped to her studio. But the strict moral regime being imposed by the mullahs meant that in some areas of life and behaviour her husband had a new power over her.

Most of Bahar's days started with a piano lesson before she went to her artist's studio where her tutor would supervise her work. She would paint most of the day, getting back to supervise meals. Her piano teacher was a middle-aged divorced woman who, despite the mullahs' back-to-basics campaign, kept a young lover. It was from this woman's home that Bahar contacted her poet, now exiled in the States, sometimes talking for several hours a day. What she did not realise was that the piano teacher's lover was listening in.

Why the piano teacher finally threw out her lover we never knew, but the young man, now deprived of his meal ticket, saw a chance to get some easy cash by blackmailing Bahar. He had managed not only to record one of her calls but to get his hands on a telephone bill listing all the numbers called from the house. This he would give to Nasser Khan unless he got his cash.

Left to herself, Bahar would have handed over the list herself. She had never cared for her husband, and as he got older she was more repulsed by him. To his credit, Nasser Khan had bought a substantial amount of property in the name of his wife and his daughters, so finally Bahar had some independence. Her Mother's death the previous year had also added to her fortunes and thus to her freedom. But Bahar had tolerated too many years of pain to throw in her marriage so easily, and she cared dearly about how society viewed her girls, who were still dependent on their Father. The scandal would have been bad enough but it would also have left her liable to imprisonment or even stoning if adultery was proved under the new strict Islamic laws. If nothing else the scandal would have ruined the girls' chances of getting into an Islamic university. Only the good, or at least the pious, were given places in the institutions of the revolution.

The lover's persistence, phoning Bahar at the House of Gloom and demanding not only money but also her assistance in mending fences with the piano teacher, forced her to confide in Auntie Homa, who was up from Shiraz to see my Mother. Bahar and Homa were very close and shared their secrets, their hopes and their fears. My Mother was somewhat stricter in her views on what was permissible within marriage and so she was shielded from the details of the blackmail. Nevertheless we were all going crazy, leaping up to answer the phone before Nasser Khan got to it.

Our nerves were well and truly on edge. Bahar stayed home more, and when she went out someone else was assigned the task of 'telephone patrol'. So we jumped at an absence by Nasser Khan to go on one of our tours of Tehran trouble spots, leaving the telephone to ring in the empty house. Not having found any excitement, we stopped near the Majlis (Parliament) for a snack at one of the many downtown sandwich bars that sell delicious food.

As usual Bahar's hair refused to be confined under a scarf and it flowed out at every point. A month earlier she had been sitting waiting at a red light when a man in the next car had motioned for her to pull her scarf over her cascading hair. She had motioned back for him to mind his own business. The man turned out to be a plain-clothes morals cop and Bahar found herself at the notorious Evin prison. Evin was where first the Shah and then the mullahs tortured and killed their opponents. They had kept Bahar in a cell with several hundred other women. As she gasped for breath, and was faced with disappearing into the prison system without her heart medicine, she gave in and signed a confession that she had worked as a prostitute. She was released the next morning into her husband's care.

While we waited for our sandwiches to be brought out, a gaggle of mullahs stepped out on to the road in front of us. As we jumped into action, checking that we were covered and Islamic, I was awestruck at the sight of real live revolutionary mullahs deep in conversation less than three metres away from us. Then the group parted, and there directly before us was my friend Raffers, otherwise known as Ali Akbar Hashemi Rafsanjani, the man destined to be President, although I didn't know then that I would grow to like the man. Then he was merely the Speaker of the Majlis, a senior mullah – the enemy – and he was standing right in our sights. I saw Bahar's hand move from her scarf to the ignition; the car slowly coughed into life.

'We can get him,' Bahar said softly. 'A push on the gas and we could destroy one of them,' she snarled.

For a moment it seemed possible, even honourable; then reality flooded back as the girls started to beg their Mother not to do it. As Raffers stood poised between a life that would make him the nation's most powerful man and death under the wheels of an ancient, crumbling Peugeot, I saw a pain I had never seen before behind Bahar's eyes.

'Think of the girls,' I told her. 'They will be taken in with us – you'll destroy their lives.' The engine revved slowly but she hesitated long enough for a brand-new Mercedes-Benz to draw up, and in seconds the future President was whisked away. I was drenched with a sweat that had nothing to do with the heat.

One cannot help but feel sympathy for those mullahs who still have to drive rust-buckets or to use public transport while they struggle along roads chock-a-block with luxury cars ferrying their more powerful revolutionary brethren about their new domain.

That evening Bahar disappeared, returning several hours later to assure us that she had sorted out her little telephone problem. After that she again felt free to go about her routine and her order book filled with commissions for portraits. Having gone blonde and lost mounds of fat, I fancied being immortalised in oils, and Bahar started my portrait a couple of days after making her peace with the piano teacher's lover. It was in the middle of one of these sittings that Bahar was seized by crippling stomach cramps. She took to her bed that night with a severe headache.

For the next two days she treated herself from a drugs cupboard that would have put most hospitals to shame. A nurse was called to administer injections while Bahar issued orders from her bed. But by the third day she could no longer talk and we called in a doctor, although her headache and stiff neck were enough to tell us that she should get to a hospital and get there soon. Easy to say but not so easy to do.

By the time we got a taxi – Nasser Khan refused to drive – it was already late in the afternoon. There then followed a mystery tour of all the Tehran hospitals, but none of them would give Bahar a bed. Mother and Auntie Homa then got to work on the phone to every contact they had in Tehran. By midnight we had her safely in a bed in one of the first hospitals we had visited that terrible day. Meningitis was diagnosed and we were sent on a search around first the chemists and hospitals and finally the black market for the drugs that would save Bahar.

Through several days when it was touch and go for his wife, Nasser Khan went about his daily routine as ever, merely adding a visit to the hospital into his afternoon, post-nap programme. This did nothing to increase my sympathy for him. But looking back on it I can see that he wasn't an evil man – in fact he is not only courteous but kind; but he really could not deviate from the straight line that he had drawn for his life. He could not adapt to the changes in his public or private lives – that is his tragedy.

Her aunts and sister took turns at staying with Bahar in hospital, as in Iran it is normal for the nursing to be done by a 'companion'. About a week after Bahar was admitted to hospital, Homa came home after a hard night's shift at the hospital to find Nasser Khan on the telephone, his eyes like those of a drunkard, although he did not drink. He had in front of him a list of telephone numbers. Why the jilted lover had carried out his threat we will never know, but it thrust us into what was at times farce but mostly nightmare as Nasser Khan pursued his prey.

Nasser Khan finally had something to occupy him. Spending every free moment at the phone, he hardly ate or slept but just dialled and dialled. Those at the other end of his calls were greeted with: 'Hassan – who is he? Where is he? What is he?' Having tried all the numbers, exhausting the list using the code for Los Angeles, he started using random codes, sometimes reaching Idaho, sometimes Mogadishu. We could hear him through the night: 'Who is Hassan?'

It was a tragic sight, an old man daily growing older and more broken and ever more demented. There was no attempt to work out which was the correct telephone number; he just dialled any number and harangued whoever replied. We were trapped in a madhouse, our nerves already in shreds; Nasser Khan's ranting and raving was unbearable.

We were sitting quietly trying to watch television when Nasser Khan emerged from his room. Unshaven and dishevelled, he raised his arms to heaven and screamed: 'Allah, kill her! I want to see her dead! Don't let her survive!' This did not do much to make us feel welcome in his home, and it didn't help the mental state of the girls whose Mother was fighting for her life. Yet no matter how angry Nasser Khan became at home he would dutifully trot up to the hospital at the same time every day. There he would sit beside his wife, kissing her hand and treating her like the love of his life.

For several days we were certain that Bahar would die. She had been in a coma when she was admitted to hospital, her heart was already bearing too much strain and her spirit seemed drained. Then one day the phone in her room rang. She talked for less than two minutes in her low, delicate and much-weakened voice. When she put down the receiver she was a woman reborn. It had been her poet calling from Los Angeles, and it was the breath of life to Bahar. From that moment she fought back, growing stronger every day.

Her poet had been one of the most influential broadcasters in Iran before the revolution but he had always kept firmly on both sides of the fence so that while the last regime tolerated him the new could not find any crime with which to destroy him. He was finally driven out of Iran by his cook, a man who had grown up in the poet's household and who had become a leading member of a local Komiteh after the coming of the mullahs. The Komitehs, the Imam Committees, had sprung up in every neighbourhood in

26

Iran in a matter of weeks after the return from exile of Ayatollah Khomeini in February 1979. Their job was to arrest local rich people and to impose the new Islamic standards on the populace. As few knew what these new standards were, the Komitehs were very busy. They depended on informants to point out the 'local tyrants' (as the rich were now known). One woman we had been friendly with was arrested and later shot after her maid told the Komiteh that the Empress Farah had attended her daughter's wedding and had given the bride a large diamond as a gift.

The poet's cook had apparently had only one desire: to own the house he had been brought up in. The two men had imagined themselves friends before the revolution, but afterwards the poet became the oppressive master and the cook the oppressed servant. This oppressed servant would arrive at the poet's door nightly, accusing him repeatedly of one trumped-up charge after another. Finally the poet could take no more, terrified that having failed to get him arrested the cook would stage a shooting, a common way in those days of removing those the courts could not convict. The poet was smuggled to the States in the clothes he stood in.

It took Bahar a month to recover enough to return home. But the woman who arrived was even more frail than before; she could hardly walk, and her laugh had been left behind on that hospital bed. Her tired heart found it increasingly hard to pump blood. For the first time Bahar was truly crestfallen, a shell where an angel had lived. Yet her desire to contact her poet soon lifted her out of her hole and her spirit lifted her fragile body above its physical disabilities. She only came fully to life when she eventually persuaded her aunts that she was strong enough to go back to work – and she was again free to start her secret life.

*   *   *

There was a sort of civil war between the factions of the revolution, and we lived our lives in between street battles, midnight ambushes and the odd bombing. It was very exciting.

Shiraz, the southern capital of ancient Persia, was the worst hit of the cities. The university had an international reputation which had drawn students and lecturers from throughout the world. This meeting of several cultures had thrown up a particularly political intelligentsia – one that had to be suppressed if the fundamentalists were to successfully hijack the revolution.

Homa's daughter Laleh and her husband, a student leader, were forced to flee for their lives to the United States. They had met at – shock – a party when she was in her early teens and had been together ever since. Her husband, Jobo, had used his position as a students' representative to spread the word of rebellion, but the very animal that he had wanted to promote, the revolution, had turned round and tried to bite his head off and by 1981 he was in exile.

The streets of most large cities were buzzing with fear, excitement and expectation. It was a great show unless you happened to be one of the players. Such a player was a senior official at a southern prison. True, he had been no angel, having stood by and watched as the Shah had crushed the meek and the defiant. 'We can't change anything without ending up in the cemetery ourselves,' he had argued while he got rich under the last regime. This man had not been above dividing the inmates into 'the payers' and 'the poor'. The former were given the best cells, and had their own food brought in to them, among many other privileges. When the demonstrators opened the doors of the prisons the latter group of inmates vented their spleen on the class they blamed for their misery. The official had thought he had been lucky when the mullahs failed to replace him. He had also imagined that he had seen the worst he could ever see, but the revolution had sent him to the brink of insanity.

In lucid moments he told anyone who would listen the story of Ali, the grandson of the ninety-year-old widow of his best friend. The boy was a heroin addict and his Mother had come to the official and asked that he lock him up for a few days to scare him into beating the habit. Ali had been in prison two days when Iran's answer to Judge Roy Bean, Ayatollah Khalkhali, came to town. It was the start of the crackdown on the Mujahedeen-e-Khalg-e-Iran, the Marxist-Islamic group who had advocated a Shia state without the mullahs. This ideology earned them the privilege of being the first against the wall after the revolution and they were arrested in their thousands. The hanging judge had been instructed to empty the cells of these idealistic, if misguided, youngsters.

His method of cell clearance was to have them taken out in the middle of the night and shot. All the cells were emptied that night, including the one in which Ali struggled with his withdrawal symptoms. Although hundreds of students were killed that night, the prison official could not cope with the death of this one 'innocent' addict.

There was little popular sympathy for those extreme factions that had fuelled the revolution. People even rejoiced at the thought that the hardline Mujahedeen were being hunted down. But in the midst of so much death there was still the odd case that touched the public heart. Such a case was that of Sombol, the daughter of a friend. This nineteen-year-old, a talented second-year medical student, had been foolish enough not to obey the call by the Islamists to boycott lectures. She was shot as she left her lecture, a note left on her body warning that this would be the fate of those who disobeyed and who refused to wear the veil. The girl watched the rest of the post-revolutionary era from a wheelchair, her spine shattered by a liberator's bullet.

Soon the attacks spread to Tehran, where many women still refused to cover themselves despite reports of acid throwing and face slashing. Although one of the sisters of Islam had once stuck a large needle into my unveiled hip, we refused to give in and cover what for years had been on show. We could not believe that just the sight of our hair or the smell of Chanel No. 5 could turn on the sons of Islam.

How we had got to this state nobody really knew; the Ayatollahs had come upon us as we slept in our self-satisfied smog of assumed progress. But the excesses of the Shah's regime had pushed the meek too far and we had to bear the backlash. On my previous visit to Iran in 1975 women had been walking about practically in the nude – even to my Westernised eyes. Sharon Stone had nothing on the minister's wife at the Tehran Hilton salon who had sent the Italian stylist into a frenzy as she lifted her feet for a pedicure, revealing unfettered pubic hair.

Now the revolution had brought us full circle. I spent most of my time in those days with my cousin Farah, the elder daughter of my uncle, Dada Jan. We had been born on the same day in the same hospital and were more like sisters than cousins. She had married at the tender age of sixteen and had never shown any inclination towards doing anything but keeping house, shopping, gossiping and more shopping.

Farah drove me mad with her constant dusting and hoovering, and I wanted to spit blood when her husband, known in the family as Useless, sat with his feet up after a hard day of losing her money on some hare-brained scheme or other, and called for 'Tea!' It seemed amazing to me that she would actually scurry off into the kitchen and come back with a piping-hot long glass of tea. Tea dominates life in Iran and every home has the samovar at full boil twenty-four hours a day. Nice wives serve tea well, and when suitors arrive the daughter to be negotiated over is commanded to show her skills in this department.

It was at Farah's flat that I met 'ordinary' middle-class Iranians. Here women worked if they wanted to pay the rent and to buy the scarce Western luxuries in the shops. These women were lower-ranking civil servants, air hostesses and bank clerks, and they juggled work and family without the help of nannies, cooks or lunches at the country club. One day that first post-revolutionary spring a group of these working women initiated me into the cause of women under Islam. Several weeks earlier the regime had announced that all government staff had to wear the veil – the *hejab* – and anyone entering government offices also had to cover up, as would schoolchildren, who were to be issued with Islamic uniforms.

It was the beginning of the end, but in those days we imagined that the people could really run their country. The new Islamic dress was about as ugly as you could get. It consisted of a wimple or *maghneh* which covers the head, neck and shoulders with an opening for the face to poke through. Under this the woman wears a loose-fitting, calf-length *mantau* (coat) over trousers that should be at least two sizes too large to ensure that no female curves show through. Under this she wears a pair of thick stockings or socks, even though Islam allows a woman to show a bare foot. These uniforms came in black, navy and mud-brown.

The ladies were planning to take part in a demonstration against the *hejab* to be held the following week outside the Prime Minister's palace. Did we want to go?

'No thanks, it's nothing to do with us,' Farah said.

'Of course we'll be there, right behind you in the struggle,' I accepted, to black looks from my cousin.

To drive the point home, a couple of the neighbours and I decided to dye our hair Marilyn Monroe blonde – a further symbol of our disdain and our defiance. Two days before we were set to march, a smaller demonstration by women against the *hejab* ended in three deaths and a lot of broken bones. Farah pleaded with me not to take part, but I was determined to be there, no matter what the risk.

So on a fresh spring morning a taxi took me to pick up Farah and her neighbours. When the driver realised that we were on the way to Palace Avenue where the demonstration was to be held, he pleaded with us to turn back. I offered him the chance to drop us off as we approached the tail end of the marchers who were converging from miles away, the car creeping through the traffic.

'This looks dangerous. I'm going to come with you,' the driver said as he found somewhere to park away from the lines of Renault 5s that fashionable women were driving that year.

As we reached the main body of demonstrators, Farah tried to drag me away: 'We've seen it; now let's go.'

But I was buzzing, I wanted to be part of this, and I pulled her ever forward. We were herded on to the narrow pavements that lined the avenue as our men were pushed, with the tips of machine-guns held by pubescent Islamic Guards, the dreaded Pasdars, into the middle of the road among the counter-demonstration by Hezbullah, the Party of God.

We marched to jeers of '*Jendeh*' ('whore') and '*Madar jendeh*' ('your Mother is a whore') and even '*Pedar sag*' ('Your Father is a dog'). Really! – such language coming from the mouths of nice Muslim boys. I had a moment of doubt when I looked into the eyes of the fifteen-year-old who was waving me on with the barrel of his machine-gun. But it was too late to run; we were in the thick of it, chanting and waving for freedom.

I was just getting the gist of the slogans when I found myself face to face with a female sumo wrestler. She had her black *chador* pinned to her hair and twisted round her ample waist. The mammoth started screaming at the little group of women around me, and they shrank from the contest. With a rush of blood to the head I launched into a heated discussion on my virtue with the old hag. Farah was looking particularly pale as the exchange intensified. In despair she threw her hand over my mouth.

'Shush, you idiot! That's Zahra the Ripper!' she screamed.

'Who?' I asked in ignorance of the lesser players of the revolution.

'She used to kill soldiers with her bare hands. They said she pulled them apart limb from limb,' my cousin explained. We quietly squeezed further into the crowd, away from the disarming Zahra.

Finally Bani-Sadr, Iran's last truly secular Prime Minister, popped his moustached head out of an upper-floor window of his office fortress to promise that he would put our views to the Ayatollah. I reflected that it was impossible to take seriously a leader who bore an uncanny resemblance to Charlie Chaplin.

Come the revolution, the Pasdars had raided the homes of the despots, the Taghoutis, and stripped them bare. It was rumoured that the best pieces were taken to Geneva to be auctioned by Mohammad Ringo, the son of the Ayatollah Montazeri. Dayee Jan, Maman Joon's brother, had left one such home. He had died some fifteen years earlier, but his uniforms had survived. The home was emptied of its treasures, his widow given the maid's room. Assorted 'oppressed' citizens were moved into the mirrored ballroom. Among the things removed were the field marshal's formal uniforms – to be redistributed among earthquake victims. The image of some half-starved victim sitting in the rubble of his home dressed in gold epaulettes and medals always tickles my sense of the absurd. It was obvious, however, that Bani-Sadr had come by his suits in a similar manner. Why else were they all at least three sizes too big?

Once the walking shoulder pads had addressed us and we began to turn for home, the thugs of Hezbullah were let loose. Suddenly the road swarmed with young men – boys really – brandishing steel pipes, stones and knives. I told Farah to keep walking calmly as if we just happened to be out strolling. Our pace was rather more than a stroll but I kept my eyes to the ground for fear that I would panic if I looked at the throng.

We were surrounded by screaming women and jeering boys when something hard hit me on the head. A second later I saw a red, round object fall to the ground. I turned to look at Farah, who was stuck to the spot with a look of horror on her face. My cheek was cold. 'My head is broken, I've been hit by a rock and the pain hasn't started yet. I'm bleeding. Oh God! I'm bleeding.'

I stared down at the weapon at my feet, a melting blob of red ice-cream. I had been injured in the pursuit of freedom by a strawberry ripple. These were nothing more than village boys, bussed in with the promise of a free sandwich and ice-cream, in exchange for shouting a bit of abuse and chasing a few women.

But panic had set in among the women and we knew that next time it could be a rock or worse. I have never been so glad to see anyone as I was to see our driver when he beckoned to us from a side street. He had been back to the car and made his way through armed guards to the heart of the protest. 'Get in and get down,' he ordered. 'They are getting killed further up.'

We hid on the floor of the car as we drove past the militia who had been lying in wait by the parked cars. As I squinted up, blood splattered on the window and the car swerved to avoid a body on the road. In the side streets vehicles were being pulled apart and women dragged out by their hair. The red was no longer strawberry.

The car jolted to a stop. A middle-aged woman stood before us begging to be saved. 'Leave her,' the driver said. But we couldn't.

As she jumped into the front seat she pulled out a giant carving-knife and started shouting at the men who again surrounded us: 'We'll get you, animals! Dare to stop us!'

I was trapped in a car with a lunatic brandishing a carving-knife, surrounded by hardened fighters hell-bent on shredding me. 'Please, please put it away. In the name of God, put it away,' I begged.

'I spit on your religion,' the woman howled as she tried to open a window.

'Put it away or you get out!' our driver ordered.

'I'll take them all with us!' she ranted, still waving her weapon.

How we got free of that hell I know not. Sheer terror ensured that I didn't register the details until, safely on the road to North Tehran, we booted out the demented woman.

Slowly I was beginning to realise just how little I really knew about my people. The next week I joined Mummy and Maman Joon on a pilgrimage to Qom, a spooky city where mullahs were in the majority and *chadors* were the order of the day.

As we arrived in the city we were entering a strange world of theological colleges and Ayatollahs' headquarters. The shells of buildings that had once housed cinemas or restaurants stood deserted. One of the Sisters of Zahra spotted Mother's nails as she entered the shrine of Hazrat Masumeh. 'Look at the harlot's nails,' the woman screamed, and others gathered. If it had not been for a young, and extremely handsome, trainee mullah we might have gone on to meet our maker that day. But the man ran to our aid with several of the shrine's cleaners and keepers. He took us home and gave us a delicious meal before waving goodbye. I swore never to return.

On the road back to Tehran that day I learnt how easy it was to walk by, to let injustice happen. I tell myself that there was nothing that I could have done but I still feel shame. An old man, perhaps the age of my grandfather, was standing between two Pasdars while the rest of his family were loaded on to a truck. An aged woman and an assortment of young men, all with their hands tied behind their backs, were driven off as the old man wept. We had wandered on to the set of a Nazi war film.

We were living in the heart of hell.

Which is probably why so many of us gathered so often to dance and drink and gamble like the passengers in the ballroom of an ocean liner not realising that we had hit the iceberg. While Tehran did a fair imitation of a police state by day, by night it was transformed into Rio at carnival time. Bahar would take me, my Mother and the two girls for midnight drives around the capital. The parties often lasted till dawn as the newly liberated nation took its last sip at the cup of freedom.

That first year the masses were waiting for the new regime to keep its promise to deliver every Iranian's share of the oil revenues to their doors. They are still waiting. There was a feeling of 'we are all going to be rich soon so let's go out and spend it.' The centre of festivities was the freshly named Park Mellat (Park of the Nation) on the northern end of what was no longer Pahlavi Avenue, though few could remember exactly what its name was that week. Everyone with a pot and a few spare chairs had set up an open-air restaurant around the park. The good citizens of Tehran – the rich of North Tehran and the poor of South Tehran – would gather here to eat, to flirt, to row on the lake, to watch the young men show off on their skateboards or just to escape the fear that overshadowed the city by day.

In the midst of this disarray Zeeba, Dada Jan's engineer daughter, decided that what we really needed was a good get-together. She was not about to abandon her luxury homes, her three Mercedes or her summer garden to 'these louts'. The seizure of the American Embassy in Tehran by students and the holding of diplomats as hostages gave many anti-revolutionaries hope. This was the excuse the CIA needed to enter the conflict.

'You are coming to my party,' Zeeba commanded on a phone line known to be bugged. Mummy and I were still staying with Bahar and Nasser Khan, whose position as a senior security official under the Shah made us certain that we were being bugged. Auntie Homa was in Shiraz and Maman Joon was in Damavand, her mountain retreat where she escaped the summer heat. Mummy and Homa had been talking for more than an hour on the subject of their eighty-four-year-old Mother's safety.

They were going over the same ground for the hundredth time when a voice came over the line saying: 'I'm sick of hearing about your Mother. Talk about something more interesting now.' At least the spooks had a sense of humour.

The spook must have been delighted with Zeeba's call. 'It will be the party of the season. Everybody will be there,' she enthused. And indeed everyone was there. Minor royals came out of hiding, Freemasons surfaced despite execution orders, and the wine flowed. The women decked themselves out in their most revealing designer leftovers and in a back room the drugs were found in plenty.

However, the local Pasdars had also decided to attend our little soirée. We were well into the festivities when the doorbell was followed by the sound of the ground-floor garage door being broken down. As the fighters made their way up past the servants' quarters and the bedrooms to the top floor, the women scrambled for their coats and Zeeba searched for scarves to give them while the men scrambled to hide the opium. I was stuffing a bottle of Bollinger into a suede boot when the door came crashing down.

We women fled into a back room while our gallant men faced the music. There was no doubt in my mind that I was on my way to seventy lashes of the whip, but, worst of all, there were several people there who would face the executioner. 'Please God, let it be OK, let them get away. If you do I promise to say my *namaz* [ritual prayers] for the rest of my life.' I prayed as I waited. I was repeating my pledge when the bedroom door opened slowly, but instead of the unshaved, dishevelled representative of Islam that I had expected to appear it was the second cousin three times removed of the ex-Empress: 'All clear,' he said. It seemed that even the dreaded Pasdars were not averse to a backhander out of the 'get-away-with-anything' fund.

Things were so chaotic in those days that almost anybody got away with anything just as long as they looked the part. I know one former minister who grew a beard, bought a mullah's cloak and a turban and went about the streets pretending to be an Ayatollah while the Islamic Court sought him high and low.

The Pasdars were not slow to profit from the new prohibition either. There was the famous case of a gang in North Tehran who made a fortune selling a case of whisky. A middle man would approach people he knew wanted alcohol and invite them to collect their devil water at the dead of night from a house at the end of a cul-de-sac. There they would be sold a case of Johnny Walker Black Label, the seller insisting it be put in the car boot. The sap would get to the bottom of the road to find one of the many road-blocks common throughout Iran in those days. The whisky would then be discovered and after a lot of begging and pleading the Pasdars would accept a bribe not to turn the poor alcoholic in. They would also confiscate the booze, which they took back ready for the next sting.

On 17 September 1980 Mummy finally gave in to the pleading of a friend who had phoned day and night for a fortnight to urge us to leave Iran, if only temporarily. We flew out on a Japan Airlines flight five days before Saddam Hussein invaded Iran, to the applause of the West.

3

Husbands and Lovers

Iran went to war and I went to Hong Kong. In England Maggie was manufacturing her 'Me Generation' while in Iran Saddam managed what the mullahs had failed to do – unite the entire country behind Ayatollah Khomeini.

I spent two years as just one more alien among so many and was making rather a good job of antagonising the Hong Kong government. Perhaps too good, since a request from the Governor's office to the owner of the *Hongkong Standard* ensured that I was replaced as the correspondent who would cover Thatcher's historic visit to China to sell one of Britain's last colonies down the river.

I resigned in grand manner, storming out of the office only to return minutes later to retrieve my handbag and a stray cat I had left behind. The strain of trying to survive so far away from my family and my roots, whatever they were, began to take its toll; depressed and self-destructive, I knew that I had to find something to give me a reason to go on. It was then that a close friend turned down an offer from *The Times* to set up as a stringer in Tehran. I saw my chance to return to 'my roots'.

Three years among British ex-pats had shown me that outside Britain I was nationless, not accepted as English yet unable to claim any other homeland. The final straw came during one of those Hong Kong drinking sprees that go on well into the early hours of the morning. As dawn broke over the Fragrant Harbour, a newcomer to my close circle of friends asked where exactly I came from. To my surprise not one of my bosom chums could answer. A boy I had gone out with for several months said: 'She's from Venezuela of course.' To which the husband of my best friend responded: 'Don't be silly, there are no Jews in South America.' I was adrift. The new threat posed by invading hordes of Iraqis merely heightened my new-found Iranian patriotism.

It was 1984 and the police state, or should I say the mullah state, was well and truly established. *Shariah* law ruled supreme and not a strand of hair was seen on the streets of God's Republic. The veil and the Islamic state were here to stay, despite wizened old men plotting its overthrow in dark Paris cellars. Deposed ministers and other leftovers from the last regime still gathered in Tehran homes to listen to the various radio stations preaching resistance and giving hope for a return to their good old days. The authorities soon started to jam these broadcasts from the Voice of America, the BBC World Service or Radio Free Iran, but the hopefuls still listened, trying to make out the words above the crackle and the thunder.

Nasser Khan would turn on his ancient radio religiously to catch the latest pronouncements of various 'governments in exile'. The Crowned Prince, or Half-Pahlavi as he was known because of the tiny gold coin of that name; Bani-Sadr; Shahpour Bakhtiar and the Muj leadership – all were promising to liberate the people within days. Often those who listened made up their own interpretations of the screeches they had heard. They still regarded the years under the Ayatollahs as a mere blip in the natural order of things. Old men would gather to listen to the crackle that was all of the Voice of America you could hear above the interference broadcast by their new masters.

'What did he say?' one former minister would ask a fallen leading civil servant.

'It was the Shah, I swear it was. Allah be praised he is still alive,' one of the terminally optimistic would shout.

'I thought it was the new Shah. He said we should be ready for a three-week siege of Tehran when his army arrives,' the third conspirator would chip in.

'How long till he comes?' another asks.

'Six months. These — will be gone within six months,' would be the standard reply.

Step into any home in North Tehran today and you stand a good chance of hearing those words, 'just another six months'. The only difference is that those glamorous houses are now occupied by the 'children of the revolution', the new rich and powerful who orchestrated the revolution, many of whom have developed too much of a taste for the high life.

In 1984 many Iranians who had stayed behind in the hope that the mullahs could not survive long were trapped by a regime that would not let them take part in society any more but who were not allowed to leave either. Passports were denied to many thousands of former officials and royals. For these people the only hope was that the CIA or the British would 'decide to change things again'. These people are still waiting for that six months to finish sixteen years later – that is the tragedy of a country that has no room for its managers, for its experts and for its educated.

But it was not all bad in those days. There were still islands of vast entertainment such as what was popularly known as the 'Gilly Show'. Ayatollah Gillani was an eminent Islamic scholar and had been given a prime-time television spot on which to pontificate on questions of religion and personal behaviour. One of his masterpieces was an example to show under what circumstances children were *halal* (lawful) and when they were *haram* (unlawful).

'Imagine,' he told the male viewer, 'that it is a hot night and you are sleeping on the roof of your house. Your aunt is sleeping in the yard underneath beside the house. That night there is an earthquake and you fall from the roof on to your aunt,' he continued, always addressing himself to the man in society. 'God forbid that your aunt then gets pregnant, would that child be *halal*?' The image of anyone falling off a roof in the midst of an earthquake and still being in any state to have intercourse caused much merriment.

We all remember the story but few remember the answer. It was a sad day when the powers-that-be realised why Gilly was so popular and finally took him off the air. Many years later Muhammad Hashemi, the head of the Islamic Republic of Iran Broadcasting, IRIB, and the brother of President Rafsanjani, told me how he had tried to get Gilly to tone down his shows.

'We had so many complaints from Fathers who were shocked at the explicitly sexual nature of the Ayatollah's examples that I decided that I had to ask him to be more circumspect. But he laughed at me and said that these were "the word of God" and to be found in the Koran, and there was no need to be embarrassed.

'I had to stop him somehow, so I said that if that was the case then we would get actors and actresses to act out his examples on the screen so people realised just what he meant. He responded with anger, saying that would be disgusting, but I pointed out that this was the word of God and to be found in the Koran.

'He laughed and said he saw my point and would take care to be more discreet in future. But soon he was back to his old self and we had to stop the show,' Mr Hashemi said.

Another source of entertainment was the many rumours about how people had tried to smuggle out part of their fortunes. For once the women's private parts found use other than that of satisfying the lust of their men. Soon the mullahs had caught on and women were strip-searched at the airport, the Sisters of Zahra using the same pair of disposable gloves to probe the nooks and crannies.

Ingenious to a fault, the Iranian nation put all their energy into ways of outwitting the authorities, who in turn found ever new ways of frustrating their plots. The maestro in this genre was a society hostess who was not about to flee to the States without her jewels. To this end she had a friend take a crowbar to her leg until the bone was broken. She then booked herself on a plane to Paris and the morning she was to leave she phoned customs to report a woman who was leaving the country with millions of dollars' worth of jewels hidden in a cast on her left leg. She was stopped at Mehrabad and the cast forced open to reveal a broken leg. After many apologies she was booked on the next flight out and given an escort to her doctor to have the leg re-cast. Few noticed that the cast was considerably larger as she boarded the flight out the next day, her fortune safely hidden in the plaster.

Meanwhile, the Islamic state was kindly holding my share of the family fortune in trust until the courts could find me guilty of a crime for which it could expropriate the lot. All the evidence indicated that the Foundation for the Oppressed, the organisation empowered to seize land and property, had no intention of handing it over to the oppressed. Being one of the 'new poor' was losing its charm and I was tired of attempting to make a living by the pen while millions in property and rents stood idle in Iran.

It was Aunt Omol, Mummy's half-sister, who persuaded my

Mother, who had not dared allow me to return on my own, to try and get back some of the property that we had lost during the revolution.

Mummy is not a woman to let anyone scare her and has never shirked from a fight, but my exploits at demonstrations on our last visit and an incident when I had tried to join in a punch-up at Iran's London embassy had persuaded her that I was not to be trusted on my own. Now she thought we might as well see what we could do to get something back. It was with high hopes that I went with my Mother and Aunt Omol to the jewel in my collection, an office block in the heart of Tehran. When my Father bought the building in our joint names I became one of the richest teenagers in Tehran. When the Royal Iranian Navy rented the office space I was convinced that I had a reliable tenant for life.

Our arrival at the building caused quite a stir. Oppressors were not supposed to turn up and ask for their money back. We were ushered into the office of an 'expert' who explained that the matter of the outstanding rent and the ownership of the building was under exam-ination by the Islamic Court. There was nothing that the navy could do. But as we were obviously 'needy and honest women' he might be able to sway the court in our favour. And as we were such honest and good people he felt sure we would like to make a donation to a cause close to his heart – £100,000 for a well at a remote village.

Not having the odd hundred thousand to spare, we left, promising to get back to him. He must have seen the error of his ways, for he chased after us as we were leaving the building. 'I almost forgot to ask you. We hold the district's lunch-time prayers in this building. More than five hundred Muslims pray in this place every day, and we need your approval as the owner or our prayers will be void. Can we have your blessing, please?' The man had just asked for a bribe to help me get back what was mine and now wanted my blessing so he wouldn't go to hell. Young Muslims had died in their millions so this man and others like him could line their pockets.

Words failed me. I just turned and made my way out of the building. Outside a group of men had gathered, word had spread that I had returned, and the tenants in the shops on the ground floor of the building had assembled to take their pound of flesh. The ringleader was the grocer with the biggest shop, and with his one good eye staring at me he accused me of being the daughter of

41

a thief and a runaway. He did not mention that he had moved into the shop after a very dodgy contract with my paternal grandfather, who had seized on our absence to earn a little extra cash for my aunt to gamble away. I pointed out to the grocer that he was the thief for moving into our property.

We must have made a strange couple standing there in the middle of the road waving fists at each other as our respective camps held us apart. I was screaming and trying to bite the hands that held me back. I had left my stiff upper lip behind in Oxford; I was a street fighter, a soldier for truth and the defender of my family honour. I demanded that the local Komiteh be called so we could see who was the 'thief and runaway'.

This exchange was invigorating, the adrenalin was pumping as never before and I felt part of the world, part of life and part of history. My aunt instructed our driver to pick me up, despite the ban on physical contact between the sexes, and shove me in the car. As we drove away the driver told us that he had been offered a large bribe to tell the grocer where I was living.

The next day a letter was slipped under my grandfather's door threatening to kill us all if we did not leave well alone. He came to plead with me. It was the first time I had seen him since my parents separated in 1976. He admitted selling off some of my property and promised to hand over the parts of the profit that my Father's sister had not lost in the world's casinos if I promised not to incriminate him. I had no intention of doing so anyway, but I did want what belonged to my Mother and my family.

*   *   *

The headquarters of the Islamic Court were in the grounds of Ghasr prison, neatly tucked away behind a boulevard lined with army barracks. To get to it you entered a military zone still tense with the fear that any day they might be fighting the Iraqi troops on the streets of Tehran.

I presented myself at the doors of this complex dressed in the natty little black, all-in-one, sacklike number popular among fashionable Islamic revolutionaries that year. There was a hole for head and hands and the get-up made me feel like a life member of the Sisters of Zahra.

I was confident that the Islamic Court would be charmed into handing back the keys to our property with a profuse apology for ever having judged such a sweet innocent thing as myself as ungodly. They might, however, have a bit of trouble communicating these sentiments to me because of my poor Farsi, so I had taken my cousin Hamzeh, Omol's son, as interpreter.

Cardboard signs directed the supplicants down a narrow lane at the end of which stood two makeshift huts and all too many armed boys in combat uniform. Pens separating the men from the women channelled visitors to gates hidden behind sandbags and protected by barbed wire and combat-clad youths armed to the teeth like Mexican bandits. Worried over what I should say at the door I went over to the men's line to consult Hamzeh, only to have the nose of a machine-gun thrust in my stomach. 'Get back,' the soldier ordered. 'Men and women must stay separate.' I thought it was a joke but as he shoved me I realised they were serious about this Islamic business.

Around us another group was gathering. These were the Mothers, Fathers, wives, brothers, sisters and friends of those who had received the midnight knock at their door. A girl wept as an old man explained to the guards:

'My daughter's husband was taken three months ago. Soldiers came for him in the night, without telling us where they were to take him or what he had done. We have been searching for him ever since. Our Komiteh sent us to Evin prison but they said he was not there and sent us here. Then Mr Alahi sent us to a prison near Damavand. We have been to all the prisons ten times but no one knows where he is.

'Please, please check in your prison, or let us search for him. For Allah's sake, the boy was only twenty years old and married for less than a month. We have never had anything to do with politics – we are peaceful, ordinary people,' he said sobbing.

There were at least thirty similar stories among that crowd.

Once through the gate I was ushered into a hut where an old woman straight out of the opening scene from *Macbeth* searched me. Taking my handbag she stamped a small piece of paper saying: 'Don't lose this if you want to get out again.' Two body searches and five barriers later I was finally outside court 29, political section.

'Name,' a man barked as we timidly entered court 29, a box-room in which two defenders of the faith squeezed behind a shared desk.

Hamzeh replied, 'This is Parichehre Mosteshar – you have her file.'

'Can't she speak?' the shorter man growled, not looking up from a file spread before him.

'My Farsi is not fluent very,' I ventured.

'Nationality?' he asked.

'Iranian of course,' I stammered.

'Then why can't you speak your language?' the man said as he waved Hamzeh out of the room.

I wanted to ask how come I could be alone with men in this room when I had not been able to queue with my cousin. But the anxiety attack I was having prevented me from uttering a sound.

The man who had dismissed Hamzeh was obviously the boss. He was all of four foot one and bore a striking resemblance to Edmund Blackadder's sidekick, Baldrick. 'I am inquisitor magistrate Babai,' he said as he closed the file in front of him and handed it to the tall, younger, but none too clean man sitting beside him.

'To Evin,' he instructed his minion before turning his attention again to me.

'Why can't you speak your language?' Babai asked as if this was enough to condemn me to eternal damnation if not an Evin cell.

'I have been in England since two years,' I said in what passed for Farsi. I had been fluent in classical Persian and Arabic at the end of three years of study at Manchester University. I could still vaguely remember how to translate passages of the Koran, but my everyday Farsi was spoken in a heavy British accent and the phrasing tended to be a direct translation from the English and therefore gibberish to my inquisitor.

'Two years and you have forgotten your language,' the other man – who was playing the 'Good Cop' – exclaimed.

'I never knew how to speak it,' I told them. 'I was here two years only. You know there are many Iranians who have only been out of the country a few moments and already they drop all these foreign words into their speech. I think I've done very well to know as much as I do,' I said, defending myself.

It took us half an hour to establish that I had left Iran when I was two years old and not two years ago. The inquisitors were sweating from the exertion needed to decipher my singular breed of their language.

'Why have you lived in England instead of returning to your homeland?' Babai barked.

'I did what my parents told me,' I replied.

'What did you do to support the revolution?' Babai asked.

'Nothing. I was not involved in politics; I just got on with my studies at University so that I could be a better person to serve my country.' I played the patriotic card.

'When did you last see your Father?' the Good Cop asked, while Babai opened a thick file with my name on it that a menial had just brought in. I didn't think it would be helpful to point out this was a famous picture and the basis of many cartoons.

'I haven't seen my Father since three years before the revolution,' I replied finally on the verge of tears. I had never been in contact with people like this before. I didn't understand who they were or what they expected and yet my life could depend on what I said to them. The Iranian working classes were a complete mystery to me, and even more so the devout classes. We could have come from different planets for all we understood of each other.

Both men had the stubble that had become compulsory if you were to prove yourself a good Muslim; apparently Islam prohibits men from being clean-shaven. Good members of Hezbullah, both men had their shirts over their trousers to protect me from seeing their bulge and thus being turned on. Good Muslim men also wear long sleeves to hide their flesh from lusting women and they are not allowed to wear that symbol of Western oppression, the necktie. Why they insisted on wearing their shoes with the back tucked in to make them look like slippers I have never found out. But on the whole they looked seedy and sinister and I did not want to be alone in the same room with them.

Babai asked another question. I understood that he wanted to know when something had happened to me, but what that something was I had no idea: the word was new to me.

'I'm sorry, I don't understand that word,' I said, feeling a real idiot.

'When were you born?' Good Cop explained.

'December the 14th 1956,' I said, pleased that finally I had a definite answer.

'No, no,' Babai screamed. 'The Islamic date, we want the Islamic date.'

'Tell us the Iranian date and we will convert it,' Good Cop offered.

I had no idea at all. I had never had to use any other calendar and was not at all sure what date it was on the Iranian calendar let alone the Islamic one. I later discovered that I had been born on 21 Azar in the Iranian year 1335.

'Are you *mojarad* or *motahel*?' Babai continued.

'Sorry?' I whimpered.

'Give me strength,' Babai said, drying the sweat from his brow. He was getting very irritated after more than ninety minutes of struggling with my imperfect Persian. 'Do you have a husband?' he screamed.

'No,' I replied.

'You are twenty-seven years old – why aren't you married?' Good Cop asked in that 'I might make an offer here' tone.

'Just lucky, I guess,' came out before I had time to think. Big mistake, very big mistake. Now there were two bad cops.

'You are lying to us,' the formerly Good Cop barked.

'Stop lying or you'll be in big trouble,' Babai added.

'Tell me about your Father's business. Who did he work for?' Babai asked.

'For himself – I don't really know,' I said.

'Who did he spy for? Was it only the CIA or were there others? Who were his contacts in Iran?' Babai fired at me.

I was in tears, and inwardly furious that I was so feeble.

'You are a very bad liar,' Babai added as he indicated that I was to wait outside – probably for someone to come along with a ball and chain.

While we waited on a bench in the now deserted corridor, Hamzeh passed the time with amusing stories about all the characters who had come out of the other rooms in that corridor with numbers on their backs. He had overheard that Ghasr was full and they were waiting for a coach to come from Evin to take new prisoners away. He then pushed some money into my hand. 'Hide this – you may need it later,' he whispered as my heart started an attempted escape from my chest.

When the call to prayer rang out in that empty hall Babai poked his head out. 'Go now. Be back at the start of work on Saturday with someone who knows the facts in your Father's case. And don't wear that outfit again unless you want to join the Mujahedeen in the graveyard.'

On Saturday morning I was outside the courts with Mummy and Hamzeh at 7.30. Two hours later we finally reached Babai's door, where we waited another ninety minutes. Eventually Mummy and I were summoned in while Hamzeh was left out again.

'You must not lie to me,' Babai said to me. 'You should be too frightened to lie to me. I have your lives in my hand and I already know many of the things I ask you.'

I tried to be too clever by half. I was trying to speak in their language, the language of Islam, but it came out all wrong. What I meant to tell him was that I would not lie because I feared God, not because I feared him.

'I'm not afraid of you,' I said, struggling with the words I needed to get my point across. I started again. 'It's not you that makes me afraid to lie,' I continued. 'I am not afraid to lie to you,' I insisted to looks of surprise from my two tormentors. 'I'm not afraid of you . . .' – but before I could finish Hamzeh opened the door. In his hand he had our passports.

'What should I do with these?' he asked, thrusting the passports under Babai's nose.

'Give them to me and get out,' Babai said, taking the documents, putting them in a drawer and locking it. 'Afraid now?' he asked me with a smug little grin.

That night I was with Babai again and he was waving my passport under my nose. But at least he looked much neater in black tie and tails. Then I was on the top of a mountain with my Mother, who was being strapped to the underbelly of a particularly bilious goat. I was dressed as a sheep and we trudged over mountains to Pakistan. There my sister was waiting with British passports. Joy surrounded me as I sat on the plane to Heathrow. Finally we were landing; freedom was in sight. But as we landed I noticed some green-clad guards on the tarmac.

'Ladies and gentlemen, this is your captain. The authorities at Heathrow have asked me to inform you that while we were in the air there has been an Islamic revolution in the United Kingdom and you are requested to observe Islamic dress codes as you disembark.'

This is where I wake up screaming.

For the next two months I had the pleasure of Babai's company on average about twice a week. Yet I was surprised when he called out of the blue to say that he wanted to see my Mother again.

The next morning we went off again with Hamzeh, but this time only my Mother was allowed beyond the gates into the abyss. Mother had gone in at 8 a.m. but by noon, when I was summoned to the guards' hut, there was still no sign of her. There was a call for me, the soldier said.

'Don't worry, darling, but they may have to keep me. I don't have much time, so hand the phone to your cousin,' Mummy said.

My whole body froze; this wasn't true, this couldn't happen. The next thing I knew I was clutching at the bars that separated me from my Mother. 'Bastards, you bastards! You can't keep my Mother. I'll kill every last one of you!' I screamed as Hamzeh tried to persuade me to stop without touching me.

'We have to get home. There's only forty minutes before she goes to the cells and we can't get to her,' Hamzeh said, and I finally let go.

In the car back to a home halfway across town, he explained that my Father had written to the court accusing Mother of smuggling jewellery and money from Iran after the revolution. Grandfather, who was trying to get the property back in his own name, had delivered this letter to the court. Babai, who had openly admitted that he did not trust my grandfather, had agreed to release Mother if we could provide bail of about £500,000. It took a good twenty minutes to get to Bahar's. Our uncle, Dada Jan, arrived with what cash he could get his hands on and some house deeds, and rushed back to Ghasr with Hamzeh.

All I could think of doing was to go after my grandfather. I knew that he kept a room in another office block that had belonged to me, which he had let. I don't know how I got there, but I remember being revolted at the state of the building as I made my way up the stairs to the office on the fourth floor. Outside what had been flats for the rich and famous, the oppressed had deposited piles of dusty and cheap shoes. It was the one thing that divided the classes most in Iran, taking off the shoes outside the door. The upper classes remained clad while their underlings went about the house in stockinged feet.

A bewildered secretary told me that she had not seen my grandfather for days. So I left a message: 'Tell that thief that if my Mother spends even one second in a cell my sisters, brothers and all our families will not rest until we wipe him and his children off the face of the earth.'

By the time I got home Mother was free.

That night my grandfather was at Bahar's door, swearing that he had only done the things he had in order to save my fortune. He said he had money he had saved, around £1 million, and that he would bring part of the cash the next morning. That night he drowned in his bath.

It is true what they say about the relationship between hostages and their captors. Over the months I came to feel quite close to Babai. He was in many ways a very innocent man, having seen little of the world before the revolution. He told me he had been plucked from his quiet life in a remote village to become an inquisitor. He had been chosen for this job because he had spent three years in prison under the Shah for distributing cassettes of a message from the Ayatollah Khomeini, then in exile in Paris. His family had been turned out of their home and his brother, also working for Khomeini, had disappeared. The job he now did was his reward for going to jail.

Babai was fascinated with the West and wanted to know every detail of daily life. He hoped one day to be sent to an embassy in Europe. 'At university in England, do they give lectures in Persian and English?' he asked. I was shocked to find that Babai had very little idea how countries differed. He seemed to think that Farsi was a universal language with regional variations just as in some parts of Iran people spoke Farsi and Turkish.

About four months into my captivity things changed again. perhaps Goodish Cop had reported on Babai's soft attitude, for when I turned up for one of my sessions there was worse than usual waiting for me in Babai's court. A boy, not more than fifteen, sat by the wall blubbering and begging for help. 'I didn't know it was loaded, I didn't want to kill him,' the boy said. He had been sent to the front as part of Khomeini's army of 20 million. While he was on guard duty with another young soldier, the boy's gun had gone off, killing his friend. He was desperate; he begged and swore to God that he was innocent as he was taunted.

'You killed him, you wanted him dead. I can help you, but you have to confess. If you do not then I cannot save you from the executioner,' the once Good Cop told him.

The boy screamed and hollered, he whimpered and called for his Mother.

'Take him down,' Babai said after I had been witness to the worst of this drama. I was looking at a boy who might soon be dead and I felt contaminated by the evil going on around me.

With the boy gone, Babai looked at me and said, 'Now for you,' as he picked up the phone and dialled. 'Get me the governor of Evin,' he said into the mouthpiece. 'Hello, this is court 29, political section, at Ghasr. Babai here.' He listened, then continued. 'I am sending you someone.' He listened again. 'We are full here,' he suddenly bellowed down the phone. 'We are not supposed to keep politicals, they are yours, so you can have them.' He slammed down the phone.

I was about to go to the notorious Evin prison, where the sound of executions still kept people living nearby awake well into the early hours. I couldn't bring myself to ask what was happening. Goodish Cop returned with a wad of paper. Babai took the papers and threw them in front of me. 'Sign at the bottom of each page,' he ordered.

'What is this?' I asked.

'A record of what you have told us,' Babai explained.

'But it is in Persian. I cannot read it,' I pointed out.

'If you want to leave here today you will sign it,' Babai told me. Remembering the phone call I signed, but in English, hoping that if these notes were presented in court I could always argue that I had no idea what they said.

Then they let me leave. I had never had such a rush of joy as I made my way through the numerous check-points. I was in that last hut, my handbag back in my hand, and had just started to open the door to freedom when the phone rang. 'It is for you,' the woman said. My heart fell to the bottom of my stomach. It was a mistake, they hadn't meant to release me, I thought, as I took the receiver and put it against the black scarf that covered my head.

'Parichehre, next time wear more than that handkerchief on your head,' a voice warned before hanging up.

There was no relief from the tension of these inquisitions. At home Bahar was depressed, even frailer than before, and unable to do anything for herself. As the home got gloomier so my spirits sank further and further. All I wanted was to get away from all that doom but we were trapped, by that bastard called Babai. I suspect he was hoping that by holding my Mother and me he would force my Father to return from hiding in the West. Babai, a man I would not have allowed to enter my home by the front door, had absolute power over me. I was surprised how arrogant I was growing as the class structure in Iran was being turned upside-down. I had been a socialist, but I was turning into a snob.

The thrill of walking round a corner to find a pitched battle had worn thin; guilt at having been privileged had been replaced by a sense of great injustice from knowing our property and land were in the hands of others. I imagined some mullah sleeping between the sheets my parents had bought for me from Italy, I saw his children playing on the silk carpets that should have been part of my dowry, and I knew that his wife's fingers were adorned with the jewellery that had been seized when the Islamic Guards raided our Tehran home.

Things could get no worse, or could they?

We were just getting over the shock of our brushes with Babai when news came that Mina, Aunt Omol's eldest daughter, had been taken from her home after a raid by the local Pasdars. Mina had been alone at home with her three children, the youngest a daughter just a year old. She was told to leave the children with a neighbour and that she would be back in a couple of hours. It was four months before she saw her children again; as with so many in those days, Mina disappeared. After much calling in of favours within the new regime, Aunt Omol, a devout Muslim and highly respected by the religious establishment, heard that her daughter was in a prison near Bahar's home. She was due to be taken to Evin the night the Mujahedeen attacked the prison where she and many other political prisoners were held.

Mina had been picked up after her estranged husband had been arrested as a supporter of the ousted pre-revolution Prime Minister, Shahpour Bakhtiar. The prison in which she was held was within a couple of hundred yards of Bahar's home, and that night we squatted in her garden as the bullets bounced off the walls.

The sensation was strange. It was part fear for the fate of the prisoners should the Muj look like winning the battle – the Pasdars were not beyond killing prisoners rather than see them freed. At the same time it was thrilling to be in the thick of battle, albeit at a safe distance. As I sat crouched on the back porch with Bahar, Mother and the girls, missiles started to rock the district, the occasional bullet finding its way into our garden. The battle raged all night, while Nasser Khan slept undisturbed. Not even revolution could rock his tidy routine, the ordered life that was increasingly driving Bahar crazy.

Mina stood trial with two other women about four months after she was taken to Evin. The newspaper said that the two women had been executed that horrific morning but there was no news of my cousin. At 3 o'clock the next morning, the execution hour, Aunt Omol got a call to come and collect her daughter. We were certain that it was a body we had to collect, but to Auntie's joy a living, breathing, but very disturbed Mina met her at the prison door.

The torture had been relatively mild: Mina had someone with money trying to get her out, so they took more care of her than some. But it had not stopped the authorities taking her out into the yard with the other women at 3 a.m. every morning; it had not stopped them blindfolding her, and it had not stopped them lining her up while they shot the women around her before returning her to a cell.

*   *   *

Homa used the excuse of Bahar's ever-worsening health to get away from her husband and visit us in Tehran. She was her niece's closest confidante, both living in a hell with men they cared nothing for. Homa was just thirteen when she was married to the Fat Man, a descendant of the prophet Muhammad (AS), in order to forge an alliance with a large and important southern family – thus extending the family's sphere of influence. Homa was beautiful with a razor-sharp mind and a poetic soul; while her husband lived only to eat and to have sex. Gossip does not circulate in our family quite as fast as it seems to in other Iranian families, but I have heard of an incident when, still newly married, Homa returned home unexpectedly to find her groom in bed with the toothless maid.

His appetite for sex drove away friends with young daughters and caused his wife a lifetime of pain and then embarrassment. In less conservative societies and less Islamic days the Fat Man might have been able to get help to control his appetites for women and alcohol. But in his world women often married without love and men were expected to take pleasure where they could.

My cousin Farah once told me that during a visit to Tehran when

Homa and the Fat Man stayed with her parents he would retire for a nap after lunch and call for his wife to join him. He would go on and on till she was so uncomfortable she would have to join him in the sitting-room where he would start to have sex on the floor, with the door wide open.

I hated staying with them as the Fat Man tended to like to exhibit the fact that he was defecating and rarely closed the toilet door. His staying with us was also a nightmare, since he was usually half drunk and would prefer to urinate in the bath-tub because it was a bigger target; if there was no bath, then the floor got its share of urine. Homa spent her life cleaning up after him.

In the good old days of the Shah these oversexed men could find satisfaction elsewhere, but the revolution brought the excesses of the husbands back into the home, and women who had been left in peace for years were suddenly called upon to perform their duties.

Five years after the coming of the mullahs, Homa had survived her own dance with death; half her insides had been removed and an infection had followed the three operations to remove most of her stomach. She had even survived having to get out of her recovery bed to try to get the Fat Man out of prison. We never found out why he was arrested, but Homa had spent every day, when she was still very ill, trying to pull the strings that would free him.

It was winter and Maman Joon was in Shiraz living in the flat on the top floor of my aunt's house. Several months had passed and Homa had got nowhere in trying to free her unlovable husband. Grandmother had gone to visit friends while Homa went to the prison in an attempt to see the governor. She had apparently been sworn at, spat at and finally pushed into those ditches that carry water along the side of Iranian roads.

The home of the couple entertaining Maman Joon not passing muster hygiene-wise, Grandmother decided to return home in time to perform her afternoon prayers. She found Homa in the bath, her wrists slashed and her blood all but drained. It was her third suicide attempt and the last to fail.

Several months later the Fat Man was released, his case unresolved. We never found out just what his alleged crimes were but they came to haunt the family for years to come. Having gone through her own personal hell over the previous three or four years, Homa planned a trip to the United States. Mother was to join her and Maman Joon in Los Angeles, where two of Homa's children lived, and then bring Grandmother back to England, allowing Homa much-needed rest.

In the meantime Bahar had finally made the decision to take up the poet's entreaty to think about leaving Iran to be his wife in the States. She arrived in Los Angeles with great hopes, the revolution having convinced her that there was no place for her or her children in Iran. She was thus willing to face a scandal in order to be free.

Bahar had arranged to meet Hassan a couple of days after her arrival. The family were staying in LA with Shirl, Homa's much-married daughter, who was also a close friend of the poet. My Mother had heard some of the gossip about Bahar and the poet but had refused to acknowledge the relationship. Maman Joon would not countenance any private contact between the loving couple, she detested the man, so it was with great secrecy that Bahar sneaked off for her first dinner in ten years with the man she loved.

Their love had started when Bahar was a young, single girl. Their relationship had been conducted through letters and his poetry, much of which was either about Bahar or dedicated to her. While in the US he had continued his courtship of Bahar, urging her to leave Iran and join him and promising to support her and her children. By this time Goldie was dead and Bahar had inherited a tidy fortune that liberated her. The poet told Bahar that he had been advised 'by a doctor' to take a lover while he was in the US for the sake of his health, and she had agreed. Their love was of the mind, not the body.

The poet swears that the woman who hounded them on that first night was not his lover. According to his version of the events that led up to that night, he had met this 'very ugly' Iranian woman when they both worked at the Iranian television service before the revolution. He had befriended her and her family after they fled to LA, as he had done for many exiles. When he got a university appointment, she took up the course and they met as student and teacher.

But she began to follow him. She declared her love and was repulsed. Then started a terrifying 'Fatal Attraction', during which the woman managed to get into his flat and empty it of all his belongings. She now had his address book and hounded his friends, family and eventually Bahar.

The night of the great reunion she had followed the ill-fated lovers to a restaurant. Here the woman hovered as the poet suggested that he and Bahar tour the States. It must be remembered that Bahar was still a married woman and had dreamed of something a little more respectable than the quick fling being offered. As they struggled to understand each other, Miss Maniac was spotted bobbing up from behind the fake greenery clutching a large bag and with a strange gleam in her eyes.

The poet swears that he feared for Bahar's life and that was why he rushed Bahar out of the restaurant, bundled her into his car and deposited her outside Shirl's home, his admirer standing in the background screeching at them.

Bahar left Los Angeles without seeing him again. She went to her uncle, a doctor exiled in the US, where after a week of tests was told that she should have died years ago and that she could keel over at any time.

She returned to Iran to put her affairs in order. She sent her younger daughter to learn French in Paris and took a break alone in Turkey to think through her life. Bahar returned from Turkey a happier woman, determined to make a change. She wrote to us to say how well she had felt by the sea in Turkey, how she had been able to walk for hours and how she was now convinced that her only hope was to move to the Caspian coast in the north of Iran, where the sea air would help her lungs and the beauty would inspire her painting. Bahar was preparing to leave her life. Early in 1991 she phoned Mother in Oxford to ask her to promise to help her younger daughter to come to England and to get her into university.

Bahar said she had a slight headache and was going to bed. She got up only to go to hospital the next day. A week later she was dead.

Homa had also gone to the United States to escape her life, to hand over the responsibility for her Mother so that she could start to think about making changes for her future. But Maman Joon had different ideas: she held on to her youngest daughter with all her might, and the gentle self-sacrificing woman could not deny her Mother's request not to let her other daughter (my Mother) take her to the land of the *kafers* (unbelievers). Thus Mother and daughter returned to Iran and a life that would ultimately destroy the younger and leave the older adrift. With Maman Joon to look after, Homa had to hang on to her home in Shiraz and the husband that went with it. She should have returned to the States to live out her life in comfort with her daughters, but her Mother would not countenance living on non-Islamic soil and begged her daughter not to leave her.

4

The Next Generation

The stench of death left by revolution and eight years of war with Iraq invaded everyday life in the Iran to which I returned in 1991 with Mummy and Mahshid. We were in black to mourn the loss of a precious cousin, but the moment I stepped off the plane I discovered a nation in mourning for its spirit and its hopes.

Bahar's death was the first in a string of losses of very dear people. By the time we reached Iran the death toll included two of my Mother's closest friends; Uncle Naj's widowed sister-in-law who lived in his home for the last forty years of her life; and an assortment of second cousins. As if this were not enough, the daughter of another cousin died in Europe, while the son of yet another was attacked by Islamic fundamentalists at his American university. To top it all, Homa's eldest daughter Shireen was discovered to have some suspicious lumps in her womb and had been forced to have a hysterectomy. All this in the two months since the first shock of Bahar's death.

I had longed to be home, to be back in the bosom of the extended family and the warmth and camaraderie of the Middle East. But surely we had landed in the wrong country. The air had always embraced me with its warmth and its smells of Eastern mystery in the past. That day it ignored the returning natives. Nor did the airport live up to my expectations. No strip searches, bags hardly touched by the customs Gestapo. Where on earth had they put the revolution?

There was a tension in the air, but it wasn't the buzz of religious zeal. 'Neither East nor West, but Islam,' the masses chanted as they waved goodbye to the monarchy. They had been left with nothing. As dawn broke over Tehran it was hard to see the energy that had created the Islamic Republic. It was so ordinary I just couldn't believe it was the same place that had once filled me with such excited terror.

In at attempt to attract back money and expertise, Raffers had promised to welcome home exiled Iranians with open arms. Most of the people on the Iran Air flight with us were the wives of exiles sent back to test the water. These women had left Iran when it was still a playboys' paradise and you could see the culture shock as they stepped into the mullahs' den. Most of them had put on the veil for the first time five hours earlier when they boarded the plane, and now struggled to keep hair and body covered. They were soon to feel more than a mite dowdy as they passed through customs to discover the multicoloured example of Islamic womanhood awaiting them.

To make travel as unpleasant an experience as possible for those lucky enough to be able to indulge in that luxury, most international flights, especially from unfriendly non-Islamic countries, arrive in and leave Tehran in the early hours. So there I was again at Tehran's now ultra-clean Mehrabad airport, pen poised to start my reporting activities as soon as I hit the tarmac. The sun rose on this new dawn, but search as I might I could not spot a single example of revolutionary zeal. The Pasdars, those once terrifying Islamic Guards, were snoozing in a corner of the arrivals hall; an old man played with worry beads under a sign that read: The Foundation for the Martyrs and Life-Sacrificers: Information point. However, there were no weeping relatives of the martyrs or life-sacrificers in sight.

The latter are the boys who have failed to achieve martyrdom but did achieve the next best thing – to have their limbs blown off or their spines snapped. With their wheelchairs they could command front-row seats at any event that attracts the cameras. There was also a new law that new businesses must have a life-sacrificer on the board before they could get subsidies.

The backlog of five flights into this would-be *laissez-faire* state shuffled restlessly towards the two passport booths. If you happen to be on the 'enemy' list and are simple enough to present yourself at Mehrabad with a passport in your own name, this is where the forces of Islam swoop down on you and cart you off to Evin. But as it is unlikely that Ronald Reagan or Salman Rushdie would turn up in the line there is no real danger. Nevertheless I felt the slight pull of stomach muscles as the inspector checked my name in the Big Book. His slight blink as he spotted the surname, then double-checked my first name against my Father's – which was on his list – started a giggle of relief deep inside me.

In that other life, the life before the mullahs, we would have been met on the tarmac by my Father and an assortment of minions who would have scurried around sorting out passport formalities and retrieving suitcases that no customs official dared open. We would have been whisked past the real people, much as now the mullahs and their kin were whisked past us. Father's fleet of American gas-guzzling cars, with their court number-plates, would have whizzed us home while heel-clicking policemen held up the traffic for us.

I had once felt a pang of pity for a mullah on one of those rare occasions on which I had seen the inside of the customs hall. We had arrived from England via shopping sprees in Paris and Rome and were anxious to have our cases. As I waited for the houseboy to get my bags I watched a wretched mullah being treated like dirt by the officials. He was ignored, and pushed to the end of the line of people waiting to have their bags checked. Each time the mullah reached a customs official he was waved away with a torrent of abuse – one and all joined in the jeering. I was filled with fury, but I had done nothing but watch, just as the new rulers now watched as my cases were emptied and searched.

It had been exciting, if you were just visiting, to be in the heart of the revolution being pushed about by people you knew must have fought in bloody battles, battles you had seen from the safety of your television. But now, instead of black crows turning your belongings out on the floor and shoving you into booths to examine your fixtures and fittings, the customs officials were polite and helpful, if lacking something in joviality.

Not once was I addressed as 'Sister', nor called a whore by a passing fanatic.

Pity the millions who had died to produce this watered-down republic. They had put an end to a society where I could have ordered the closure of a man's shop if I didn't get the service I felt I deserved. A society where I had seen a man beaten to a pulp by two goons working for a powerful general, and all because the man had parked in the general's parking spot on a public street.

When the police arrived it was the motorist who was arrested. The anger of being thus disempowered had led the people to the streets, had made them beat their enemies to death out of generations of suppressed outrage.

Now, in contrast to those of us who returned to God's Republic in our greys and blacks, the women of the new Iran sparkled under the airport lights. They paraded in pinks and reds and bright, bright green. Hems were down to the ankle on the long baggy coats that were required to hide those curves that drive the male wild. Veils were big and colourful and hair was making a comeback. Bouffants that Joanna Lumley would die for held up scarves, sometimes as much as eight or nine inches above the head. Badger was the in look for the trendy Tehran girl that season. Jet-black hair streaked with thick lines of blonde was the order of the day. Make-up was an obligatory two inches thick.

There was a handful of women of the revolution, the ones who showed 'the face of a man' in public – that is they left their moustaches and other facial hair untouched. They draped their bodies in long black sheets, the more devout only allowing a nose and one eye to show through. They may have been Monroe lookalikes under those *chadors* but the only men who would ever know would be their husbands or blood relatives.

Despite the early hour whole families had come to the airport to welcome home the passengers. We were met by my uncle, an aunt and an assortment of cousins. The reunion awakened all the feelings of sorrow over Bahar and the many others who had died in those revolutionary days.

By the time we reached Bahar's home it was clear that the country had changed fundamentally since the heyday of the revolution. For one thing the slogans were gone. Walls stood tall and clean with not a sign of the 'Death to America' that used to be scrawled on them. The stalemate in the Iran–Iraq war explained the disappearance of the 'War, War, War Until Victory' slogans. But surely there were still a few good old enemies we could insult. Wasn't there anybody out there who still cared?

With Bahar gone, the House of Gloom was plunged into a chilling spiritual darkness. Its heart was gone and those who were left drifted through it like lost ghosts. She had taken what little life there was in that house with her when she went. The lights were rarely on, music was never heard and dust gathered on her piano. Bahar's portrait stared down beyond the long entrance hall reminding all who entered that she was gone.

Bahar's death had overwhelmed her daughter Nastaran. She went through the motions of welcoming us and she scurried about cooking and cleaning, but her eyes screamed to be left alone. Every attempt to reach out to her was rewarded with a rebuff. It was impossible to penetrate that hard exterior to discover what was going on within her soul. Nastaran had not shed a public tear since her Mother's death. As far as one could tell, she had only a handful of friends, all female, and all in the process of finding husbands and new lives, while Nastaran was plunged into the mourning process.

In her late twenties when her Mother died, the young woman had known as much about the world as the average fourteen-year-old. She had spent the best part of her life taking care of her ailing Mother and her handicapped brother. Her goals had been set by her Mother and she had struggled to turn into the academic she was expected to become. The two girls were expected to be beautiful and elegant and great hostesses as well as academics and career women. As they cooked, Bahar played Linguaphone tapes in English, French and German. She had pushed her girls to achieve at school and at university, but the pressure seemed to have left the elder daughter terrified and tired.

Nastaran was teetering on the edge. She had lost the centre of her universe and overnight she had been forced to take on the role of the woman of the house under the scrutiny of a society that would be only too quick to find fault. Bahar had planned for her daughters to go to the West, where they could reach for everything she had been denied. She had made all decisions for her girls and taught them what they should hope for without properly equipping them to go after their dreams alone. Now all those hopes were dashed; the young woman had inherited the chores of running a home for a Father increasingly disabled by Parkinson's disease.

The pressure to be the perfect hostess is great in Iran, where women are still judged on how they look and what they can do in the kitchen. This suddenly very lonely trainee woman knew that everything she did would be talked about, analysed and criticised. Her insistence on managing the household singlehandedly became unbearable in the end. There is nothing quite so annoying as not being allowed to make your own tea, do the washing up, buy food or drink and other normal things of life. Yes, it sounds wonderful, and it is for a week, even a month, but after seven months it gets beyond a joke.

There was the day when Mahshid and Auntie Omol's daughter, Minu, went out shopping for material and made the great mistake of buying some cakes for tea on their way home. Nastaran was a thing demented. She ranted and raved and accused us of implying that she was a bad hostess. That night she cried at the dinner table as she took us all to task over the cakes. 'Don't ever bring anything into my house again,' she said to a stunned audience.

Bahar's daughters had not been brought up to be just wives but they were trapped in a society that expected them to fulfil that role before any other. The elder sister had achieved the almost impossible in the post-revolutionary days: winning a place at Tehran University despite being the daughter of a former security chief. She had graduated top of her year, winning the President's outstanding-achievement prize. She had framed her degree and her award and then set about keeping house. 'I have a maid with a university degree,' Bahar used to joke. The two were often seen on shopping trips, Bahar sitting in her prehistoric Peugeot outside the grocer's while her daughter, inside the shop, held up vegetables for approval.

Nastaran coped with her Mother's death by turning into an efficient machine, going through the motions of taking over and pushing her sorrow so deep it was impossible to see.

Yet, if there is anything that Iranians do best, it is mourning. We are totally fascinated with death – why else would we have watched as millions of our young were sent to their deaths over the last decade and a half? Death is a time to plunge ourselves in black from head to foot and indulge in abundant wailing and screaming. Few people, these days, go as far as dyeing everything in sight black, but mourning is still a serious and exhausting process. No news spreads faster than that of a death, which is the go-ahead for all and sundry to make their way to the bereaved's home. The family are then required to feed the stomachs and souls of these hordes. It is supposed to help the bereaved forget their sorrows as they panic over how they will ever recover from the cost.

Conversation is dominated by views on the hospitality following the latest death. 'Their rice wasn't quite as good as the

Mohammadis'' or 'They can't have spent much on hiring that mullah – his voice was terrible', and so on. The money spent on Bahar's ceremonies could have kept the average working-class family going for a good six years.

The cost of death is reduced if you are fortunate enough to have been martyred. Not only do you and your nearest and dearest get a reserved place in paradise, but the state takes over the ceremonies, providing mourners, all hospitality and the very best in mullahs to work your guests up into a frenzy of crying. A learned friend, whose Arabic is up to understanding Koranic readings, tells of the day he arrived at the funeral ceremony for a colleague to find the men crying their very guts out, unaware that the passage being read was not a tale of the death of some Muslim martyr but an observation that 'the cry of the donkey is the ugliest noise created by Allah'.

On the third day after a death the body goes to be washed and then on for burial. In Tehran every corpse has to be washed at the massive graveyard of Behesht-e-Zahra (Zahra's Paradise) where acres of martyrs are buried. While the corpse queues up to be taken into the undertaker's, mourners are sent to a waiting-room to watch the television monitor for their turn. The body-washers work behind a glass wall stared at by families there to see the body for the last time. Much fainting and frothing at the mouth goes on in this viewing-room.

Once washed, the corpse is wrapped in a shroud and taken out to the praying area, where mourners line up behind the body and pray. Pole bearers then carry the body to the grave, where the eldest son of the deceased, or the Father, opens the shroud to reveal the face in the grave and turns the head toward Mecca.

A week after the death, the mourners again hold ceremonies that involve a great deal of eating and wailing. On the fortieth day after the death there is yet another ceremony with the best feast. Deprived of the freedom to throw the great parties of the past, where men and women used to drink, dance and sleep together, Iranians have taken over the mourning ceremony as an occasion to pull out all the stops.

Normally, one would wear black for a year after the death of a parent, a husband, a sibling or one's child; between three to six months for a cousin, aunt or uncle; and forty days for a close friend or distant relative. For the first forty days close female relatives are expected to ignore their looks, not wearing make-up, dyeing hair or plucking eyebrows, etc. Parties unconnected with the death are out of the question for at least six months, and weddings are banned until after the very last ceremony to mark the anniversary.

The death of his wife had left Nasser Khan a broken man, and his Parkinson's disease meant that he needed constant care. Keeping her promise to Bahar, Nastaran had arranged for Nasrin to go to a college, in Europe, in the autumn. Thus Nastaran, at the age of twenty-eight, was trapped, carrying the burden of her Mother's life. She had stepped into shoes that no one could possibly fill. For the next seven months I was to live in this house over which she ruled with all the warmth and grace with which Mrs Danvers presided over Mandalay after the death of Rebecca.

*   *   *

In the good old days, servants had done the shopping, cooking and cleaning, while secretaries, estate managers and houseboys had sorted out the other practicalities of life. In the world of post-revolutionary Iran my family and I were social cripples, lost in a nightmare of not knowing how to get our passports renewed, where to go for fresh bread and how to get from A to B without a driver. This new republic had no identity that I could perceive and I could not get to grips with how things worked. Even the street names had changed and I was more or less trapped in the House of Doom. Nastaran was not helpful in explaining the mysteries of Tehran life – she seemed almost as lost as the rest of us. But instead of saying, 'I don't know', three words Iranians loathe to say, she would just stare if you asked her anything and often walked away without giving a reply.

The seal was set on my ever-worsening relationship with Nastaran soon after our arrival. We had been searching for somewhere to have our legs waxed – the latest activity outlawed by the regime for no understandable reason. We finally traced a salon carrying out this illicit activity and were sworn to secrecy as we were given an address on the other side of town.

Nastaran wanted to have her face waxed and so we set out in Bahar's banger one afternoon during the Big Sleep, the daily siesta hours. The streets were empty as we turned into a boulevard on the rim of what could still be called North Tehran. Lying on the other side of the boulevard was a man, face down and writhing like a fish out of water.

'Stop!' I screamed, but Nastaran ignored me and drove on. 'There is someone in trouble. Didn't you see him?' I babbled.

'It's not my problem,' the cool voice replied. 'He'll say we hit him if we stop.' We were getting ever further away.

'But he may be dying. Look, there are shops here. Stop so I can phone an ambulance,' I demanded.

But the car went on.

'You have to help people. I always think if I help someone then one day, if my loved ones are in trouble, someone will go to their aid.' I tried to reason with the rock now turning on to the motorway.

Resistance was indeed useless, so I held my tongue until we reached our destination. 'I'm off to get a taxi and find that man again,' I huffed.

'OK, OK!' she yelled. 'I'll take you back.'

When we reached the spot, the man had disappeared – but would I give up? No. Poor Nastaran sat in the car as I searched every ditch, wandered out on to wasteland and accosted passers-by. I finally went back to the shops we had spotted in a nearby square. Well, it was a dusty road actually, with a grass roundabout in the middle, the fledgling trees providing shelter for sleeping workmen. A dusty old man sat in the doorway of his shop, a clay pipe in his mouth, his skin folding in great furrows of age. There was dust trapped even in those wrinkles.

'There was a man hurt near here. Do you know if he was found?' I asked the man, who sneered up at me.

'Get away, you naked whore!' he snarled.

'A man hurt, just up the road – did you see if they found him?' I jabbered.

'My son died to rid us of you. But what did he die for – so you can still parade naked in the streets and drive your fancy cars? You people should have been wiped off the earth,' he spat out.

How could I ever make him understand that I too hated the Shah's regime and that I was just as disgusted as he was to see that the players had changed but the game was still the same, the powerful getting rich and the poor being stepped over? However, I had finally grasped that I was not exactly wanted. The little bit of hair showing under my scarf had marked me as an evil woman to this Muslim who didn't want to know that yards away someone might be lying in trouble and pain.

That was not the end of my discomfort. For when we got back home Nastaran stormed into the house claiming that I had called her a murderer for not stopping.

'Who, me?' I asked, reeling from the shock.

Somehow a simple drive had turned into a major drama and I had missed most of the action. Eat your heart out, *Dallas*; a day in Tehran makes the antics of JR look normal.

Even the road-sweeper frowned at me as the story spread and changed out of all proportion. Before I knew where I was there were two camps supporting one or other of us. I had no idea how I had got into this war. From that day, living in that house became a continual battle. To have left would have been a major snub to Nasser Khan, who was a perfect and generous host.

I was now also trapped by modern Iranian manners. Most of that first month in Tehran was spent at home, the summer heat not mixing well with the layers of clothing we had to wrap around us before venturing out. Going out to dinner was more trouble than it was worth; sitting in some hot restaurant eating with your coat and scarf on was not my idea of fun. But beyond the bother of it all there was a deeper despondency among my family.

Corruption was everywhere, even at the heart of the revolution. I was to come face to face with the unacceptable side of the revolution in the form of the lawyer who had been instrumental in presenting the case against my Father and thus allowing the Foundation for the Oppressed to grab our assets. Having destroyed so many people, he had turned from gamekeeper to poacher, setting himself up in a private practice specialising in getting capitalists' money back from the Oppressed. I suspect that he had a colleague at the airport tipping him off when Tyrants returned, for he just happened to phone us at our last-known address less than a week after we reappeared. His offer: 'To try and put right the wrong done.'

I had expected to find someone racked with guilt; a khaki-clad son of the revolution with a couple of days' growth and the Marco Polo shirt that was so popular now ties were evil. What I found had walked straight out of a Medallion Man catalogue. His shimmering-blue, Thai-silk suit complemented his gold-striped silk shirt. The light caught the jewels on his gold Rolex and the rather large diamond in his gold wedding ring. I could have wrung the neck from which that squeaky voice explained how the confiscation of my property had been a terrible injustice.

He declared that although the judgement against me would not hold up in any international court 'it would be a brave judge in the Islamic Republic who would sign the order reversing it'. But, as luck would have it, he was still in close touch with important people in the relevant ministries and foundations. These people would be willing to help retrieve the properties in return for a percentage.

Nice work if you can get it!

'Don't let him handle it. I know someone much better. He knows all the top people and is related to Ayatollah Yazdi,' my cousin Farah insisted.

Her Mr Fix-it had helped a string of important exiles for a mere 10 per cent of the profits, she claimed, dismissing my reservations after I found out that he was her Mother-in-law's tenant. A man making millions on land deals could surely afford his own place. 'He wants to keep a low profile,' Farah explained.

Three days later I was in Hadji Amini's sitting-room confirming for myself that he certainly wasn't spending the money if he was making it. He was sixty if he was a day and the wife, who came to serve tea, was a good thirty years his junior. I had taken my shoes off beside theirs at the front door.

Hadji announced that he would need a power of attorney to allow him to act on my behalf – buying and selling and dealing as he wished. He also explained that Raffers was the only man that could reopen the case, but the President received thousands of applications a day. However, Hadji knew a man in Raffers's office who could move my file to the top of the pile for a mere million and a half tomans (the exchange rate was about 230 tomans to the pound at the time).

I struck a deal with the man on the basis of his assurance that no bribery would be involved, although without bribery it might take several years. Don't get me wrong, I wanted to be rich again and I wanted to be able to pick and choose who I worked for and when. But I was still naïve and thought that things could be done without backhanders.

The Shah's Iran had been corrupt and immoral to its core, and our monarch and his entourage had seemed to spend more time in St Moritz than Tehran. Drugs had been a normal part of life and the only qualification you needed for high office was to be related to the right person.

There had been a rather plush all-day party given by one of the more powerful army generals on my visit in 1976. Everybody who was anybody was there. Our clothes were by Valentino, Dior, Chanel or whatever designer was most popular that season. The drink flowed, caviar was available by the bucketful, and the rich and privileged were losing fortunes at gaming tables in the garden. I was taking a rest from the festivities, hidden away in an alcove of the hall in the general's lavish third home, when I saw another general sneak in to make a phone call. It was obviously to some official, for the general said: 'I am here with Minister So-and-so who has instructed me to tell you that the company I represent is to be given the contract for the new tanks', or words to that effect. The minister had never spoken to the general and had no idea that he had just made him a multi-millionaire. The official would never dare question the deal.

It seemed the new Iran had not changed a great deal. I had expected to find some bribery but not on the scale of the past. What I found was a system that turned on the backhander for everything, and unashamedly at that. At least in the last regime people had tried to hide their corruption, knowing that it was wrong. But in God's Republic they considered it their due.

Even the shops had two classes of goods: the stuff in the front, or the better-quality goods at the back that could be bought at a premium. Hailing a taxi had become a question of trying to be the highest bidder. Set-route taxis used to take you over certain stages at 10 tomans a journey, but in the new Iran you were expected to stand at the side of the road waving a 100-toman note before the driver would even consider stopping. Once you were in the cab negotiations would ensue and the highest bidder would set the route.

This performance was stressful enough in itself, without trying to do it in the summer heat with your head wrapped nice and tight and your body encased in a long coat that inevitably got caught on any inconvenient surface. On my first attempt to get around Tehran by public transport, after forty minutes at the side of the road, with the sweat pouring into my eyes I decided to risk taking a bus that had stopped in front of me as if from nowhere. The bus was mixed-sex and packed, so I grabbed the running rail inside the back door and held on for dear life.

'Give me your ticket, I'll pass it up,' a bonny-faced woman in a floral *chador* said to me as I squeezed into the few inches of space left.

'Oh, do I have to have a ticket? Can't I just pay the driver?'

'Don't worry – someone will have a spare ticket. Anyone got a ticket our sister can have?' she shouted.

Three people came forward to offer their spare tickets over the heads of other passengers. I accepted one, asking how much I needed to pay the woman.

'Just say a prayer for me at your *namaz* tonight,' she told me, returning to her own scanty bit of space.

I was thinking what nice people my fellow Iranians were when I felt something dig into my buttocks. I turned to see a shortish man with greenish-yellow skin grinning at me with a mouth full of several gold teeth, his groin burrowing ever further into my back. I could not believe he was doing it on purpose, but I fled from the bus at the next stop, for the first time understanding the wisdom behind the segregation of the sexes on some of the bus routes. Of course this kind of experience is not exactly unknown to women travelling on the London Underground in the rush hour.

Nasrin told me that night of how, in the days before segregation on the downtown routes, she had stayed behind at university for an extra two hours a day to avoid the rush hour on the buses and thus escape being manhandled.

That evening my Mother's Uncle Naj, a leading journalist and an MP under the last regime, came round to see us and tell us some of the latest jokes.

'A woman passenger on a crowded bus suddenly turned round and slapped the man standing behind her,' Naj said. 'They carried on their journey, but before they had gone much further the woman turned round and slapped the man again before getting off at the next stop. A woman next to the man asked him what had happened: "What did you do to make her slap you twice?"' Naj chortled. 'The man said: "Oh, nothing. I noticed her skirt was caught between her buttocks so I pulled it out for her and she slapped me." "But why did she hit you the second time?" someone asked. "Well, I realised that she obviously hadn't liked me removing the skirt, so I just slid it back where it had been before."'

The British are notorious for their love of lavatory humour, and

Iranians have a similar fascination with sex. Jokes in the Islamic Republic centred on Islam and the mullahs, and had many of them been repeated within the hearing of the Pasdars the teller might well have found himself up against the wall as a blasphemer.

There was almost nothing to do on a summer evening in those days, the television being dominated by religious programming and *Secret Army*.

Now that's another thing that made me mad. There we were, hiding hair from the sun, and our men could go home and watch bareheaded girls in British TV programmes.

The cinema was better controlled and showed films on uplifting and pious themes. The night clubs having been burnt down or turned into cake shops, we also made our own entertainment, which involved gathering over supper to eat and drink the latest meths-like substitute for vodka, and telling the latest jokes. Even these couldn't raise a smile among those of my family who were worn out by years of waiting for change. But we still went through the motions, playing a pathetic farce of trying to keep the Pessian spirits up.

Few of our jokes translate into English, but I was very fond of a series of jokes aimed at the disgraced Ayatollah Montazeri, who had been removed as heir to Khomeini's place on the Peacock Throne by Ayatollah Khamenei. Jokes directed at the disgraced former spiritual successor were in the mode of the Irish joke in Britain. My favourite was one where the Ayatollah goes for a cruise on a British ship with his entourage.

On this cruise the Ayatollah was to be seen up on deck every morning taking his constitutional. As he passed the ship's officers they would say, 'Good morning, Sir', and Montazeri would reply, 'Sir, morning good.' After a few days one of his entourage turned to the Ayatollah and said: 'Your eminence, I had no idea you spoke English so well, what is it that you say to these people every day?' Ayatollah Montazeri replied: 'Oh, it's nothing really. They just say *Salaam Alaykum* and I reply *Alaykum Salaam.*'

I wonder if the Ayatollah was aware of his reputation for mental dexterity as he sat under virtual house arrest in Qom.

5

Under the Veil

Despite my reservations about the new order of things, it was with great expectations that I leapt out of bed at the crack of dawn on the first day of my quest to become Journalist of the Year. I hadn't written a word yet but I had memorised my acceptance speech.

I was going to write about the real Middle East, I was going to show that Iran was not the Evil Empire but was made up of real people with ordinary hopes who feel the same love and pain as the rest of the world.

As ever, Nasser Khan's home was plunged into the gloom of the tomb. I knew that he hated to waste electricity, but this was a new start and I had to throw some light on my search for fame and fortune. This was the big story and there were precious few of us able to write it. With wild abandon I pressed the light switch in the hall – nothing! I tried another switch and still no light. The bathroom light gave the same response as the one in the kitchen, where the only light came from the flame burning under the samovar.

What fun! My first power cut. This was life on the front line indeed. Never mind the light, I would just get washed and dressed before setting about finding out where I had to go to register as correspondent for the *Independent* and the *Observer* among others. I knew not to tell them I worked for *The Economist*, which was not much loved by the mullahs.

In the guest bathroom, where tiles left over from other rooms were mismatched but at least there was a working Western loo, the pipes snarled and groaned – but no water. OK, so I was also in the midst of my first water cut. No problem. Who wanted to be in a boring old country where everything worked, anyway? A touch of breakfast – tea, flat Iranian bread, jam and feta cheese – and I was ready to tackle the Ministry of Culture and Islamic Guidance, hereafter known as 'Interference' or 'the Ministry of Bribes', both more accurate descriptions of its real function.

An hour later, at 8 a.m., the time I had been assured all Iranians were at their desks and ready for work, I attempted to phone the ministry for instructions. But why was the phone dead?

I shook it, I hit it, I put it down and picked it up but to no avail.

'You have to hold on till you get a line,' Nastaran responded to my suggestion that I go next door and report a fault. She then disappeared, her favourite trick, not to be seen again until about noon, when she was discovered making lunch.

So I held on, and on and on and on. She had been joking surely – I had held on for at least fifteen minutes and the phone was as dead as the dodo. Phone lines are property, you buy and sell them, and the more you have the more important you are.

The line I was hanging on to the end of was not in fact Nasser Khan's. His telephone line had been seized by the Martyr's Foundation, which had taken over the assets of the general from whom Bahar had bought the line. We thus had to resort to sharing a line with the upstairs neighbours.

I soon found that I was not alone, as the owner of the line picked up her receiver. It was a bit of a shock at first, this voice coming from nowhere. But I soon realised what had happened.

The voice liked to chat. She told me that actually it was near impossible to get a line in Tehran before noon. As we waited she told me her life story. Having lost her husband ten years earlier she had lived with her daughter until two years ago when her son got a divorce. The child of the marriage stayed with the Father, as was normal in Iran, and Grandma had moved in to look after the child.

We were on to the story of her second heart attack when the phone sprang to life, buzzing the signal that it was ready to serve our every telephonic need. 'Would you mind if I just phoned my daughter? My heart has been hurting all night, so I want her to come over just in case,' the woman asked. No trouble now that the phone was alive.

Forty minutes later I heard the tinkle that meant that she was now dialling another number. I finally got back on the line two hours later when the line took another of its little naps. Three hours after I had first lifted the receiver I got a dial tone all to myself.

I had dialled half the Interference number when the line went dead again. This time it only took a couple of minutes to get back on line and I could actually hear ringing at the other end. A voice replied to my request to speak to the person in charge of foreign journalists with the Persian equivalent of 'Piss off'.

Before I could redial, the phone rang. 'Mehr Hospital?' a woman's voice on the verge of tears asked.

'No, sorry, this is a private home,' I stuttered in my out-of-practice Farsi before she slammed down the phone.

Seconds later it rang again. 'Mehr Hospital?' she asked.

This happened another three times before she really lost her rag and I was subjected to a stream of abuse mainly questioning the legitimate birth of myself and the mullahs, the Shah, Ronald Reagan and 'those blasted British who are behind all our troubles'.

She slammed down the phone once again. Telephone repairs are a growth industry in Iran these days.

I started to dial, but the woman was back. 'Mehr Hospital?'

'Sorry, it's just me again,' I said.

'Your accent is a little strange. Where are you from?' she asked.

'I've lived abroad since I was a child,' I replied, fearing the use of the word 'Britain' in case I set her off again.

'You are here on holiday?' she asked.

'No, I have come back to live,' I said with pride.

'Are you mad?' she snapped. 'This is hell – get out while you can. I would give everything I have in life for the chance to live in America.

'My husband used to be an army officer under that bastard the Shah, who ran away like the scum he is and left us to pay for his stupidity. Now my husband runs errands in an office in the morning and drives a taxi in the afternoon. If he could find a night job he would take it,' she ranted. 'My Mother was taken to hospital last night. My sister is with her but I can't leave my baby. Can you hold on to your receiver for a few minutes while I redial?' she almost begged.

The woman never called back, so I presume she got through to her Mother, or perhaps she just got another crossed line.

Her pain and bitterness shook me. It was all very well accepting the loss of position and fortune in Iran from the safety of North Oxford, but my experience of being passportless in this land had taught me how hopeless and frightening life can become. I imagined that woman pushing her husband to make something of himself. I could see her revelling in the position of an officer's wife, of suddenly being able to afford the Paris fashions no respectable middle-class Iranian woman would be seen without. She must have gone to parties where the wine flowed and ended the evening in one of the many exclusive night clubs that abounded in Iran in the seventies. During the summer she probably went to the Caspian at the weekend, spending the day showing off her bikini on the beach and the night losing her husband's money at the casino.

Even I had found what went on in those night clubs and discos a little too advanced for my palate. One evening I had been on the verge of being kissed by the gorgeous son of a family friend who had been brought along to act as my partner. Before the boy could plant his kiss my Father jumped out from behind a pillar and ordered me to return to our table; as I walked away, I saw one of the many women standing around in the dark of the club sidle up to my beau and start rubbing herself against his crotch.

The people I had now returned to were in an earthly limbo but I had not appreciated their paralysis. I had, when all is said and done, been a foreigner discovering a quaint little Islamic state from which I could escape if the going got tough. But Iranians were living in their own country, with their own people; yet they understood little of the new rules that had arrived just thirteen years earlier and which slowly changed as power shifted from fundamentalists to reformers to right-wingers.

Much of that morning's enthusiasm had waned as I finally got through to Interference. 'You have to come here,' the voice said, putting down the phone before I could ask exactly where 'here' was. Drained, I abandoned my quest for the rest of the day. I would familiarise myself with the territory before again venturing to introduce myself.

The next obvious step was to order all the newspapers to be delivered to the House of Doom every day. Easy matter – just go the newspaper booth and order. You could find them on every other street. But which booth? Every paper vendor within a mile refused to deliver. But someone was bringing Nasser Khan's evening paper. Nastaran, as usual, claimed not to have any idea how to order the paper. There was nothing for it but to lie in wait for the delivery man. For three days I didn't hear his motor bike until it was zooming away. Then one morning I heard the 'vroom, vroom' of his bike, and I threw myself out of the door and into his path.

He looked more than a little stunned to see this woman clad in black cheesecloth shorts and tube top appear before him in the land of the veil. I could see Nastaran cringing in the doorway as I told the man what I required.

The next morning came, but no papers. That evening Nasser Khan's paper failed to arrive. This paperlessness continued for a week, with Nastaran blaming me for offending the paperman's religious sensibilities. Then there came a notice; I saw it on the front step and recognised the picture of the paperman. It advised us of his funeral and memorial services. On the day I had placed my order the man had finished his rounds, gone home and dropped dead.

We spent most of that first month in Tehran with the family in our homes. But as the time for Mahshid to return to England approached Minu insisted that she should at least go out to see some of the sights. Mahshid just wanted to get the visit over with as quickly as possible. What little of Iran she had seen on this, her first post-revolutionary visit had not inspired her to see more. She hated the heat under most circumstances, but to have to endure it thus cocooned was unbearable, and she preferred to stay inside and safe. But she finally gave in and we were off on a tour of the royal palaces, now opened to the public.

When we arrived at the Sadreabad, an enclosure of five palaces, I recalled how many angry evenings I had spent watching the excesses of the Shah's regime. I had almost knocked over the former Prime Minister, Amir-Abbas Hoveyda, in these grounds. I was thirteen and my parents had taken me to my first party at the royal court. I was not much impressed by the tables laden with oysters, caviar and all those other exotic dishes that mean nothing to you during your hamburger-and-chips years. The royal family had settled to listen to the cabaret of top singers that graced these occasions, and I joined the children of the rich and famous in a game of hide-and-seek.

I was in hot pursuit of the Crown Prince, several years my junior, when I came around a shrub to find a rather chubby man telling the prince to be careful as he clutched the newspaper he was reading by one of the garden lights. Too late I tried to stop, but only managed to cling to the paper, tearing it in the process, and cause the Prime Minister to totter in his tracks. Sadly he was left behind by the monarch he had served for thirteen years, and his life was ended by the executioner's bullet.

A year later, outside this very palace, I had stood with my cousin watching the royal helicopter take off. The policeman clearing the crowd ordered us to move. Unaccustomed to being addressed like that by anyone, Naz, the daughter of the Shah's cousin, turned on him with a torrent of abuse. He rewarded her with a swipe on the head with his baton. We rewarded him by telling our Fathers, and the officer was removed from his job and perhaps even jailed. It was strange to be a child with powers to change, and even destroy, the lives of others less well connected.

I was remembering the good old, bad old days as we sat on the veranda of the Shah's palace with a group of tourists waiting for the next tour. One of the men waiting with us asked an ancient decorator why he was painting the building. The man shot a quick look to check that the Pasdar wasn't within earshot before saying: 'He's [the Shah] coming back, and I'm just cleaning up for him.' A group of those within earshot began to cheer.

Six weeks had passed, Mahshid was back in the UK, and I still wasn't registered with the Ministry of Bribes. But I had seen the inside of almost every government office on the Vali-e-Asr Avenue, which a phone call by Minu had identified as the location of Interference's Foreign Media Department. At first I didn't even know where to find Vali-e-Asr, unaware that it was the new name for Pahlavi Avenue. On my first post-revolutionary visit it was something else; at one point I believe it was Khomeini Avenue, but just for one night. Roads changed their names at the drop of a hat. During the war the roads were named after the latest martyr to have lived there, so one week it was Martyr Hassan Ali Road and the next Martyr Muhammad Ali Lane.

The joke goes that Raffers was on a visit to the poor south of Tehran when he spotted a sign reading Pimp Street. Outraged, he demanded that the name be changed by the time he finished his tour. An hour later he returned to see a new road-sign reading: Rafsanjani, the former Pimp.

Call it Vali-e-Asr or Pahlavi, it was the heart of the city as far as I was concerned. Looking down the tree-lined avenue that stretches from the centre of downtown Tehran, through exclusive North Tehran to the foothills of the snow-capped Elburz mountains that ring Tehran, on that road it is always spring, people are always free and Persia still has an empire. It is majestic.

I finally discovered the Interference offices along its lower belly. The building was clean but tacky, the walls were bare, the tables broken and the floor covered with documents discarded by officials who resented any request that would mean they had to work. But when I walked in I imagined that they were razor-sharp, dedicated soldiers of the revolution who would cut me down – professionally – if I put a foot wrong. Well, they would if I could find anyone to register me.

Minu, who had come with me, had made a visit to the place the previous day and discovered exactly who we had to see. He was, of course, not at work. Nor was the head of the department, although his secretary was. As I waited in her office for someone to return, Minu excused herself; ten minutes later she had tracked down an official and I was dragged in to see a woman whose surname loosely translated as 'Lunatic's Friend'.

The two women hit it off instantly, and soon they were lamenting the decline of standards in the Civil Service. Minu, sister of that very Hamzeh who had submitted my passport all those years ago, was a former diplomat based in the US who had resigned after the revolution. I smiled and grinned like an idiot as Minu wrote out my application for a press card and her new friend promised to have the process completed within two weeks. I had not yet learnt that when an Iranian official said two weeks they meant 'some time in the next couple of years unless I can find a way of not doing it at all'.

Three weeks later I still hadn't heard from Interference, which nevertheless had not stopped me doing the odd story for the *Independent*, despite Ms Loony's dire warnings not to put pen to paper until I was officially registered. I took to haunting the corridors of Interference in the hope that they would get so fed up with me that they would give me my card just to get rid of me. That was my first mistake, for it was during one of these visits that I met the man who was to become my husband.

I saw his shoes before I saw him. I had been sitting with my Interference keepers, the boys who ran the press section and who had to give their seal of approval on everything I did, for more than an hour waiting for some indication as to when I might have my press card. I was trying to get into a press conference being held by visiting Azerbaijanis, but without a card I had little hope. Central Asia was the story of the moment, with the press back in Britain divided on whether Iran or Turkey would have more influence in the newly independent Muslim republics.

Then a pair of white, but tattered, patent shoes appeared attached to white socks and a cheap pair of khaki trousers. The next thing I noticed was a pair of Mick Jagger lips under which a set of gigantic stained teeth were attached to black gums. 'What big teeth you have, Grandma!' I thought, grinning to myself. I later discovered that he had interpreted the smile as an invitation to familiarity. I had always wondered why some Iranian women were so po-faced in public.

Before I came to know him I thought of him as 'Grandma'. Nicknames were my way of sorting out one Muhammad from another Muhammad. There are a limited number of names shared among the officials of the Islamic Republic. If you want to confuse the receptionist at any ministry, call up and ask for Mr Mohammadi. Of these you could usually choose between a dozen named Muhammad Mohammadi, an equal number going under the name Ali Mohammadi and a good sprinkling of Mohammadis named Reza and Ali Akbar – although the last seemed to be reserved on the whole for ministers. Intereference was no exception to this rule, the foot soldiers tending to be a Muhammad, an Ali or a Reza – or any combination of these. The chiefs preferred less Islamic names such as Said or Faramarz.

The abundance of the surname Hashemi might have had something to do with its being the President's family name and thus reflected the profusion of relatives in places of power and influence.

Grandma snapped some instructions at the boys of Interference, then turned his attention to me, introducing himself as one of the department's 'experts'. I extended my hand towards him and then checked myself as I saw horror sweep over the faces of my two keepers, Junkie and Sleepy. It would be my downfall, this forgetting that to shake hands was a 'vertical sin' (a sin committed while standing) punishable by loss of one's press card – which I still didn't have. It was a sin I was to commit time and time again; one felt such a ninny pulling away when innocent foreign interviewees extended the hand of friendship.

My attempt to shake hands with Grandma was purely instinctive, but he saw it as a massive come-on, despite my premature withdrawal.

The next day he called me at Nasser Khan's. 'Hello, Miss Gharai?'

'Miss who?' I asked.

'This *is* Miss Gharai, the *Independent*'s correspondent?' enquired Grandma.

Although my full name is Parichehre Mosteshar-Gharai, I had gone under the name of Cherry Mosteshar for so long that it took me a while to work out that this Miss Gharai was in fact me. In the new, supposedly classless Iran, I would find people more often using my tribal name, Gharai, instead of my status name, Mosteshar.

'Yes, yes, it is me,' I said, rather shamefaced.

'It's me, Muhammad.'

Terrific – that narrows it down to several million possibilities, I thought. I said: 'I'm sorry?'

'About your press card,' he whispered. 'We met yesterday.'

'Great. Has it been approved?' I asked.

'Not yet. It takes time, as you have been told. But there is an interesting meeting tonight that I thought you would find useful,' he said.

'Fantastic. What meeting?' I enthused.

'It is private, very, very private, but I have got you an invitation,' he said, a little too smugly, I thought. 'Can you come? I advise that you do if you want to become a famous reporter,' Grandma added.

'Of course. Where do I go?'

'Be outside the ministry at seven tonight. Please be careful – don't tell anyone about this. You know I am taking a risk, you are not allowed to work yet, and you have no permission to meet the people tonight. This is a great chance for you.'

Oh, my God! They were going to kill me, or else I would disappear. But why should they want to? I hadn't done anything yet. They must know about my Father and wanted to hold me again in case he returned. No, that had failed last time, and they must know the papers I worked for would kick up a fuss. But what if I just disappeared? Who would know that I had been lured into a trap? My Mother would know. OK, so what else could go wrong? They could arrest me for meeting a strange man for immoral purposes. But then they would have to arrest him as well.

I agreed to meet him; I could always not turn up once I had more time to think about it. For the rest of the day I worried about that evening. Surely they needed journalists like me, so why set me up? Perhaps they wanted to have something with which to blackmail me into writing pro-regime stories, or to use if later on they needed to get rid of me. At 6.30 the journalist got the better of the coward and I called a taxi.

One of the advantages of going out in the Islamic Republic is that there is no need to dress up. Just pull on the scarf and the coat and you are ready to party. You don't even need make-up.

The strip of Vali-e-Asr Avenue on which Interference lived was lined with shops selling cheap Western goods and jewellery catering mostly to the lower middle-classes. At that time of night it was teeming with life. Families strolled along the wide pavements as if they were out on the Champs-Elysées, the only difference being that the store lights illuminated tired and fallen faces.

In the middle of it all stood Muhammad in an outfit even more tasteless than before. The white socks were still there but this time under baggy grey Oxfords and a deck-chair-striped shirt totally inappropriate for a secret assignation. We shook hands and Grandma led me to an ancient red car, species unknown, held together by mounds of rust. I had to wait for him to open the passenger door from the inside, using a screwdriver.

Half an hour later I was walking through a hole in a wall covered by a blanket into a small yard strewn with children's toys. The clothes on the line across the yard were little more than rags. Around a small basin in the middle of the yard four barefoot, ginger-haired children, aged between two and six, sat and stared at the new arrivals as if we had come from Mars. This was the home of a Lebanese man called Ani and his second wife, Gisu. This Iranian wife, not the Mother of the children, welcomed us. I had already spotted her on my first visit to Interference, where she also worked, and her presence that evening made me feel a lot easier.

What little of her I could see under her *chador* was stunning. Large green eyes were bordered by long, jet-black lashes below thick, slightly bleached eyebrows. Her nose was small and perfectly formed and her lips looked as if they were the model used to develop the

Paris lip. I was jealous: I wanted to look young and stunning even under the veil.

The house was just a long corridor with three rooms running off it. On the left there was a kitchen and a back room, and opposite these was one long room in which the other guests sat. Outside the door were piles of shoes to which we added ours. Muslims do not allow shoes into their homes as they fear the floor on which they pray might be contaminated. There was no furniture in the main room and everyone sat on the floor on surprisingly expensive Persian carpets. At the far end of the room there was a pile of mattresses and bedding, which would be pulled out when the day was over to convert the room into a bedroom for the family. Revolutionary Muslims adopt this way of life even if they are able to afford the trappings of Western culture, such as furniture, as a symbol of their culture and their piety.

I joined the circle of women sitting round a *sofreh* (tablecloth) while nineteen-year-old Gisu brought tea and fruit. Iranian women tend to keep their maiden names and will often be introduced as (let's say) Miss Qomi, wife of Mr Naghash, so I had no idea when I met her at the office who her husband was.

Her *chador* was pinned to a scarf that was tied tightly round her face, and she also wore a long coat under the *chador*. There was no chance whatsoever that anyone was going to catch a glimpse of her flesh that evening. There were three other women, a Lebanese and two older Iranians. The six men sat at the other end of the room next to the bedding. Three of them were from Interference but I had no idea who the others were. Interference were all in shabby brown suits and those dreaded white socks. The two strangers were in tan fatigues, the off-duty uniform of the Pasdars.

The women were eager to hear about England and how Iran was regarded there. They had all lived in Lebanon and one had 'been trained' in Syria, but they were fascinated by the West, especially how easy it was to get a divorce. They delighted in stories of women who had been acquitted of murdering their husbands because of the men's abuse of them. I hope they heard about Mrs Bobbitt, for I am sure they would rejoice.

When the meal arrived the men joined us around the *sofreh* and the conversation became much more general. As they came to sit on either side of me, Muhammad told me our host's real name.

My blood turned cold, for it was a name that anyone who followed the course of Middle Eastern terrorism would have known.

I had believed Yasser Arafat when he had argued that terrorism was the only way in which the Palestinian people could bring their cause to the attention of the world. I had wept as I read *My People Shall Live* by Leila Khaled, who was a member of the Popular Front for the Liberation of Palestine. I had even named my cat after George Habash, the PFLP leader. But face to face with this man I felt terrified and disgusted by the idea. Someone had been full of life, they had breathed and loved and eaten, and done all the other things that meant they were alive. Then this man sitting next to me, this Lebanese freedom fighter at whose table I now sat, had taken that life. He had raised his hand and existence had escaped a body as he watched. I felt contaminated as if death was like dust on this man and it would brush off on to my soul.

But I was a journalist and these were the people that made history, so I sat and listened to him explaining the international Islamic struggle. I let him try to convince me that his revolution would free humanity by subjugating them to the rule of Islam. He accepted that the movement was 'at the beginning' a device of the political reaction against what the Third World perceived as Western imperialism rather than a spontaneous desire for a world dominated by Islam.

'Islam is the tool just as communism was before it. But it is the best tool and the only one that can be triumphant because it is the word of Allah,' he insisted.

He had a natural charm that almost overcame my revulsion at the acts he must have carried out. I was sharing bread with a handsome, articulate, passionate and cold-blooded murderer. In another setting I would have argued the toss with him all night, but although our conversation was in English I could not help thinking that this might have been a set-up to draw out my opinions, and so I said little and tried to resist challenging the core of his philosophy. For me, freedom did not mean the act of giving people the right to agree with whatever system you chose to inflict on them.

By the time we were tucking into our food I was thoroughly uncomfortable. The last time I had spent the whole evening sitting on the floor was at university fourteen years before when my body was still supple and young. Now I had cramp and my back was beginning to ache. Although there was cutlery the other guests ate using pieces of bread to pick up their food. I had never seen people eat with their hands and I quite liked it; there was something comfortingly primitive about it. They had all washed their hands before sitting down to eat and the food never came into contact with flesh, but when I tried I got grease up to my elbows.

The men dominated the conversation, discussing high matters of philosophy and quoting great Muslim scholars I had never heard of. As usual they used 'big words' and I was soon lost. After the plates were cleared away by Gisu and her younger sister, who had been hidden in the kitchen, our host Ani brought out the implements for smoking opium. Call me old-fashioned but I have a natural aversion to all types of addictive drugs.

We ladies retired to the safety of the kitchen and while Gisu did the washing-up she told me about her life. She was the daughter of a minor bank official. Her Mother had worn the veil but none of her generation had adopted it – that is, until she was introduced to Ani by one of her colleagues at the ministry. He had offered her status in the new Iran, as the wife of a famous revolutionary, and she had snapped it up, allowing herself to be persuaded that the *chador* was a sign of political defiance, not of female submission.

'It was good at first. I learnt so much and I took to the *chador* as the price I had to pay. Ani has broadened my outlook – he's given me books to read that have changed me as a person. But the more I see the more I want to see and the less I can just accept,' she told me. 'I love my husband and I want to obey him, but often I wish he was a little different. I wish he shared his life with me, but since we married I have been on the outside. He teaches me but we don't always share. Sometimes I feel like a maid, even though I know it is a wife's duty to serve and to honour her husband. The Arabs are so different from us, have you noticed? They are very strict you know,' she confided in me.

To my shame, I judged the girl harshly, not yet understanding the pressures that keep women trapped in their roles as wives and Mothers which come ahead of their needs as people. I could not grasp why she didn't just say no, or leave.

We were just starting to analyse the plight of Muslim women when Muhammad announced that it was time to go home. I asked to use the bathroom before we set out. Bathroom! I was shown to a shed on the far side of the yard. To my horror it was one of those hole-in-the-ground jobs. Iranians had gone back to this form of toilet more and more since the revolution. I always teetered on the brink of falling in as I struggled to hold everything up while trying not to splash myself.

By the time I emerged it was well past 11 p.m. and the road-blocks were in place. The first time we were stopped my heart missed several beats before Muhammad flashed a card at the Pasdar and was allowed to drive on with a salute. I was surprised that they would treat a civil servant with such respect, and I said so.

'It's a card I have kept from my war days,' Grandma explained. 'I was an official of the Foundation of Islamic Thought in the army. My job was to go to the front and lecture the fighters on the reasons they had to fight the war.'

The story of Muhammad's life followed. He was the sixth of nine sons and three daughters, born into a 'noble' family of the nomadic Qashqai tribe of southern Iran. He was born in a village outside the southern capital, Shiraz, but had moved to the city when he was sixteen. The man beside me looked no more than twenty-seven, even though I had nicknamed him Grandma, so he must have come to the big city well after the Islamic dawn.

He had lost two brothers to disease – I later learned that they had been retarded. Another brother had been killed in the revolution and yet another in the war. He and his cousin Sleepy, one of my keepers at Interference, who had also lost a brother in the war, had been married off to the wives of their dead brothers. Muhammad was only nineteen when he took on the responsibility of a wife ten years his senior and his brother's two sons. He told me that he had never wanted children and felt the two he had inherited were more than enough.

'I hated them calling me Father. When we went out I pretended I wasn't with them,' Muhammad said.

Getting surprisingly intimate, he went on to tell me that his wife had tricked him and become pregnant. He had tried to divorce her for betraying him but was persuaded that it had been an accident and that she would never allow it to happen again. Two years after the birth of a daughter she became pregnant again, and they were again at the divorce court. The night before they were to finalise the divorce his wife had come to his family home with their tiny daughter. His will had been melted by the tears in his little daughter's eyes.

A year later he had taken the family out for a day in the mountains on the girl's birthday. He did not say where he and his wife were when the little girl ran on to the mountain road and into the path of a truck. Muhammad said he could still hear the sound of the impact as the car hit her. She had died in his arms before they reached hospital. I felt so very sorry for him.

'There was nothing then to stop me divorcing my brother's wife,' he told me bitterly.

'What about your sons?' I asked.

'The Martyrs' Foundation looks after my brother's boys and I give all I make for my son. They live in my house in Shiraz, so they are fine.'

I wanted to ask where he lived but I held my tongue; this strange man had already grown more familiar than I found comfortable. By this time I had decided he really was quite ugly, despite his large brown eyes. His features resembled those of Mongols rather than Iranians, and he was shorter than I like in a man.

Muhammad then turned to the subject of my press card. I ranted on about how inefficient the ministry was: how could it take more than a couple of days to check someone out? I had been told that my case had been passed to security.

'You don't understand our system,' my new confidant told me. 'The people you deal with in Guidance probably earn less in a year than you get paid for a single article. You cannot blame them for thinking that they should get a little more from you,' he explained.

'But it is their job. I'm not asking for more than they are paid to do,' I argued.

'Your card is very valuable. You can get to see all the ministers and ask them for favours, so it is worth a lot more than the 10,000 tomans men like Ali earn,' he told me.

He was right. I thought: at the present exchange rate I would earn six times Ali's monthly wage for an average article in a Sunday paper and about four times his wage for 1,000 words in the *Indy*.

Muhammad said he wasn't telling me to pay a bribe to hurry things along. 'But a colour television as a gift would be a nice gesture,' he advised.

I stayed up all that night debating the issue in my head. Yes, it was a pittance to live on. Why shouldn't they make a little bit extra? It comes off expenses anyway. But it's wrong; corruption was one of the main reasons that the people rose up and died for the revolution. Didn't we owe it to the young who had given up their lives to act by their principles? By dawn I had decided that I could not join the world of bribery and corruption, not just because of my ideals but because I wouldn't have had the first idea how to go about it. No, it was best to leave the dirty stuff to those who had the stomach for it.

*　　*　　*

From the beginning I was fascinated with President Rafsanjani, sometimes admiring him, sometimes hating him. But what was sure was that he was the best, as far as I was concerned, of a fairly uninspiring bunch.

I first saw him in action giving out prizes at Tehran University. In a speech in which he encouraged science and learning, Raffers challenged those fundamentalists who argued that there was no place for modern science in the Islamic Republic on the grounds that if it isn't in the Koran you don't need it.

Once he had said his bit, it was the turn of a group of male lecturers to receive awards for outstanding work. As Raffers extended his hand to shake the hand of the first don, the man grabbed it and bent over to kiss it. The President quickly pulled his hand away, placing it firmly behind his back in a gesture to show this hand-kissing was not required. But as if this had never happened the next recipient also bent over the hand in an attempt to kiss it. Each of the lecturers tried this hand-kissing. It was astonishing to see how subservience to authority had become so ingrained that intelligent men could behave with such lack of personal dignity.

The spectacle of grown men groping for Raffers's hands sent my mind back to a time under the Shah when my Mother had taught us to respect but not to grovel. We were off to the wedding of a second cousin, to be attended by the Shah and Empress Farah. Mummy had taught Pari and me how to bow when presented to the imperial couple – just a quick step back with one foot accompanied by a quick bob of the head. My curtsy was a disaster, almost knocking over the Light of the Aryans, but Mummy and Pari executed theirs with dignity. The rest of the gathering scraped noses against carpets in their efforts to be the most respectful. Now Iranians were at it again, bowing and scraping before a leader until he began to believe in his own overblown importance.

Ali Khamenei, the present Spiritual Leader, behaved quite differently to Raffers. He was after all Khomeini's successor and to many ordinary Muslims the most holy man on earth. On one of his frequent trips to the provinces locals strewed the road with flowers before his Mercedes. At the end of every day they lined up to be blessed, the men kissing his hand without shame. When it was time for the women to meet Khamenei, who had become something of a pin-up boy among some otherwise normal women, a white cloth was spread over those long, white fingers of his only good hand (the other had been blown to pieces by a terrorist bomb). As I watched fascinated, a woman handed something to the Ayatollah which he put in his mouth, sucked and then spat out into her hand. The next day the newspapers explained that the woman had given the Ayatollah a sweet and had asked him to make it 'holy'.

Gisu had promised to get me a temporary card to attend one of the mass audiences given by Khamenei, and she was true to her word. It was one of those many special days that have sprung up after the revolution and of which it is impossible to keep track – Support of Palestine Day, Woman's Day, Mother's Day, Great Aunt Twice Removed Day, Glorious Defence Day, Pasdar's Day, Nothing Else to Celebrate Day, and so on. This one as far as I recall was something like Solidarity with the Third World Day, an occasion shunned by Raffers, who, like myself, refused to accept that Persia had joined that collection when only thirteen years earlier it was on the brink of joining the First World.

Masses of guests had been flown in from friendly nations and they were all converging on the Bait-al-Rahbar, the House of the Leader, from where the late Imam Khomeini had issued so many of his edicts. It is tucked away down a labyrinth of alleys and side roads to protect it from ground attack. Journalists from the Third World joined locals for the ten-minute bus ride down the road from the Laleh Hotel. I was the only woman on this bus, Gisu having made her own way to the event. There was no sin in my sitting next to 'our brother Muslim journalist' from Pakistan, since the male representatives from Interference stood over us in deep conversation. But once the bus had stopped and we approached the home of 'the Fragrance of Khomeini', as the great revolutionary's successor was known,

I was sent round to the women's entrance, where Gisu was waiting.

It was one of those affairs one attended stripped to the bare essentials – no watches, rings, notebooks, pens, etc., allowed. As we made our way up to the still relatively empty women's gallery, Gisu started to bad-mouth the leadership present and past: a dangerous activity so close to its heart. Was she genuine or was she just trying to get me to incriminate myself? These are the fears that have always, and may well always, divide the Iranian people. I listened but kept my own counsel.

Women were consigned to a gallery at the back of the great hall above the ranks of faithful men who squatted on the floor and awaited the arrival of their leader on the big stage before and above them. We sat ourselves down at the very front; a puny iron rail was all that stood between us and the sheer fall into the arms of our brothers below.

The men were already there in their hundreds, the Iranians to the left, those from Pakistan and Afghanistan to the right and the centre taken up with assorted Muslims. At the centre were the Lebanese, whose leaders were working their flock into a frenzy of devotion as they beat their chests in hypnotic thudding rhythm and chanted: '*Allah o Akbar, Khomeini Rahbar*' – 'God is great, Khomeini is the leader'.

Suddenly several thousands of men were chanting in unison between the great 'thud, thuds' of their fists hitting their chests. '*Marg Bar America*' ('Death to America'), thud, '*Marg Bar Israel*', thud, '*Allah o Akbar*', thud, and more chants to that effect.

The gallery was beginning to fill up, and a rather large woman came in leading a group of at least 700 women, all giggling and chatting under the wrappings that characterise the *hejab* in the sub-continent. Their heads were encased in layers of once brightly coloured scarves in the prints of India and Pakistan; their *chadors* were colourful and worn loosely over layers of jumpers and blouses.

'Get up,' their leader told me.

'I beg your pardon?' I blinked.

'This is reserved for my group,' she growled as her ladies swarmed round me.

'I don't see a sign,' I replied.

'Ignore her,' Gisu told me, waving a card in the woman's face.

We sat resolutely looking forward while the woman huffed and puffed and her clan piled on top of one another in order to get a prime-site view of the great leader.

Now, Farsi has a letter *zeh* that our Indian sub-continent brothers and sisters cannot get their tongues round and so they replace it with *jeh*. *Zendeh* means 'to be alive' in Farsi, while a *jendeh* is a prostitute. As the mass of the faithful started to chant, '*Khomeini zendeh ast*' – 'Khomeini is alive' – the women who were sitting on my legs and on my hand and any other surface they could find, were chanting, '*Khomeini jendeh ast*'. It was most unfortunate, and someone really should have told the poor women.

I was reflecting on this when a voice rang out: 'The Fragrance of Khomeini has arrived.' A door opened on the stage to reveal the Leader of the Revolution. As the multitude sprang to their feet the women surged forward to get a closer look and in doing so crushed my chest against the gallery railing. For a couple of seconds I could not breathe and my chest felt it would snap, but as the panic built up inside me the woman pressing on my back moved enough for me to free an arm and elbow her and her sisters aside sufficiently to allow me to breathe again.

I was raging at these vixen to no avail when they suddenly sat down as the great man motioned that he was ready to speak. I tried to sit, only to find a woman's head where my bottom should fit. There was not a single centimetre for me to fit into, nor was there any room for me to move away.

So there was no choice but to stand and reflect on the contrast between the calm that descends on those waiting outside the Vatican for a glimpse of the Pope and the frenzy inspired by our own dear leaders. Soon my reflections were interrupted by my sisters shouting for me to get out of their way so they could see their Rahbar. They had battered me, I was bruised, tired, saddened and very angry, and I am embarrassed to admit that my language was not what you might call saintly as I asked how they suggested I carry out this miracle.

*　　*　　*

We Iranians are a spiritual race and nothing will ever remove that instinct for the holy from within our soul. Even those who have never got up at dawn to perform their morning prayer would not dream of walking past a hospital without asking Allah to help the sick. I have never started up my car without saying, 'In the name of Allah', I always call to Imam Ali for help as I try to lift a heavy load and I always add the greeting, '*Alyeh salaam*', after the name of the Prophet Muhammad (AS). These things are ingrained, they are cultural as well as religious, and we would be the poorer for their loss.

I cherish religious ritual; the pilgrimage to Imam Reza fills me with joy, and I always shed tears on the anniversary of the deaths of Hassan and Hussein, Imam Ali's sons. Shia Muslims believe that Imam Ali, the cousin and son-in-law of the Prophet, should have directly succeeded the Prophet himself instead of being merely the fourth Imam. Ali and Hassan were assassinated, and Hussein and his followers were slaughtered on the battlefield at Karbala.

One of the rituals that I cherished more than most is the annual *samanu* cooking ceremony, and I have tried to be present in Iran for it whenever possible. As a teenager, eager to be in the midst of the excitement of Tehran, I had hated our weekends at Maman Joon's summer retreat on the slopes of Mount Damavand, but I grew to love them. It was the closest you could come on earth to the Garden of Eden, deadly quiet, fresh air in abundance, and every fruit your heart desired dangling from the trees that created a canopy over this secluded world.

In the *bagh* or gardens, the ancients in the family and their weekend guests would gather under the marquee in the middle garden to talk of wine, women and song. The food and the *sharbat*, a sweet drink usually made with fruit juice, would be as fresh as the air. There would be a lavish lunch, then those who wished to would snooze in mosquito-net-covered beds placed under the trees beside the brook that runs from a mountain spring through all the gardens on the mountainside.

Step out of the garden, cross a mountain road, and you are suddenly in a barren land leading to the foot of various minor peaks and then on to Damavand itself. Less than a hundred yards from the border of the Pessian garden there lies a graveyard out in the wilderness. In those early days I would spend the sleeping hour climbing up to this graveyard, where memorials to the dead bore the pictures of young men taken before their time.

But going back after thirteen years of revolution I discovered that Damavand had become a very different place. The calm of the Sabbath – Friday in Muslim countries – was shattered by the blare from the loudspeaker installed in the village mosque so that the faithful could not escape the mullah's sermon. The graveyard had grown tenfold, the bodies of the martyrs swelling it to within yards of Maman Joon's realm. Villagers stubbornly used her lower garden as a short-cut in faint-hearted defiance of the family that had dominated their lives for generations.

Months after the revolution Maman Joon's gardener of twenty years had tried to blackmail her into giving him the lower garden, threatening to expose her as an enemy of the revolution. Then well into her eighties, Maman Joon had turned them out that night, telling them to do their worst. It had been quite frightening, cowering in the summer house as revolutionary guards and villagers, who had worked for us since my grandmother was a young bride and before, turned up to turn us out of the gardens. Mummy and Maman Joon took on the hordes as Uncle Pessian and I hid. The crowd soon dispersed and by the next day a new gardener was installed.

Nine years later all was forgiven and forgotten and Mashed-Ali, the gardener who had been so intent on seeing us carted away, was back to help in the annual ritual of cooking the *samanu*, a thick sweet made from germinated wheat and nuts. He had bought a more modest garden further down the mountain with my grandmother's help. His sons were now professionals working in Tehran and his daughters had been married off at thirteen to village lads. His first wife was dead and so at the age of sixty-three he had taken another wife more than thirty-five years his junior – it's not every day a girl gets the chance of a husband with his own garden.

I had been having a lot of trouble with my back and legs for a few weeks, and by the time we made the hour-long journey to Damavand I could hardly walk unaided. Stress had been diagnosed as the cause of my problem and a weekend away from the big city had been prescribed. That weekend most of the family gathered in Damavand for the ceremony.

This ritual had started when Maman Joon made a pact with God more than sixty years earlier. After the birth of Aunt Goldie, Maman Joon had been unable to get pregnant for more than six years. She had still not produced an heir and was desperate to have more children, so she made her pact. If God gave her more children she would cook this sweet every year in honour of the daughter of the Prophet, and would distribute it among the poor and the hungry. She had three more children, none of whom was eager to carry on this time-consuming tradition.

The wheat had started to germinate the previous day and the village women had turned up to help liquidise the ingredients while their husbands dug a pit over which a massive cauldron, in which the *samanu* was cooked, would be placed. By dawn on Friday everything was ready; the fire was lit in the pit and the cauldron filled and placed over it. By lunchtime the ingredients were bubbling and guests were arriving with pistachios and other assorted nuts to pour into the mixture in the hope that God would grant their wishes as well. We all took turns stirring the mixture with massive, person-sized wooden spoons while making our wishes for health and wealth. Maman Joon wished that I might finally find a husband and I wished that I would win the Journalist of the Year award. She obviously had more pull with the powers that be than I.

The new incumbents of the gardener's home, a family of Kurdish refugees, ran around serving tea and cakes as guests came and went throughout the day. Maman Joon was not altogether happy to have Kurds to work for her, believing the stories, of the bitter, that they would cut your throat as soon as look at you, but explained: 'Iranians are too good to be servants today. No, they all want to be ladies and gentlemen,' she said with a snigger as if this were obviously ridiculous.

I watched the gardener's six-year-old daughter as she half hid behind doors, watching us in our designer clothes, and I wondered what the future had to hold for her. Would she be handed over to a stranger, like all the other village girls? Would she spend the rest of her life serving that man and working in some noble lady's kitchen to feed nine children, as her Mother was forced to? Would she ever have the chance to stir the *samanu* and ask God to let her win an award or to publish her first book or to close an important business deal? I took the giant spoon and as I stirred I prayed that she would.

Aunt Homa had managed to escape from the Fat Man for a few weeks and had come to town to see us and her doctor. It was her birthday, but sitting on the veranda of the lower house, a chocolate birthday cake in front of her, she looked so sad and so tragic. She had given birth to six girls and a son, but only four daughters remained. Her only son had been born in the back of a taxi and suffocated before she reached a hospital. Her youngest daughter had died when only twelve years old. The child had gone to the kitchen to ask the maid to bring tea for her visiting uncle, Dada Jan, the giant samovar had been knocked over by an over-excited pet dog, and the girl died of her burns three days later. The Fat Man never spoke to Dada Jan again and did not allow his wife to do so for many years.

I asked Maman Joon how she had ever come to give Homa to the Fat Man, as we watched Auntie swallow a couple of tranquillisers without which she couldn't get through the day. Maman Joon blamed her husband, which caused a chorus of protest from her assembled children.

The whole fiasco had started when Uncle's nanny had left to start working for the Fat Man's brother-in-law. His Father had come to Tehran from the provinces, where he had managed to marry a woman of high birth, and it was her daughter for whom this nanny now worked. The nanny heard that the brother of her new master was looking for a wife, and presuming that the family back in the provinces were also of good stock, she suggested the thirteen-year-old Homa.

One sight of the Fat Man, a penniless and then uneducated youth, and Agha Joon refused to give him his daughter. He had argued that it was out of the question anyway because she was below the age of consent. Dayee Jan was Interior Minister at the time and he dispatched a ministry doctor to examine the girl's mouth and declare her old enough to be married. Grandfather was forced, under pressure from his wife and Mother-in-law, both very strong women, to agree to a marriage ceremony. Iranians separate marriage and wedding, the bride not going to her husband until after the latter. Agha Joon would not allow the wedding for several years. Year after year he delayed the wedding but was finally forced to surrender – something he had never done on the battlefield – when his daughter reached sixteen. The night of the wedding he had cried till dawn.

As dusk fell on Damavand some twenty people remained around the *samanu*, their expectant faces illuminated by the glow of the golden embers. As the air turned from fresh to freezing, some coals were shovelled out of the pit and placed in bins around which we gathered to share warmth and hope. By dawn the mixture was ready, the fires were extinguished and a large muslin cover was placed over the cauldron while the mixture was left to settle.

The next morning, in the cool shade of the walnut trees, the mighty and the humble gathered in the Pessian *bagh* with their pots and pans as Maman Joon presided over the distribution of the *samanu*. After everyone had gone the gardener prepared freshly picked walnuts and his wife set a meal of fresh village bread and white cheese made from the milk of a neighbour's cattle. It was a wonderful moment of pure calm before we made our way back to the pollution, the noise and the restrictions of Tehran.

For the first time in months I felt refreshed and positive about life. It seemed as if I had left behind in Damavand all the fears brought about by the recent deaths. But the calm lasted less than a night. We were woken at two the next morning to be told that the family doctor, a dear friend, had died in a car crash near the Caspian.

6

The Doctor as God

Doctors are not for healing, they are for marrying. They study for seven years in order to fulfil young girls' dreams of being called Khanoum Doctor – 'Lady Doctor'.

'We'll have to find you a nice doctor,' the two aged women, whom I had never set eyes on before, said in unison.

'That's so kind. Perhaps after we come out of mourning,' Mummy replied.

'These days you cannot afford to wait. All the good men are gobbled up straight away. And poor Parichehre has waited so long already,' the elder of the Sisters Grim said with compassion.

'She's not married because she hasn't wanted to. She is too busy with her work,' Mummy retaliated. 'Anyway there are few men that I would consider good enough for my girl.' Which was the story of my life.

'What would be the harm of letting the girls meet someone?' the younger sister asked.

'The girls?' Mother asked feigning puzzlement, although Aunt Omol had already filled her in on the women's plot.

'There is a really wonderful young man, a gynaecologist with a very successful practice in . . . er . . . where was it?' the eldest asked.

'The very best part of Los Angeles. Another chance like this may not come up for years,' the younger enthused.

'He is only in Tehran for a month, and is looking for a wife he can take back with him. He's perfect, handsome and tall, and he has the lightest skin. He is not from one of the best families, so marrying into a good family will be a great advantage for him. He has two girls from his first wife, a terrible woman who just wanted to go out and who neglected their children,' her sister explained.

'Going to the US goes to some of these women's heads – they think all of a sudden they have to have their own life and be like American women,' the younger continued.

'But she only managed to give him daughters, so a wife that produces a son will get his fortune for her children,' her sister added.

'I really don't think we could consider him,' Mummy said in the futile hope that she could put an end to the subject.

'What is the harm in meeting him?' the elder sister asked. 'He will be at our house for lunch on Friday with his Mother; you could bring the girls,' she suggested.

'The girls?' Mother enquired again.

Laughing slightly nervously the younger Sister Grim explained: 'We thought he could have a look at Parichehre and Nastaran and choose which one he likes.'

The fury that erupted from my Mother was something to be seen. She didn't raise her voice, didn't move at all in fact, and yet the anger wafted over the room. Her eyes said 'Die' as she told the two meddlers: 'I have raised daughters, not horses.'

'Perhaps we could have a picture to show him,' the older and bolder sister said as they were shown to the door.

Matchmaking had always been a prime occupation for Iranian women of a certain age, and most families still arranged marriages, no matter what their class. However, before the coming of the Ayatollahs more and more girls were choosing their own mate. But, when it became 'illegal' for the opposite sex to mix, this practice of marriage by photograph had become quite common.

Once the god-like male had chosen a handful of possible wives, he would go about meeting the candidates to pick the lucky lady. Should the groom be an exile, unwilling to return to the Islamic Republic, the girls would meet him in Turkey and the lucky lady be given a quick marriage ceremony before her spouse returned to the country of his exile to arrange for her visa. Many of these girls would be back within a year disenchanted with the man and the West.

Women could provide in their turn two things: inheritance and respectability. Bahar's daughters had both in abundance. Educated and beautiful, they had already come into a considerable fortune from their Mother's estate and their Father looked as if he wouldn't be long for this world. While Bahar was alive she had fended off any attempts at matchmaking, but her death convinced the women of Tehran that finding the girls a husband would earn them extra Brownie points.

A good matchmaker is never deterred in her quest to tie two lives together. The sisters, very distant cousins, were widows with a string of prestigious marriages to their credit. They may have been willing to give up on me, but Bahar's two girls were too good to abandon. Yet Nastaran was adamant that she would never marry, somewhat undiplomatically saying in front of her aunts and married cousins that to be married was to be a servant and a slave. She had been so indoctrinated against the sort of marriage that her Mother had suffered that she had developed a phobia about marriage as a whole.

In contrast to Bahar's experience, Maman Joon had an idyllic marriage. She had been married to build a dynasty and it had worked, for she had adored my Agha Joon, although she had seen him for the first time at their wedding. Maman Joon would talk of the day her Mother told her she was to be married. She had said nothing but her maid had asked: 'Is he handsome?' Khanoum Maman had told her to be silent or have her mouth split open, or words to that effect.

Maman Joon was terrified that more of her grandchildren would end up like Shahnaz, unmarried at forty and now unlikely ever to marry. I was fast approaching the watershed and showing little prospect of catching a mate if left to my own devices. It was this dread of spinsters that caused her to conspire with the Sisters Grim to bring about the meeting with this magnificent catch.

I had been out on one of my raids on Interference, trying to get my press card, when I returned to find Mummy in such a fury that her chest was exploding with pain. She met me at the door and told me to go straight to our room. Before I could get there Maman Joon called: 'Chehreh Jan, come here please.'

There were the Sisters Grim and between them a middle-aged, hunchbacked, scruffy-looking man. The light from the crystal chandelier was reflected in his bald head, at least adding a little light relief to his sullen complexion. Tiny eyes bulged out from behind thick glasses and I had doubts about his teeth being the originals. He couldn't have been far off fifty which might be just about acceptable for a woman in her late thirties, but to suggest him for Nastaran was grotesque.

I excused myself as soon as it was polite and the party left soon afterwards with promises to call soon. The next day Agha Doctor (Mr Doctor) phoned to ask if he might meet Nastaran again. My heart was broken and so was the phone when Nastaran slammed it after thanking him very much but saying that she had no intentions of ever getting married.

Maman Joon was appalled at the girl's audacity and turned her attention to me. The popular view was that I was dying to get married and give birth but that Mummy was determined not to allow it. I was thus a worthy cause, and Maman Joon stepped up efforts to find me a match. To this end one of my Mother's cousins and husband were invited to tea. During the course of the visit the husband, widely thought of as rather a common match for a family such as ours, mentioned that his nephew was in Iran to find a wife. He was not a doctor, of course, but he did run a very successful business in Los Angeles, and thus was a very good catch. It would have been quite useless to tell him that I wouldn't live in LA if you paid me. He would have said that no one in their right mind would turn down the chance of going to the USA.

'I would like your permission to arrange a meeting,' he told me. 'He would be very good for you. He is very rich. You would also be good for him.'

'In what way?' I asked politely.

'Because if he wanted a wife who lived in Iran it would cost him thousands of dollars to get her to the States, but you are British and he could get you over for the price of a plane ticket.'

Truly a match made in heaven.

It took all my ingenuity to come up with excuses why I could not make time to meet this dream husband. I understand that he went away empty-handed and subsequently married his American girlfriend with whom he had been living for six years. Many a man, despite having live-in girlfriends in the West, would return for an Iranian wife that they hardly knew.

A male friend explained this as he searched for a wife for his brother, who had lived in Idaho for more than twenty years, the last ten with a girl called Mandy. 'He just wants a wife who is untouched by another man. Every man wants a virgin if he can get one,' he said, with the assurance of someone stating a universal truth.

There are only three categories of women in Iran: the unmarried virgin, the wife or the unmarried whore. Many of the 'virgins' I met over the years have admitted to allowing boyfriends to enter them by the back door, thus giving pleasure while hanging on to that physical virginity that assured them of a good husband. In England one would feel shy of admitting to being a virgin at thirty-five, but in Iran it is compulsory even at sixty-five if the woman is unmarried. In many, mostly working-class, families it is still customary to gather outside the bridal bedroom and wait for the groom to hand out a blood-stained sheet. Many a marriage has ended on that first night when the woman has not bled and therefore could not be virgin. It also explains the occasional noise of a chicken being beheaded coming from the bridal parlour.

*   *   *

Every paper and magazine in Christendom wanted a story about the treatment of women in Iran. They wanted guts and gore, they wanted subjugation, repression and degradation. Many of my colleagues had provided just that, a picture of women as slaves and as chattels. But that was only half the story. No one came and looked inside the hearts of these women to see the real anguish. They just came and saw what they wanted to see, and these articles lost their power because they ignored the deeper truths.

They looked at the veil, and they said, 'This is disgusting', and then went away to find something else that was disgusting. They said things like 'Women who want to be doctors cannot, so they become hairdressers', so the women who were doctors derided them and the women who were hairdressers despised them. They did not see that it takes money and contacts to get a place to be a doctor; they did not consider that Armenians made up the bulk of the country's hairdressers, a tradition handed down from generation to generation much like coal-mining in the past. In Iran, class dictates profession far more strongly than sex.

I wanted to talk to real women, the kind of women that were taking a full and active part in this revolution. I wanted to see if the devout, pious Muslim woman had an axe to grind. In fact, what I found was that she was unhappier than anyone, for she struggled to see good in a system that made her a second-rank citizen. She had borne arms like a man and was now expected to retreat into the home. A token nine women were members of the Majlis and Raffers's only female adviser restricted herself to matters concerning her sex.

'Islam is, in many ways, a religion full of rights for women,' a woman university lecturer told me.

I asked her to give me an example.

'A woman does not have to breast-feed her child; it is not her duty in Islam, while it is in the West. In Islam a woman has to be paid by her husband to breast-feed. He also has to pay her to do the housework. If he does not pay, she does not have to work. The money she makes is also hers. She does not have to spend it on her home or on her family. Islam says the money is hers and she can spend it on herself. Also her husband has to buy her gold and jewellery with any spare cash he has,' she told me.

However, she admitted that no wife, unless she was a fiend, would actually demand money before feeding her child or working in the home. The lecturer also had a few reservations about the *chador*.

'To get any promotion you have to wear the *chador*,' she explained. 'The scarf and coat are not signs of real dedication to the revolution, and those women who do not wear them will never get the top positions. But can you imagine me in the morning, on my way to work, trying to hold my books in one hand, my son with the other and also keeping my *chador* on my head. It is torture.' She giggled.

She did not accept that there was an alternative interpretation of these so-called feminist perks: your husband paid you to feed the child because it was his child. The woman is used as a mere instrument to produce his family and to keep his house, and like a servant is paid. Once divorced, she takes her belongings and her bride's price and leaves his home and his children. The purpose may have been to liberate women but the practice has disenfranchised them.

The Iranian men I had been brought up with were centuries apart from the men I met in God's Republic. Women could parade naked in front of my brother and he would not raise an eyebrow. He had always encouraged me first to study and then to work. I remember many a night during my adolescence when he and Mummy had stayed up till dawn arguing with me and telling me that a university degree in the hand was worth ten husbands in the bed. From childhood my Father had taught me to fight like a man – if the need arose – and to change fuses, operate videos, repair car engines and all the many little skills that Fathers normally teach their sons. Ask any of my parents' friends who was the manliest man they knew and the odds are they would name my Father; but he would cook, do the washing up, hoover and even shop for those embarrassing items women used – and all this long before the New Man.

Our friend Masoud was another of the men I had grown to admire, for he was kind and fair and behaved like a perfect gentleman. He respected my sisters and me and always treated us just like our brother. Masoud was sent to Oxford as a teenager and grew so close to us that we regarded him as another brother. A brilliant student, Masoud went back to Iran to assume responsibility for his Mother and sisters after the death of his Father. He was now the head of an old and influential family from the province of Khorasan, on the border with Afghanistan. They had a long and illustrious history and even with the coming of the mullahs their vast lands and wealth were untouched.

His three sisters and two female cousins had married the sons of another noble Khorasan family. Generations of inherited wealth made the girls independent and forced them early into the world of business and finance. Fatieh, Fatimeh and Faatan were the very model of the modern liberated woman, as were their cousins and sisters-in-law, Mahnaz and Shomez. Later, when I was alone and lonely in Tehran, it was these lovely women who provided me with the only feelings of family warmth and support. I spent more time with them than with many of my own cousins and found I had more in common with their cosmopolitan lifestyles than with the traditional ancestral attitudes prevalent among some of my kin. So it came as a real shock to find that these women had also succumbed to the pressures of being a 'good Iranian wife'.

Mahnaz had thrown a family gathering to welcome Masoud and his wife home from Canada, where he moved when the revolution started to founder under the weight of the war with Iraq. Mahnaz's home was like a museum of good taste and fine art. I marvelled at the collection of ancient Islamic artefacts and gasped at the latest addition to her collection, a magnificent silk carpet. She giggled as she told us of the trouble she had taken to track this particular carpet down. The search for just the right item had taken years and sent her to far-flung corners of the mullahdom.

'I finally found exactly what I wanted last week. I had put the dealer through the wringer for months, getting the carpet checked and authenticated. Then it came time to pay for it and I had to tell him – like a naughty little schoolgirl – that I had to go and ask my husband's permission,' she said, while her husband sat and grinned in embarrassment. 'Fatieh also wanted a carpet from the same man, and we two grown-up, rich women had to go to our husbands and ask them if we could please spend our own money.'

'What?' I asked in astonishment.

'Yes, we are too silly and too stupid to be able to write a cheque, so we handed all our money over to our clever husbands. When we want something they come and inspect it and huff and hum and we flutter our eyelashes until they agree to let us have some of our *own* money to buy what we had chosen,' she said mockingly.

'But why?'

'Well, my dear Chehreh, you know men are delicate things with frail egos and we have to be very sure to bolster their pride.' She laughed.

I could not imagine that the tiny little man married to Mahnaz would ever dare refuse anything his dynamic and commanding wife asked of him. The innocent in me still thought how strange and unreasonable this behaviour was. I would never yield to that sort of pressure; I would never be in the same boat as these women. I must have misjudged them – they were not the strong women I had always imagined them to be. The women I had known would never give in to such rubbish. But what of my Mother and her sisters? They were also strong and intelligent, but they had handed their wealth to their husbands.

Even those who believed themselves to be Westernised and fully paid-up members of the decadence of the Shah expected their daughters to hang on to their virginity. What they did afterwards was up to them, but a promiscuous daughter could kiss goodbye to any chance of getting a decent husband. Get beyond a certain age without a husband and tongues would begin to wag. The girl was either having illicit sex and therefore a trollop, or she was not interested in the opposite sex and by implication was interested in other females.

One of my new and very dear friends had two daughters whom she guarded against the taint of romantic contact with men. At twenty-one her eldest daughter, Soosan, had never been out with a boy; she had never been to a party without her parents or her twenty-five-year-old brother – himself proud of being a virgin. She had yet to be allowed to go out after dark on her own, even if it was just to the next tower block. After leaving school at seventeen, Soosan had sat at home waiting for the day she would be wed. She didn't have the talent or the inclination to go to university, nor could she work for a living in an ordinary job – this would be considered to shame her middle-class parents, who would appear as if they could not support their daughter. So she spent her days with her Mother's friend or with the daughters of a neighbour, particularly the nine-year-old daughter. It was at the home of this neighbour that I saw a sight that at first turned my stomach and then filled me with sorrow.

While the two girls' Mothers discussed their fascinating morning of shopping with me, Soosan and the little girl sat on the floor. Slowly the elder girl put her head on the younger girl's lap and then to my horror I saw them in a deep mouth-to-mouth embrace. The kiss was passionate and I squirmed in my seat as their Mothers paid not the least bit of attention to the 'snogging'. I wanted to lash out, to tell them that they were allowing the child to be sexually abused. I felt physically sick for at least two weeks after the spectacle and tried to avoid both the parents and the children. Was my revulsion due to ingrained homophobia? I believe not, although not having seen such an act between two females might have accounted for it.

However, my rage was directed at a society that is so obsessed with the 'sin' of sex between men and women that they force young women to satisfy their needs by whatever means possible. Had Soosan kissed a boy in front of her family she would have been disgraced and her life would probably never have been the same again. But she could do what she liked with this child, at an age when the child most needed the protection of adults.

*   *   *

Nastaran had thrown herself into taking care of us and her Father, who was getting worse by the day. His pills didn't seem to do anything for him and Bahar's death had plunged him into a deep depression. Mother grew very concerned for him and persuaded him to get an appointment with a new doctor who was famed for his expertise in dealing with Parkinson's disease.

This was easier said than done, as we discovered on talking to the doctor's secretary. 'You will have to be here at 6 a.m.,' she informed us.

'What for?' Mummy asked in amazement.

'To queue for an appointment. The doctor is very busy and his appointment book is filled up for the next six months. Anyone arriving after 7 a.m. is unlikely to get a place,' she said, as if this were the most reasonable behaviour.

'But it is an emergency and we have been recommended to the doctor by his friend.'

'That is why I am fitting you in without an appointment,' she said, with a new charm in her manner.

'What time should we come?' Mummy asked, now she had established that we had contacts.

'To see him the same day you must queue from 4 a.m.'

'But you said 6 a.m. before.'

'That is for people with an appointment,' she replied.

'When does the doctor start his surgery?'

'It is from 10 a.m. to 1 p.m.,' she said, and then the phone went dead.

Nasser Khan could hardly stand. It took him a good ten minutes to get from one side of his bedroom to the other. He often had to make six or more attempts before he managed to get up from his chair, and his voice was all but gone. The idea of his turning out at four in the morning to wait for someone who would not even turn up for another six hours was ludicrous. There had been a day, before Nasser Khan really needed them, when the best medical minds in the land would have trampled over each other for the chance to treat him.

After much calling in of favours he finally found a doctor who could see him. He returned from his appointment with a prescription for an array of new drugs – drugs that could only be found on the black market. The pill dealers gathered on Nasser Khosrow Avenue in downtown Tehran, a place that takes half a day to reach through the lawless traffic and requires a healthy bank account to be able to negotiate. The cupboards at most of the city's chemists were bare, but on Nasser Khosrow bags were bulging with every drug on earth.

A pill that would cost the patient a mere two tomans at the chemist could be purchased for 200 tomans or more on this street.

On the whole it was not a good idea to get ill in God's Republic unless you happened to be a mullah, a cabinet minister or related to one of these powerful men. Perhaps it had been the same in our heyday – it probably was – but then we were the pampered and the privileged, and we imagined that, just because we could pay for our servants and staff to be treated and educated and housed and employed, then everyone could get these things.

*   *   *

Mummy had been finding that the smallest upset would result in short breath and an acute pain in her chest, and Nastaran was providing much cause for upset with her rudeness and her stubbornness. So when Maman Joon came down from Damavand for her annual check-up Mummy went along to see a tame but elderly doctor.

I heard them return as I sat in the back room writing one of those articles I still wasn't officially allowed to write. I went out into the hall to say hello but the first thing my grandmother said was: 'Your Mother has had a heart attack. She is very ill and might die at any time.'

I was too stunned to move as Mummy came in laughing and saying that it was rubbish.

How could this be? She had been fine, she didn't even want to go to the doctor, and now she might be dying. I couldn't stand it: Mummy was the centre of our lives it was inconceivable that she was in danger. This had been the first month in the last six that had been clear of a death and just as I was beginning to think I could relax – this! It was obvious she didn't have a chance; she wouldn't see out the week.

Oh God, Mahshid and the rest will kill me, I thought, somehow having convinced myself that it was all my fault for bringing her to this unreliable land.

The doctor had told her to go straight home to bed – after she had refused to be admitted to the Cardiac Care Unit at the hospital where he was a partner. She was instructed not to leave her bed for at least a month. She was to avoid salt and fat and was not to lift anything heavy. She wasn't allowed to sit in front of an open window or to stay up later than 8 p.m. Most of all, she must not get angry, for it could be fatal. And she certainly could not fly to England unless she wanted to kill herself. For the next month I rarely slept, staying awake to listen to her breathing in case it should stop.

A second doctor confirmed that there had been two heart attacks and that Mummy had acute angina. Not convinced that there was anything wrong with her, Mummy went about as normal, while we watched with trepidation. She finally agreed that if a third doctor, Dr Jalali, considered to be Tehran's top heart specialist, gave the same diagnosis she would take it easy.

This Dr Jalali had been Bahar's doctor, the man Bahar had phoned that last week to say she was not at all well, but he had been about to go on holiday and had told her to get in touch in ten days when he returned, rather than refer her to another doctor. She was dead before he returned. This was not a history that filled one with confidence, but he was considered the best, and Homa insisted that Mummy should see him before she would agree to come to Tehran. I desperately wanted my aunt there; I wanted a 'grown-up' to take charge.

There was a free appointment in three months' time, the reception-ist told us. But a phone call from Farideh, Homa's daughter, an eye surgeon, got us an appointment the next day at 2 p.m.

The surgery was in a building given over to doctors, situated just yards away from one of our confiscated properties. This soured our mood from the start. An ancient lift made for 'Nine Bodies Only' took us to the sixth floor, where Dr Jalali plied his trade. We walked past the half-dozen people waiting in the corridor and knocked at the door.

'Wait there,' a nurse growled through a half-open door before slamming it shut. We knocked again and explained that we had an appointment. 'So has everybody else. You'll have to wait,' she replied, slamming the door with even greater vigour.

An hour later we were still waiting but had been joined by twenty others. Around 4 o'clock that afternoon all the seats lining that corridor were occupied and women swapped heart horror stories.

'I've been to every doctor in Tehran,' a grey-haired granny, who could do with losing three stones, told us. 'They take your money and then the sons of whores tell you that there is nothing wrong with you.' She took our her collection of reports to illustrate this point. A woman in her early twenties then started comparing cardiograms with the granny.

A young couple carrying two enormous palm plants arrived and were ushered in by the receptionist, a woman we had all come to hate with a vengeance. Mummy started beating on the surgery door again and the abominated one appeared.

'Some of these people have been waiting since this morning. When are they going to see the doctor?' Mummy demanded.

'I'm sorry, but some guests are with the doctor at the moment,' she said, again closing the door and thus missing Mummy's explosion of wrath.

By 6 p.m. this particular 'son of a whore' still hadn't seen more than a handful of people, and my usually ultra-calm Mother was in a rage and encouraging the assembled patients to mutiny. She was just launching on a speech starting, 'What are you? Sheep?' when the electricity went off. From the bowels of the building patients with dodgy hearts could be heard wailing with fear – the lift was stuck somewhere far below us.

It took twenty minutes to winch the lift to just below our floor and at least twelve battered men and women climbed out. An ancient couple had to be handed up. Mummy relaunched her attack on the system: 'They cannot treat you like this if you don't allow it. If you all go home now, the next time this so-called doctor will have to treat you like human beings, not cattle.'

There was a lot of cheering from the forty or so people gathered there in the dark, but as we could not see beyond the end of our noses we stayed put. By the time the lights came back on I had lost all track of time. But as we turned to leave the door opened and Mummy's name was called.

'I have changed my mind. This is not a doctor,' Mother said as the rest of the assembled faint-hearted urged her to go in.

Once inside the receptionist explained that none of the doctor's nurses had arrived that day and she had been left to do all the tests on patients. When she took Mummy's blood pressure it was 'dangerously' high, so some drug was administered before the untrained receptionist struggled with the cardiogram.

Finally we were in with the doctor, who took three minutes to say that the other doctors had given Mummy the right diagnosis but the wrong treatment. The number of previous attacks rose to at least three. He wrote a new prescription with about nine drugs on it and we were on our way out. As Mummy left the room in front of me this monster grabbed my arm, put on his best sorrowful look and said: 'Take very good care of her. Keep your eye on her all the time.'

When we left the building Mummy clung to her chest as the pain hit her. Two pills later and it settled, and she spent the entire drive home cursing the man who had just made me think that she was about to topple over.

The next month was a constant battle to keep Mummy in bed. I did not dare leave her alone for too long and I was not getting a great deal of sleep.

Although Homa had promised to come to Tehran if the doctor confirmed the diagnosis, there was no sign of her. I had expected my aunt to be at our door the moment she found out that her sister was ill – a sister who was a guest in this country, who was far away from most of her children and who knew nothing of the system. But I was slowly beginning to realise that even those living in Iran still didn't understand the new and ceaselessly fluid system imposed by the mullahs. Half the nation were suffering from paralysis while the other half were trying to make enough money to get out.

In fact, the woman who heard that her sister was ill could no longer cope with life. The once pampered woman was worked like a puppet by her demonic mate. He kept her on her feet from morning to night, calling for her to hand him something every time she tried to take a rest. He fell out with anyone who tried to share the burden of nursing him and would drive most hired help away within a week. That year he used his age and heart condition as a powerful weapon to keep his wife at home in Shiraz as much as possible. The news that Mummy was ill caused a dramatic decline in the Fat Man's condition, ensuring that his wife could not leave him for a second.

The sisters spoke only by phone and late at night when he was asleep. 'I'll leave him one day – just let me get my hands on my money' had become Homa's catch-phrase, but that summer it had lost its urgency. It was as if she had finally surrendered.

The only woman to visit Mother regularly was her childhood friend Ghodsi, the victim of yet another bad marriage to an over-dominant male. She stayed with Mummy while Nastaran and I went shopping for food – the excuse Ghodsi had used to get out of the house. She always left after a couple of hours.

Ghodsi even cared about the strain that the illness was having on me. She turned up on the doorstep one day, insisting that she take me to lunch, since I had not been out of the house for ten days. The meal was rushed because Ghodsi was keeping an eye on her watch. She had told her husband, known by her friends as the He-Devil, that she needed a new outfit for when she took off the black she was wearing in memory of her Mother, and that we were going out to buy some material.

That evening Ghodsi phoned. 'If Seyma phones you, tell her we went to buy some material together today,' she said in a panic. 'When I got home he [the He-Devil] asked if I bought anything and I said yes. Then Seyma phoned and her Father told her I had been out buying material. I couldn't tell her I hadn't because he was listening. She wanted to know the colour and what type, so I said grey jersey. Then she asked me how much and I had no idea how much material cost so I said 4,000 tomans a metre,' Ghodsi said, beginning to giggle now.

Then it got really bad, for this was a true bargain, and Seyma wanted to know where her Mother had bought the fabric. 'I told her I had no idea. I said, "You know me, I never concentrate on where I go." Then she wanted to know the road at least so I told her it was Yazd Street where I know they have a few material shops. She started to ask what the shop was like. She described one of the shops and I said, "Yes, that was it." Twenty minutes later she was at the door wanting to see if the jersey was any good. She said she wanted to go and get some first thing in the morning, but I know she wanted to see if I was lying. I told her that you had taken it home with you. So if she phones just say you are not well enough for her to come round.'

Next day Ghodsi escaped again and spent four hours searching for the right fabric. She had finally settled for a light black that could pass for grey if you squinted. Inspired by her success at getting away with the lie, Ghodsi bought some navy jersey to have a suit made for her other daughter, Shahpari.

Now the two sisters were mortal enemies and Shahpari was out of favour with her Father while her sister was in. Thus we were launched on another sham. The day the suits were ready I went round to fetch Ghodsi with my cousin Minu who was playing chauffeur. But Seyma was on one of her rare visits to her Mother and insisted on coming to the dressmaker with us.

In the car Ghodsi shoved some money into Minu's handbag and hurriedly begged her to claim that the second suit was hers. The poor dressmaker was completely confused as Minu, whom she had never seen before, enthused over how much she loved her suit. Now Shahpari is a very petite size 8, while Minu is a fullish size 16 – I didn't know whether to laugh or to cry.

'Try it on,' Seyma said, obviously suspicious.

Her Mother turned several shades of red, and I tried to suppress manic laughter. Only Minu kept her head, saying calmly that she had her period, which made her swell, and she would try on the suit at home. Ghodsi downed a couple of Valium on the drive home.

How the Fathers and daughters had managed to break this woman so completely was unbelievable. She constantly maintained that she stayed in a life she detested because she wanted her money. The He-Devil had succeeded in taking control of her fortune and throwing much of it away on his ego, buying houses in exotic places they would rarely visit. Meanwhile he subjected his wife to very subtle torture.

One day, on a visit to their Riviera home, the He-Devil told us a tale that made my blood boil, but he merely thought it was funny. The couple had decided on a day out to Monte Carlo. Once they were on the motorway he suddenly claimed there was no petrol, blaming Ghodsi because she was the last to drive the car. Instead of finding a garage he continued on his way, constantly warning that they would run out of petrol soon. Ghodsi, her nerves weak at the best of times, was chain-smoking.

'As she reached to push the car lighter I snapped at her that she was wasting petrol,' the He-Devil told us. Ghodsi giggled nervously. 'She pulled her hand back as if she had an electric shock. I laughed so much when she finally realised it didn't affect the petrol.'

It was a small example of the methods he used against his wife. She was never allowed to relax and he used every opportunity to unnerve her.

About six months before Mother's illness, Ghodsi had tried to kill herself. It was not her first attempt but it was the closest to success she had got. Aunt Homa and the Fat Man had been in Tehran for the funeral of a friend and had spent the evening with Ghodsi. In the early hours of the next morning the He-Devil phoned to say that his wife had taken some pills. Homa rushed back and found her friend in a coma. It was several days of intensive care before she came round again.

When she recovered she finally made the decision to leave her husband and she went to Shiraz with Homa. There were days when her resolve was strong, but the longer she was away from her husband the weaker she became and the more she started talking about going back 'to get her money'. Within a month she had returned to her solitary hell, within two she was threatening suicide again.

*   *   *

Mummy was gathering strength but she still needed vast amounts of medication. This we obtained through the brother of a friend who was a doctor. He had treated Mother several times on previous visits and was a friend more than a family doctor. That autumn he would pop in from time to time to keep an eye on Mummy. One morning he turned up early to tell her he was going away to the south for a few days. That night his sister phoned in a panic, saying he had had an accident and nobody knew what had become of him. By the next morning we knew that he was dead.

This was getting ridiculous.

It was to Shiraz that we took Mummy when the doctors finally gave permission for her to move. We both needed a break: the tension of her illness, meeting deadlines for various magazines and living in the House of Gloom was getting to me. The summer was over, I still hadn't got my press card, and Muhammad had promised to try to hurry things along. Maman Joon was going to Shiraz for the winter and so we went with her.

Our first night and day in the City of the Rose and the Nightingale went off without incident. The granny flat we shared with Maman Joon was a good deal scruffier than when I had last stayed in it in 1980. It was as if it had been caught in a time-warp – the air-conditioning controls had fallen off the wall and been stuck back with tape, the wallpaper was peeling off the walls, and the carpet was frayed and worn. The kitchen had turned into a laundry-room where

Maman Joon washed at a stained sink. To reach it she had to stand on a precariously balanced soap-box.

The second night we were sitting downstairs watching a video of the wedding of a girl we had never met when Maman Joon decided to go to bed. She wouldn't let anyone go up with her and so we settled to watch another video. Two hours later we heard someone banging on the ceiling. I was upstairs within seconds to find Maman Joon flat out in the middle of the sitting-room. She had fallen off the soap-box and had tried to drag herself to the phone. She was screaming with pain and clutching her right hip. It was 2 a.m. when my aunt phoned a friendly doctor, an ENT specialist, who rushed round. He assured us that nothing was broken and advised us to leave her on the floor until morning, then have her carried to hospital for an X-ray.

He left the three of us huddled up on the floor around Maman Joon, who kept shouting that her leg was on fire. She finally got so bad that we decided to call an ambulance and try the hospital anyway. The ambulance arrived and the driver, who I presume was also a paramedic, pulled Maman Joon's leg about a bit and pronounced it intact. He moved her to her bed and left us to try to lessen the pain by moving the leg till it was comfortable. The next day an X-ray showed that there was nothing broken, and Maman Joon was prescribed some physiotherapy. Her shrieks of pain and constant moans of agony were put down as hysterics from an attention-seeking old woman. No matter how much she insisted that there was something very wrong with her leg and that it was getting worse by the day, the doctors insisted that she should be ignored.

With Mother's bad heart and Aunt Homa's bad back, I was the only fit person around, and I wasn't exactly Miss Healthy myself, so we had to bring in Homa's driver to carry Maman Joon to the bathroom, a place she visited every half-hour or so. She moaned and screamed twenty-four hours a day, never sleeping for more than a few minutes at a time. There were moments when I longed for just an hour of silence.

Mother was at her wits' end, already having ample reason to distrust doctors, but Homa insisted that her Mother had the very best attention. Every few days we would go to the doctor again and be sent away despite Maman Joon's obviously weakening condition. No amount of painkillers, including morphine shots, would put her to sleep at night, and if she did not sleep nor did anyone else. Maman Joon was getting frail and desperate and we were lost as to what to do to help her.

While we struggled with Maman Joon in Shiraz, her sister-in-law, Khanoum Sepahbod ('Madam General'), Dayee Jan's widow, was fighting for her life in Tehran. She was one of the last of a breed of great, noble ladies.

I really thought that one more piece of bad luck and I would go mad. And then Goodi, Dada Jan's ten-year-old son, phoned from Tehran to see how his grandmother was. Mummy and Homa were busy massaging the painful leg, so I spoke to Goodi.

'If I tell you something will you promise not to tell anyone?' he asked me.

'Of course,' I said, sitting at the foot of Maman Joon's bed.

'Khanoum Sepahbod is dead,' he said.

I was stunned. I wanted to scream and shout, I wanted it not to be true, but it was, and I didn't even dare look sad. This was news no one needed. But try as I could I had to tell someone, so as soon as Homa went downstairs I followed and broke the news. She cried for about a minute, then suddenly her tears dried up.

'I'm going to tell Ghodsi. I'll ring her and tell her right now. She always gives me bad news, now it's my turn to give her some,' Auntie said with a resentment and bitterness in her voice that was new and uncharacteristic.

Maman Joon took the news well and seemed even more determined not to risk slipping away in her sleep. Few of us got any sleep in that household, except for the Fat Man, who used the chance of so many captive Pessian women to display himself at his most vulgar. On the evening after we had returned from taking Maman Joon for the X-ray and Mother and Homa were upstairs putting her to bed, I found myself alone at the dinner table with him and the driver, a young man called Hamid, whose sister Fati was the woman whose wedding video we had been watching the night before.

'So did the doctor have a good look at your grandmother's fanny?' the Fat Man said.

I was stuck there at the table with this fat, frog-like man, whose pants showed through the fly of his pyjamas as he sat there stuffing his unshaven face and just beginning to get into his stride. The flood of sexual fantasy that issued from his lips had me rushing off in tears like a complete ninny – they were tears of rage. I had seen him reduce

Homa to a similar state with his outbursts. I should have bluffed it out, I should have played the hard-nosed journo who had heard it all, but I was just too shocked.

All I wanted was for Mummy to be well enough to fly to England where I would again be safe and secure. But the nightmare seemed to have spread to England. Although I had not seen Robert Maxwell's sons since I was at school, I took their Father's death as another incident in the assault upon my sanity. Everyone I had ever come across seemed to be dying. It got worse as Mahshid, now safely back in Oxford, told us that my nephew's childhood friend had been found dead in bed and no one knew why.

I was just taking in the full extent of this tragedy when she added: 'Freddy Mercury died last night.' I was devastated: this death seemed even more personal than all the departures of the last year. Freddy was a nice Zoroastrian boy, and we all know that Zoroastrians were originally Persians. We Persians had been so proud to see one of 'our boys' doing so well. Despite the mullahs' outlawing pop music and Western culture, Freddy can still be seen in the opening sequence of the Friday weekly news summary on Iranian television.

I had decided that this attempt to settle in Iran had been a terrible mistake and that I should pack my bags and go to England when Muhammad's cousin at Interference phoned to say I was expected for an interview with 'our brothers at Islamic Thought' in two days' time. I had no idea what 'Islamic Thought' was and what sort of questions they might ask. A friend in Tehran, who knew about these things, suggested that this might be a session where I had to prove I was a good Muslim. Panicking, I started to try to learn the names of the Shia Imams and similar religious details. This time, perhaps, they would catch me out and I would be going nowhere but Evin prison.

7

Hating Robert Fisk

The road to gaining a press card in the Islamic Republic was a long and slippery one and it had been set back months by one Robert Fisk, superstar. Let me confess from the outset that I had been insanely jealous of Mr Fisk for some years. He was doing exactly what I had wanted to do – cover the entire scope of the Middle East – and, worse, he was doing it well.

I had grown to resent him even more when as a sub-editor on the *Independent* I had been told that his copy was sacred and I was to treat it as if it were the word of God. Other people's articles I could massacre to my heart's content, but with Fisky I had to be pretty sure I had a very, very good excuse before I dared to change even the most lowly comma.

On my return to Iran I had pledged to make my name synonymous one day with coverage of things Islamic. Having ruled out bribery I had returned to 'undue influence' to try to hurry Interference along. An old friend, recently returned from France, knew a boy who knew a man who was related to a woman whose best friend knew a man who was married to the cousin of the wife of the man who ran the section that was to issue my card. A word in the right ear and my application had been put at the top of the list.

I imagined that the waiting was over when Muhammad said I was to be issued with a 'temporary' card. This entitled me to attend selected press conferences and to cover any stories brought to my attention by Interference. But I was not, under threat of dire punishment, to write anything not sanctioned by my keepers.

Taking no notice of these warnings I had been filing stories for several months. The forthcoming Middle East peace talks, to be held in Madrid, were the big Middle East story in 1992 so I had rejoiced when the Islamic Republic decided to hold an alternative conference. This I wanted to attend more than anything; not just because of the news value but because there was some talk of the likes of George Habash and perhaps even Yasser Arafat attending. However, Interference, in its wisdom, decided that it was not necessary for me to attend this terrorists' shindig at the Hotel Esteghlal – the Hilton. After much righteous indignation and threats that I would embarrass the regime by telling the world that they had barred me, I gave up the attempt to get their blessing. I was going to get in despite them.

The Hilton had been my base since I arrived, I met all my contacts there, and I used the hotel fax to send my stories – surely I would have no trouble getting one of the staff to smuggle me in. It had not occurred to me that the Ministry of Bribes was depending on this conference to boost its yearly earnings and that a nice stereo for one of my keepers or a gold coin or two could open the doors of the hotel. As the world's freedom fighters converged on Tehran I imagined that no really meant no. Think they could keep me out, did they? Better men than these had failed, and faint heart never won awards. It would be easy; I would just stroll into the hotel saying I wanted to collect a fax – and I arranged for one to be sent there on the first day of the conference.

The commando unit of the Islamic Guards that was positioned at the entrance to the Hilton had other ideas. No blustering about being 'the *Independent*'s correspondent' could persuade them to remove the barrel of the machine-gun they were – yet again – pressing against my nose.

'This is not a very Islamic way to treat a lady,' I complained as I withdrew to the safety of my hired car – which was now blocking the route of officials' cars off the highway and into the conference. I had to try another strategy.

A fleet of radar-fitted, armour-plated American limousines ferried in the great and powerful of the terrorist circles. Lesser figures were driven back and forth in a fleet of matching navy BMWs and the odd top-of-the range Mercedes-Benz. If I couldn't get in I could at least watch the show. So I set up on the wall for my vigil, ignoring the soldiers' instructions to 'go away'.

One of the advantages of Islamic tradition is that men cannot touch strange women, so as I sat there the guards could do nothing but frown at me and wave their weapons. Finally they decided if I was mad enough to sit there under the midday sun I was mad enough to risk being shot and they withdrew to the shade of their makeshift shelter.

A group of Afghan Muj wandered out at lunch-time and gathered in front of me trying to decide how to spend the afternoon. My Pushto wasn't nearly good enough for me to follow the conversation but I gathered enough to realise that they considered this visit to Tehran as a bit of 'rest and recreation' from their own civil war. They were about to move off when the guards pulled back the barrier to let a particularly luxurious Mercedes pull out. In the back the Afghans spotted one of their leaders, and as they roared with laughter and approval the tiny figure in the back waved a stump where a hand had once been. This raised even greater laughter. After these fighters for the faith finally dispersed I pondered on the benefit their little break had brought to the people back home suffering the consequences of these men's war games.

From time to time the odd Iranian would arrive, unaware that the Hilton had been declared part of Palestine for the duration of the conference. Without exception the Iranians cursed the government that was throwing away their money on 'this rabble' or 'these peasants' or 'these murderers and savages'. To the mullahs' credit, such criticism would never have been tolerated under the Shah.

A grovelling fax – sent from the main post office – to my editors at the *Independent* apologised for failing to cover the conference received no reply, and I was convinced that they must have decided that I was totally useless. I was to learn the reason for the silence not from my colleagues but from Interference.

An early-morning call from Ms Loony summoned me to an interview with Interference the following day.

'We have had a report from London that you have been writing without permission,' she told me. I could not deny it. 'There is no more I can do for you,' she told me before assuring me that there was no way I would now get my card.

A call to Muhammad confirmed that I was in deep trouble, but he was sure I would just be asked to leave.

The next afternoon I was ushered into the office of a short, moustached and not unpleasant-looking man dressed with style in spotless beige. He asked if I wanted to talk in Farsi or in English, and I chose my native tongue, thinking it would count against me to appear too English. The fact that I could not fully express myself in Farsi did not deter me. In fact I am sure that this quaintness in my speech may well have saved me from a worse fate then and on many other occasions.

'We have had a report that you have written an article damaging to the reputation of the Islamic Republic and its leaders,' he said solemnly.

'I have always not been against my homeland and my people, which I was ready to be dead for. I am from a family of people who have been dead for their country,' I spluttered forgetting the word for martyrs. I could see from his eyes that he had idea what on earth I was babbling on about.

'There has been a highly damaging report and we think it was in the *Independent*,' he told me.

'I have not written anything bad. How come that it is you are not knowing what paper?' I said as my grammar deserted me.

'The name on the story is Robert Fisk, so it must be the *Independent*. You are the *Independent*'s correspondent here,' he replied, as if this were making sense.

'Do I look like Robert Fisk?' I asked outraged. The expression meant nothing in Farsi and he just stared at me. 'I am not Robert Fisk; I don't write as Robert Fisk. If Robert Fisk wrote something you do not like you should tell Robert Fisk, not me.'

'Robert Fisk is no longer in Iran,' he told me, as if this explained everything.

'You can't get to Robert Fisk so you pick on me! President Rafsanjani asks Iranians to come back and help their country and the revolution says Iranians must be put before foreigners. I leave a secure position on the *Independent* to come and serve my country, and reverse the wrong things said about her, but just because some foreigner has done something I have to suffer. You shouldn't have let him in anyway. You had an Iranian who is registered as the *Independent*'s person here. We should be cross at you for still bowing to foreigners above Iranians,' I ranted, beginning to warm to my subject.

The inquisitor then went on to reveal, rather shamefacedly, that Robert Fisk had been banned from entering the country. According to Interference he had sneaked in with the Lebanese delegation and had not been spotted on the visa list. He then sent me away saying that they would have to withhold my card for at least two months. But he added that I should not worry; he would tell security that he believed me when I said I loved my country.

London were amazingly silent on the subject of Mr Fisk, whom I was coming to hate with a vengeance. Although I had got away with writing articles up till then, I knew that now I would be under closer scrutiny. I was thus restricted to publications that did not advertise the names of their correspondents.

My experience with Interference did not fill me with confidence as I finally turned up for my all-important interview with Islamic Thought, whatever that was. I had briefly studied the Koran at university and listened intently to my parents' and Maman Joon's version of Islam, but I could not stray beyond the very basics.

It was with some trepidation that I entered the room given over to my inquisitor. The last time I had seen a figure like the one that sat behind the broken desk was on one of those newscasts from Tehran during the revolution when hairy men beat their chests and other people's heads in devotion to Khomeini. This enormous man, in the compulsory combat jacket and designer stubble, was straight off the bloody streets where crowds had ripped 'servants of the tyrant regime' to pieces.

The scene I walked into came straight out of some cheap spy novel. He sat against the light of a large window. On the desk in front of him a lamp shone, despite the sunshine flooding into the room. I presume his features were supposed to be obscured and I was at this stage expected to be quivering in my shoes. But the obvious set-up made me want to laugh and set me at my ease. I had had such a bad time of it up until then that I would have accepted a decision against me with relief.

I thought the figure standing in the corner was a particularly realistic version of those wooden Indians you see outside shops in westerns, until it moved to sit opposite me. For the next ninety minutes it sat staring at its feet with an impenetrable expression on a much-creased face. Sitting Bull, as I came to call him, for another name was not volunteered, was to become my shadow for the next eighteen months, eventually giving up attempts to hide behind pillars when I spotted him – which was often.

The scene may have been poorly constructed, but his boss was no cheap-novel spy; he was the real article. By the time he had finished playing his mind-games with me that day I was convinced that I really was a British spy sent to topple the Islamic government. He never suggested any such thing, but his eyes said 'We both know what you are'.

I explained how I wanted to put the record straight on Iran and Islam, how I meant to redress the balance of prejudice and misrepresentation that had dominated in the Western press.

'We don't want people who just come here to make money and then go back to the West,' he told me once I had stopped babbling about my good intentions.

'I am here to stay and to serve my country,' I assured him.

He started the interrogation at my birth and took me through the next thirty-four years in microscopic detail. Just when I got into my stride on one subject he would jump to something I had mentioned in passing earlier, and grill me on exactly what I had meant. While I was telling him about my days at university he would suddenly ask some question about my parents. He must have known of my family history but he did not mention the courts or our convictions. As we spoke I was terrified that some hair would make its way out from under my keffiyeh, the tablecloth headscarf as worn by Yasser Arafat. Did I clean off all my mascara last night? I thought, as I reeled off the list of jobs I had since leaving Manchester.

I thought of repeating the white lies I had told Babai in order to avoid admitting that I was a journalist, even though every Muslim knows that 'the liar is the enemy of God and will go to hell'. On that occasion I said that I had been in Hong Kong on a work placement studying harbour management – it was the first thing that came into my head. Having told the first lie I had to continue, saying that I studied port management at university. This time I played safe and went back to being a journalist.

Neither of us mentioned that I was supposed to be the daughter of a notorious CIA agent – for that is what it said on the Islamic

Court's judgement that had deprived us of our assets. He didn't mention that I was on the list of those barred from any financial transactions, meaning that I could not open a bank account, buy a car or rent a flat.

I was used to my broken Farsi causing much hilarity, but the more this guy got into our interview the more he was enjoying himself, and the less I understood what he was saying. His enjoyment reached its peak when he asked me: 'Are you in a hurry for me to give you your press card?'

'I don't think you could say I was rushing you – I've been waiting for four months already,' I said somewhat irritably.

His face was suddenly covered with an enormous smile and his eyes twinkled. 'It's actually three months and ten days,' he managed to say before bursting out into uncontrollable laughter. Even Sitting Bull had squeezed on a grin.

'You are making a mistake – it is exactly four months,' I replied.

'No, no, no,' he giggled. 'It is *exactly* three months and ten days today,' he chortled.

Had he gone mad? I searched in my bag for my diary. 'Look,' I said, opening the diary at the entry that said, 'Went to get my card, met mad woman who talked to ghosts.' By this time he was laughing so hard he almost fell off his seat. He could hardly get out the words as he explained that I would have to return for another appointment in 'a few weeks', and as I was waved out of the room I could hear him bursting his sides.

That night I told Minu of this extraordinary performance.

'The dirty dog,' she said, turning red. After much urging she explained that three months and ten days was the time a woman had to wait between temporary marriages to ensure she was not pregnant. 'He was flirting with you, the bastard,' Minu added, in case I hadn't got the message yet.

This could not be, this was the Islamic Republic and the man was so obviously Hezbullah. In a country where men and women are not allowed to shake hands surely an official would not dare *flirt* with an innocent young journalist.

Shia Islam is unique in allowing *seegheh* or 'temporary marriage'. The two sides agree to be married for an hour or a month or fifty years – whatever they want. The man can end this marriage at any time and the woman is not allowed to marry another man for 100 days in order to be able to know who the Father is if she falls pregnant.

Muslim men must never be deprived of their sex. Years earlier I had heard Ayatollah Khomeini advising wives to find their husbands a *seegheh* during their periods or when their husbands went on trips. I couldn't believe what I was hearing. The practice was especially well developed at pilgrimage sites such as Qom and Mahshad where male pilgrims would take a *seegheh* for the duration of their visit. In my great-grandfather's time, when rich men sent their wives out of the city to avoid the summer heat, they would take a *seegheh* to ease their carnal urges. Many claim that the Foundation of Marriage, set up after the revolution, is just a legalised brothel through which the regime provides women for the faithful – mostly as a temporary wife.

*   *   *

It had been a brief interlude in the drama that was just about to move into a new act.

The day after my encounter with Sitting Bull and his boss Bright Eyes, news came from Shiraz that Maman Joon had seen a new doctor who had confirmed that her hip was indeed broken. Once this had been diagnosed they had to pull all the strings they could to get her admitted into 'the best orthopaedic hospital in Shiraz' before searching high and low for the replacement bone, which Homa had literally handed over as the surgeon walked into the operating room.

It was the hospital from hell. Walking into it for the first time, I started sobbing. The paint was peeling off the walls and the whole place stank of the toilets. Moans came from rooms where cock-roaches shared the beds.

Maman Joon was in a room for four, just opposite one of the reeking toilets. Her orthopaedic mattress had a crater in the middle; the torn and stained hospital sheets had been replaced with ones from home. The sink by the door dripped all night and would not have won any cleanliness prizes. The floors were filthy, the walls were filthy – the whole place was squalid. A large bin under the sink held soiled dressings from patients present and patients past, this in the era of AIDS. It slowly smouldered in the corner, threatening to infect us all.

The room was shared for the first few days by only two other women. In the bed next to Maman Joon there lay an enchanting nineteen-year-old girl from the Lar tribe, a colourful and beautiful people. She had no idea that she was no longer a Mother, her baby girl having died in the crash that had seen her rushed to that Hades with a lump of metal embedded in her spine. It was fascinating to watch her visitors. When they came together they held hands, bobbing and bowing and repeatedly kissing each other's hands in a carefully choreographed ritual. Her Mother and Mother-in-law took turns nursing her day and night. It was the latter who told us that the girl had lost her son the year before; he had fallen into the village well and drowned.

It was not clear if the girl would ever walk again. On her second day the surgeon stopped long enough at her bedside to ask if the dressing on her wound had been changed. It hadn't. That night, around midnight, as my Mother kept vigil, they were woken by the girl's screams. A nurse stood over her with a soiled dressing in her hand. 'If you don't like it here you can get out now. Come on, get up and get out,' she bellowed as the patient whimpered with pain. This 'angel' had sneaked up on the sleeping girl and ripped off the dressing.

'Who can we report her to?' Mother asked my aunt the next day.

'There is no one to complain to,' the sister of the third patient told us. 'You complain and they will just make things worse for you.'

This did not stop Mummy finding the hospital administrator and telling him that she would be reporting him to the International Red Cross. Suddenly we started getting four-star treatment in our little corner of torment.

The third corner of this demi-Hades was occupied by Nosrat, an octogenarian street trader, and her sister Tooran. Nosrat was a shadow of a woman, years of opium addiction having left her a wafer topped with waist-length hair, white at the roots but with the bright copper-orange residue of a henna tint on the ends. The sisters had been abandoned by their husbands, who had also been brothers and the women's cousins, more than thirty years earlier. Tooran had once owned a trailer from which she sold fruit and vegetables on street corners.

'Our neighbours hated to see two women surviving on their own. They did everything to make trouble for us,' Tooran told us. They had finally been forced out of business and lost the trailer. The sisters had been selling cigarettes from a tray at the side of the road when a mule went mad and delivered a kick that broke Nosrat's hip.

On the odd occasions when she was *compos mentis* Nosrat would pull herself up in her bed and tell anyone who would listen: 'I don't have any luck even with my bad luck. Other people get knocked down by a BMW and can get some money out of the rich driver. Me – I get broken into two after a collision with a mule. Musa Agha [the mule's owner] hasn't got the string to keep his own trousers up let alone pay for me to go to hospital,' she would say with a giggle.

If anybody had reason to give up it was Tooran, who had been abandoned not only by her husband but later by her children. Despite her age she still had to work to support herself and her sister, who would now need constant nursing. However, she was probably the most cheerful woman I have met, her smile slipping only twice and her humour helping us through some of the worst days. I'll always remember the time I ventured into the fetid toilets to find that the person using it before had emptied her bowels on the floor. I had thrown up in the big bin that stood beside the sink in our room. The sight of the blood-soaked dressings in this bin turned my stomach even more. Tooran wasted no time cleaning me up, organising the removal of the bin and then taking a hose to the mess in the toilet while making one think she considered it to be a favour to be allowed to do this.

This just made it worse when she finally did cry. It was late one afternoon and the assembled patients and relatives were swapping hospital horror stories. Tooran suddenly started raving about doctors being butchers.

'It's not the doctors, it's the system and we who allow it to treat us badly,' I said in my complete ignorance.

She rushed across the room, shouting, 'How could I stop this?' as she pulled up her jumpers to reveal a grotesque series of scars where her right breast should have been.

Even to an amateur eye it appeared that this was the work of a butcher, not a surgeon, the scars uneven with lumps of flesh dangling from between the stitches. They ran from her right shoulder to her belly button and from the top of her other breast down into the waistline on the opposite side. Another scar ran down the middle.

'I'm nobody, I'm nothing! They can cut me and throw me away. Our nephew died in their war but some fat official tells me he doesn't know when the Martyrs' Foundation will have the money to pay my sister's hospital bills. I owe 30,000 tomans which I had to borrow before they would let us in this stable,' she sobbed.

Just as we were getting really depressed, things got worse. A woman abandoned on the hospital stairs was unceremoniously dumped in the fourth bed. Her legs were crushed and she was obviously delirious from the pain. The first day she was shot full of drugs and taken off somewhere – we presumed to the operating room. On her return the doctors and nurses proceeded to ignore her. She was filthy and the room stank even more than it had before. Tooran took on the responsibility for this woman, who constantly soiled her bed, and had to be force-fed – often resisting by burying her teeth in the hands that fed her.

The Islamic revolution had promised to humble the mighty and exalt the meek and the oppressed. Well, the general's wife was surely humbled but the meek were right down there with her. The players may have changed, but power commanded the best, while the oppressed, the street sellers, the village girls with crushed legs, the grieving young Mothers, were still at the bottom.

I was never happier to see the back of a place. Once Maman Joon was back home we could afford to have a 24-hour maid to help with the nursing, we could afford home visits from the surgeon and a physiotherapist. If she could not bear the pain in the middle of the night we could still afford to call the man with the morphine injection. Despite all these advantages we were all falling apart, so how were those poor, helpless people feeling?

I had only been in Iran for five months but by now I was ready to throw myself out of the nearest window.

Homa got more depressed by the day and we often found her crying in some corner. She would sob and tell us how she had hoped to give us such a good time in Shiraz and now we were housebound, nursing an aged woman and tolerating her husband. He took full advantage of the situation knowing that whatever he did no one was in a position to get up and leave. So he started accusing Auntie of adultery with all and sundry. If any of her friends called to visit he would torment her with the most vulgar of allegations. I remember waiting for two bachelor brothers to turn up to dinner while the Fat Man described in graphic detail sexual acts he claimed they performed on each other.

What a relief when the call came to return to Tehran for my second interview with Bright Eyes.

The last thing I needed just then was to return to the House of Gloom, so I turned to Mrs Mo, a very old and close family friend. She came to my rescue by offering me some space on her floor. Mr Mo was one of those dear friends who had died that year. His widow lived in their one-bedroom flat with her forty-year-old divorced daughter, who had abandoned her two children in Spain, and her thirty-five-year-old son, whose second wife had absconded to Sweden with the contents of their bank account. The two women spent their day moving from one chair to another trailing cigarette ash behind them while the son taught English between bouts of sleeping that could last three days at a go. But they were generous people and at least there were a few neighbours to pop in and keep us amused. They even had a video-hire-man whose nocturnal visit was the highlight of the week. I was starved of Western culture and I missed the cinema and Radio 4 more than any of the 'other instruments of decadence' I had left behind.

The only snag of living with the Mo family was that if you once put something down in this flat you were unlikely to find it again. My first day I lost a pair of shoes which were found six months later when a pile of clothes had to be moved from the bathroom floor after the bath flooded. These were night people who only came to life after midnight, which meant that I rarely got to bed early enough not to look like one of the living dead if I happened to have an early start the next day. But it was better than the House of Gloom, what with the stereo and the video and real people coming in and out rather than Nastaran's tired glare.

We were living in a 'luxury' tower block on the trendy Jordan Expressway – now called Africa by the mullahs – along which you could find some of the most fashionable boutiques and restaurants. A three-mile stretch of this road has become a gathering spot and pick-up point for stylish youth, and thus the inevitable morals police. An expert eye could differentiate between those women who, like myself, were innocently trying to flag down a taxi and those who were out to meet men for recreation and a third group who were in the oldest profession. Unhappily most of the men that crawled along those curbs lacked this expertise and would flash their lights at anything in a scarf. This made life even more confusing as Tehran's shortage of yellow taxis, growing unemployment and rocketing inflation had driven many ordinary citizens to taking passengers. So, was that man who was flashing his lights at you a pervert or an entrepreneur?

At least three women took credit as the star of one of the best stories going round Tehran that winter, so I cannot vouch for its truth, but if it isn't true it should be. The tale starts as Madam X waits on Jordan on a cold winter morning for a ride when a car flashes and stops to offer her a lift.

There were three women wearing the full, black *chador* in the back, so she felt safe as she popped into the front seat, delighted that the driver was going right to her front door. But instead of taking the road north he pulled on to the motorway south, assuring the woman that this was a short cut. She started to get scared and demanded to be let out of the car, but the driver only went faster and her screams were ignored as the car headed ever southward. Spotting a morals-police patrol, Madam X took her scarf off to reveal long blonde hair. Just to make sure she had attracted their attention Madam X threw off her coat to reveal bare arms and cleavage. The sex-police rushed to arrest her, only to end up taking away the driver and the three men disguised as women in the back.

Shiraz was full of great Pasdar stories. The following story came from one of Homa's friends. He sat there, still able to laugh after three months in prison, and told how he had been stopped by an Islamic Guard on his way home from a boozy party one night. Beside him, in his Range-Rover, was his eight-year-old son, who worshipped his Father as the real-life model of his hero, Rambo.

The guard motioned for the Father, who was admittedly a tad drunk, to get out of the car. As he opened the door he could hear his son saying: 'Hit him! Give him a quick chop to the neck! Go on, Daddy, beat him to a pulp!'

'Be quiet, son,' the terrified man ordered.

Father and son were taken to the nearest Komiteh and the man used his only phone call to ask his brother to come to his aid.

The brother was ushered into the Komiteh commander's office where he was told that both Father and son would have to stay overnight.

'But the boy has done nothing wrong,' the brother protested.

'It is from the lips of babes that we hear the truth. We need him to get to the heart of the matter,' the commander said smugly.

The brother asked to be allowed to see his nephew so that he could at least comfort the child and explain what was going on. As the boy was brought in and sat on his uncle's knee, the commander dialled a number on his phone and started discussing arrangements for a demonstration planned in support of Palestine.

'Tell me what happened,' the man asked his nephew.

'We were driving and this soldier stopped us, so Father opened the door into the soldier's stomach, sending him falling on to the ground. Then Father sprang on him and kicked his head before picking him up and throwing him across the road. The soldier tried to get up but Father was on top of him with a chop and another chop – kow, wow – till the soldier started to bleed and to beg for mercy.' The boy was just getting into his stride.

'That's enough, enough! Don't tell such lies,' the commander shouted, forgetting his call. 'Get the boy out of here,' he instructed as he lost hope in his star witness.

*   *   *

I was ready to face my second interview with Bright Eyes, this man whose name was apparently too secret for me to know and yet who seemed to be intent on getting a little more familiar than one would expect from a pillar of Hezbullah. He looked no less repulsive than on our last meeting. There is something about designer stubble combined with a dark skin that is irrationally frightening. I could not understand half of what he said to me in the over-flowery and Arabicised language used by the mullahs and their sidekicks. But, to my relief, the first thing he said was that he had decided to approve my registration as a foreign journalist.

The second thing he said was not so reassuring, for I was expected to report my every move to this man, who now revealed his name as Mr Mousavi. I later found out that he was also Mr Jabari, among other pseudonyms, and that his main function was to keep track of journalists believed to be working for 'the Big Satan' (the USA) and 'the Little Satan' (Britain).

He was most convincing when he explained that the small band of journalists, photographers, cameramen and translators working for the foreign media – forty in all – were divided into fiercely competitive groups that would stop at nothing to put the rival camp out of business. It was in order to protect me from these plots that Mousavi insisted that I consider him as my best friend and guide.

'When someone comes in who is clean, I like to shield them from harm, to guide them and to promote their interests,' he told me with a twinkle in his eye that I did not altogether like.

In order to be thus protected I was to phone Mousavi at least once a week to tell him what stories I wanted to write. I was also to tell him if any of the other journalists approached me to recruit me into their camp. I was not to attend any event without clearing it with Interference. He claimed that rival journalists had been known to phone up newcomers and give them bogus meetings at entirely the other side of town to where the real news was to happen. Private interviews I had to clear with Mousavi. And if I wanted to travel, even for pleasure, I had to get his permission.

He said this all with the air of a person talking to a child who would not dispute that she needed guidance. This was how women were seen – as people to be allowed in to improve the country's human rights image, but incapable of doing the job like a man. Often I had to force myself to smile instead of cringing when some well-meaning soul tried to compliment me by saying: 'You are as good as a man.'

'These other journalists, these conspirators, are mostly ignorant. They are not professional like you,' Mousavi said to flatter me. 'Many of them do not even have their high school diploma. So why do you think they have been allowed to work?'

'I don't know.' But I could guess what he would say.

'They are agents of those groups in the government that want to see certain leaders fail and who want to gain power and to make trouble. They will try either to recruit you or to burn you. Just keep away from them. But let me know when you have contact with them. Then when they try to make trouble for you I can say that I knew this or that. If I am warned I can protect you. It is very important that you carry out my instructions. Do not mention me to anyone, especially not to the people working at Guidance: they can't be trusted either.'

'So who can I trust?' I asked.

'Me.' Mousavi grinned.

There was no censorship of stories, he told me. But he warned that anything 'against the national interest' would be punished. He thus very cleverly ensured that I was constantly censoring my own work but was unable to accuse the authorities of specific censorship.

'What would be considered against the national interest?'

'Oh, nothing special – just the same sorts of things that Britain or France would consider against their national interests,' Mousavi explained. He then gave me a telephone number at which to contact him – a number that I later discovered was a direct line into the Ministry of Security. Should you ever wish to contact these shadowy people their number is: Tehran 236555.

What I did not realise was that you got nothing for free at Interference. I may have gained the security police's permission for my card, but Mr Petty Official was not about to put my name on his list of journalists without a little 'gift'. Foreign dignitaries came and went, conferences were held and speeches made, and I only found out about them when they appeared in the local press. When I complained to Interference they would shrug, apologise and say the omission would be put right. But it never was.

The section that dealt with the everyday torture of foreign journalists was manned by four men, some of whom were honest and some of whom were not. Most of the work was done by Matt Busby – well, that's what I called him because of his love of soccer. Matt was the man who took all the risks by receiving the 'bribes'. At the New Year journalists were expected to give the officials a gold *azadi* coin worth about 12,000 tomans.

A television set hurried along card applications, while a stereo got you into sensitive conferences. About $50 would gain you a private interview and $100 permission to travel within the country. Foreign journalists could expect their agents in Iran to pay $300 to secure them a visa, interviews could go for as much as $70 and travelling would cost them at least $100 a day plus expenses for the official picked to travel with them. Interference pays its officials only an extra $4 a day to accompany foreign journalists.

Everybody in Iran was after the mighty dollar. Rents had to be paid in dollars, bribes also, and many goods could only be bought if you had US currency.

Among the officials at Interference, Reza was responsible for befriending the journalist and pointing out that the others expected a little extra on the side, always claiming that he had nothing to do with it when it was he who in fact set the price and distributed the spoils among this little gang. Then there was Ali, whose reluctance to do a stroke of work gave away the fact that he was the security service's spy. Yet another Muhammad seemed to be the only one to do any real work but he made his money out of running an illegal video-hire service from the office. I saw many a banned film, both foreign and Iranian, courtesy of this other Muhammad, whom I came to think of as Rabbit because of his protruding teeth.

Then there were minor players such as Sleepy, whose only function appeared to be to gather information about foreign journalists and brief the Foreign Office on whether to grant visas or not. He spent many an hour interrogating me on various British journalists. The regime appeared to be afraid of David Hirst, who writes on the Middle East for the *Guardian*.

My first session with Sleepy started with: 'What do you think of Robert Fisk as a journalist?'

'I hate Robert Fisk,' I replied from the heart.

8

Nice Girls Don't Laugh

I was happily writing the twentieth version of my authoritative piece on women in Iran when the radio newsreader announced that Turgut Ozal, the Turkish Prime Minister, would be in Tehran the next day for an ECO conference. At last there was some real news and I was going to be there no matter what.

'How come I don't know about this ECO conference?' I demanded as Matt mumbled something about the old list of journalists going to the Foreign Ministry by mistake. Several dire threats of exposure later he finally vouchsafed the information that press cards would be issued the next morning at the Strategic Studies Centre – formerly the Foreign Office Club, where as a teenager I had danced many a night away.

I turned up at the gates of my old stamping ground bright and early the next morning, loosely covered by my keffiyeh, which signalled my solidarity with the Palestinian cause, and a drab brown ankle-length coat, which said I was oppressed. No one here knew anything about arrangements made for the press and I was told to go away before I was arrested for interfering with their preparations. Two hours of arguing – which I was to find was the norm if you wanted to get anything done for free in Iran – and I was left to stew in the porter's lodge while they tried to discover where I should go. Twenty minutes later I ventured out again. More shouting into walkie-talkies followed and half an hour passed before a neatly bearded, fashionably suited official appeared claiming to be a member of the Foreign

Office public relations staff. My joy at seeing him was short-lived, since he told me that he had no idea where press passes were being issued and that there was no one around who could help.

By now I was on the verge of losing my temper, never having been a morning person, and it was well before the hour at which I liked to rise. Already exhaustion had set in and I was emotionally drained. My arrogance ran away with me and I started to pontificate on the sorry state of the new republic.

'Did thousands of our young die so that you could be as incompetent as the last lot?' I said, and did a lot of other ranting in this vein. To my surprise it was going down rather well with the handful of security guards and sundry minions gathered around me. Question the route the revolution was taking and one of two things could happen: (1) you get what you want; (2) you go to jail.

This was my first contact with the men of the Foreign Ministry, who were a completely different kettle of Muslim from the Hezbullah shock troops. These men had expensive haircuts and elegantly sculpted beards. They wore clean, dark-navy suits rather than camouflage jackets and combat trousers. Spotless white collarless shirts were buttoned up to the top to prevent some innocent woman from being turned on by a glimpse of chest hair. They wore – oh joy of joys – thick navy socks inside polished brogues. This was more like it.

Finally someone was found who thought that the cards would be issued at the Hilton. Twenty minutes later I was at the hotel, from where I was sent back to the research centre. Here I managed, after more foolhardy ranting, to extract the number of the hotel room from where these evasive cards were being issued.

Back again at the Hilton I was challenged at the lifts in case I was some hooker going up to service one of our foreign visitors. Finally I fought my way through the security and other lost card-seekers at the door of suite 1242. Here I was informed that I was not on the list of journalists for the conference. I was ready to kill as yet another Mr Mohammadi slammed the door in my face. I hammered at the door, only to be told to go away, there was nothing they could do.

'Like it or not I have to write a story today,' I said in my best Farsi. 'In London my editor wants a thousand words tonight. I can write about your conference, which is what your government wants, or I can write that you kept me out of this conference.' I had just got the last word out when the door slammed again.

However, I had become something of a folk hero with the press gathered outside the room and many of them cheered as others shouted that I should ignore the conference and write the other story. Frankly I was surprised and pleased to see Iranians feeling so free to express their opposition and frustration within earshot of officials. Perhaps it wasn't all bad in God's Republic.

I still had absolutely no idea what an ECO conference was, but I was determined to cover it. By noon I had been back down to the lobby to phone Interference and back up to demand my rights half a dozen times. The former told me there was nothing they could do because the conference was in the hands of the Foreign Office and all the relevant officials were out. Iranian officials spend a lot of time being 'out'.

'You journalists shouldn't depend on us so much. A good journalist goes out and gets the story despite everything. They pounce on a story like a tiger,' the cretin Reza sneered over the phone.

My mouth had developed a mind of its own and I retorted: 'In places where there is freedom that is the case, but here you're liable to cut our hands off if we sneeze without your say-so.' I regretted it as soon as I said it, but it was too late, it was out there, and there was no taking it back.

You must understand that I was hot and exhausted. I had rushed here, there and everywhere, I had fallen flat on my face twice as my foot got caught in the hem of my coat, I could not hear half of what I was told through the rag around my head and when I did hear it I did not understand half the words.

As the call to prayer filled the corridors of the once luxury hotel, now run by the Foundation for the Oppressed, I stormed back to suite 1242 and once again pounded on the door.

When the head reappeared I heard myself saying: 'I have just been on the phone to the Foreign Office and Mr Hashemi said you are to sort out this mess yourself or he'll want to know why not.'

I had never heard of a Mr Hashemi at the Foreign Office, but as Raffers had found jobs for his family at most ministries I took a chance that there would be someone using the first part of the President's double-barrelled surname.

I had just said 'Open Sesame'. I was ushered in and taken to the top of the queue waiting inside to have their photos taken for their passes. Many months later I discovered that a certain President's brother, one Hojat-ol-Islam Mahmud Hashemi-Bahramani-Rafsanjani, was director of the Foreign Office Fourth Political Office. It seemed that people could still get what they wanted by dropping the right name. No one was going to question an order given by Raffers's brother.

Ten minutes later I left with a pass to the ECO conference. Now all I had to do was to discover what it was.

ECO turned out to be an acronym for the Economic Co-operation Organisation, made up until that year of Iran, Turkey and Pakistan. But following the break-up of the Soviet Union the Central Asian republics were to attend with a view to joining the pact. As a result of Turkey's competition with Iran for the hearts and minds of the newly independent republics, the meeting had taken on an international significance and the delegates arrived with the world's press in tow.

This was to be the occasion on which I first met most of my fellow journalists and I was soon to learn that there were indeed four main gangs among the foreign correspondents – all championing one or other of the few professional journalists at work in Iran. Most of the correspondents lined up to be counted behind either the Reuters man or his main competitor, the Agence France Press correspondent. Both were charming, intelligent and conscientious journalists and I could never commit myself to one gang or the other. I have never been much of a joiner as far as factions are concerned, finding it more rewarding to keep on good terms with all. The photographers made up the other powerful group and were the most fiercely competitive.

Finally there was the most nauseating group: those who worked for Japanese newspapers and television services. They were paid enormous amounts of money to sit in expensive offices – often with swimming pools. They were driven to press conferences by the office driver in brand-new Japanese cars and had access to all the news wires. They were mostly contented, carefree and altogether far too happy to abide.

Of the forty 'resident foreign correspondents' only three of us were women – a former architect; an attractive Hungarian married to an Iranian; and me. I had been at Interference when the Hungarian came to have her press card renewed. She could not understand the conversation so she didn't know that Matt and his cronies were keeping her waiting because they wanted to have 'longer to look at her'. She caused quite a stir wherever she went, with her lily-white skin and her ash-blonde fringe showing under her nonchalantly worn scarf.

Three other women, from the Iranian press, were covering the conference and, since security frowned at us every time we so much as walked past one of our male colleagues, we instinctively banded together. During one of the long breaks in business, while the leaders met in private, we women sat in a row chatting and laughing in restrained tones over the asinine rules that govern women. The local girls explained that until fairly recently they had not been allowed to work outside the office and certainly not to cover any event which Raffers attended. However, of late they had been allowed to cover Raffers even when he travelled about the country; although they were still banned from foreign trips. One of the girls had been forced to get married before she could get a grant to travel abroad to study because the Islamic Republic would not 'contribute to the corruption of our women'. She had us in fits, when one of the FO henchmen appeared before us: 'Sisters, keep your voices down. Mr Rafsanjani may hear.'

'What's wrong with that?' I asked one of my local colleagues.

'If he hears our voices it's going to turn him on and Ozal is going to get the wrong idea,' she explained, only half joking.

Afraid to talk I took out a cigarette and joined a group of male journalists to plan a joint strategy for covering the afternoon sessions. The henchman appeared again: 'Put your cigarette out,' he ordered. Nice girls don't laugh, they don't speak and they don't smoke.

The henchman returned later that afternoon full of apologies. 'Please understand, it is not our fault. I hope you were not offended. You wouldn't have thanked us for letting you get a bad reputation so early in your career here, would you?'

How did this complete stranger know what stage of my career this was?

At the end of that first day the heads of state present were to say the evening prayers together. This was going to be a good photo-opportunity, and even those of us who could only draw the scene with words were ushered down to the centre's mosque. As the most senior cleric at the prayer session, Raffers was to lead the worship. But as he stepped out in front of Ozal the Turkish leader shouted an order to his bodyguards, who started to herd the reporters out of sight. A scuffle broke out and several of the photographers had their cameras broken.

We were told later that Ozal did not want to be photographed behind Raffers because it gave the image that he was inferior and there was some fear that the Islamic Republic could use the photo in its crusade to win influence in Central Asia.

The next day I met Muhammad again. He was hanging around the grounds of the research centre and was rather vague about what he was doing there.

'I work a little for Islamic Guidance and a little with the Foreign Office,' he told me. He was amused when I told him of my reprimands the previous day. 'You will learn soon enough what you can and cannot do,' he said laughing.

'But none of the men were told not to smoke,' I complained.

'These people are very backward – they still believe that it is not a woman's action, smoking,' he explained, and then advised me to move on before we were spotted and rumours about us spread.

I felt there was nothing to be gained by pushing the point: not smoking was a small problem beside the many that women had to face and overcome, so why make waves? But the more I stayed in Iran the more I realised that it was these little points that added up to a system that set women aside. It was a means of control by disempowering women in tiny ways. Had the Koran said, 'Woman shall not smoke,' I might have been willing to accept the ruling as part of a deeply held theological tradition. But, as with so many of the methods used to control women, this was man-made, not decreed by God.

I appeared to have become quite a talking point, for not only was I one of so few women in public life but I spoke the language with a thick British accent and had been 'mad' enough to return to Iran at a time when most people – certainly most of those I met – were desperate to get out. The fact that I had lived abroad made me even more fascinating to the new breed of Iranian officials, many of whom had not left their village before the revolution. Everywhere I went people I had never met already knew about me; it was rather enjoyable, this new-found fame.

Between sessions the delegates at the ECO and the assembled world press were lavishly entertained. I was getting particularly irritated with the head waiter, who insisted on trying to shuffle me towards cake and coffee every time I started to interview anyone. I finally had to tell him in no uncertain terms to stop pestering me. That second afternoon, just after my brush with the waiter, the conference was to be opened with a speech by the Deputy Foreign Minister. I was eager to find out who he was, since he was alleged to be a very informative and articulate source of accurate information. As I waited, the head waiter took the podium and started making a speech welcoming the various ministers to Tehran. This was the man it had been so important for me to get on my side.

The classless society created by the revolution had made it almost impossible to tell the minister from the tea-boy, but you have to admire a nation where a deputy minister is humble enough to double as a waiter. I was so embarrassed that I never had the nerve to face the man again without feeling some shame, although he continued to offer me help and refreshments.

I was not in any fit state to tolerate another Interference hindrance campaign, which is just what I was about to face as I once again slipped off the journalists' invitation list. As assorted dignitaries from the Muslim world gathered to celebrate the thirteenth anniversary of the revolution at Azadi (Freedom) Square, I therefore found myself among the ordinary people marching from all points on to the square instead of sitting in the press enclosure.

Here at last was the feeling of togetherness and revolutionary zeal missing so far. Millions marched shoulder to shoulder with their leaders. For half a day everyone was truly equal; this was why the revolution had appealed. Gone were the helicopters and cavalcades of limos that had ferried the Shah and his family and officials around the country, oblivious to the lives and worries of ordinary people. That day Raffers marched from his office to the square with the lowliest of citizens, while I made my way between a handful of ministers and a battalion or two of chanting Islamic Guards. The revolution may have become famous for its anti-US chants, but it had also inspired some rousing songs and marches which had taken the place of the banned pop music. These were now being sung as the masses made the most of this holiday.

Gradually I became aware that I was the only woman not wearing the black *chador*, but instead of my standing out as an enemy, as I had expected, the crowds turned to look with warmth and friendliness. As I passed the many stands handing out free food and drink, officials would call on me to take something. Women started conversations and only one man whispered 'Whore'.

The most impressive part of the march for me was the protection I received when a spotty young man decided to harass me. He started to follow me and pushed against me, staring at where he imagined my breasts would be. Eager to test the new morality I motioned to three passing Islamic Guards – all about fifteen years old – and asked them to reprimand the boy. They laughed as he quickened his pace. There had been no one in earshot but suddenly a Hezbullah henchman appeared at my side, and asked casually: 'Was it the one in the black jacket?' He then made towards the boy, who knew the game was up and walked even faster. The man spent the rest of the march positioned between me and the boy. Being followed by security men does have its uses after all.

Once I arrived in the square some quick talking and card waving got me into the official enclosure and among the benches reserved for visiting dignitaries. Before us lay a sea of humanity; millions of Iranians chanted 'Death to America, Death to the Zionists and Death to the Serbs' in perfect unison. A band struck up a tune and schoolchildren waved coloured flags and sang revolutionary songs. Then a hush fell upon the square, but the mood was somewhat spoiled when that well-known revolutionary anthem 'Jesus Christ Superstar' rang out as Raffers stepped on to the podium to the roar of the crowd. It was clear that these people loved this man.

'Hashemi, Hashemi, we will follow you to the death, Hashemi!' they roared as he grinned that simpleton grin of his that was so endearing. His expression always seemed to be saying: Is this me, this man they are making all this fuss about?

The humble of the nation were obviously deeply involved in a love affair with Raffers. This was a world away from besieged North Tehran where people waited for the past to return and bemoaned the common but increasingly wealthy mullahs, moving into their exclusive tower blocks.

It was becoming obvious that I would have to put my foot down with Interference or they would never take me seriously. So it was a seething, but determined, *Independent* correspondent who stormed into their offices the day after the anniversary bash ranting over being excluded once again. The room in which Matt and Ali operated was lined with men, who were there either to chat or to get clearance to send out film or to have their cards renewed – which had to be done every six months. I was surprised that despite Iranians' usual very strict adherence to etiquette none of these men rose to offer me their seat. I stood in the corner waiting to be dealt with. Finally one of the photographers vacated his seat. As I made a bee-line for it, my back problem having been worsened by the difficulties at the ECO conference and the previous day's marching, Matt shook his head and moved to block my way.

'You cannot sit there,' he whispered.

'Why not?' I asked, somewhat perturbed.

'It is still hot from the heat of a man's body,' he explained.

I laughed. 'Stop fooling around, I'm not that stupid.'

But he was in earnest. Matt explained that many 'fundamentalist types' would see it as my trying to become sexually aroused from the body heat and I would have been marked as a whore for such an act of indecency. I had never in my life heard such utter rubbish, but sadly this 'belief' was confirmed by those more familiar with the sexual preoccupations of the zealots.

*　　*　　*

Mummy was finally fit to travel back to England; Maman Joon was out of hospital but unable to walk, and I was launched on the road to prize-winning journalism. Nothing could go wrong now.

Mummy's departure was going very smoothly. The taxi arrived spot on 3 a.m. and we were at the airport the obligatory four hours early to find her wheelchair waiting as arranged. A porter took her through to the check-in and baggage area, and I watched with Minu through the glass that divided the arrivals and the departure hall. The porter took her cases to the back of a queue waiting to be checked by what he had promised was a benevolent customs official. Every suitcase is hand-searched for prohibited items, such as rice cookers, backgammon boards and the odd bar of gold. While her cases waited to be inspected, Mummy was wheeled over to collect her passport. Iranians wanting to leave have first to obtain an exit visa and then to hand in their passports at least five days before their flight for security clearance. The official behind the bullet-proof glass looked in his pile of passports, then at his list.

As Mummy was brought back she looked at us, smiled and shook her head. I wanted to vomit from the shock when I realised that she must be on the 'Prohibited Departure' list. I couldn't believe it. We were trapped *again*!

The flight was to leave at 7 a.m. but at 6.30 we were still trying to persuade the soldiers outside the passport office, on the other side of town from the airport, to let us in.

'There is no one here, sister,' a pubescent soldier said.

'Look, I write for the *Independent* newspaper and my Mother has a flight in less than an hour, so let me in to sort it out,' I commanded, waving my press card at him.

I was no longer a supplicant at the mullahs' door; I was the heir to a great military tradition, and I was going to force these people to sort out my problem by sheer willpower. But the drowsy soldiers waiting to be relieved from night duty were blissfully unaware who they were dealing with and refused to let me in.

Minu and Mummy returned to this fortress the next morning to find that my Father had withdrawn his permission for Mother to travel. It mattered not that my parents had been divorced in a British court over ten years earlier; it mattered not that my Father had fled the Islamic Republic and that he had been branded an enemy of the state. Here a man had power over his woman even if he was supposed to be a CIA agent, be she ever so pure.

We were given a copy of a letter from the Friday prayers leader of London confirming that she was still married to my Father and that he was entitled to stop her travelling. There was also a letter from my Father withdrawing a 'lifetime' right to travel.

Even under the Shah, women needed the written permission of their husbands to get a passport and to leave the country – things considered fundamental human rights in other parts of the world. It amazes me that the debate over human rights violations is often restricted to how many people are kept in prison or physically tortured, while many states administer a more subtle torture, the denial of identity and of power over one's life.

Mother was lucky, since she was an educated, strong and determined woman unwilling to accept the ludicrous situation.

Fortunately we also had Minu, the only one of our clan who could work the system.

Two days after my Mother's confinement to the borders of God's Republic we presented ourselves at the family court in downtown Tehran. We were taken to an office in the bowels of the building where two women took Mother's details while their children sat in a corner of the room doing their homework. We were then sent to a room down the corridor where some twenty supplicants were struggling to attract the attention of the clerk. Men and women climbed over each other to be heard, flinging pieces of paper over heads and pulling at the legs of those squeezed in front of them. The clerk resolutely blocked the door into the room where yet more officials assigned people to the various courts.

The clerk was obviously from Azerbaijan, the northern province my forefathers had made their home after falling out with the tsars. It took only a few choice words from Minu in Turkish, a language she had picked up from the servants, for us to be shown into the room and our file attended to.

'Give him something,' Mummy whispered as the clerk personally escorted us up a narrow staircase to a courtroom.

'I can't do that in front of everyone,' Minu replied.

'He wants a tip – give him something,' Mummy insisted.

'We'll be arrested for bribery,' Minu replied.

'I'm telling you to give him something. He won't help us get the right decision if he isn't given something.'

'Auntie dear, I can't. I don't know how to do it. We will get caught and we will all spend the next ten years in prison. It is not like the old days; people don't take bribes any more,' Minu said, looking on the verge of panic.

'Don't be so naïve – the people may have changed but the system has not,' Mummy said.

We were shown into the outer office of the Islamic Court family section.

'We will see you later,' Mummy whispered to the clerk.

He smiled, and went to a man sitting at a desk at the end of the waiting-room. They started a long discussion, occasionally turning to look at us. Meanwhile we had squeezed on to one of the two benches that ran along the walls of the room. Two doors led off the room, one to the family court and the other to a criminal court. Mummy started to chat to the woman next to her, who was waiting to go in to be tried for attempting to kill her abusive husband.

The courts were little more than large offices with three or four judges at desks hearing the supplicants plead their case under the obligatory pictures of Khomeini, Khamenei and Raffers – which had replaced portraits of the Shah, the Empress and the Crown Prince. This was a far cry from the courts in which my brother Said, my sister Pari and her husband David practised in England.

Mummy was lucky, the woman next to her said: the clerk had sent her to a non-mullah, a judge who had survived from the last regime and who interpreted the law without the prejudices of the spiritual establishment. While I waited outside, my Mother was ushered in to her fate, and the woman sitting next to me in her black *chador* asked what we were there for. Even under that shroud it was obvious that she was beautiful and sparkling with vitality, her nose delicately sculpted in fine bones covered by flawless, milky-coloured skin. Thick brown brows topped the large hazel eyes, and she had a pair of cheekbones you would die for. As I told our story the woman, who couldn't have been much more than twenty-four, frowned. When I finished she said: 'Sons of dogs! They are a load of sons of whores. If your Mother is allowed to leave, go with her. This is no place to live – they are sons of dogs.'

She added: 'I hope to go to Sweden myself as soon as I finish my sentence.'

'Your sentence?'

'I am on leave from Evin for two weeks,' she said, as if it was an everyday thing. Perhaps for her it was. 'I want to ask the judge for another week so I can sort out a visa to join my sister and her husband in Sweden when I am released. I have no life here.'

She explained that the sons of dogs had put her in Evin for three years for doing nothing. 'These bastards put you in prison just for drawing a few false cheques. I never went to jail for that before. Their Mothers are all whores,' she spat out. 'I wanted to extend my leave from prison for another week, but this judge to-day is no good. I'm going to come back tomorrow to see Hadji. He always gives me more time. He is a good man and has been very good to me whenever I have been in prison,' she said. Then she leant over and whispered in my ear: 'He always gets a little comfort from me when he needs it.'

She had been in and out of prison for more than nine years and blamed the mullahs for arresting her and locking her away from her daughter. She longed to go to live in a country where they don't 'lock people up for nothing'.

'What is Evin like?' I asked.

'It is not so bad for us, but there are some who are treated very badly,' she said conspiratorially.

'Are there many political prisoners? What is life like for them?' I asked, now fascinated at being next to a woman who practically lived in this prison that puts fear into the souls of all who hear its name.

'There are special prisoners. But they have their own section. We don't see them, but sometimes we hear them,' she told me.

'Hear what?' I asked.

'You can hear screams sometimes and there is a lot of crying from the special section. At night we are sometimes woken by the shots in the yard, but we don't see the specials,' she told me, as if she was discussing the price of beef.

Was she just telling me what she thought I wanted to hear or was she telling me the truth? I desperately wanted a chance to visit Evin – not as an inmate – and I had been working on a scheme for some time.

Shamefully I soon forgot the plight of the women of Evin as Mummy emerged from the room. It hadn't worked; her face was dark with rage. *Oh God, we are trapped again! Why on earth did I come back? Why did I bring Mummy back? Now she will die in this place and it will be all my fault*, I thought, as all those gathered in that anteroom looked up in expectation.

Finally a man sitting closest to the door asked: 'What happened?'

'She can go,' Minu said, and cheering and clapping broke out. The woman from Evin hugged and kissed me while a few others slapped me on the back. They were united, these people living in adversity, rejoicing in the escape of one of their number, drawing hope from her freedom.

The judge had concluded that the law giving men power over their wives' movements was meant to keep families together, not to keep them apart. As my Father was not in the country in which he was trying to trap my Mother, he was actually using the law to do the opposite of what it was for. He signed her exit permit.

So why was she so furious?

She was being 'allowed' to leave; someone else was giving her that right which had almost been taken away by her ex-husband. That judge had warned her that if she came back she might not be so lucky next time.

The clerk did not get his tip.

It is unimaginable looking from the outside, this dehumanising of the female, this presumption that others had the right to determine her life.

Mummy was now free to leave but the blows of the last few months had left me nervous and a little frightened. I had reached a point where I was no longer sure I could fit into my Iranian identity. This was not the Persia I had loved; this was a land where strange people with strange beliefs had power over my life, where I could not influence the events that shaped my life. I knew I wasn't ready to stay there on my own. After some pleading, Mummy agreed to stay on for a few extra weeks.

*   *   *

By now Muhammad had taken up my cause and we were meeting at least once every ten days for 'an exchange of ideas'. He explained the factions and divisions of the regime. I told him about the West and how journalism worked there.

Despite the winter snow we would meet for lunch in one of the restaurants at Darband, the district nuzzled into the slopes of the Elburz mountains, now deserted by the multitudes that thronged there to escape the eyes of the morals police during the summer.

Everyone in Iran that year wanted to fill me in on their version of the world under the mullahs, but some could not risk being seen with me in public. Government officials were repeatedly warned not to socialise with foreigners on pain of imprisonment, while ordinary Iranians were told to stay away from all foreigners unless they were forced to meet them on business. Muhammad explained to me that he was risking his freedom by meeting me but, like myself, he loved his country and felt that I was 'to become very famous and important' as a writer on Iran. Intrigue and flattery: it was a tantalising combination.

Our meetings were straight out of le Carré. I even changed taxis three or four times in a vague attempt to lose the tail I was not even sure I had. I was investigative journalist, patriot, hero and liberator all in one. It was becoming obvious that Muhammad pulled the strings and Interference jumped. He was still vague about exactly who he worked for and what he did. But as long as he handed over internal government bulletins and memos I wasn't going to complain. Much of what I got was 'for my eyes only', he would tell me, adding to the illusion that I was in the world of George Smiley.

Shirazi, my favourite Interference keeper, just happened to be Muhammad's cousin, and I soon found that being friendly with Muhammad meant I had no trouble getting on the lists and learning the news even before the givers of gold coins and Japanese stereos.

For once my inability to speak the language properly started to work to my advantage as Matt and Shirazi took on the task of teaching me the language and the ways of the new Iran. I was invited to eat on people's floors in communal dishes from which we ate with our hands. They also delighted in my ignorance of expressions and customs. I was sitting with Matt in Interference when one of the ministry drivers popped in and asked Matt if he had 'a thread'. I started ferreting around in my bag for my travel sewing-kit. As I proudly handed it over the two men doubled up in uncontrollable laughter. 'A thread', it transpired, is slang for a cigarette.

When the United Nations bandwagon arrived in town I was witness to yet more Iranian efficiency. The UN had chosen Tehran, conference centre of the Third World, for a conference on something immensely boring and with little news value. But again the Central Asians were coming to be integrated into the world fold and I was going to be there to see it.

The day before the start of the conference we were at the Hilton again, this time from noon to three the following morning as the delegates and journalists tried to register. First of all, the camera used to take the photos for the conference ID cards – operated by security agents only – failed to arrive until ten that night. Then the search began for the colour-coded backdrops that differentiated delegates, translators, secretaries and the press. But by the next morning we all had our cards and had assembled at the Hilton to be ferried, in BMWs and Mercs, to the television centre where the conference was to be held.

'Women round the back,' a soldier screamed as the handful of female officials and journalists were dumped at the front of the building. Three body checks later we were through to the main door, where two women inspected us.

'You cannot go in wearing that scarf,' the uglier woman said, pointing at my keffiyeh.

'Why not? It is covering my hair,' I argued.

The discussion went on for ten minutes until the woman finally said: 'You have to wear black, and that ends the discussion. White is *haram* [forbidden] in Islam.'

Now I had her!

'The day President Rafsanjani replaces his white turban with a black one, I will change my scarf to black,' I told her.

It did the trick: she looked appalled but she let me through without a whisper. Only those mullahs directly descended from the Prophet Muhammad (AS) can wear black turbans. Raffers is not a descendant and so he wears white. I was feeling rather clever and pleased with myself until that night, when I got a call from Shirazi.

'What did you say today? You have caused a very big stir,' he said in a panic.

'Nothing,' I assured him.

'We have had a report from Intelligence that you insulted the President,' he explained.

'I didn't even see the President,' I replied.

It turned out that my comment had been reported to SAVAMA, the successor to the Shah's secret police, SAVAK, and they had interpreted it as an arrogant oppressor calling the President an upstart. Which was ironic, because he was about the only one of our leaders about whom I didn't hold this view. But the incident did a great deal for my image. A woman that dared challenge the highest in the land must have someone important and strong backing her.

Many Iranians still believe that if you lift the beard of a mullah you will find 'Made in England' written on his throat. I worked for an English paper and dared to challenge the President, therefore I must be a British spy. This was illustrated when the arrival of a BBC television producer who worked on the *Living Islam* series inspired *Keyhan*, a radical daily newspaper, to run the headline: 'Infamous British Spy in Tehran to Brief Agents Masquerading as Journalists'. I heard of this story in the Laleh Hotel while I was having a chat with that so-called British spy. He had seemed harmless enough, this good-natured jolly television producer whose loose tooth flapped as he told me about his many trips to Iran.

We were thrown together as we waited for a Foreign Office press conference which had been scheduled for that afternoon. First it had been put back an hour, then we were told it would take place four hours later. Once we all gathered again, Interference officials apologised: the official we were waiting for had not arrived yet, but they were trying to find him. At 10.30 that night they finally gave up on him and told the press corps to go home. That evening I further confirmed that I was truly a spy by having dinner with my 'spy-master' at the hotel.

Suddenly I was very popular at parties as new-found friends basked in what they felt was the glory of influence. It was at one of these very parties that I was first approached to become what everyone already thought I was – a spy.

9

Factions within Factions

Playing at Mata Hari had fulfilled all my childhood fantasies. It gave me all the power and the glamour without any of the risk and trouble of actually being an agent. But things were beginning to get out of hand as reality encroached on fantasy.

The charming diplomat inviting me to spy for real had me nonplussed. Was he genuinely making an approach, or was I reading more into his words than was actually there? But no, there had been no mistake. I was being approached to spy for a European power. But spy on what? I couldn't even get the ordinary news out of the Iranian system let alone secrets. Muhammad gave me access to some documents that might be interesting, but surely anyone with a bit of initiative could get those.

I confess that for a second I wanted to be part of this secret brotherhood: Cherry Bond – licensed to play at espionage. But I knew I would probably have dropped dead from fear on my first outing. The only thing to do was to laugh it off. I told him he would be very foolish to recruit someone whose favourite book happened to be *Our Man in Havana*, Graham Greene's story of a reluctant spy who fooled his masters with fictitious agents and reports.

'Think about it,' he told me.

I did think about it, and what I thought frightened me.

Two of my closest friends in Tehran were the British chargé d'affaires, David Reddaway, and his delightful Iranian-American wife, Roshan. We spent some very happy times together and I spent many a pleasant evening in their company. They are the most delightful people I have known, and they became like my family, my oasis of sanity and enjoyment. But Iranians cannot mix with foreigners in God's Republic without someone like Mousavi trying to get something out of it. I was becoming rather unpopular as I turned down requests from people – great friends who had not mentioned my name for the last twenty years – to get them a British visa from my friend Reddaway.

'David wouldn't give his own grandmother a visa,' I told Farah, who wanted me to help a couple who planned to become refugees to get a visa to England.

But that was nothing compared to the pressure put on me by Mousavi to record my visits to my friends' home. He finally drove me to abandon my friends and to cut off my only lifeline. I mention the Reddaways here for two reasons: the first is that their friendship was the only thing that kept me sane; and the second is to put on record that they had no part in any of the advances made towards me to spy. The British never asked anything of me but to be fair and honest.

I thought about the approach in every waking minute for the next week. Part of me was excited and part was outraged. I knew it was immoral and I certainly could not feel loyalty to a country I had never even set foot in. If I had wanted to make money at any cost there were better and safer ways of going about it. But beyond my moral reservations there was a far greater constraint, the fear of execution.

I could not go anywhere without someone trying to recruit me to one cause or another. To cap it all old Mousavi was getting in on the act. He had already hinted at possible 'closer co-operation' several times during our weekly meetings at Interference. I was planning to return to Oxford for a break and re-evaluation of my position when Mousavi called to say that he would have to change the venue for our weekly meeting. He said he would meet me in the lobby of the Hilton the next morning.

But there was no sign of Mousavi – just a receptionist summoning me to one of the in-house phones. 'Miss Gharia?' Mousavi's voice said. Strange! He normally used the first half of my surname. 'I am in room 1215. Could you come up here please?'

A million alarm bells began to ring. This was, after all, the man who had flirted with me so outrageously and now he wanted to get me alone in a hotel bedroom. Iranians often believe that women living in the West are promiscuous, so I feared that this man might be after a bit of recreational interviewing. Would he dare try to seduce or rape me? Surely not. Not in the pious Islamic Republic. He couldn't possibly hope to get away with it, could he? Good sense said, *Turn around and run*, but the journalist said, *Don't be such a ninny: you are a professional; you can handle anything.*

As this debate raged in my mind I made my way to the lifts, only to be challenged by the hotel's morals security man. Thank God I have an excuse not to go up; he will never let a woman go near bedrooms, I thought. I explained that I had been told to meet Mr Mousavi. That was obviously not his Hilton name, since the security man stood his ground between me and the lift.

'Mr Mousavi from Islamic Thought. From Guidance,' I said, not yet realising that Mousavi was actually from somewhere completely different.

Still the stoic stare.

'Here, look, I'm a reporter,' I said, searching for my newly acquired press card.

Still nothing.

'In room 1215,' I explained.

Recognition dawned in those oval brown eyes. I thought I saw a little panic as he said, 'Yes, yes', and leapt out of the way.

What had he meant by 'Yes, yes'? What was room 1215 – the official rape room; the room of no return?

Turn back, said the voice of good sense as I entered the lift. *Don't get out*, it told me as I arrived on the twelfth floor.

My knees went weak and my hands shook ever so slightly but I went ever forward towards room 1215 and whatever fate awaited me. By this time I had convinced myself that Mousavi had somehow learned of the spying offer and had planned my disappearance. Poor, poor Mother, this would kill her. *Turn back, turn back*, the voice said. *No one really cares about what is happening in Iran. Why throw away your life for stories that people will forget as soon as they have read them?* the voice argued as I got ever nearer to 1215.

The numbers stared down at me: 1215 – the prison number to be tattooed on to my arm . . . I was ready to run as my imagination carried me into a world of intrigue and conspiracy.

I knocked.

Joy! There was no reply.

I knocked again; still nothing.

It was a trap. If I turned the doorknob the door would open and inside I would find a body – perhaps that very diplomat who wanted to be my controller. Mousavi would then arrive and I would be dragged off to jail and all protest would be useless because I would be on a criminal charge, not a political prisoner.

'Goodbye, Mother, do not cry for me, for I went doing what I believed to be right,' I whispered as I turned the handle on that door. I held my breath and pushed.

Nothing. It was locked.

I was about to turn and flee when I heard a distant voice calling: 'Miss Gharai!'

At the far end of the corridor I saw the green-clad, slightly podgy figure I knew to be Mousavi. He had changed rooms so no one would know it was him who raped and killed me. My knees were jelly and my heart was forcing its way up my throat and out of my mouth as I stumbled across the vast chasm between us.

Then I spotted Sitting Bull sneaking a look around the door frame. Thank God! There are two of them, I thought in naïve relief.

Instead of rape and death I was treated to a feast of hotel food and flattery. I was, it appeared, obviously a patriot without rival and an all-round model of purity and ability. As such I must be anxious to protect my beloved homeland from attack by 'enemies that would destroy our young and besmirch our guiltless people'. The long and short of all this adulation was that Mousavi had chosen me from among the many who would 'volunteer' to grass on my fellow journalists and friends and the diplomats with whom I mixed. In return for this small favour, Mousavi would introduce me to agencies looking for a little information and willing to pay for it. He would get me appointed as the stringer for some of the world's best publications and reward me with lashings of money. We were, in short, to set up as a semi-mercenary intelligence special squad, feeding information to the mullahs and in exchange spreading their version of events in the world.

None of my excuses for why I would be the worst person they could choose cut any ice with Mousavi. He had noticed that I had found a place among all the groups into which the journalists divided and that I had become close personal friends with 'influential' diplomats. And of course I needed money to cover my debts in England.

How did he know all this? Was Barclaycard supplying credit information to the world's secret agencies? Did SAVAMA have an agent at the NatWest?

'My editor is no fool – he would spot any story that was not 100 per cent accurate. If I got a reputation for being your spokesman no one would take my stories,' I argued.

'Of course.' Mousavi nodded. 'We are not asking you to tell lies, but to work with us so that I can give you the real information – information that no other journalist can get.' I had been starting to relax, but Mousavi added: 'Don't forget what I told you when I approved your registration. And don't forget that you are an Iranian. You're not like those other foreign journalists that we'd just expel.'

In the taxi home I passed Evin prison and my blood went cold when I realised how close I could come to ending up there.

My mind was in a whirl. I needed some advice but was by now convinced that someone was watching my every move. Perhaps if I just ignored it they would give up on me and offer this great privilege to someone else.

That night I phoned a friend in England who was not inexperienced in such matters.

'I've been asked to join Smiley's People,' I told him, alluding to the spy novel that I knew he had read.

'Us or them?' he asked.

'I'm not sure who *we* are and who *they* might be, but so far it looks like two opposing camps,' I said.

'Do you want to do it?'

'I'd rather marry Boy George, but there is some question over whether I will be allowed to keep breathing if I don't,' I quipped. In fact Mousavi had not threatened my life, just my livelihood, reminding me that he could take away my press card.

'Then play them along. Don't say no but don't tell them anything,' he advised.

'I'm not sure I can get away with that,' I said.

But I did. For the rest of my time in Iran I managed to string Mousavi along, always leaving enough hope that I would turn over anything I discovered to him. It cost me my private life as I started to avoid other journalists and friends; it was the price I had to pay for staying alive professionally. There were days when I doubted that I could hold out until my trip back to England, which was just three weeks away. But these three weeks turned out to be some of the most eventful so far.

They started with the news that another dear friend, the woman who had carried me out of hospital after my birth, was riddled with cancer. There were days when I just wanted to hide in my bed for fear that there would be more bad news waiting in the real world. The lack of any support for me and my ailing Mother from family and friends just enhanced the feeling that I was in hell. I was emotionally bruised and very disillusioned.

During the day I had to struggle with the obstacles of everyday life in Tehran and the added aggravation of a hostess who was becoming increasingly unhinged and antagonistic. I woke from one of many sleepless nights to find that I had a rash on my arm. By the evening I was covered in hives, which grew and grew until I was just one red and swollen mass. Despite covering myself in everything our district herbalist could supply, taking pills that turned out to be for the treatment of schizophrenia, supplied by a mad doctor, and consuming all the water melons in town, the hives stayed.

So a maddening itch was added to all my other troubles. Every time I went out on a job I was terrified that something might have happened to Mother in my absence. My Farsi had improved but it was still slow, and every contact was a real drain as I struggled to be understood and to understand.

On the way home from dinner at the British Embassy one night, in the days I still went there, the taxi driver who picked me up observed that my Farsi was 'excellent'.

'Thank you. So it should be,' I replied.

'Why? Have you lived here long?' he asked.

'No, I've only been in Tehran for about six months,' I said.

'Then it is really exquisite,' he enthused.

'I am Persian,' I added in shame.

'Allah! Then it is appalling,' he replied as I felt the blood rise to my face.

Finally a cousin, herself a doctor, suggested that a few tranquillisers might help me. Two nights of Valium later the hives were gone.

*   *   *

Things were getting interesting politically as the 'fundamentalists' or hardliners tried to cling on to power under an onslaught from the 'moderates' – the men of Rafsanjani.

But in Iran nothing is ever straightforward. Those hardliners, the men of the Left, who were so antagonistic to the West and against economic reform, were not averse to having the nation's women parade the odd strand of hair. The moderates, on the other hand, cared little about the economy as long as it made them lots and lots of money; they were the men of the bazaar and the shopkeepers of the middle classes who wrapped their women up in those black shrouds. These were the men who were aroused by the sound of a woman's singing voice and who believed Michael Jackson was of Satan's seed but secretly watched *In Bed With Madonna*. It was this latter breed of chauvinist that was emerging under Raffers and who would ultimately thwart him and his masterplan of reform.

We were back at the research centre where I had become quite a celebrity after the ECO conference. Word had spread of my stubborn pursuit of entry and I had become something of a heroine. The doorman's eyes would light up whenever I arrived and he would relate the story of our first meeting to anyone who would listen. 'I never thought she would get in, not after some of the things she said. But they were afraid of this little girl,' he would say with glee. Thus, I believe, much so-called bravery results from sheer ignorance and stupidity. I had not had enough sense to realise that shouting my mouth off would land me in trouble.

On this visit to the centre, just days before my planned departure, we were again gathered for a conference to discuss the fate of Central Asia within the Islamic family and I had another chance to get in close to Raffers. Minu had dropped me off nice and early that day. On the whole it was a boring gathering. Its only amusement was a short press conference by Raffers, who entered with his characteristic smile which seemed to say: Is this really me being President of Iran? We have really suckered the fools.

There is only a half-mile uphill hike from the research centre to the nearest main road, but on that dark and cold January night it felt like ten miles as my back and legs began to throb again. The end was in sight when the man who had followed me out of the centre caught up with me and asked: 'Can I give you a cigarette?'

Oh, no! Another picker-upper.

'No, thank you,' I replied, staring straight ahead.

'Who was that woman who dropped you off this morning? Your sister?'

He had my attention. 'No.'

'Why didn't you ask Mr Rafsanjani any questions?'

'Were you watching me?' I asked, exasperated.

'It is my job,' he said.

'What is your job?'

'I'm the President's bodyguard,' he replied casually.

'Really? What is he like? Does he really believe in these reforms?' Many other questions spilled over in my excitement.

'Don't you have a car?' he asked, ignoring my questions.

'No, I will get a taxi at the road. Are you going now?'

'No, I just came out to buy some cigarettes. But I will come with you and get you a car,' he offered.

Danger bells rang again and I declined his kind offer, making some crack about liberated women, but there was no deterring him. By this time we were standing in the dark on the side of a badly lit main road. Before I knew what was happening a red car, full of hairy men, pulled up. The back door opened and my companion said, 'Here you are, Mr Mousavi will take you home', and he pushed me into the back of the car. Not *another* Mr Mousavi, I was thinking as the car sped away.

I should have been terrified, but instead I thought of what an adventure I was having at last. The fact that they did not ask my address did not worry me; everybody in this country seemed to know my business. However, when we started to make our way south and away from my area of safety and knowledge I began to think of escape. The car headed for the deep south of the city and I fantasised about using any decrease in speed to fling myself out of the car.

The man in the passenger seat in front of me was particularly horrendous-looking. His three-day growth of beard sprouted in all directions from a face covered in moles and pock-marks. He turned in his chair fixing me with tiny eyes and a deranged grin.

'Don't worry, Miss Mosteshar,' he said.

'We are journalists just like you,' said the driver, who was just a mass of black facial hair from where I sat.

Next to me was the Middle East's answer to Billy Bunter, with teenage acne hiding a cherub's face. In the far corner I spied Al Pacino. I abandoned plans to throw myself from the car.

'Why didn't you ask Mr Rafsanjani any questions?' the driver asked.

Had the whole world noticed?

'I had my name on the list but I wasn't called,' I explained.

'You should insist. Not everyone has the advantage of working for the *Independent*,' Pacino commented.

'Especially as Iran owns that paper,' Billy said, and they all started to giggle. This was not the first time that I had heard this bizarre and unexplained view expressed by Iranian journalists.

'I don't think that is true,' I said defensively.

They just giggled and put on that 'We know better than this silly girl' air that Iranian men have perfected.

I finally felt it was time to ask where they were taking me.

'For a talk,' the driver told me as he turned into Shoush Square and headed yet further south. I had little idea where I was but I recognised Shoush from the occasions when I took foreign guests in the old days to show them 'where the poor people live'. I'd like to say that I was still cool and collected, but my heart was beginning to beat faster than usual and my thoughts focused on how my Mother would react if I failed to turn up.

We drove around for several hours while my 'kidnappers' interrogated me on my political leanings. I suggested that they meet me halfway by telling me who they were and what they wanted from me. Once we were back in their territory among the slums of Tehran the four men were quite open. They were journalists from a number of opposition papers very close to Raffers's main political rival, Hojat-ol-Islam Ali Akbar Mohtashemi, the former Interior Minister who took Hezbullah to Lebanon and the very man who had caused me so much trouble by giving an interview to Robert Fisk. As Interior Minister, Mohtashemi had been in charge of the regional governors, the police and the Komitehs. He had also shared responsibility for the security services.

You learn very quickly in Iran never to talk about what you believe, especially to strangers. This mistrust was a leftover from the days of the Shah, who turned half the population into informants. So I stayed quiet, no matter how these men pressed to hear my views on Raffers and Khamenei.

'Don't be afraid – we are patriots like you,' the driver told me.

159

'How do you know what I am?' I asked, for want of anything more intelligent to say.

'You have the blood of Colonel Muhammad Taghi Pessian – that makes you our sister. We share his vision for our nation,' he explained, as my mouth fell open. These guys had done their homework.

'We thought we could share some information with you . . . put our side across,' Pacino said.

'Oh yes, of course, I'd be delighted. Good idea,' I gushed, hoping that now I could return home and forget this ever happened.

But it was not to be, not quite yet anyway, for these men were not letting me go free until they had delivered their political manifesto and were convinced that I had taken full and accurate notes – not as easy task in the dark, crammed in the back of a small car, beside who knows who.

Mohtashemi and his supporters still held to the economics of central control, the closed nation as the only defence against imperialist influence. They were the Young Turks of Islam, deeply committed to the anti-imperialistic tradition. Young students, progressive mullahs and many of the Islamic Guards pledged their allegiance to this group. To know them was to know the heart of radical, insurgent Islam.

In the early hours of the morning I was finally delivered to Bahar's house and they waved goodbye with a promise that they would be seeing me again soon. My Mother was already in a state when I finally got home. She had imagined any number of terrible fates befalling me. I just told her the bare details of my adventure, hoping this was the end of it. The next morning Nastaran shook me awake at seven with a sneer. I had a phone call, she told me, as if she were accusing me of mass murder. It was the driver, who introduced himself as 'Hussein, your driver last night'.

'There is something very important you have to see. Meet me at eight on the corner of Vali-e-Asr and the Modarres Expressway,' he instructed.

This was my chance to get in with the real revolutionaries, the very people who held the world to ransom, who pulled the strings wherever Islamic fundamentalists took up arms. It was also extremely alarming, for I could not rule out the possibility that I was being set up. A family conference was convened and the general opinion was that I stay well away – but then few of them understood the motivations behind modern journalism. None of them had any desire to get to know these aliens that had invaded their country any better than they had to. In the end I felt that any surreptitious meeting could be too easily interpreted as something other than journalistic endeavour. I had a vision of the other Mousavi being handed a file of my meeting with pictures as I got into the car of a group that was the biggest threat to Raffers. It was obvious that the President intended to crush Mohtashemi and his like, and I was not eager to be branded as one of them. So I stayed at home.

Daily, for the next two weeks, one of the four would contact me to urge me to meet them. Finally I agreed to meet Pacino, although I did not realise that it was him. I was not going to be picked up at any street corner so I suggested an after-dinner coffee at the Hilton.

As bad luck would have it the first person I saw as I stepped into the hotel was the other Mousavi. However, it took me some time to realise who he was. He had caught my eye because he was the smartest man in the lobby. He was beautifully dressed in an obviously expensive and modern navy suit, his white, collarless shirt was starched to perfection, and his hair was transformed. As I stared, my jaw dropped around my knees, Mousavi chatted to yet more visiting foreign dignitaries. Then he noticed me, and a slight shake of the head and blink of those shining eyes said, 'You don't know me'.

Before I could pull myself together, Pacino was at my side, obviously pleased that I had actually turned up. The Hilton lobby has two seating areas: Men Only and Family. The head waiter – the former head waiter at the hotel's former Hunt Bar in the days of the former Shah when alcohol still flowed – regarded it as his aim in life to make my life miserable. No sooner had we sat down than he bore down on us to complain that my scarf was 'not correct' and he had to ask me to leave.

I had fallen out with Chubby – as I affectionately knew him – early on in our post-Shah relationship. When, on first arriving at the hotel, I had innocently – honest! – wandered over to the windows that were the lobby's back wall and tried to look out, Chubby had dashed across the vast lobby screaming: 'Stop, stop! Naked men!' My joking attempt to get a better look had not been appreciated. What I had been in danger of seeing was the hotel swimming pool where I had once turned nut-brown and frolicked in the clear water. Women are not allowed to see naked men any more than men are allowed to see naked women, so mixed bathing was a thing of the past. Since then, Chubby and I had gone through this ritual whereby he told me to go and I told him I had just come from interviewing the President or a minister or an Ayatollah, and if my *hejab* was good enough for them it was good enough for him. I was certainly not going to be branded a Jezebel by a man who had served me with more than a few G&Ts and had as good as kissed my Father's feet for one of the over-generous tips he was famed for giving.

Surprisingly for a leftie revolutionary, Pacino seemed totally at home in this luxury hotel now owned by the Oppressed. His suit was also navy and well pressed, if a few years out of fashion, and his Islamic stubble would have been at home on *Miami Vice* – a programme it transpired he had loved during his three years at the London Embassy. On closer inspection he looked more like a malnourished Dustin Hoffman, his sallow, stretched skin clinging to his bones like a thin, dry parchment. I could tell he was a hairy man because he was wearing those ultra-sheer socks through which his foot hairs were trying to escape.

He had enjoyed England, spending most of his evenings at home in front of the television. The movements of diplomats were closely watched to ensure they did not trip the light fantastic in the flesh-pots of the West. We talked about *Cheers*, which was great if you ignored the drink, and *Casualty*, which led our conversation to the war and his experience on the front line.

Doctors, when not finding a suitable mate or overcharging hypochondriacs, mostly tended to keep well back from the mortars and bullets of the Iraqi foe. Despite having had half his thigh blown away, Pacino had helped treat those worse off in the trenches. It took three days for relief to arrive after he was wounded; in the meantime he pumped morphine into any remaining vein.

'We were given plenty of drugs at first, but without any real doctors and few ambulances by the last years of the fighting. Right from the start we had very few weapons and ammunition in any case, so I made my men keep quiet. Every time we sent the Iraqis one rocket they sent us a hundred in reply,' he told me with a humour that belied a deep pain beyond that of the body.

He then started to ask me if I could honestly say that what I found in the Iran of President Rafsanjani was what had motivated hundreds of thousands of young people to die for freedom. He was right: there was no way I could reconcile this distorted version of Islam and this corrupt and affluent society with the vision that had inspired the downfall of the Shah. That is not to say that I was in any way in agreement with that vision, but it had been the will of the people and it had disappeared as soon as the people were no longer required to lay down their lives.

Hassan, as he told me he was called, laughed and called me a foolish innocent. 'They did not promise just Allah and a place in heaven. They promised them that they would deliver every citizen's share of the oil revenue to their doors. They promised that the beggar in Shoush Square would be housed in the palaces of the Shah and they promised that no official would ever again take a bribe and no policeman would ever take a pay-off. Most of all, they promised to make us as rich as people like you used to be. That is the reason that Mothers and Fathers sent their children to be slaughtered by the Shah and by Saddam. Those who had real ideals were hounded and slaughtered or driven into exile when they were no longer needed,' he said with passion.

Hassan was being amazingly honest for someone talking in a very public place to a complete stranger. Alarm bells rang again. This suspicion of one another is the saddest aspect of Iranian culture and one of the main reasons that we are so easily divided, conquered and manipulated.

He told me of people living in the sort of poverty that the mullahs had promised to eradicate, of twenty people living in one room with no electricity and no water. Sensing my reluctance to believe that things were quite so bad in Tehran itself, he offered to take me to see how the poor lived along the railroad tracks. I agreed to meet him again when I returned (if I returned) after my break in England.

At last Mummy and I were on the plane for London, but back in England I did not feel the rush of relief that I expected. Instead I felt awkward at being uncovered in public. The dark days plunged me into a deep depression and the British reserve made me long for the streets of Tehran, where every passing stranger at least says hello, and more often than not gives you their life story. Part of me never wanted to set eyes on another mullah while the other part was dying to know what was going on in my absence. Who was stabbing who in the back? Which faction was gaining the upper hand? What scoops were my rivals getting while I was away? In the end professional curiosity overcame personal frustration and after a mere six weeks I went back 'home'.

I had missed the first round of that year's parliamentary elections, which swept Mohtashemi and most of his faction out of the Majlis, but I was in time for some rather exciting riots.

10

Bonfires of Futility

The smell of rice filled the small flat as Farah slaved over a variety of boiling things in her colour-coordinated kitchen. Unfortunately the colours were dark, dark green and mahogany. The entire two-bedroom flat was sealed off from natural light; a few table-lamps provided a dusky glow by which we moved around the place. Despite the glorious sunshine outside, I was in a melancholy world where drowsy people came and went and waited for their lives to start again.

I'm the sort of person who puts on the lights even during the day. I know it is very irresponsible, what with global warming and all, but I have found that light is the best antidote to depression. Yet in the homes of my family all was dark; they locked out the rays of the sun that could have lifted them out of their collective misery. At least I didn't have to go back to the House of Gloom – that would have been the last straw. Instead I watched my 'twin' cousin, Farah, do those wifely things while her two adorable six- and eight-year-old boys showed me their worm collection.

Farah was born three hours before me, in the same ward of the same hospital, and ever since we have been more like sisters than cousins. That is, until I made the mistake of taking up her invitation to live with her, her loquacious husband, Useless, and her three children.

I shared a room with the boys while the four-year-old daughter moved in with her parents. It wasn't perfect but it would do. For the first time in almost a year I had a whole wardrobe to myself and

I could stretch out. There was only one snag: Farah was a shopaholic and together we were the shopkeeper's dream.

Farah had inherited a small but useful fortune on the death of her Mother. This she had handed over to her husband, the only man she had ever known and who she got engaged to at fourteen and married two years later. He was not quite 'our kind of people', but he was educated to be the next best thing to a doctor, an architect, and she loved him. Uncle was happy enough to be relieved of the task of marrying a daughter off to someone she did not care for. Her husband earned the nickname I gave him, Useless, by failing in every venture he ever undertook. Much of Farah's fortune went down the drain because of these failures.

Useless was an ethnic Turk, a race that has been the butt of Iranian jokes about their alleged stupidity, much in the genre of the Irish joke. But with Useless sometimes it seemed it was no joke. Over dinner at a friend's home one night another guest had told Useless about a scheme to build a large shopping complex and promised to give the young man the contract to build it – once he got government permission for the project. Delighted, Useless went straight out to hire the equipment and a workforce. These he kept on standby as his 'partners' continually promised them that work would start any day. After almost six months of paying for men and equipment that he did not need, Farah's remaining piece of property, a small flat, was in hock, and Useless was facing ruin. So they fled to Turkey, where his parents saved and scraped up the money to pay the debts and thus to rescue Farah's flat. Five years later the debts were paid and the couple came back home with no more than they had left with, unless you count the sweetest little angel of a daughter that ever set foot on Iranian soil.

They had been back for about three months, much to his dislike and her relief. As far as Useless was concerned, Turkey was the centre of civilisation and Iran the last place on earth he wanted to be. For her part Farah loved home, with all the gossip and back-stabbing that you can only truly indulge in among your own people where you know everybody's secrets. I was soon to discover that my cousin was not beyond making up a tale or two in order to fulfil her need to create enemies of people who had once been friends.

That night she was preparing to entertain a couple they had met while living in Ankara. Jahanshah and his wife, Firouzeh, were middle-class wannabes who believed that the streets of LA were paved with gold. They had been trying to escape to America for seven years, and despite losing everything on a series of failed attempts they had not given up hope. Having accepted that they would never get a US visa as a family, they had faked a divorce with the help of a crooked mullah, and Jahanshah was going for a Green Card on his own.

The flat was decorated in the same green and mahogany as the kitchen. A balcony had been converted into a reading-box and was now my office. As ever, the air-conditioning didn't work that night because there was no oil for the generator – no oil in Iran; that was really something. It was only April but it was already hot, yet we didn't dare open the windows for the stench from the sewers outside. Most streets in Iran are lined by two *jubs*, ditches through which water runs. Well, in the old days it was water, but as the capital had grown and its development was turned over to the forces of anarchy the multitude of new buildings taxed the sewage system and many turned their sewage pipes into these roadside *jubs*.

'That bastard mayor,' Useless would fume as the sweat dripped off him and he was forced to change yet again before his guests arrive.

Why was the mayor a bastard? You might well ask.

It was simple really: he would not give a certificate to say that the construction of the building in which Farah and Useless lived was complete. Without this they could not get deeds for their homes and without deeds the value of the property was almost halved. Thus they could not sell up and move.

But why leave?

To get away from the stench of those *jubs* of course.

So why no certificate?

'The bastard says we cannot have the certificate until we install a sewage-processing machine in the cellar and stop pumping it into the *jubs*,' he complained.

'Very unreasonable,' I agreed, having been taught that it was rude to contradict or argue with your elders.

The guests arrived an hour late, but that is more or less usual. As we settled to chat over a bootleg vodka and Coke, Jahanshah agreed that the mayor was indeed a bastard.

'He won't let us cut our own trees down. He taxes us at ridiculous rates and then goes and squanders it by building parks and putting up fountains in the south. I can't sleep at night for the sound of the trucks and the dustbin men, now that they are only allowed into town after eleven in the evening.'

'But the city is really very beautiful and very clean nowadays,' I ventured.

'What good is that? What we need is money, not beauty,' Jahanshah snapped at me. 'They have the right idea in Mahshad,' he said, turning to Useless. 'There have been riots all week and the people have burned down all the local council buildings in protest at the behaviour of the mayor.'

'Well, actually there was a bit more to it than that,' I started to say to the air.

It was obvious that I was not to be included in this 'man's talk', and a nervous Farah called me into the kitchen. Never mind that I was one of the only people to tell the world about what happened in that city, no matter that some of the world's most prestigious publications had asked me to write on the riots. These men knew better, and I had to set the table as I listened to their uninformed ranting.

Mahshad had been turned over to Basij (volunteer militia) forces after four days of rioting. Despite a virtual press blackout, Muhammad told me that at least nine Islamic Guards had been killed by protestors. The masses marched through the country's third largest city setting fire to all government buildings in their path. He showed me dispatches that claimed more than 300 people were under arrest and two thirteen-year-old boys had been shot. But Mahshad had been just the worst in a series of clashes between people and government; there had been eruptions of discontent in at least four major cities. Muhammad had witnessed the uprising in his home town of Shiraz, while throughout the nation there were reported outbreaks of violence in the cities of Arak and Tabriz, in the north.

Mahshad had erupted on a quiet Saturday when a group of landowners confronted city officials and police as the latter tried to knock down a number of 'illegally constructed' buildings. Shots were fired, and crowds gathered to watch the commotion on a long, lonely stretch of road which ended abruptly in barren land on the edge of the city. When the shooting stopped, two young boys were left dead. The boys' bodies were paraded around the town, inflaming the masses, and soon all the frustration of ordinary life broke out in furious violence.

The regime blamed the trouble on the *Tondro* (hardliners), who had suffered a massive defeat in the general elections. 'In each case the trouble started on the pretext of economic protest, but we believe it is the work of those who failed to keep their seats in the Majlis,' an official said.

'Was it you?' I asked Hassan during a picnic in a remote wood.

'They were our guns,' he admitted. 'But the people did it themselves. We do not need to inflame the people – they are very angry and very sad without our help.'

He claimed that the flashpoint, Arak, was a warning shot by hardline candidates opposed to Raffers's reforms who had their candidature turned down by the Council of Guardians.

'Shiraz started with the *Janbazans* [Life-Sacrificers] who were protesting about their low allowances and benefits. But very soon they were joined by other groups, and they began setting fire to petrol stations,' Muhammad told me in a back room of a suite at the Laleh Hotel taken over by the Foreign Office during anniversary ceremonies for the death of Khomeini.

A demonstration in Arak, to the east of Qom, led to the first bloodshed, and martial law was imposed. However, the average man on the street only learnt of all this through the rumour grapevine; not a word was said by the official media.

Then came Mahshad, where 'anti-revolutionary' rioters set fire to the city council building, burnt down the main library and several police stations before starting on a rampage of arson and looting. The Interior Minister, Ayatollah Nouri, a very nasty piece of work, was quick to blame the break-up of law and order on the freedom given 'by the revolution towards the people'.

'From now on all the new freedoms will be removed. We will go back to the strict rules on the streets,' Muhammad predicted. Rafsanjani and his supporters, he said, blamed the radicals. 'They will not say so openly, but this is the understanding. The economic factor is an excuse. There is no doubt that this is the work of the radicals.'

The Tehran Spring that Rafsanjani had promised with the removal of the hardliners from political power was turning into a Summer of Discontent.

I had started seeing rather a lot of Hassan that spring and thus a lot of the troubles of the poor and the powerless. He popped in to see me at Farah's almost every day and Farah was thrilled by the idea that we might get married. No amount of assuring her that this man was just a professional contact and platonic friend would deter her; he was a man so it must be sexual. He gave me daily Farsi lessons and acted as my guide and my escort wherever I went. Hassan had been doing this for about a month when Farah informed us that my uncle wanted to see us both. I was frankly surprised because it was Farah who kept inviting Hassan round and I could not see any way in which it affected my uncle. But it is not the done thing to refuse one's elders in Iran, and we duly presented ourselves at the Pessian home.

Without any reference to me, the two men started to discuss my future and Hassan's intentions. I was amazed to hear that this attractive and intelligent man was hoping to marry me; they were all quite dotty.

You cannot be serious, I thought as the two men continued the process of bartering me away. Hassan admitted that he could not afford to keep a wife and that he wanted to be 100 per cent certain that I could live in Iran. Dada Jan then instructed us to stop compromising Farah by meeting at her house. This made me mad, for it was she and her husband who constantly invited Hassan to the house. We had spent the last two days searching Tehran for spare parts for Farah's iron – after I broke it in a pathetic attempt to help with the chores.

Who cares what these people think? This is preposterous. Anyway our family is not like that; we do not see sex everywhere. How dare Uncle do such a thing? I told myself, fuming inside. I felt as if I had been attacked. They had stripped me of my dignity and accused me of things I had not done or even thought of. Who in their right mind could read so much smut into perfectly reasonable behaviour? How pathetic and bizarre. I was an adult who had made my own decisions for years, despite my strict upbringing. And yet these two men were taking it upon themselves to know better than I what I should do with my life, and they had no idea that they were doing anything out of the ordinary.

'Since when have we been anything but friends and colleagues?' I asked once we were safely back in the rusted shell on wheels that passed for a car.

'Don't worry. It is normal here when a man and a woman are together that they should get married. No one understands friendship between the sexes. We just have to play their game and pretend we are to get married or you will get a bad name,' he explained.

'I've never heard of such a thing!' I barked, but dropped the subject.

Determined that in the future no one would get the chance to poke their nose in my business I resolved to meet Hassan out of the sight of the small-minded. Thus our meetings moved to street corners, suburban woods or deserted roads at the dead of night. It was during one of these meetings that Hassan declared his love for me and his desire to live with me for the rest of his life. We were in the back of his wreck down a narrow street in the Darous district of Tehran. The rain drenched the entire city that night, and the car windows dripped with condensation as he declared his love and his respect.

'Do you think you might want me one day?' he asked.

My little voices said: *Not on your life*. But when I opened my mouth I was giving him hope, saying that I was confused and not at all sure that I wanted to stay in Iran for ever.

'That doesn't matter. I will live with you anywhere, even in England if you want,' he told me.

Not another one, not another poor trapped soul who would do anything to get out of God's Republic! It was all so simple, this love at first sight; it was really freedom that they were catching sight of.

The next time he mentioned love we were sitting in the middle of the Nature Jungle, a manicured wood on the road to Karaj, sharing pizza and water melon that Hassan had cooled under a tap placed among the trees and barbecue pits. The melon stain on my notebook will be there long after this fragile, radical and impetuous young man burns out.

Hassan really cared about people, be they rich, poor, Muslim or godless. A realist-communist, Hassan preached the testament of responsibility. He argued that those who had more than their essential daily needs had a duty to ensure the well-being of others.

'I don't blame anyone for being what they are. Your Father was rich so you accepted the life he gave you without question, that is natural. What good is it going around telling those who have that they must give up everything to those who haven't? All that happens is that you get what we have in Iran now – the rich are not the same people as before, but there are still rich people.

'You are a little poorer, that is true, but my sister's husband is still poor. He was poor yesterday and he will be poor tomorrow. He will be poor until those who are rich accept that they have a duty to serve others.

'I would rather sit at a table with a good person, no matter how rich he or she is than one of the mullahs who fill their pockets promising ignorant people a quick route to heaven,' he told me.

'You won't write all this in your paper, will you?' he asked.

'Why not? I thought you were telling me so that I could write it,' I replied.

'I am telling you so that you understand it, that someone knows and that one day others will know and will think. I have escaped death once in my life already and I am not ready to face it again. Tell the story later, when there is some distance between us, when they cannot trace it to me,' he almost begged. But the second after he had said it he changed his mind.

'Tell it now, tell them it was me, I don't care. Someone has to take us back to our ideals, to the spirit that made us go out on the streets in front of the Shah's bullets.'

He sat in front of me, a skeleton with burning eyes. His pastel-pink shirt was soiled from days of repeated wearing. I should have been taking in the enormity of this man's disappointment, but I could not stop thinking about the ring of black grime that had built up on the back of his collar and which peeked out as he rolled his head in the intensity of his speech.

'I thought you told me the people did it for money,' I reminded him.

'Not all of us – only the ones who survived.'

'When did they nearly kill you?' I asked.

'She was beautiful,' he replied, his eyes light-years away in another time and another place. 'She looked a bit like you. I have never loved as much as I loved her,' he declared.

Oh no, he is about to make another pass!

Shame on me for the thought; this boy was reliving pain.

'There were eight of us in the group,' he mumbled.

'What group?' I asked, my mouth full of pizza.

'Mujahedeen. We were Mujahedeen. Eight of us – two women and six men. We had fled to hide in the north in the jungle,' he said, as if he was back in that jungle. 'Golestan, it was called. Golestan [land of flowers] Jungle. We were really happy there, the eight of us. But then it got dangerous and a friend put us up in a house in the city. They must have been eating when the Pasdars came,' he continued.

I was silent; he needed no encouragement.

'Our commander had sent me to do a job in Tehran. We had made a successful raid, the eight of us, and had been sent to safety out in the jungle. But there was a job and I was needed, so I went back.

'They were having lunch, sitting around the *sofreh* on the floor. My best friend died at once. He had a gun and they shot him down. They took her away. We heard nothing for six weeks, then her parents were told to come and get her body,' he said, with tears rolling down his cheeks.

'They said I must have reported them. They say that is why I am now in politics instead of in a grave beside her,' he sobbed. 'We couldn't fight them from outside – better to get inside and try and keep them on the right path.'

'What is the right path?' I asked. He just gawked at me.

The Mujahedeen-e-Khalg-e-Iran, the People's Combatants of Iran, proved the old axiom that the first thing any revolution does is to turn on its own children. They died in their hundreds of thousands under the reign of terror of the Shah; then they died in their millions at the hands of the people they had helped put in his place. The Muj were Islamic-Marxists, as the Western press dubbed them over television footage of the revolution. At first they had advocated Islam minus the Ayatollahs, but they gradually had to accept that they needed the impetus that a figurehead such as Khomeini could give their rebellion. Once the Shah had been ousted, the Muj presented a very real threat to the mullahs' authority. They were every bit as Islamic as the clergy but they believed in a nation controlled by a young volunteer force with arbitrary powers of arrest and execution.

The Party of God, Hezbullah, had won the ensuing civil war and the graveyards filled up with more young bodies. As the Muj lost public support, mainly due to their targeting ordinary people, their corner of Zahra's Paradise was literally turned into a public toilet. The Muj rebellion was crushed ruthlessly; the youngest victim of this purge was a ten-year-old girl, Zahra Maqsadi. Prisoners were taken out of their cells and shot night after night. Evin became the mullahs' Killing Fields.

'Have you ever killed another person?' I asked, pen poised for a Pulitzer Prize-winning article.

'Of course.'

'Do you regret it?'

'Sometimes.'

'When?'

'When I see the fate to which I have condemned my people.'

'Will it ever change?'

'We are doing our best to change it.'

'How?'

'Look and listen and you will find out. We are in the middle of something that will rock this nation very soon. People cannot take the pressure that the mullahs are imposing.'

'What would you put in their place?'

'Freedom.'

'The freedom of the Mujahedeen?'

'No, they have corrupted themselves. They should never have gone to fight with Saddam. We cannot survive unless we let people choose how they want to live. I believe people will choose Islam. They will live good and pure lives if they are moral and unsullied. If they are not they will wallow in debauchery and obscenity whatever the regime does.'

'What do you want for your own future?'

'Not to question my actions as I lie waiting to die. I believe Allah gives every person three days in which they know they are about to die and in those days you get a chance to look at your life. I want to be able to see a life in which I have served society and helped people. I don't want to think that all my life was about was to make myself richer,' he said, as if it was a speech he had delivered many times before.

'Yes, yes, yes,' I agreed, feeling that he had articulated exactly the things that were in my heart. He was a lovely man, a truly honourable person in an unscrupulous world.

*   *   *

It had been raining non-stop for three days and I had been drenched as I made my way to our assigned meeting place; I was not going to risk his being seen picking me up. The car windows were steamed up again and so was Hassan. I began to say that I was very flattered, however, before I could get to the 'but' he lunged forward and started suffocating me with what was the most amateurish kiss I have ever received. I quickly tried to push him away.

We were thus engaged when both front doors of the car opened and two Islamic Guards stared in, saying: 'What are you two doing?'

'This is my wife. We have come out to try and resolve a row,' Hassan said, quick as a flash.

'At 10.30 at night?' the second guard asked.

'We live with my parents. There is no room to talk, and they always want to butt into our business, so we needed somewhere quiet to solve our problems,' Hassan continued to fabricate with ease.

These young protectors of the faith had heard it all before. Giving me no time to recover from the extreme terror that had seized me, the two were in the back of the car and instructing us to go to the nearest Komiteh. There, the younger guard assured us, we would have to prove we were married or be flogged. 'It is only seventy-six lashes since Mr Rafsanjani came to power,' the youngster said.

'We are married and we are both important journalists,' Hassan said. 'It would be in no one's interest for you to arrest us.' He took a card out of his pocket and showed it to the guards.

'Stop here,' the older guard said. The three men got out in the pouring rain and started a heated discussion. After about ten minutes the young guard came back and asked me if I knew Hassan's Father's name. I mumbled something about always calling him 'Father'. The boy laughed. 'He probably has a wife. Why waste yourself on his type? Has he promised to marry you? Well, don't believe him if he has. I am not trying to make trouble, but you are like my sister, I advise you very strongly not to see this man again,' he warned with feeling. 'When he comes back tell him I was asking about your work and home. Be very careful please.'

When the drenched Hassan returned he wanted to know what the boy had said. I told him the lie and he asked me how much money I had. 'They want money to let us go,' he said. I had 1,000 tomans (about a tenth of the average monthly wage), which Hassan took to give to the guards. I presume he handed the money over. We headed home with a sense of relief.

The next morning Farah decided that it was time to enter stage two of the marriage game, that of checking up on the prospective bridegroom. I had finally told her that I was still seeing him and also about our close shave with the Islamic Guards, after which he had told me where he lived and the name of his parents in case we were stopped again. Hassan was very slick in some ways, the ways you learn when life has to be a lie, when you have to hide your true self for fear of the executioner. He had made it sound so credible when he told me never to phone him at home because of his jealous and suspicious Mother. I had believed all the stories of how she had manipulated him into living just for her, how she had stopped him staying in England and how she would threaten to kill herself at the least provocation.

'She will force me to marry some cousin or other for fear that I might get involved with someone like you who would take me abroad,' Hassan told me.

He claimed that when he went to London he had not told his Mother until he was at the airport, then he phoned and left a message with an aunt for fear that her tears would make him turn back.

But Farah was not to be deterred, and for once Directory Enquiries produced the telephone number without delay. Before I could stop her Farah was on the phone pretending to be from one of the papers on which Hassan worked. I went and hid in my room while she pretended that they needed him urgently. She spoke to his brother, who said he had no idea where he was – I knew he would be at an economic seminar all day.

Then, according to Farah, the brother said: 'Hold the line and I will ask his wife if she knows.'

My gossip of a cousin came rushing into my room, shouting: 'The bastard is married! He is married!' Then she turned on her heels and before you could say 'Long live Khomeini' she was on the phone telling the whole story to her Father, then to her best friend and then to a neighbour. By that evening my aunt in Shiraz had heard it and by the next day strangers were talking about it on every bus and in every taxi.

A call from *The Economist* came just in time and I gladly agreed to go to Mahshad to confirm the reports of the riots and to try and see who had been behind them.

*   *   *

FOR THE ATTENTION OF MR S. KUSHA, FOREIGN JOURNALISTS
SECTION, MINISTRY OF CULTURE AND ISLAMIC GUIDANCE

Dear Mr Kusha

Further to our telephone conversation on Thursday, here
are the details you asked for.

Firstly, I must say that I find the behaviour of the law
enforcement agencies involved in my detention reprehensible
and contrary to the ideals of the Islamic Republic. However,
I also accept this sort of harassment as an occupational
hazard.

I phoned your section several times on Saturday and
Sunday of last week to see if you could arrange for me
to travel to Mahshad. Finally I got through to someone
in the ministry, who told me that your section was closed
for several days. I was therefore unable to inform you of
my intention to visit Mahshad.

I travelled to Mahshad overnight on Sunday/Monday,
arriving on the Monday afternoon. During the half-day
I was in Mahshad I took a tour round the town and
spoke to some residents about the recent troubles. I did
not meet anyone directly involved in the recent riots, and
my intention was to write a piece about the mood of ordinary
people caught up in troubled times.

I then spent the evening with friends, and visited the shrine
of Imam Reza. I slept at my friend's home and left the holy
city at 3 a.m. on Tuesday morning.

At 7 a.m. Tuesday the taxi I was travelling in was stopped
on the northern road, at a check-point shortly after the
Golestan Jungle – which I was later informed was where
many of the Mujahedeen hid when they were outlawed after
the victory of the Islamic Revolution. I informed the officer
in charge that I was a journalist returning from Mahshad.

Despite showing my press card and explaining my trip, I
was subjected to a strip search, without any reason being
given for my being stopped. I was also subjected to verbal
abuse.

I had some 25,000 tomans in my handbag to pay my
taxi fare. This was piled on the table – I was allowed to

remove the rest of my belongings. The officer in charge then examined the pile of money on the table, while warning that I could be held for some time.

I was sent out of the building where a soldier suggested that I might solve my problems with cash. The officer in charge then got into my car and asked to be driven some hundred yards down the road. I felt he expected to be offered some cash; he appeared rather angry when no such offer was made.

We stopped at several posts on the road, and again a junior suggested money should be offered. I was finally sent off to the army barracks and security headquarters in Minoodash. A young soldier was sent with me in the taxi, and he openly offered to let me go, again if I paid his debts. I may well have saved myself a lot of time and trouble if I had paid the 4,000 tomans he had demanded. However, I find the practice of bribery to be one of the most inexcusable customs and would under no circumstances play a part in encouraging one law for the rich and one for the poor.

Once in Minoodash, I was cross-examined for several hours by two officers who refused to give their names. I gave them all the names and telephone numbers of Guidance officials in Tehran, but they refused to contact you.

All my notes were read and I was asked to point out the word Mujahedeen. When my notebook was returned the pages containing this word had been torn out. My personal letters, receipts, diaries, etc., were removed and even my dirty underwear was closely examined.

I was forced to sit outside with no shelter from the sun for five of the hottest hours of the day. Private camera film in my handbag was removed and has been kept, as has a cassette tape; this contained merely hypnosis therapy which I use to relax.

I waited a further couple of hours for my personal papers to be returned – I am sure copies have been made. I was then made to sign two pages of handwritten notes although I informed the officers that I could only read printed Farsi and then only very slowly and it had been a good fifteen years since I wrote in the language. However, as they

The past: My paternal Grandmother, Akhtar Iran Ansari, never wore a dress without a Paris or Milan designer label. She was considered one of the most elegant women to grace the royal court.

General Heydargholli Pessian: A good German military education and a spell in the German trenches during the first world war made my Grandfather as much an outsider in his society as I became in mine.

Out and about in fifties Iran: Mummy and Aunt Homa (*centre*) with my brother, Said (*front left*), my sister, Mashid, and Pari in the arms of her nanny, Fatemeh.

New Years' Eve 1957. My Father, Muhammad Ali Mosteshar Gharai, with his sister, Houri.

Top left: Happy days: Maman Joon's gardener, Nasser, makes a wish over the Samanu pot watched over by his mother, Saffi, in the gardens at Damavand.

Top right: The veil is still new and exotic for me as I pose in the grounds of the great Persian Poet, Saadi, in Shiraz.

Left: Happy days in Oxford: Charlie helps me get into the party mood as we prepare the marquee for Nader's 21st. Muhammad later took this photo as proof positive that I had been having a "sordid" affair.

A girls' night out under the tyranny of the Shah (*top*) and Islamic style (*bottom*).

My Father's Limo rushes me past a typical mud hovel on the outskirts of Tehran during the peak of prosperity under the Pahlavi dynasty.

Snow covers the dome of a Tehran mosque in the shadow of the television centre from where Raffer's brother broadcast the word of God to the masses.

I had Tehran at my feet and I should have been on top of the world, but the view from my flat will always take me back to the nightmare of waiting for hours on end to see Muhammad's car on the road below on its way to take me to my wedding.

IN THE NAME OF GOD
ISLAMIC REPUBLIC OF IRAN
Ministry of Culture And Islamic Guidance

Card No.

Ms/Mr. PARICHEHRE MOSTESHAR-CHARAI
REPORTER OF INDEPENDENT

Position:

Press

validity   signature   validity   signature

16July1992   1992 APRIL

FL-observer

Please Return This Card Before Depature

RIDZUAN IBRAHIM
BERNAMA
MALAYSIA

K.NARAYANAN
UNITED NEWS OF
INDIA SINGAPORE

The Ministry of Culture and Islamic Guidance Press Card could be had for the price of a colour television. That's me in the second row sporting my Yasser Arafat headdress and wondering who warned the boy sitting next to me in black not to talk to me because I was a spy.

Me and Raffers at the Press conference taken from the T.V. transmission. I have just asked him to give women their freedom and fear that I may finally have gone too far.

Alexei Sayle and Bob
Hoskins get day jobs
protecting Raffers.

I thank my mother-in-law
for finally finding me an
outfit that totally hides
my ever more ample
figure.

Modern times: The eyes that seem to say "Don't mess with me girls". He heads the system that is crushing my native land and yet the President may be its last hope.
Credit: Kamram Jebreili

Women in their proper place. A curtain separates the sexes at Friday prayers.
Credit: Kamram Jebreili

threatened to keep me until I did sign, I had no option but to do so.

My captors were not only rude but ran a barracks that was a disgrace. They did not take kindly to my suggestions on how my grandfather would have beaten them into shape. I must say that I find it appalling that Iranian soldiers are so scruffy, that men on duty are allowed to wear plastic slippers and that those who do have boots are not required to keep them clean.

However, I would like to thank the young conscript who had enough humanity to provide me with tea and water despite orders not to. If it had not been for this young man I believe my health could have been seriously affected.

I now hope that the matter is at an end. I do not expect an apology, nor do I expect compensation for my time or for my coat, which was ripped during the initial search.

I do very much hope that one day it will not be necessary for such things to happen on the free roads of Iran and that our citizens can go about their lives without hindrance.

Best regards,
Parichehre Mostehsar-Gharai

The ordeal of being arrested on a remote northern road and kept in an army barracks beyond the known world had failed to inspire in me the sort of fear that was proper to the situation. The fact that my driver had been one of the elite Imperial Guard under the Shah and had spent three years in a revolutionary prison would not exactly have helped my case if my captors had decided to keep me for longer. Things might well have been very different if I had showed any fear, but I had automatically slipped into Pessian mode, imagining myself as my grandfather the general and thus empowering myself rather than seeing myself as a victim.

As we finally drove away from the barracks that night, my driver told me: 'God really loves you.'

'Why?'

'Whenever I go out of town I carry my gun. This time I went home to get it and I had lost the key to the chest I keep my service revolver in. They would have had us shot if they had found a British journalist and former Imperial Guard on their way back from the area of serious unrest with arms.'

On the sixteen-hour journey back to Tehran I had time to reflect on what a foolish thing I had done by going to Mahshad, and by car at that. Never mind the risk from the bandits who had once again returned to Iran's roads; never mind the floods that had swept away parts of the road and thus made a hazardous journey along mountain roads even more dangerous; never mind that I had been branded in the *Keyhan* newspaper as a British spy; never mind that I was being driven by a former member of an elite commando force loyal to the Shah. What if they had realised that a member of the Pessian clan had returned to the very province from which her distinguished second cousin had launched a coup attempt a generation earlier?

We were stopped twice again, once at a check-point outside Tehran. 'This time don't mention journalism,' the driver told me after he had been interrogated.

I confirmed his story that I had been on a pilgrimage to the holy city. He wanted to know why I was alone and I explained that I had no family in Iran. Two hours later I was on my way again.

I was more than a little fed up when we were stopped again on the mountain road four hours away from Tehran. This time it was a traffic cop and the offence was merely speeding. The official fine was 5,000 tomans, but in a private deal with my driver the officer took 250 tomans for himself and we were back on our way.

Back in Tehran there was a general panic among my family and friends as news of my adventure spread. Farah had already worked everyone up into a lather because I had been missing for more than fourteen hours. Once they heard about my arrest, the panic spread and people were rushing out to deserted mountain roads to bury video machines, films, playing cards, booze and other assorted prohibited possessions.

I had thus been left alone to write my article when the doorbell went. I opened the door to find the hall in darkness, and as I hit the light switch I saw a classic Hezbullah lackey standing at the top of the stairs.

'Can I help you?'

'I am asking questions about one of your neighbours, Mr and Mrs Emami. Do you know them?'

'No, I don't know anybody,' I said, not believing a word of it.

'Mr Emami is due for a promotion so we are asking questions,' he explained unconvincingly. 'Is your husband at home?' He was trying to find out if I was alone or not.

'No, I am a guest here, and the people who live here are out,' I said without thinking.

I then slammed the door and waited for it to be kicked down. For the first time I was scared, for I had heard of how they surround people in their homes, then send someone to the door to assess how easy it will be to take the person and then they pounce. I waited for over an hour for them to pounce.

Later I learned that there was a neighbour called Emami, and Mrs Emami confirmed that her husband was to get a promotion; he was in the security service, and there had been a man in the building that morning asking questions about their habits. Everyone was rather worried because another neighbour had gone to the door in a strapless dress and no scarf and was now terrified that she would be arrested for indecency. Another told of the questions the man had asked: 'Have you ever seen Mrs Emami without proper *hejab*? Do the Emamis drink? Do they go to Friday prayers? Do they say their prayers regularly?' This, it appears, is normal practice, and even Nastaran had had to go through this sort of moral investigation before she was given a place at university.

On the subject of my arrest, Mousavi, Muhammad, Matt and Ms Loony each assured me that it was only their direct intervention with SAVAMA that had saved my skin and ensured that I had not been locked up for going to Mahshad without permission.

*   *   *

Death was everywhere that year, and I could not escape it in my private or public life.

It was an average day in Iran as I left Mehrabad for Bandar Abbas, a southern port, to commemorate the anniversary of the downing of the Iran Air AirBus over the Gulf by a US ship, killing more than 300 innocent passengers.

I spent the day with weeping and angry relatives who wanted to know why the man who had ordered the attack on the plane had been given a medal for valour by the US President. I had struggled to keep my scarf on my head as I stood on a battleship being ferried out to the spot where the plane had come down in the Gulf and by the time I was sitting in a taxi in Tehran on my way back home I was exhausted and dejected.

It was a Friday and Vali-e-Asr was deserted when my taxi came to turn into it from a side road. My driver slammed on his own brakes as we watched a brand-new navy Range-Rover skid, trying to check its speed along the deserted road.

We were only yards away from the two boys whom I now saw being thrown up and down as the car rolled, once, twice, three times. I saw the windscreen smash and the bodies get caught on the metal frame as they came through the gap left by the glass. I saw them hang there, trapped, as the car rolled over them, once, twice. I saw the blood on their bodies as they finally came untangled as the car went over for the fifth time, leaving the ground every time it turned. I saw their young bodies fly through the air in front of me and I could see the bones of the youngest boy's broken neck. I could see the red mess that was all that was left after the road had scraped off the flesh of the other boy's face.

I was shaking as I got home to find Useless curled up complaining of the flu that he could not shake off. I was crying, but he dismissed what I had just witnessed as just another day in sunny Tehran. They were just two more young men among the hundreds who die on the roads of the capital every day – who die for want of a little common sense, who die because it's cool to drive like James Bond and who die because people know they can buy their way out of the fines imposed in the attempt to introduce some law and order on these, some of the wildest roads in the world.

I was still shaken when Farah and Useless took delivery of a brand-new Renault 5 the next week. They had ordered a white car but soon learnt that to actually get it they had to bribe the dealer. They settled for a smaller bribe and a grey car.

The day it arrived, the caretaker of the block of twenty flats in which we lived brought a lamb to be sacrificed. The animal had its throat cut in front of the car, which was then driven over its blood. The blood was smeared on the steering wheel and two bloody hand-prints were placed on the back of the car. This ritual was to protect the good Muslims from accident.

Then these good Muslims took me out for a ride in this new car. Farah got in the back with me while the three children were allowed to stand in the passenger seat at the front. It seemed ludicrous to me that educated people should go through an ancient blood ritual to ward off accidents but not take an elementary step such as putting on a seat-belt.

'You know it would be illegal in the West to have the children in the front like that,' I remarked casually.

'Yes, I know,' Farah replied. 'They are so much more civilised than us.'

I wanted to scream: 'You stupid woman, if you know it's better why don't you do it?' I kept quiet but it was eating me up inside. Every time I got in that car and put on my belt, Farah and Useless would laugh at me and say things like: 'Really, Parichehre, you are so funny.'

Not so funny when you are lying on a hospital bed fighting for your life and your family are preparing to plunge themselves in black once more.

It is this inability, or refusal, to calculate the consequences of our actions that has been our undoing. We hated the Shah so we wanted him removed, so we spilled on to the streets without really thinking of what we wanted in his place. Our revolution had been one of hate; hate for the Shah and his like, rather than one of love, love for our nation and its future.

11

Sex, Drugs and Friday Prayers

After the fiasco with Hassan, I took refuge in a block of flats where Goli, my closest friend in Iran, lived, and it was there that I met Nahid.

At the age of fifteen Nahid had been forced to marry her cousin. Four years later she left him and their six-month-old twins, to become the wife of another woman's husband. She was moving uptown and nothing was going to stand in her way.

Hadji Abbas was the chosen vehicle of her transportation from poverty to wealth. Never mind that he was thirty years her senior, and that he already had a wife and eight children. Never mind that her family disowned her. Nahid was going to be the wife of one of the most successful iron dealers in the Tehran bazaar.

Tall, white-skinned, with piercing green eyes – all qualities that are much prized by the Iranian male – she had little trouble attracting the esteemed Hadji, who had little to recommend him other than his money. An ugly man by anyone's standards, Hadji was not the stuff of any young girl's dreams. The prefix 'Hadji' denotes a person who has been to Mecca – a duty of all Muslims. But it is also used by the merchant middle classes as a mark of respect for those who are particularly devout or particularly rich. Hadji Abbas was both.

Nahid had believed that in time her charms would win Hadji away from his elderly first wife. Hadji was smitten, but he also feared God, so the two relationships were conducted by the letter of Islamic law. One night he spent with Nahid, the next he was with his first wife. Whenever he made love to Nahid she knew he had just done the same 'on the other side', or would be doing so the next night. Much to the fury of his young wife, Hadji treated both wives exactly the same, as is required in Islam.

When I first met Nahid the revolution was a year old, and her veil-wearing, prayer-saying model of the traditional Muslim wife was still a novelty to the circles in which I moved. My great-grandmother's generation had been the last in our family to have worn the veil. During my childhood the only people who wore the *chador* were servants. In those days the *chador* was not this black crow-like outfit, but a beautiful, bright-coloured garment. Our cook used hers as a shield against dust rather than against lust, draping it over the back of her head and then wrapping it round her ample belly; this was a cultural outfit, not a sexual cloak. However, when I met Nahid I was eager to find out what sort of woman lived behind those black folds. We met at an all-girl lunch party given by Goli, who found herself living next to Nahid and her two children.

'My life is very interesting – you should write about me,' said Nahid. Hence, as her prospective biographer, I was privy to the most intimate details of her courtship, marriage and subsequent life.

Nahid's conversation was crude and rarely left the area below the waist. Before long she had grilled the assembled women on the exact dimensions of their husband's penis, the frequency of their love-making and the size of their jewellery collection. She had also kept us in fits of laughter with tales of the lengths she would go to in order to retain her husband's sexual interest.

'Men never stop being children,' she proclaimed. 'You have to keep them interested with something new every day . . .

'I served Hadji's dinner dressed as a belly dancer last night, and after he had eaten I got up on the table and danced for him . . .

'Young men make me sick. My Hadji has everything a woman could want. And, believe me, every bit of him works better than my first husband,' Nahid chortled.

She was quite oblivious to the hurt she had inflicted on Hadji's other family, and often boasted of the day the other wife had come to beg her to reconsider her engagement.

'The old hag offered to marry me to her eldest son,' Nahid said. 'She begged me, she fell on the floor and kissed my feet. She said Hadji would tire of me, and when I was old another wife would do to me what I was doing to her. I shouted that I loved him and nothing would make me give Hadji up. The witch then showed her real self. She started spitting and trying to pull my engagement ring off my finger. Hadji gave her a good beating that night,' Nahid smirked.

'I was only fifteen when I married the first time. I had no say, I was just told one day that I was going to get married to my cousin. When I refused, my Father beat me till I said yes. I had no one to stand up for me. We had very little money – thank God you have never been so poor that you have to go to bed hungry,' she told me as we tucked into the feast Goli had conjured up for us. 'At the wedding my Mother sat beside me, prodding with her needle to make me say yes,' Nahid had explained with tears in her eyes over that first meal. 'At that age you are still playing with your dolls, not wanting sex. I hated him and I hated the children.'

Ten years passed before I saw her again. She had undergone a metamorphosis. A new nose, a skirt that ended a millimetre below her pants and a cleavage pushed out of the tight Lycra top she had squeezed into greeted me as I arrived for yet another of those all-girl parties. Around her she had gathered assorted wives of the lower middle classes, who had now colonised the block of flats in which Goli lived.

The lives of these women, mostly married off in their early teens, consisted of sleeping with and feeding their husband, gossiping with their friends and bringing up their children. But they had all escaped traditional backgrounds, and had adjusted very well to a Westernised lifestyle of that other Iran, when at a stroke in 1979 the revolution dragged them back kicking and screaming to the Middle East. They had aspired to the values of the Shah's court, but found themselves back in the harem and the Middle Ages. They had never been told that they could work, that they had their own place in society. They looked down on their poorer, working sisters but had been left behind by their more educated and therefore more liberated countrywomen who were free to pursue a high-status career.

The gatherings of women had become their only outlet. They laughed and danced to black-market tapes of the new breed of Persian singer and groups, such as Andy and Kouroush, our answer to Wham. These artists were now making a fortune in Los Angeles with songs of longing for a country few of them had any intention of returning to. Behind the smiles of the women left in the homeland there was nothing. Outside those walls they ceased to exist in their own right. Under such pressures, and with no other outlet but the home, they would surely go mad.

I was staying with Goli, her two overactive children and a husband who had refused to work again the day the mullahs took power. He had sat at home getting quietly drunk for the last thirteen years while Goli struggled to earn enough to keep her family fed and clothed and to ensure that her children had an education. Her reward was to be constantly criticised by friends and family for neglecting her duties as a woman.

'Look at you,' her Mother would say. 'You look exhausted, you never do your hair and your clothes are dowdy and unfeminine. No wonder Malaki beats you.'

I never saw her being beaten, but I saw her rush home from work at nine each night to prepare the evening meal, to help her children with their homework and then to do the housework, while he sat and philosophised and told me how he had been very, very influential once.

It was about a week after my second meeting with Nahid, and for the first time in a month I was left alone, so I was eager to catch up on some work. I was tempted to let the phone ring. But it might be urgent, perhaps even a news conference, I thought.

It was urgent, Nahid said. 'Please come up right away.'

For a moment I was convinced that I had rung the wrong doorbell. This was the mad wife from *Jane Eyre*, finally having escaped from her attic cell. I looked at the number on the door again. It was Nahid's flat. So who was the possessed creature answering her door?

The woman before me was wrapped in a sheet, once white but now covered in black, red and green scrawl. On her forehead the word 'Allah' had been written in blood-red lipstick.

'There is only one God and Muhammad is his messenger,' she chanted. Swivelling, her hands caressed her body and her eyes flicked open, then shut.

This was surely the threshold to hell.

Suddenly she disappeared into the bowels of her house. What demons and goblins could be lurking beyond that hall? A less avid reader of books on the supernatural might have entered with nothing more than curiosity, but all my senses told me that retreat was the better part of valour.

'Come in, I need your help. Hurry, it will spoil,' Nahid said, momentarily appearing in the hall before twisting back towards her bathroom.

Do Muslim demons shrink before the sign of the cross? Should I pop back to the flat for a clove of garlic?

'Come,' the demented one instructed.

With trepidation I stepped across the threshold. I found my deranged neighbour in the bathroom ripping off her shroud. She stood in front of the mock mother-of-pearl bidet, her head slumped on her now bare breast, the bowl of the bidet filled with the now discarded shroud.

Nahid turned to me, lucid again. 'I have to set fire to this,' she said, pointing to the mess in the bidet. 'When I set it on fire, wait till the sheet is charred so that you can no longer make out the writing, then take that bowl and pour the water over the flames,' she instructed.

At times like these it is better to humour the disturbed. So the flames were duly doused, the charred remains settling to mar the plushness of the colour-coordinated suite.

Then, as if nothing had happened, Nahid picked herself up, slapped a handful of cold-cream over the lipsticked 'Allah' and wiped if off on a daisy-patterned towel. She wrapped a silk kimono around her and smiled at me. 'Tea?' she asked.

What can one say? 'I want an explanation,' would have been the logical reply, but all I managed was: 'Yes, please.'

Installed in her kitchen with a cup of sweet tea to settle my nerves, I waited for an explanation.

'Can you lend me 250,000 tomans?' Nahid asked as she offered me a piece of her home-made cake. She explained that she owed the money to a local sorceress who had given her several love-charms.

Open-mouthed, I stared at her. The request for a loan of about £1,000 might not have seemed so excessive had we been in the UK, but in Iran it was more than the average civil servant earns in a year. 'What is going on here?' I finally managed to ask.

'You remember the boy you met in the lift last week? The one you told Goli was good-looking?' she asked.

I nodded. Goli had pointed the boy out as Nahid's lover, but I pretended not to know of her new sexual adventurism.

'I love him,' she said. I produced the appropriate look of amazement. 'He loves me very much. We want to be together, always,' Nahid gushed.

'But . . . but . . . but your husband,' I stuttered. 'You have children . . . This is Iran. How?'

Through tears Nahid garbled: 'You can't know. You are so lucky, so free. I want to die. I have nothing. Imagine an old man next to you in bed. He can't do anything. All night he rubs his thing against me, hoping he can make it rise. Look at me, I am a young woman, I have to live.'

In order to do this, Nahid had picked up the phone and dialled a number at random. On the third try she had reached a man. He was a twenty-four-year-old footballer, and destined to become the first of her lovers. They had met in the Mellat Park the next afternoon, and had ended up consummating their passion in the back of his van.

Her affair had gone well for the first few months. They met every day – first in the back of his van, then in the homes of friends. Finally, Nahid started bringing him home on the nights that her husband was 'on the other side'. Then the footballer had started missing dates. Afraid that she could not keep his interest once he had his fill of her, Nahid had enlisted the help of the sorceress.

'I went to Mariam Khanoum, and she gave me a prayer from the Koran. I said it all night before I was to see him again. Then when he came I put a tiny bit of my urine in his drink. He changed overnight. Now he comes two or three times a week,' she said, with childish innocence.

This was one cup of tea that I was not going to finish.

Today's performance was guaranteed, by this crone, to block any effort by the footballer's family to marry him off until he reached his fortieth birthday.

'I had to wait until I got my period, because this makes women much more powerful. Then I wrote passages from the Koran on a sheet that I had put underneath us that last time we made love. This morning my period finished, and I collected the water from my bath in a bowl. The water put out the flames as it will put out his desire for other women,' she explained, as if this were completely rational.

'If Massoud leaves me, I will kill myself,' Nahid threatened. 'Look at this place,' she said, pointing around her at the home Hadji had made for her. It may not have been a palace, but the three-bedroomed flat was respectable. The furniture, although unfashionable, was new and clean. The fitted carpet, in deep pink, was expensive and exactly matched the velvet on the sofa.

'Nahid, it really isn't such a bad life. Look at the people around you; no one has anything these days. You are still very lucky.' I tried to comfort her in my broken Farsi.

'Nothing is mine,' she screeched. 'This house is in Hadji's name. Can you see any Persian carpets here? My son has no car, no money for Reeboks. Look at my hands,' she said, thrusting them in my face, the tears building up in her eyes. 'They are ruined. I've slaved for this man for twenty-three years. But he gives me nothing. I have no rings, no gold. What I had from the first years I have sold to buy clothes. I paid for my own nose operation, and he wouldn't even give Layla the money for hers. I had to save out of the housekeeping to make my daughter look beautiful.

'Without Massoud, I might as well be dead. If I lose him I will kill myself. Keep my rings until I pay you back,' she said, thrusting her wedding and engagement rings towards me. They had appeared from somewhere within the kimono, and they disappeared just as quickly. 'I can't ask Hadji. The old skinflint needs an account for every little thing I spend. He even does the shopping himself rather than give me the money. He'll kill me if he ever finds out.'

The sooner the better for all concerned, I thought. I hated the hopelessness and ignorance that made some women resort to magic, charms and spells. It was medieval and had always been associated in my mind with the dregs of society. Suddenly I remembered that I was expecting an urgent call from the paper in London. I promised to see what I could do about the loan and shot out of there like a bat out of hell.

From the day of the burning, most of the news of Nahid's exploits came to me second-hand through Goli. Goli, the product of a strict upbringing, delighted in Nahid's tales of sexual adventure. She ignored my dire warnings of impending disaster, and continued to skip in and out of Nahid's flat for constant updates. This was, after all, the Islamic Republic, and dear Nahid was not exactly discreet. Should the Pasdars raid Nahid's home, they would surely round up all known associates. I could see the headlines: '*Independent* correspondent picked up in raid on den of vice.'

Our conversation over the wisdom of befriending Nahid was cut short as Goli's husband came into the kitchen with his son's history book in his hand and a look of blind rage on his face. Goli's ten-year-old son had brought his history textbook home to ask his Father, a Harvard graduate, for help. The book opened with the words: 'The history of Iran is the history of Islam and the Imams.' With one sweep of the pen 2,500 years of Persian history had been wiped out and replaced with the history of a religion. Children were being taught to think of themselves as Muslims, not as Iranians. Mehrdad had ranted and raved and forbidden his son to read the book. That night I found the boy crying in his room. 'Why doesn't my Father know these facts? Why isn't he intelligent?' he moaned. A new generation were doomed to be indoctrinated with a knowledge they were not equipped to doubt.

*   *   *

It was around this time that I began to get crippling pains in the general area of my ovaries. Several months before going to Iran I had been rushed to hospital to have a cyst removed from a twisted ovary, and I was rather obsessed with the idea that I might lose them before I could use them to reproduce.

Goli suggested that I go for a check-up with her gynaecologist, who was about to perform surgery on Nahid. There was nothing wrong with Nahid, but after four children she was about to become a 'born-again virgin'. Iranian surgeons specialise in this particular miracle, not only sewing back the hymen but narrowing the entrance to enhance the pleasure of the man and in the process often making sex unbearably uncomfortable for the woman.

I arrived at the surgery to be ushered into a dark and gloomy room where a troll of a man sat behind an enormous desk. I went through an examination that I'd rather not think about. Then I was sat down, given a cup of sweet tea and told that I had a large immovable growth that was in all probability malignant.

'Don't worry,' the white-haired troll told me as he saw me out with his arm round my shoulder. 'I'll just cut from here to here,' he continued, sweeping his hand across my groin along the line of entry. 'No one will be able to see the scar.'

I was devastated. I stood at the side of the road as taxi after taxi slowed down to offer me a ride, but I could not remember where I was living. Perhaps I should go and buy a ticket for London and go home. Over and over again a voice was saying, 'You might have cancer.'

I was standing there with my heart pounding in my throat when a car drew up and a man asked me if I was all right. It was Ahmad, a young security service agent I knew only by sight. That day he must have been assigned to follow me and I must have looked really bad for him to blow his cover. I would never have got home if not for him.

The next morning I arrived at the hospital at the crack of dawn to await the troll. By nine he still wasn't around and my bladder was bursting from the water one has to consume before having an ultrasound scan. The nurse at reception kept fobbing me off as I demanded to have my scan before he arrived. However, the sight of 400 tomans changed her mind. I hated resorting to the language of bribery, but I had not slept all night and I was frantic to know the worst.

An hour later the doctor carrying out the ultrasound was telling me that he could not find anything that could be a large lump. I was normal, thank God. It was just then that the troll arrived and insisted that the examination be carried out by another doctor.

'That man is no good. I always use Dr Bahonar. That is why I was late – I had to find him to come and do the examination,' the troll told me.

He was still trying to persuade me to admit myself at the hospital and to have more tests when I made my escape.

It turned out that this creature specialised in the sort of operations that no other doctor would do. He was one of the few doctors to risk carrying out abortions despite the death penalty. Back home I urged Nahid to have nothing to do with him but she was determined; she wanted to keep her toy boy. She told me that having a narrower front access might discourage him from demanding the very painful anal sex which she had been forced into recently. She smiled as she told me how he had taken her right where I was seated in her sitting-room, while he watched a porn-movie video. I still had no idea that he had been paying for the pleasure. Noticing my rather shocked look, Nahid claimed that I might also resort to such lengths in her place.

'This wrinkled old man gets in beside me every other night and wants sex; but he can no longer get it up. So for hours he puts his cock between my buttocks and rubs, while I have to say dirty things to him to make him erect,' she told me, sobbing.

I was sympathetic to a point, but no amount of advice could make her accept that she was again the victim, that she was just making the same old mistakes and that there was a path to happiness other than having a man between your legs.

By this time Nahid had recruited the wives of two neighbours to join her escapades. The three would meet at Nahid's on the nights that Hadji was at his other home to entertain their various men. There was Nasrin, the sensual wife of a businessman, who started her life of vice by sleeping with the man she had wanted to marry before her family forced her to marry a cousin. Soraya was the eldest and the richest of the three and unashamedly admitted to Goli, who in turn told me, that she had taken a lover for a bit of excitement. A woman in her late forties, she had two daughters who often accompanied her during her sessions at Nahid's. The teenage girls would keep Layla, Nahid's daughter, company while their Mothers enjoyed their lovers.

The Three Tarts, as Goli called them, were all to have the tightening operation, which cost 150,000 tomans, and Nahid was the first to go. She was ecstatic the day she came out of hospital, only lamenting that she would be out of action – or should I say business? – for at least two months. It was this inability to perform that forced her to expose her new profession when she tried to urge Goli to meet with some of the men she could not service. She didn't put it in quite those words but that is what it amounted to. Goli was outraged at the idea.

By this time I had moved back in with Farah, but I was visiting Goli one morning when Nahid pounded on the door in real distress. She was as white as a sheet and blood was pouring down her leg. As we bundled her off to hospital in Goli's car she explained that her latest lover had been unable to wait till she had the stitches removed, and had tested out the new Nahid despite her screams of agony. He had torn her to bits with his attempts to enter the passage which the troll had proudly told Nahid was now narrower than his little finger.

On the way to hospital Nahid recovered enough to tell us about a new man in her life. 'Nasrin and I were in her car, parked in front of a sandwich store, when this lovely navy Jaguar stopped behind us and sounded the horn. Nasrin didn't want to go, so I got in with him. I was wearing large sunglasses and he begged me to take them off so he could see my eyes. He begged so much that I took off the glasses and he said they were the loveliest eyes he had ever seen. Then he begged me to pull up my coat so that he could see my legs. He was so sweet, I did it, and he felt my calf. You should have seen him – he was in heaven.

'He asked me to go with him to his brother's house near the Niavaran Palace. I had to tell him I had just had an operation and could not go home with him,' she told us, wincing from time to time from the pain.

'I have to phone him at six tonight at a number he told me to use only at the times he said. Could you phone him for me and meet him instead of me?' she asked, turning to me. 'You're so lucky, being free. Don't ever give up your freedom, will you?'

'No,' was all I could manage in reply to both questions.

Whether Nahid was delirious from the pain and loss of blood or whether she was just beyond caring I could not tell, but she then went on to tell us a story that would show us 'how filthy these mullahs are'. She said that she had been picked up by a mullah in one of the holy shrines at Tagrish Square, North Tehran. He had approached her after she had finished her worship at the shrine and asked her if she would be his *seegheh*. She had agreed, not telling him that she was already married.

'He was enormous,' she claimed. 'What energy that old boy had! I was on my back for five hours while he did everything he wanted to me. We went to this room over a shop in the bazaar where there was just a bed, a sink and a fridge. Before we started he got a bowl and filled it with iced water. Every time he wanted to come he would pull it out and dip it in the water to keep it hard. I wish Hadji had such energy. He came three times – once in my mouth, once in my ear and once inside me,' she confided, without any shame or reservation.

'He is very generous, and Nasrin and I often go to be with him and some of his friends. He likes to watch women together and sometimes a child will join us. All these men are so filthy, they all want to get in from the backside,' she continued.

My prudishness overcame my curiosity at this point and I urged her to be quiet, to save her strength. At the hospital I acted rather badly, for I did not want to be associated with the woman after all I had heard on the drive, so I helped carry Nahid to the emergency ward and then left Goli to deal with her while I waited outside in the car. An hour later they were out, and Nahid looked pale but less hysterical. There were to be more revelations on the way home. The doctor who had treated her had known her from a visit to the hospital a month earlier – after a suicide attempt. I pitied the woman but I also despised her; it was a strange sensation.

Back at home and with Nahid safely in her own bed – alone – I was ranting at Goli for mixing with her oversexed neighbour in this atmosphere of Islamic piety when my uncle phoned to tell me that Aunt Omol was in hospital and not expected to survive.

Omol passed away after three days of fighting for her life. Cause of death: contaminated fruit.

We were back in black, and the clans had gathered at Auntie's house. Farah and Useless dropped by, and Farah spent the forty minutes she stayed complaining that the refreshments were inadequate. Auntie had said that the money that would usually be spent on feeding mourners should be donated to the disabled. 'What rubbish; it is disgraceful,' my cousins whispered as the poor bereaved children served tea and dates to the guests streaming through their home during those first days.

On the morning of the funeral I woke up to find Farah on the phone to her best friend. She was claiming that she could not find anyone to mind her children and would have to miss the ceremony. I made the mistake of pointing out that when it was a matter of going shopping she seemed to be able to leave them quite alone, and at least that day the caretaker's daughter was around in case anything happened. But Farah insisted she could not get away.

I left after borrowing her cool black coat, advising her: 'Try and find someone, please. You know what people are like – they will say you didn't care because Auntie was only a half-sister.'

So there I was in the middle of a hospital lobby waiting for my aunt's body to be handed over when my uncle came up to me. The entire Pessian clan were gathered within earshot when Dada Jan horrified me by saying: 'Farah has been on the phone to me. She is in tears and says that you have made her life hell.'

Before I could take in what was happening he had delivered a stream of abuse and walked away. What on earth was going on? We were friends when I had left her house that morning. I was on the verge of tears of rage when Farah arrived, marched up to me and demanded her coat back. She was carrying my black plastic coat. When I handed over her coat I informed her that I would not be returning to her home. I was furious with her: there had been no argument, but even if there had been we were adults for heaven's sake, not pathetic children who go running to their parents every time they have a row. I would think about it later: this was Auntie's day and I felt guilty being in tears over something other than her death.

Auntie's body, wrapped in sheets, was handed over to the waiting, wailing mourners at a side door of the hospital. In the skirmish to get closer I was knocked over into a pile of hospital refuse chucked on to the street. As I tried to get up I slipped again on a pile of used hypodermic needles buried among soiled dressings.

A hospital ambulance took the body to Behesht-e-Zahra cemetery, and we followed in a couple of coaches. I wasn't sure if the tears were for Auntie or from fury. What I did know was that I felt very lonely among these peculiar people. Body tourists roamed this macabre mausoleum asking the bereaved for the details of the death, and life, of their departed kin.

In the long concrete building the body-washers worked on the corpses behind a glass wall as the mourners wailed and howled and screamed.

'Don't hurt her,' Mina and Minu said in unison as a woman scrubbed their Mother's heels with a pumice stone.

Next to us another woman screamed: 'Look at her poor body! Oh, Mummy, Mummy, look at your poor bruised body!' Then she began to beat herself around the face and head.

Auntie's body was then wrapped in a shroud, taken to a reception room and placed on a stretcher. Auntie was then carried out by men who were blood relatives – even in death women cannot be touched by men not of their kin. She was displayed in a small enclosure before being placed under a canopy where a mullah said the prayer of death. Then we all got back in the car and on to another graveyard where Auntie Omol was to be buried in the same grave as her Mother. Here we were elbowed aside as mullahs rushed to earn a crust by saying prayers over her.

At the grave I was surprised to find my cousin Shahnaz giving me the cold shoulder, but not because she had heard that I had been 'cruel' to Farah. Her reason was quite different and was to cause a family feud of soap-opera proportions. Every death is announced in the newspapers with a list of the bereaved families in order of importance. As Auntie Omol's sisters, Mummy and my aunts and their families were named in order of age. Shahnaz took it very badly that my Father's name should have come before hers, and I was thus shunned.

I was back with Mrs Mo that night before moving to a patch of floor at Hamzeh's home. This had the advantage of being within walking distance of Guidance, where Muhammad seemed to have taken up residence. We started meeting there every day; the atmosphere in the house, what with the bereavement and all, was not conducive to gaiety and I needed to get out, I needed to forget the tragedy and despondency.

Muhammad and his cousin Mr Shirazi were to return to their home city for the traditional nomadic wedding of the latter's fifteen-year-old niece and were eager for me to go along. It would be a splendid affair and a good chance for me to see how the Qashqai tribesmen lived. It was important that I did not mention this trip to anyone, Muhammad explained, because of the ban on officials mixing with debauched spies.

I was growing closer to Muhammad and our mountain trips were getting more frequent and much longer. About a week after my aunt's death we were again setting out on the climb from Darband at 7 a.m. It was cool and clear and for the first time in a long while I felt free in the majesty of those mountains. There was no need to look over your shoulder for an Islamic Guard or to worry that a strand of hair might escape. The magnificence of nature seemed to drain away some of the tension of life and I had someone who was paying me attention, who listened to what I was saying and, best of all, who agreed with every word I said.

On the flat streets of the city the pain from my back meant that I could hardly walk, I wore my back-brace for at least five hours a day and on a really bad day I would drag my left leg behind me from the pain. But in those mountains my mind and my body were whole and free; an extra dose of painkillers also helped.

The path wound past a small valley forged by a rushing mountain stream, the waters swelled by the melting snow from the peaks as winter gave way to spring. A trickle made its way down the path itself and Muhammad stretched his hand to help me over the mud. This first meeting of our flesh was charged with sensual tension. He, after all, had only ever touched one other woman: his ex-wife. And I had not so much as flirted with a man since I arrived in God's Republic. At the top of the path the mountain gleamed in the sun like the golden dome on a sacred shrine. Here Persia was the shrine and the rays were God's promise of liberation.

Tehran seemed a galaxy away. Up on that peak you could almost believe that nothing had ever changed, that the martyrs and the tyrants were still walking those streets instead of being dust in a grave. Muhammad's martyred brothers would be tending to their crops outside Shiraz, and Bahar would still be painting.

'Someone was telling me about Mr Shirazi,' I ventured, trying to resolve a new suspicion that was eating away at the back of my mind. 'His life sounded a lot like yours, what with marrying his brother's sister and his child dying.'

'That is why we are so close. He is the only one that can feel what I feel,' Muhammad said before bursting into tears.

'What's wrong? Please don't cry – tell me what's wrong,' I urged as I took his hand.

He guided me down to a hidden ledge overlooking the river. As we sat together in the shade of the fledgling trees he told me that it was the anniversary of the death of his daughter. To make things worse she had died on a mountain road during a climbing trip such as this. I felt so guilty for having been suspicious, this man was in such obvious pain. Before I knew what was happening we were kissing and he was telling me I was his last chance at happiness. I'd never been anyone's last chance before.

The arrival of a couple on the path below us put an end to this embrace and we made our way back to the real world in silence.

Why did you do that? the voice inside asked me. I had wanted the warmth and the comfort of a man's arms round me; I had wanted to feel I belonged to someone amidst the strangeness of this new world. Up in the clouds I had heard the tick, tick, tick of my biological clock. I had an overwhelming need for succour. When it was over I just wanted to run and hide, but I also wanted to be part of a couple and thus whole by the standards of this society.

Muhammad told me later that he had seen a triangle of flesh on my neck from under my scarf that morning, and the sight had turned him on, exciting him so much that he hardly knew what he was saying or doing. I was touched and yet slightly disgusted at the thought of his crying over his dead daughter while he had a 'hard-on'.

When we reached my home Muhammad suggested we meet again the next day. I was in mid-excuse as he said: 'I want to show you what becomes of the degeneracy of your society.'

'My society?'

'Not you, of course. But those people like your family who held themselves to be so high and mighty,' he said, and drove off before I could say no.

The next morning we travelled to a newly developed 'rich people's' colony about forty minutes east of Tehran. Here villas sprang up at the centre of luxuriant grounds in the middle of nowhere. We stopped outside one of the most lavish of these and my escort rang the bell in a gate set into tall stone walls that made the enclosure a fortress. Dogs started to bark, and their keeper shouted for them to 'Shoo'. Muhammad said something into the intercom and more barking followed before finally there was silence and the gate opened.

A beautiful young man stood before us. He looked breathtaking in grey flannel and tweed over a silk shirt and cowboy boots. These were the largest, and greenest eyes I had ever stared into. Lashes that I would die for bordered these piercing orbs.

Then he convulsed; his whole body dipped to the left while his right arm shot out as if to pull himself upright again.

'Come in, come in, come in. Shut up, Rostram,' he said. He led us past six Alsatian dogs penned up in a mud-and-wire cage. A gravel drive twisted through lush lawns and fruit trees to a Spanish hacienda. The sound of water flowing through small irrigation channels along the lines of trees was in stark contrast to the thirsty rasping of the sterile earth beyond the wall.

The boy's Mother greeted us from where she was reclining under a rose-covered veranda. Beside her the steam rose from a glass of tea. She got up as we approached but her eyes held no smile of welcome; in fact they held no life at all, no sparkle. She was about fifty, very dark, with a pock-marked olive complexion. She had had the obligatory nose job, and the tiny upturned stump looked sadly out of place in the middle of her plump face. How had she given birth to such a handsome son?

'You have met my wife, haven't you?' the boy asked Muhammad as the woman sat again without uttering a word.

Obviously seeing the surprise in my eyes, she smiled, a cold, barren smile. 'He is forty. He just *looks* like a little child.'

The Spanish style gave way to Middle Eastern opulence within the house, the walls covered with fine tapestries and paintings of battles and hunting scenes. A couple of steps led down to a living area crammed with the treasures of the past. Silk cushions were dotted around the floor next to fine antique furniture. The value of the textiles in that room alone would have kept a small nation afloat for a couple of years.

'My Father's legacy,' the boy said, pointing to his belongings as if he were pointing out a cancer.

The wife followed us in and was now crouching in front of an immense fireplace in which a blanket of pure white ash covered still-glowing coals. She slipped her hand under a blanket and pulled out a tray, tongs and some sort of ornate pipe. As we settled down on the cushions, she took something from the tray and loaded the pipe. Then she seized a glowing piece of charcoal from the fireplace with the tongs, held it to the end of the pipe and took a deep breath. The smell of opium wafted over the room.

'You see this coal?' the boy said. 'It is the finest coal for opium. It makes the smoking much better when the coal is good. I spend a lot of money to get this coal.'

His body was racked with another spasm.

'My Father taught me to have only the very best in everything.'

Rashid, our host, was the eldest son of a nobleman who had been secretly married to one of the royal princesses. He was not the princess's child but he had nevertheless enjoyed the spoils of court life.

'My Father was a great gambler – a very great gambler, in fact the very best gambler. And he left me in this hole, in this hell, with nothing,' he said, as his body was convulsed by a double spasm. 'He gave me three flats in London, behind Harrods, for my eighteenth birthday. They were beautiful flats ... beautiful ... My flats ...

He was a great gambler . . . he lost a million dollars in one night in London. "Son," he said to me, "I need your flats." '

Another spasm.

'I gave them to him without question. My flats,' Rashid said, as his wife handed him the pipe.

The pipe seemed to age him as he drew it to his mouth. The woman went out to bring the thick, sweet tea that accompanies the smoking of opium. She came back with an older man, who looked as if he had just woken up.

'How many pipes have you had already?' the man asked.

'This is my seventh,' the boy said. 'She is a little ahead of me.' He nodded towards his retreating wife. The effort brought on another of those body-rending spasms.

'When have you got to go for your test, Amoo?' the woman asked the older man after returning with a Thermos and five small glasses.

Rashid explained that his paternal uncle (*amoo*) had been caught smoking opium at a party and had spent two months in jail.

'Not as much as me,' he told me. 'I was in jail for five years.'

He dropped the pipe and jumped to his feet, pulling off his jacket and shirt. No one, least of all Muhammad, seemed to object to this display of semi-nudity. His bare back bore the marks of many beatings.

Rashid's uncle now had to turn up for regular blood tests to ensure he was not back on the opium. He hadn't smoked for two days, and was therefore more than a little edgy, and had taken a large number of contraceptive pills, which apparently hide the signs of drugs in the blood.

'I've been in jail twice and had more than two hundred lashes in the last fourteen years. They come to my house at least once a week, so I have to smoke in the night and the early morning. At nine thirty a man will come and take all this paraphernalia away and then bring it back after midnight,' Rashid explained.

It was awful to sit there and watch the decline of a young man, the leftovers of a vanquished aristocracy, and yet you could not escape the conclusion that all the ills of the nation were rooted here in this decadence.

But when we left Muhammad started to harangue me over Rashid's lifestyle, saying he was one of my kind. Part of me was furious at this man who dared to judge me by the actions of others, yet there was that guilt buried away in the corner of my mind: guilt at being part of that extravagance, when he came from hardship. Our way of life had been disgraceful; I had been repelled at being part of a set that discarded designer clothes after one outing, that spent a fortune each night at trendy clubs and bought whatever their hearts desired, then salved their conscience by putting a servant's son through college.

Nevertheless, I was not letting Muhammad get away with such generalities. There had been one or two homes in that other life where I knew there was an opium room. But in God's Republic the stuff was everywhere. Despite the execution of thousands of 'drugs gangsters' by the mullahs, you could get whatever you wanted whenever you wanted it. Almost every house I visited these days, except for my immediate family, had the pipe and other instruments for smoking yourself into oblivion.

*　　*　　*

At last I was renting a flat of my own, and a luxury flat to boot. A friend had agreed to rent to me without registering the transaction, thus avoiding my financial-transactions ban and his need to pay tax on the rent. I grabbed it before I had time to think if it was entirely wise for someone with vertigo to live on the nineteenth floor of a tower block on top of a steep hill; a flat with floor-to-ceiling windows along one side with precious little edge between you and a sheer drop.

It was a simple little pad. There was one bedroom with two single beds; an open-plan hall leading to an L-shaped dining-sitting-room; to the right of the front door a tiny kitchen; and next to that a duplex bathroom. The bedroom and the sitting-room both opened on to a large, private balcony ideal for clandestine sunbathing. The furniture was new and white, and the place was filled with light.

Goli arrived to help me unpack, and to do a spot of cleaning, because 'I know you hate it so'. She was right: I did. I do a lot of recreational cleaning when I have writer's block or I am very, very angry and have to put my energy into something other than spitting venom.

'Nahid moved out last week,' she informed me as we sloshed disinfectant over everything. 'She has moved in with a man she met in a sandwich bar.'

'I don't believe it,' I said, genuinely shocked.

'The children are suicidal and Hadji has reported her disappearance to the Komiteh. We have Pasdars crawling all over the building.'

'But why?'

'She phoned me one morning about a week ago and asked to borrow a trunk. When I took it up for her, she had the entire house packed up and was getting ready to leave. When I asked how she would live, she pointed between her legs and said that she would earn more through her cunt than from Hadji. The poor man looks a hundred years old.'

It turned out that Nahid had moved into a flat in a newly built block just across the road from me! Much to my relief, I never bumped into her, but I was constantly on the look-out.

I had not been in residence for more than a couple of days before word spread that there was a lone woman in the two-block complex of luxury flats on the Jordan Expressway, a mere stone's throw from the Mo residence, and assorted male 'neighbours' started popping round or phoning to see if I needed any help.

'Thank you very much, but what sort of help do you imagine I would need at three o'clock in the morning?'

'It really is so kind of you but I like being lonely – I came here with the express intention of being lonely.'

'No, I don't cook dinner, and I don't eat it either, and I wouldn't eat it with you even I had been starving for a month.'

'If you don't stop phoning at this time of the night, or rather morning, I will phone the Komiteh.'

Nazi, a divorced lady doctor who lived alone on the third floor, came round one day after I had threatened the receptionist and guards with dire consequences if they gave anyone my number again. She had heard about the calls and wanted to share her experience. She knew most of the characters who now bugged me. It seemed I was lucky to be just out of sight of a man in the opposite tower who had terrorised her by watching her through his telescope. For a week I sat in my flat with the curtains firmly shut against the peeping Tom. That is, until all of a sudden the calls stopped and a note dropped in apologising for the 'rudeness' of those pestering me.

The night before I had been spotted on the news at a press conference with the Foreign Minister and Nelson Mandela and by the next day the word 'spy' was being whispered in the corridors among the still-rich who could afford to live towering over the misery that existed downtown.

It had been my finest hour. After I had followed this childhood hero from reception to reception for two days, the great man had come to recognise me. On his final day he had made his way towards me in the crowd and said hello in front of the cameras. I was so happy I could have died. Back in Oxford I had a trunkful of 'Free Nelson Mandela' T-shirts and I had learnt to ski to the strains of the song with the same title.

Nelson Mandela, the man the press had said was bringing a message for Raffers from the US President George Bush, had said hello to me; therefore we must both be agents of the West.

12

On the Road to Ruin

Having my own flat made a world of difference. After more than a year shuffling from one home to another and living out of a suitcase, I was thrilled to have a place where I could wander around in just lipstick and a smile. Not that I ever did, but I could if I had wanted to.

I was also free to be alone for days on end, to spend three days throwing up over the loo without a single 'How are you?' My stomach had always been 'nervous', as my doctor put it. This was so that it would not feel out of place next to my 'angry hip' and my 'irritated bowels' which went well with my 'aggravated piles'.

I had celebrated my first evening at the flat by preparing a very spicy dinner for an Indian couple who had entertained me lavishly over the last year. They had suffered no ill effects but I was plunged into an episode of non-stop vomiting for ten days. Close friends and family occasionally phoned to see how I was, but not one of them put a foot across my doorstep – no one except Muhammad, who either phoned or visited every day. I had lost about a stone in weight before Muhammad persuaded me to see a doctor.

The doctor he took me to had armed guards at the entrance of the building from which he operated. I was searched twice on my way up by women who looked impressed when they saw the security pass in my hand with the doctor's name on it.

'You are getting the best today,' Muhammad assured me. 'This is why our leaders never die.'

After a million tests, X-rays and a string of questions, this doctor, a frog in white clothing, told me that I had a 'nervous stomach' and I should avoid spicy foods and getting upset.

Despite the suitcase full of pills and injections he gave me, I continued to throw up everything I ate. To the stomach trouble was added the Mother of All Migraines. Muhammad came round every day and phoned most nights to see if I was feeling OK or if I needed him to get anything for me. A week later I was not feeling much better, but getting to feel a lot closer to Muhammad, whom I began to see as my only friend. By the time I was eating again we were discussing the possibility of marriage.

Ignoring the dire consequences if we were discovered, Muhammad persuaded me to go with him to Shiraz by overnight coach for his fifteen-year-old cousin's wedding. I hardly noticed the twelve-hour drive as Muhammad told me of the plans he had for our future. Exactly when I had fallen in love I could not tell you, but on that trip I was travelling on cloud 9. Everything he said made sense to me and I failed to notice that it was I who paid for our tickets and for the meals along the way.

Once in Shiraz, the jewel of the Persian empire, the city of wine, roses and the nightingale, I went to stay with my Aunt Homa while Muhammad went to his family, promising not to say anything about our 'engagement' until we were 100 per cent sure. On my own with Muhammad the idea of marriage had seemed exciting, but face to face with my aunt I couldn't bring myself to say that he was more than a colleague from work.

Part of my reluctance might have been due to the fact that I knew that if word got back to Mummy she would be on the next plane out to Iran and would move heaven and earth to break it up. Mummy isn't a great fan of marriage. Since childhood I have been taught that it was just something that might or might not happen while women went about the real business of life – their careers. Many a general's son or deposed prince had been turned away at our door before I even knew I was in demand.

As always, the Fat Man, sat around the house like a withered bulldog in his pyjamas with a cigarette hanging out of the corner of his mouth. At least he had stopped dyeing his Afro-curled hair and the white gave some relief to his clouded features. As Homa rushed around serving him it struck me as tragic that this tall, fair, elegant, amusing and intelligent beauty was chained to this shrivelled, dark, seedy and vulgar little man. To hold family and home together she had put up with a lifetime of his jumping into bed with anyone who would open her legs. The home was crumbling around them while they sleep-walked through life, the misery numbed by a constant flow of vodka. Shiraz always has a soporific effect on me and I slept the entire day.

The next morning Muhammad arrived behind the wheel of a rather smart, borrowed jeep. I soon discovered why we needed the jeep when he drove across barren land with little more than a dust-track leading out of the city to one of the growing villages in which these once nomadic peoples were being forced to settle. After an hour driving through desolate semi-desert we came upon an oasis of colour. Beside two scanty brick structures that passed as houses, more than 2,000 Qashqais gathered in all their finery. The layered, multi-coloured clothes of the women in bright yellows, oranges, golds and greens glimmered in the desert sun. Their sunburnt faces reminded me of the Cherokee and the Sioux.

When we drew into the settlement, men who would not have looked out of place in Ghengis Khan's army rushed towards us, shooting off rounds from enormous rifles.

As a child I had been fascinated by the stories of clan life recounted by my paternal grandfather. His grandfather had been a Khan of one of the eastern people who had been at war with a neighbouring clan for many years. Finally great-great-grandfather had called for peace and invited his enemy and his family to a peace meeting. While the guests slept after a sumptuous meal, my great-great-grandfather ordered his warriors to slit their throats. I have no idea if this was really true but there are times I can feel a certain ruthlessness deep within my soul.

Nevertheless, I had always imagined that this sort of thing goes on all the time beyond the city limits. So when I saw these marauding tribesmen I was sure my end had come. My life flashed before my eyes as Muhammad jumped out of the car, to embrace our attackers.

Such are the fears of the naïve, much the same as the fears raised in the hearts of those of my colleagues who had infuriated me by imagining that Iran was populated only by international terrorists.

We were ushered into one of the makeshift brick houses, where Muhammad's brother-in-law introduced me to his Mother and his deaf-and-dumb sister. I was to meet numerous disabled members of this tribe during the day, products of generations of inbreeding. The welcome I received was overwhelming in its warmth and generosity. At once I was pulled into the family, made to feel at home and yet treated like a visiting dignitary. We were shown into a crudely built room, the bricks of the wall uneven and bare and the concrete floor covered by handmade bedouin rugs.

After a meal of bread, goat's cheese and herbs washed down with lashings of hot tea, we were taken out to join the main party.

'Where is Mr Shirazi?' I asked.

'There has been a bit of a tragedy,' Muhammad told me. 'The bride's little brother was knocked down by a car and Shirazi is at the hospital with his brother. The boy might lose his leg.'

I couldn't believe it; even here at this celebration tragedy and pain were following me. Was I some sort of bad omen? But I also felt anger when I learnt that this nine-year-old boy had been allowed to play next to the road unsupervised, even though both Muhammad and Shirazi had lost their own children in similar circumstances.

Sideless tents were dotted around a large clearing under which women in fluffy tunics and multi-layered bouncy skirts swapped gossip. Their heads were covered with flimsy veils of the brightest colours, two braids of hair falling down the side of their faces. Opposite them men crouched in the sun, smoking, and firing into the air to welcome new arrivals. Large trays of grapes were passed among the guests as a folk band played the instruments of the Middle East. Muhammad's Mother and three sisters finally arrived and he brought them straight over to me. His Mother hugged me and told me she loved me already, and the sisters made a great fuss of me, sending their numerous children to bring me tea and grapes and to find me shelter in a place of honour.

Finally Shirazi arrived with his family and another woman, Ahmad's Mother – many village Muslim women are referred to by the name of their eldest son. Ahmad's Mother was also Muhammad's first wife. I was relieved to find that she seemed cheerful and relaxed, and every bit as friendly towards me as the other women. Muhammad was a good six years my junior but this woman, who had been his eldest brother's wife, was at least ten years his senior. She was deeply sunburned, as were all these people, from a lifetime of being in the open. With her was Ahmad, the eldest son from her first marriage, and Mishu, Muhammad's natural son. Somewhere the other children played – probably next to the road.

Women and men took turns to perform folk dances, while Muhammad's Mother treated me like the guest of honour. Lunch was served to the family elders on the floor of the schoolhouse, and I was given the privilege of joining them. After lunch Muhammad's sisters and, as far as I could see, about twenty or so nieces dressed me up as a Qashqai woman and taught me to dance like one of them.

Ahmad's Mother, whose own name was Sepideh, followed me everywhere, introduced me to all of Muhammad's family and even insisting on washing the outdoor toilet before I use it. How on earth did they manage to go to the loo wearing all those skirts?

Towards dusk the bride was brought from a nearby village. Disappointingly she was dressed as a 'city bride' in the white frills you could find in bridal shops on any British high street. She was shown into a specially prepared room where handmade rugs served as wallpaper and all the windows had been covered to create a world apart. She would have to remain here for the next week while family and friends came to visit and pay their respects. Here her husband would take his fill of the fruits that had been forbidden him outside marriage.

As we waited to pay our respects and give our presents of gold jewellery, I started to talk to a woman called Touran, a tiny woman in her early thirties who was nursing newly born twins. She told me that she had once been a Revolutionary Guard and had spent two years in prison before the revolution.

'Sometimes I get very angry. I was a fighter in the revolution and again in the war. They taught me how to kill and made me expect to be part of the nation's leadership once victory was ours. But we are not needed any more, we women who gave up our femininity to liberate our people. Now they tell us to sit at home and be women. The Imam Khomeini comes to me in my dreams to tell me I have been part of a great struggle. My children shall go to heaven because of what I have done,' she told me, showing me the stump that replaced the foot she had lost in the war.

Both this woman and Muhammad's youngest sister explained that their place in heaven would depend on their husbands' approval of them.

'If I am a good wife and my husband approves of my actions, I will go to heaven. But if he is displeased and loathes the way I treat him my place will be in hell,' Touran said of the husband she had met at Shiraz University, where they had both studied chemistry.

Muhammad's eldest sister, Motaram, was the Mother of six children, all of whom milled around her in the dust of the wedding feast. 'How on earth do you manage?' I asked her.

'I have to manage, so I do,' she said, laughing.

'But why did you want so many children when things are so hard?' I enquired as I watched her collection of four daughters, aged fourteen, twelve, ten and eight, and her two sons, aged six and four.

'I was ready to stop after the fourth girl but my Mother-in-law said I would either have to try for sons or give my permission for my husband to take a second wife.'

'What if you refused?' I asked.

'Then he would be entitled to divorce me, I'd lose my children and then be disgraced,' she told me smiling. 'It's no problem. I am glad to make my husband happy.'

Her younger sister, Fatemeh, told the same story, except it had taken her five attempts before the first son, and her husband was not satisfied until she produced the third son.

Soraya, the youngest of Muhammad's twelve siblings, had been lucky: she had produced two sons at her first attempt. Unlike her sisters, she had learnt to read and write and had become a nurse. She now worked day and night to support her unemployed husband.

'It's not unusual,' Motaram confided. 'Many husbands in our tribes like to sit around and eat and talk to their friends while their women work.'

Muhammad then took me to meet his grandmother, who was also the groom's great-grandmother, and who sat guarding the bride's room. That night she would be the first of the crowd gathered outside the room to be handed the bloodied sheet that would prove that the girl was a virgin.

'Some women don't bleed even if they are virgins,' I told Muhammad.

'Rubbish! That is just lies put about by the whores in the West to hide what they are,' he told me.

Muhammad's grandmother was a truly horrifying sight. I felt most uncharitable as I recoiled from the sight of this crippled crone, dried into a crouching position. She moved by dragging her body along the floor using infirm claws that had once been the hands of a young bride.

If I married this man and then died, my children would be brought up here with this woman, in this dust. They would learn to sit on the floor and eat with their hands; they would be forced to marry a cousin and give birth to possibly physically or mentally impaired children. Pressure to show they were blessed by Allah would make them procreate like rabbits, and some idea that they could buy their kin a place in heaven would make them go to war. If I found I could not live with this man and eventually got the divorce he had already told me he would never give me, my children would be taken from me at seven, under Islamic law, and brought up by these nice but primitive people.

'If we get married and I die, promise that you will give our children to my family to bring up,' I asked Muhammad on the drive home that night.

'*When* we get married, you mean,' he replied.

'Do you promise?'

'Yes, of course I promise,' he promised.

*   *   *

Auntie Homa seemed worn and deeply tired on that visit. The youngest of my Mother's siblings, she looked old and weary. Although she still laughed and joked, the spirit seemed to have gone out of her.

Before leaving Tehran, Farah, to whom I was reluctantly talking again, had told me that Shirl, Homa's much-married daughter, had got married for the fourth time – to Bahar's poet. The family was rocked by the news and the gossips did their best to make Homa feel as if her daughter had betrayed all the norms of decency. Perhaps that was why she was so unhappy – not at her daughter's happiness but at the family's negative response to it.

Homa was also exhausted by ten years of looking after Maman Joon, who was due back in Shiraz any day. My grandmother had spent her whole life being looked after by servants and had developed exacting standards. As the society changed and fewer people were willing to be 'in service', especially after the revolution, the burden of doing things Maman Joon's way had fallen on Auntie Homa and Bahar.

In Damavand one of the many gardeners once told me: 'Your grandmother, God bless her, thinks it is a sin to let anyone rest. I am sure if one day she found nothing left for me to do she would throw my hat into the garden and tell me to go and fetch it rather than see me sit for a minute.'

With Bahar gone, Dada Jan reluctant to lift a finger and Mummy in Oxford, it was down to Homa to look after her Mother, just when she most needed rest herself. It was obvious that Homa was becoming increasingly dependent on a quick drink to ease the pain that was always there in her eyes. The Fat Man had again fallen foul of the authorities and his passport had been withdrawn, thus ending a lucrative business he had been running between Iran and the Arab states. His printing business was also in trouble, since the authorities had warned that his licence might not be renewed. The burden on Homa, alone in this city without her children and her family, must have been almost unbearable.

On my third evening in Shiraz, the day after the wedding, my aunt began to look like her old self as she prepared for a visit from an old friend and her husband. Everything had been going well until the guest started to ask the sort of personal questions that for some reason Iranians feel free to ask when others would never do so.

'Tell me, Homa dear, why are you still living in this part of town? It really isn't very respectable, is it? Not with all these refugees from the war being moved in next door,' the poisonous hag asked.

'It is convenient here,' the Fat Man put in quickly.

'How so?' the hag asked.

'Well, everyone knows us here and it is much safer for Homa when I go away on business,' he replied.

'Oh really, where do you go?'

'To Dubai mostly,' he said.

'But didn't you say you were on the exit-prohibited list?' the fishwife's grotesque husband asked.

'I go to Tehran a lot,' he mumbled.

'But you said earlier that you never went to Tehran,' the bat sneered.

'Oh, but he used to go quite a lot before the passport business. Now we are thinking about moving. We haven't found the right place yet,' Auntie added, while I raged inside, dying to emulate Winston Churchill and tell the hag that, whereas Auntie could move tomorrow, she herself would still be ugly. Why didn't Auntie fight back? Why didn't she tell her to mind her own business?

We stayed in Shiraz for ten days and for the first time I began to like this city, seeing it in a new light. I had hated the place, but now I loved the lunches in nomadic tents and dinners with mullahs. I was learning so much and it was all because of Muhammad. He was my guru and I sat like a pupil at his feet.

Soon I began to mistake the instrument of learning for the knowledge itself and I began to see him as all-seeing and all-knowing. He had devoted so much time to me, always wanting to do what would please me and making sure that I got the best view, the best food and the most comfortable seat. He agreed with every view I voiced, be it on women, religion, politics or the quality of Islamic television programmes. He argued that the obsession with sex could only be overcome with more freedom, and he saw no real reason why women should be veiled. He got me interviews with doctors critical of the regime; mullahs eager to allow a more lenient social order; Revolutionary Guards opposed to public flogging; and much, much more of a side to Iran I had never imagined existed.

When Muhammad arrived to take me away at the end of our visit I looked with new tolerance on the white socks, cheap trousers and torn, fake-leather jacket. All my reservations were pushed to the back of my mind as, for the next twelve hours, Muhammad told me how much he needed me.

We decided the first child would arrive the following year in order to give me a chance to have a couple before it got dangerous. He insisted that I should have them by Caesarean section, which he claimed would do me less harm. I later discovered that this way of giving birth was much favoured by Iranian men who believe that natural birth made the vagina too big to give them sexual pleasure later.

He told me that the most important thing in his life was to study and that he wanted to go to university in India to study for his master's degree. Nothing would prevent him studying, for it was his greatest love. 'I feel ill if I go through a day without reading something intellectual,' he told me, taking out some sort of textbook. He read one page before returning to our conversation.

Before long we were in the middle of a fantasy where he would come to Oxford, get his MA and go on to do a doctorate.

'Don't tell your family that I want to come to England. Let them think I am reluctant and you have persuaded me. It's better that way. I don't want anyone to think I married you just to go to England and have someone pay for my education,' he explained.

Just a minute now, what was all this about paying for his education? my secret voice piped up.

'Do you think I can get a job?' he asked.

'Of course you can, darling,' I said, much relieved.

'If I can make a couple of hundred pounds a month I will have enough to send to my wife and the children,' he added.

'What wife!?'

'I can't just abandon them because I have a new wife,' he said, and I accepted it as enough explanation. Of course he had meant his ex-wife, and what sort of man would he be if he was willing to abandon his children? 'She asked if we were getting married,' he said.

'She asked me if I was thinking of getting married. She didn't mention you, but she smiled conspiratorially and looked towards you as we talked,' I told him.

'Sepideh says if we marry and stay here we must have the children,' he said casually.

'What!? She wouldn't give up her children, surely?'

'It makes no difference. We are going to England,' he said, turning back to his book.

Ten minutes later he was back on the subject of his degree. 'I don't think I can study and work. It's better I go to India where I can afford to study and send money for the children.'

'But everybody works and studies. It is normal in America and England,' I told him.

'Oh yes! For people who just want to get a degree with which to make money. But if you want to study like me, to really learn and to grow, you cannot spend time at work. You have to be in front of a book every hour of the day,' he claimed.

Stupid, stupid, stupid. I should have moved my seat there and then and once we reached Tehran I should have walked away and never looked back. But the pathetic creature I had turned into argued that I would not have been the first wife to pay for my husband to go to college. I had been rich all my life, surely I owed it to this man, whom

I loved, to give him the advantages that I had taken for granted.

'I'll have to come back at least twice a year to see the children,' he told me.

'Of course, darling.'

This established, our imagination took flight and landed in a log cabin in Alaska where he would write his thesis and I would write my books. We chose names for our two sons and our daughter. Well, he chose the sons' names – Aristotle and Socrates. Never mind; I had plenty of time to win him over to Pierre, Nikolai and Natasha. I was still living out my *War and Peace* fantasy.

'I'd like you to do something for me. You don't have to, but it will make me feel very happy,' he asked slyly.

'Anything.'

'When men come to your flat – men who are there on business or an unmarried man – could you please wear your *hejab*?'

'I've never ever had to cover myself to keep a man away,' I said, finally indignant.

'You are as pure as milk, my sweet. But men in Iran live by other rules; they think that if a woman appears before them with her hair showing she is giving them a signal that she is available. I don't want any man to think he can have my wife,' Muhammad said.

Change seats! Go now, before it is too late! the voice screamed.

My ovaries replied: *it may already be too late; don't lose this last chance.* They were sending crippling twinges into the centre of my being again.

After some discussion he exploded, saying that at least no other man had seen a strand of his first wife's hair, she had given him that great gift, but I was too proud, too decadent and too spoilt to give anything for someone else.

Run! Run now while you still can.

I crumbled and agreed to remain covered in front of the video-hire-man, convinced by the argument that his nocturnal visits might give him ideas. I had started out on a slippery slope, for once I accepted the idea that it was proper to cover myself in some circumstances I laid myself open for extensions to the edict.

We were a couple of hours away from Tehran when our coach stopped for petrol. Muhammad got out to have a cigarette – on the filling-station forecourt! Was he mad?

As I watched him crouch in the half-light of dawn, smoking a cigarette in his crumpled clothes, I tried to shake off the sudden revulsion. I couldn't stand another false start; I didn't want to run away from another relationship. Most of all I didn't want my Iranian friends to suddenly stop talking when I walked into the room because they were discussing the dangers of having babies after thirty. I did not want Iranian women who had known me since childhood to look at me with pity every time they talked about someone getting married or having a baby.

We finally arrived back at my home only to find that the entire complex had been turned into a military barracks. There were soldiers everywhere, and armoured vehicles blocked the steep road up to the half-finished multi-storey garage through which we had decided to go to gain access. Muhammad took one look at the hardware, and decided that the taxi, which I had paid an arm and a leg for, should drop him off first and then return to deliver me.

Muhammad told the driver to stop at the top of his road – not so much a road as a dust-track in the middle of nowhere where someone had put up a line of brick buildings. He didn't even kiss me goodbye – well, this was the Islamic Republic – before he dashed out of the car and up the track, the mud spraying up to stain his beige trousers as he walked. I made the taxi pull out of sight but not far enough away that I could not see the love of my life for a few more minutes. Instead of entering the block of flats he had pointed out as his home, he went on further down the road to another, almost identical block.

He probably just got the wrong house in the half-light, and after all he was very tired, I told myself.

*   *   *

The German businessman who had built the complex in which I lived had been arrested the night before my return from Shiraz. Now the army, the Revolutionary Guards and the Islamic Court, with a little help from the Foundation for the Oppressed and Life-Sacrificers, had taken over management of the complex. Officials and officers from these organs of 'freedom' were busy trying to assess which homes they could confiscate for the state. With its customary expertise the Foundation found more than twenty flats owned by people not living in God's Republic. The tenants of these flats were duly asked to move out and the flats 'handed over to the oppressed' – mainly oppressed judges, magistrates and army officers.

I saw Muhammad again the next morning at Interference. A tall woman in the dreaded black *chador* was busy flirting outrageously with him in full view of the entire department. This, in a climate of fear and distrust, was quite something. I stood in the corridor out of sight and wondered how she dare make such a display in front of everyone. Muhammad had been too engrossed in the woman to notice me; he was calling her 'Mishmooshy' and she was laughing.

'I'd better go and write my story on temporary marriage,' she said with a wink and a giggle before leaving the room.

I was furious and yet crushed. He must be having an affair with her, I thought, as I walked into the room and greeted my Interference pals but ignored the man I was considering making the Father of my children. He smiled at me, and I scowled back and went to sit beside Matt, who started to whisper in my ear about an interview he could set up for me as long as I promised not to let my fellow journalists know that he had arranged it. Muhammad looked furious and I imagined that my slight had hit home.

That evening he risked the blockade and turned up for dinner in a filthy mood. No matter what I did he would not talk to me, but just sat and watched a video in silence.

'What's wrong?' I asked, forgetting my own fury over the woman.

'Nothing,' he growled.

'Just lost your voice, eh?' I quipped.

It was a quip too far and Muhammad leapt to his feet, his eyes shining with anger. 'No, I am just ashamed to know such a woman,' he hissed.

'What?!!'

'You cheapened yourself today, letting that nobody treat you as his whore,' he said.

'What nobody?' I said, genuinely puzzled.

'That son of a dog who you let whisper into your ear like some tart,' he said. 'The whole office is talking about it and how cheap you are.'

'It was work. What on earth are you talking about?' I shouted.

'So you work with your cunt, do you?'

I was stunned. Where had all this come from? What on earth had I done that was so bad?

'Nobody calls me a tart, especially not you!' I roared. 'I don't understand what you are so angry about.' What I should have done was open the door and tell him to leave and not to come back. But instead I tried to defend myself, to prove that I wasn't a whore.

'In this country a decent woman does not let a man whisper into her ear. If you want to be my wife you will have to learn to behave as a Muslim,' he told me. 'Everyone is talking about you. I am telling you this for your own good. People are commenting on your *hejab*, saying you show too much hair and that you smile and laugh too much with the men.'

'I smile and laugh with everyone. I am a very friendly person; that's my character,' I said, defending myself.

'If you go on like this they will take your card and even put you in the cell left empty by Roger Cooper. You are giving my enemies ammunition to attack me. Being with you is dangerous for me. At any time they might arrest us for spying,' he argued, changing direction.

'I'm damned if I am going to change to please a load of bigots who cannot raise their minds above the waist,' I told him as I stormed into the kitchen, now no longer angry at him but at a mythical 'them'.

Muhammad followed me a couple of minutes later. 'These soldiers make it very risky for me to visit you here. I think we will have to stop seeing each other for a while.'

A chasm of loneliness opened up in front of me.

'I don't see why. We are working together. What can they say?'

'They can say we are spies. They can put me in prison for years and they can make you disappear. Not that I care. I'd like to go to one of their prisons and spend all day just reading. It would enhance my reputation, so I have no fear. But for you it would be different,' he said.

'I'm not of the torturable classes,' I said, remembering a passage from my favourite Graham Greene.

'Your class makes me sick. You think you are above real life. But didn't you learn from the revolution?' he snapped at me.

It was no good trying to explain that it was just something someone said in a book about spying. I was angry and yet I didn't want to be alone so I set about making his dinner.

Before I had even cleared the plates he had his coat on and was going out of the door. As he was leaving he said: 'My wife and children are in Tehran for a few weeks. I won't be back until they go,' he said closing the door behind him.

I wanted to die. I wanted to beat him about the head. I wanted to know why his ex-wife and children had suddenly turned up.

Two agonising days later he was back to explain. He said his ex-wife wanted a reconciliation. She had told him that she had lost one child and it was up to him to give her another one. 'Sepideh made me marry her the first time, and I am afraid she will do it again. He followed this with an ultimatum: I had two weeks to decide if I would marry him or not.

*   *   *

I tried to put my troubles behind me by immersing myself in my work. Most days I spent more than eighteen hours running around interviewing people, writing stories or attending meetings in mosques and back rooms.

Much of my time was taken up with the various women's groups and their attempts to gain some sort of rights as individuals rather than just as bits of flesh that had to be covered until it was time to have sex with them. But I was soon to find out that there was a section of the Iranian female community who welcomed the imposition of the veil for reasons wholly unconnected to theology or politics. These were the criminals who found that stealing was considerably easier when carried out under the *chador*. The government had put women under the veil, and only afterwards realised that it had provided ideal cover for those who wished to break the law. Much can be hidden under those black, flowing sheets that the devout pull over their heads in public. So security had to be increased at all department stores to ensure that women didn't walk out with the goods.

I was blissfully unaware of the measures imposed to prevent shoplifting as I walked into the government-run Ghods department store. I was not in the best of humour because of the padding I was wearing to stem the monthly flow and the constraints of my back-brace, which made me look like a pregnant walrus. With so many fetters I had dispensed with my bra, leaving little but brace and pants under my coat.

It had been a bad day. The press corps had been kept waiting for more than three hours for Ayatollah Hakim, a sort of Iraqi Khomeini who was exiled in Iran, to give a press conference. We had finally given up and walked out in protest, and all I really wanted to do was to go home, but custom ordered that I pay a visit to welcome home a cousin recently returned from the States. Custom also lays down that one goes bearing cake, and the store was the only place on my route that might have something I could take as an offering.

'Take your bags to the desk,' an old crow ordered as I walked into the store.

'Sorry?'

'Take those bags to the desk. No bags allowed,' she barked.

I reluctantly deposited my briefcase – brimming over with confidential documents photocopied for me by Muhammad – at the desk just inside the main doors.

The shelves were laden with goods, and rich and poor alike queued to purchase cut-price luxuries and affordable essentials. An hour later I had paid for a box of *nan nokhochi* – sweet chick-pea bread – and tried to leave from whence I entered.

'You go out from the back door. Your case will be waiting for you there,' the keeper of the gate explained.

Some twenty women were waiting ahead of me to enter the small room created by curtains at what had once been the fire exit. Once I got into that room I was told to produce my receipt. I delved into my coat pocket and finally found the piece of paper among the tissues and crumpled banknotes. Then another woman told me to come forward, and she started to give me a cursory body search. Feeling the brace and the padding, she instructed me to take off my coat.

'I'm not wearing anything under this,' I confided.

'Take it off,' the vixen shouted, and she undid my buttons, helped me take off my coat and started feeling between my legs as I stood there trying to cover my bare breasts. My fury knew no bounds and I gave the woman a good piece of my mind, using some choice words to express my contempt for her and her leaders. I then hurled my purchase into the bin before re-dressing and storming out.

Halfway down the road I realised that I would have to arrive at my cousin's home empty-handed. I swallowed my pride and returned to the store to retrieve my sweets.

'What sweets?' the woman said as I delved into the bin now oddly missing a box of *nan nokhochi*.

It was just too much, being constantly mauled. Every press

conference I attended, every ministry I entered, every time I went to the airport or to a bus station I had to submit my body to the searching hands of some woman. You came to dread being summoned by the Majlis where they separate you from the smallest bit of property that makes you feel like an individual. No pens, watches, rings, chains, even loose change can pass through those portals. I have lost count of how many times I have had hands probe between my legs for hidden Kalashnikovs and squeeze my breasts to ensure that they were flesh and not Semtex.

We had long been taught that what Iranians did to Iranians was no one's business but that of Iranians. However, despite all the slogans wishing death on all and sundry, we remain a nation anxious to entertain our guests in style and with honour. It is shameful to a host to have any mishap befall a guest – unless they happen to be spies for the Big and Little Satans of course.

The young Czech-Canadian journalist who came to Tehran at the invitation of the Islamic Republic to cover yet another anniversary was no spy but an honoured guest, and she should have been accorded all the respect and hospitality the country could give.

It was with great dignity and in relative comfort that she was escorted to the Imam's shrine for the main ceremony of the visit. The woman who handed back her shoes at the exit to the shrine did so with courtesy and reverence. The women who gathered round her as she placed her head on her bag – which she had placed on a table before which she knelt as she put her shoes back on – were also considerate and polite. The woman who brushed against her, throwing her back on the ground, did so with civility and deference; her friend, who grabbed the woman's bag and tucked it under her *chador*, also showed great decorum as she vanished into the sea of black.

The young man at the Azadi (Freedom) Grand Hotel was a picture of manners as he informed her that she would have to pay 200 dollars before he could give her a replacement key so that she could open the safe and remove the dollars she had deposited inside.

Sleepy was attentive and cordial as he told her that there was nothing Interference could do. He was gracious and obliging when he assured her the head of the Pasdars corps had taken personal control of the search for her handbag.

Two weeks later the *Keyhan* newspaper told us that yet another gang of female thieves operating in the capital's shrines had been discovered and the women sent to Evin.

Devout Muslim women took to the veil gladly as a sign of their piety and to ensure that only their husbands had the great pleasure of viewing their body. But for women like Nahid and her ever-growing band of happy hookers it had another advantage: they could ply their new trade on the streets of their own neighbourhood without fear of being spotted by a passing neighbour or relative.

One night long after I left their little world, Goli phoned to tell me that Nahid had exceeded herself. She had been standing on the side of the road when a car that seemed familiar had flashed its lights at her – the sign that the driver was in the market for a little love and companionship. It was not until she was pressing the handle of the car and preparing to get in that she realised that the man was the husband of her closest non-professional friend. There had been a few moments of extreme embarrassment as the two came face to face and recognised each other. Never one to let an opportunity go by, Nahid persuaded the man that they should carry on regardless. But as she told Goli she had laughed and praised the *chador* as the greatest aid to her profession since the invention of the condom. I presumed that as she was still in business the man she had moved out to live with must be her pimp rather than her boyfriend.

*   *   *

A week after the row Muhammad phoned late in the afternoon to say he would be coming round that evening for dinner. I was so delighted and excited that it was almost pathetic. A hairdresser living in my building came round to do my hair and I washed and groomed myself as if preparing to attend one of those balls at the royal court rather than dinner with Muhammad. I changed outfits at least six times before deciding on chic but casual.

When the doorbell went that evening I didn't stop to look through the peephole in the door before flinging it open with a welcoming smile on my lips. Muhammad stood before me with his head bowed, and behind him stood a bearded giant clad in what the smart Islamic Guard commander was wearing that year. Before I knew what was going on Muhammad shoved me backwards into the kitchen as the man made his way into my flat, his grim face flashing past me as Muhammad started to explain that we were in real trouble and would probably spend that evening in jail.

It couldn't be happening. We had talked about the possibility of being picked up for spying several times, but I never really believed that things like that happened – not to me anyway. But it was happening; we were caught and about to be carted away to God knows what fate.

'Make some tea,' Muhammad instructed. 'Then you will have to answer his questions.'

As I made tea in my tiny kitchen, Muhammad explained that Mr Javan, for that was his name, was from the investigations unit of the Ministry of Intelligence. 'He came to my office this morning. He has been questioning me all day; now he wants to talk to you. Just tell him the truth. I will be leaving with him for further questioning.'

'But you haven't done anything. We want to get married,' I said, still unable to absorb the fact that this was happening to us.

'*Wanting to* means nothing to these people. He thinks we are spying and, if you cannot persuade him that we are not, we may be spending the next few years apart. He is already certain that we are spying,' Muhammad said.

'What should we do? What shall I say? I'll phone the paper and get them to protest,' I said – now getting more than slightly scared. A mixture of panic and disbelief gripped me as my thoughts raced. There must be something I could do, some way I could make this all right again.

'It's no good. I will go to prison, probably today. They may just ask you to leave,' he said.

Selfishly my first thoughts were that I was going to be alone again and also out of work. My little voice was saying: *This is bloody typical, I finally find someone fool enough to marry me and he gets put away for life.* But the pounding in my heart showed that I was truly frightened.

How could things keep going so wrong? I was angry and I was scared. My knees were jelly and my stomach was overwrought. I wanted to throw up as I carried out a tray of tea and cakes for my unwanted guest.

He stood looking out of the window over Tehran, this man who had my future in his hands. If I didn't do some fast talking I would disappear that night. Before I could open my mouth he turned to face me; his grim expression and obvious membership of the inner circles of Hezbullah turned my fear to terror. I was staring at a fate I had feared since childhood, a fate I had seen in the thousands of war and spy movies that I so relished and consumed with hunger as a child – loss of my lover, torture in prison and perhaps even execution.

I opened my mouth but no words came out.

Then I heard Muhammad giggling behind me. Obviously the fear had driven him mad. I would have to be strong for both of us and get us out of this somehow.

'Mr Javan, you may not realise it but you are about to arrest us and take us away to prison,' Muhammad said, laughing.

Javan grinned.

'It's a joke, my darling,' Muhammad said as I reeled round, spilling the tea I was still carrying, to see him collapsed in mirth.

'A joke – what do you mean a joke?' I stormed.

He just grinned.

'You utter, utter bastard,' I said, resorting to English as the truth penetrated the wall of horror that he had set up.

'Oh, poor little darling, were you scared?' Muhammad said. 'You shouldn't be such a coward.'

'I wasn't afraid, I just wanted to find a way of solving our problem,' I spluttered, again going on the defensive when I had every right to be on the offensive.

Muhammad had found all the right buttons to press to get me into line. I had told him that I feared nothing so much as being afraid, and now he was using it to deflect my anger at his cruel joke. I was on alien ground and it was all too easy to pull the rug from under my feet. For a foreigner I was very streetwise but I was no match for a man trained to persuade battle-weary soldiers that they should go to their deaths with joy.

Mr Javan turned out to be another cousin whom Muhammad had arranged to be transferred from Shiraz, where he was indeed a commander in the Islamic Guards, to a research job in Tehran. I was beginning to question Muhammad's numerous links to people in the intelligence world, but it was too horrific to imagine that he was in any way involved himself. The suspicion never really left me, however, rearing its ugly head again whenever his actions didn't add up and his words were flawed. But I kept pushing it away, telling myself that to think such thoughts was a disloyalty worse than adultery, a crime worse than theft. Muhammad had spent hours telling me how he was opposed to what he called the 'oppression' of this regime and was working from within to 'restore democracy'. And I didn't want to be wrong again; I didn't want Farah spreading gossip about another of my male friends.

I was still smarting from the 'joke' the next day when I finally got a call from the lawyer I had first seen almost a year earlier. He said the Foundation for the Oppressed were willing to consider giving me a place to live and that I should present myself at the offices of the 'exceptional grants' section the following Saturday. Thirteen years after the revolution I had officially moved from being a tyrant to being one of the oppressed.

This particular outpost of the Oppressed was housed within the brand-new headquarters of the Revolutionary Guards outside which I duly presented myself on the appointed day.

'You can't come in here without a *chador*,' the guards said barring my entry to the compound.

The next day I got as far as the women's search hut. 'You are not allowed in with white shoes. Everything must be black.'

The third day the woman lifted up my *chador*. 'Coloured socks are not allowed,' she snarled.

'Look, I have been here three days running, and every time I have been sent away. I am wearing trousers and a *chador* and my socks are thick sports socks so no one can see through them. Tell me where the Koran says colour is not allowed,' I ranted, having learned by now that anger was the best form of attack.

'It is not my fault, sister,' she replied, rather more meekly. 'The men inside say don't let them in like this, so we obey. There are some spare stockings you can wear.'

On the wall was a box full of sheer, black pop-socks. They had obviously been used by months' worth of summer visitors and were stiff with the residue of hundreds of sweating feet.

'Don't let them see that colour on your toenails,' the woman said almost kindly as I pulled the nylon over bright red nails. Nails cannot be painted in Islam.

Once inside I was dismissed within minutes with some fatherly advice from my case officer to wait three more weeks. He said that the Majlis was about to pass a law that would result in my gaining more compensation. He promised to phone me when the time was right and I left confident that I was on the road to vast wealth.

A month later I was still waiting and so fed up that I told Muhammad about the many frustrations on the road to winning back my fortune. As luck would have it he knew a man who knew a lawyer who specialised in getting back people's property from the Oppressed. Two days later a toothless, mature student called Said was taking me to see these lawyers. Muhammad explained that Said would get a commission from the lawyers for introducing me, but as he was a very good friend of both sides he could negotiate an excellent deal for me. Said knocked down the lawyers from a cut of 30 per cent to 22 per cent of any monies or property recovered.

Finally it looked as though things were moving for the better. I had a prospective husband, I was writing for some of the world's best newspapers and magazines and I was doing something positive to get my property back.

That week a friend returned to Iran from England where he had first gone twenty years earlier to seek treatment for his haemophilia. He was coming back with an English wife, and more than 60,000 dollars in compensation, and AIDS. Several days later he slipped into that good night.

A few days after the death I was summoned to cover a conference to mark World AIDS Day where Iran's then Minister of Health told the assembled doctors from the Muslim world that all the 240 AIDS cases in Iran were due to men travelling to the West and other countries where moral decay had seen the spread of the condition. He told the world that there was no AIDS from homosexual sex in Iran, since there were no such 'deviants' in the country.

The minister should have paid a visit on any Monday afternoon to the Revolution Public Baths (not its real name) in North Tehran. On the outside wall of this crumbling edifice pictures of young cherubs beam out at passers-by from their martyrs' Olympus while inside their outcast brothers take furtive comfort from the love that dare not speak its name. I came upon this shelter for the homosexual community through a whim to relive a tradition long ago made superfluous by the advent of the in-house bathroom. There had been a day when those who did not have their own bath-house went out to wash, be washed and to socialise. The poor would wash in a mass bath, while those who could afford it would be shown into their own cubicle, where a minion would scrub them till their skins were squeaky clean. These bath-houses used to be grand structures, all marble and gold-leaf. But time and progress had taken their toll and the few surviving bath-houses tended to be dilapidated and grubby.

As my cousin Shahnaz and I waited to be shown into our cubicles, a young man with a dreadful limp arrived, paid his ten tomans and was shown into a cubicle. Ten minutes later he was joined by an older man. Then they arrived in groups, mostly young men with older partners, and two by two they went to do whatever it was they did hidden away from the eyes of the revolution.

A week later I went back and there they were again, the same boys and men, but this time a few young couples were walking hand-in-hand in open defiance. It was one of these couples that I came to know. Both were married and had children, and both wanted to flee to somewhere they could be free to be gay. Hamid asked if it was true that homosexuals could get married in England. He was very disappointed that it was not true and wanted to know where he could go to be able to marry and live openly with his lover.

'If I have to live this life with a wife and this hidden love for ever, then I would gladly die instead,' he told me, while his lover held his hand, nodding vigorously.

According to these men, homosexuality is still punished by death in the Islamic Republic; I could never get an official confirmation of this – their response always being that there is no such problem in Iran so no need to punish it. 'Muslim men are not homosexual,' the Health Minister had insisted.

'I used to work in the mayor's office, but someone told them that I was an opium addict and I was thrown out. I do a few "dirty acts" to make money for my children and for my drugs,' Hamid's friend cried. 'I should die for making love to a man, but there are books by Ayatollahs that tell Muslims what to do if they have sex with a camel,' he said, laughing at the image he had drawn. 'Tell me how that can be right, to have an animal if you are in the desert but not to love a human?'

These men were already in hell and they had no way out.

13

Till Death Us Do Part

Muhammad's spoof with the spurious intelligence man had shaken me more than I cared to admit. I had to make up my mind one way or another and do so quickly before the hoax became a reality.

There had been many wonderful men before this one, men who made a difference to the worlds in which they lived, men who had loved me more than I deserved and men who any woman would have given her right arm to marry. But not me, I had always found some excuse to run away – his eyes were too green; his politics were too conservative; his hair was too greasy.

Muhammad was not the sort the man who would fit into my strict but progressive family easily. The surer he became of me the more demanding and unreasonable he grew. All the things I took for granted were new and strange to him and he obviously resented everything people like us had achieved. All that apart, I could not see my family jumping for joy that I had decided on a man whom I had to support, let alone finding out that I had to support his stepsons, his ex-wife and their sons.

If only I could be sure that I wanted this man. There had been a time up on that mountain and on the drive to Shiraz when I was head over heels in love. The feeling had dimmed; now I just didn't want to be out of love. But I found myself biting my tongue every time Muhammad spoke, for fear of saying something that would make him feel small or stupid.

Was I doubtful because of the poverty I saw among his people? Not me, not this socialist, a card-carrying member of the Labour

Party. So I pushed all my reservations to the back of my troubled conscience. I allowed my fear of discriminating on the grounds of class and wealth to cloud my real doubts about his cultural attitudes; I was about to say yes to cruelty and oppression because I didn't want to be a snob. But above all I wanted to reproduce before it was too late. It had been more than ten years since my last 'serious' relationship, and certainly since the last time anyone had proposed marriage. There had been other boyfriends in the meantime, but I had only managed to fall in love once, and he was already taken. And, most of all, I didn't want to be alone in Iran.

These were all the wrong reasons for saying yes, so I went into this marriage with my eyes shut.

Muhammad was so overjoyed at my acceptance that he disappeared for a week leaving me to conclude that this was another false start in my troubled path to married bliss. I was forbidden to call him at Interference for fear that 'they' might get suspicious. So I was left to brood and to worry for seven days (which I managed to fill with work) and seven agonising nights. If only I had taken this last chance to run, but I had already told my neighbours and, even worse, I had told Farah, who had shared the news with the entire civilised world. So instead of running I stood at my window every day at five, the time he usually arrived after work, and watched the junction below where the Jordan and Modarres Expressways met. My heart leapt at the sight of any red car that could possibly be his, and fell again as it passed without turning up the steep road to my home.

He finally phoned me from Shiraz, where he said he had gone on 'urgent business' to do with his factory. This was the first I had heard about any factory, but apparently he owned a quarter-share in a yet-to-be-built factory to produce pectin.

'Where were you all this time?'

'I was here, of course,' he snapped.

'You could have let me know where you were going – I've been so worried,' I told my love.

'You're just like all the other women,' came the furious voice on the other end of the line. 'I thought you were different, but you are just the same. You know I need my freedom, I don't want some nag telling me what to do all the time. If I wanted that I would have stayed with Sepideh.'

'All I ask is that you have the decency to tell me what you are doing and when I can expect you at my home,' I said in a fury. Big, big mistake. Now I was in the wrong, I had thrown the fact that it was my home in his face, and he had reason to be hurt and to make me feel guilty.

'That's right, that's the best I can expect from you. But, my dear, you are going to be an Iranian wife soon and will have to learn that it is *my* word and *my* command that count. Here I am trying to create something that will allow me to keep you in the spoilt way you are used to, and instead of helping me you are nagging and wanting more. You are so selfish, you always want more, and all you think of is Me, Me, Me,' my hero ranted.

I felt guilty; but not that guilty, and I put the phone down on the maniac. But as soon as I did, I regretted it. I didn't want to be alone. I wanted my husband-to-be no matter how mad he was. I didn't want to fail in a relationship again, not even this most unsuitable of all matches.

Two hours later he phoned again just as if nothing had ever happened. The whole project was in danger of collapse for want of about £500, my knight told me. 'I can't come back until I have sorted it out,' he moaned as I racked my brains to think how to get the money. I was already paying off a very large loan and was selling my personal possessions to meet lawyers' bills.

Two days later he was back to try and raise the money from friends at work. I still made no offer to cover the debt, merely listening to his worries with a look of sympathy. I knew that if I got my money from the Foundation for the Oppressed I could buy into the project, but I was still not stupid enough to offer.

'It is my only chance to ever be able to support you, and I may lose it because of a temporary shortage of money,' he told me.

I had this uneasy feeling he was waiting for me to offer to bail him out. He was suddenly very eager to tie the knot, again playing the spying card and saying that he could no longer control his passions. Could it have been a coincidence that my new lawyers had recently hinted that settlement was in sight?

Although I was coming up to my thirty-sixth birthday I still needed my Father's permission to get married. But Muhammad had a way of getting round everything. This time it was a tame mullah willing to perform a *seegheh* marriage for us. I had been brought up to consider a *seegheh* as little more than a mistress or tart. Nice girls from good families did not consent to temporary marriages. But it did have its advantages; well, the way Muhammad explained it, there were advantages. To start with it was 'temporary' and would run out at the end of an agreed period, so I had a chance of getting out if it was a disaster. He told me that even if the marriage was set for several years either partner could end it at any time without having to go through a divorce. It also meant that I could get to know Muhammad better without risking arrest as a spy or a whore.

It was perfect.

We met our little mullah outside a mosque in Tehran Pars, a predominantly lower-middle-class enclave. All my prejudices were at work that night as an unusually cheerful Muhammad took me to my new fate. The mullah was of the grubby variety; not for him the silk and cashmere favoured by his more prosperous and powerful brothers in Allah. He must have been at least five foot five, but he was so thin and frail I felt I could have lifted him with one hand – that is if I had wanted to get that close to the soiled cloak he wore over his scrawny shoulders. I liked him instantly and my affection grew as he got into an object that in a former life had been a VW Beetle. The sole remaining patch of paint showed that it had once been a merry and bright yellow. We followed this jalopy as it wound its way into the wretched gut of the suburb.

Our mullah stopped outside a house that was disintegrating before our eyes. 'Do you think it will survive long enough for us to be married?' I whispered to my groom. We were led up a rickety flight of wooden stairs that twisted round the skeleton of the house. Then we were shown into a room on the third floor, divided into a kitchen and bedroom/sitting-room by a wall of sheets.

As we entered the mullah's home five little urchins popped up from behind books strewn over the floor, then scurried behind the barrier. They were obviously doing their homework on the bare floor. A woman's voice asked if she could bring tea, and a minute later a shy teenage girl wrapped in a bright flowered *chador* brought two small glasses of tea and a cupful of coloured sugar-cubes. She withdrew, and her Father started to write the document that would make an honest woman of me.

'How long shall I make the marriage for?' the mullah asked.

'Fifty years,' Muhammad said, frowning at me when I tried to protest. 'It looks better, but we can end it any time you want,' he told me.

So when the mullah asked if I would give him power of attorney to marry me to Muhammad for fifty years I said, 'Yes.' Though I wondered why he hadn't asked Muhammad for permission. How come I was the only one who needed someone else to do the business for me?

'If it had been for any less time Intelligence would never believe it,' Muhammad said as we drove home.

It was the happiest drive of my life; I was married at long last.

Now I don't believe in telling tales out of bed, but it was my big night, the one all girls dream of. But nowhere in those dreams had I ever imagined I would be confronted by a plucked chicken on this night of nights.

Muslim men, my new love assured me, all shave their pubic hair – it's cleaner that way. It is not a pretty sight, especially when the prickly little bastards are making their way to freedom.

'Where else do you shave?' I said, affectionately mocking this practice.

'Under my arms.' He grinned back like a child who had done something clever.

The next day Muhammad got up bright and early to go to work. I prepared an 'omelette' – scrambled eggs to you and me. There was no 'please' or even a 'thank you'.

As I kissed him goodbye when he left for work, my new groom said: 'I can't come tonight. My wife and children are still here.'

I was devastated when he explained that he had not told all their relatives that they had divorced 'as a kindness to her'. Her cousin was in Tehran, so Muhammad had to put up a pretence of their being a couple. 'I'll persuade her to let me tell them soon, I promise,' he said as he left me waving down from my balcony – crying.

Stupid, stupid, stupid. I had just ignored the fact that she had come to town, I had almost forgotten her request to get back together with her – sorry, my – husband.

Could they still be married?

No, it was too horrible even to consider. Nothing that bad could happen to me, could it?

By that afternoon I had pulled myself together and had a plan. I was going to put an end to this marriage no matter how stupid I looked in front of everyone. So I borrowed a black *chador* from Bibi, my new neighbour, called a taxi and went to the local mosque to discover exactly what I had to do to get out of this mess.

It was not good news that awaited me at my friendly neighbourhood mosque. It was true that a temporary marriage could be cancelled, the fatherly mullah told me, but only by the man. The woman had to see out the full term.

Could he stop me from travelling?

The mullah didn't think so but he wasn't sure.

This could not be happening to me. How could God let me get into this situation? Of course it had nothing to do with God, it had been my hormones and my stupidity that had landed me in this ordeal. I walked straight past the waiting taxi as I left the mosque in a daze. I couldn't understand why this man – the taxi driver – was following me asking for money. I finally gave him what he wanted to get rid of him; I had to think, but my mind could only achieve blankness.

Go straight to the airport and get on a plane out of here, my inner voice said.

But I haven't got my exit visa, and there isn't a flight to England for three days, my weaker self argued back.

You've got money in the flat. Three months' rent will buy a quick exit visa and a flight to anywhere. Just get out!

What about my work and my things and my lovely flat? If he can't stop me now he won't be able to stop me in a few months' time. I'll leave in my own good time.

It was dark by the time I found myself climbing the stairs back to my flat. The Foundation for the Oppressed had sacked all those who had worked for the German businessman, but before they had left they had sabotaged the lifts, the water supply and the electricity. Nineteen flights of stairs later all I wanted was a bath, but we were not to have water for more than an hour a day for the next fortnight. Anyway it also appeared that my block had no electricity source of its own and had therefore been illegally wired up to neighbouring blocks, thus doubling our neighbours' bills. As more and more tenants moved in, the overload had got too much and the fuse had blown.

'We should have the electricity fixed in a couple of hours. But please don't use more than one bulb from now on until we get a new source,' the management committee chairperson told me.

'I'm not paying seven times the average monthly wage for this flat just to have to live like a pauper with one light and no water,' I screamed.

That night I argued myself round to believing that Muhammad's behaviour was not all that bad; in fact he was really kind to agree to protect his wife from disgrace. The poor woman had lost her husbands and her child. How could I be so selfish?

I was beginning to feel better when the phone rang. It was my family in Oxford. I couldn't tell my Mother what I had done, so I broke the news to Mahshid. I remember little of our conversation other than that Mahshid wasn't exactly ecstatic at the news of my being a *seegheh*, and that as Mother realised what had happened she felt faint. Mahshid hung up in order to attend to a distraught Mother. I cried for a couple of hours, then went to bed with a couple of sleeping pills.

Married and still sleeping alone.

The doorbell woke me twenty-four hours later as my newly acquired husband returned to the marital home. I looked an utter mess in the knee-length leggings and T-shirt I had been wearing when I fell asleep, and frog-eyed from too much crying and sleeping pills. This was what I had looked forward to since I was sixteen, so why was I so miserable?

As I fried liver for his dinner, he came and started to cuddle me, and told me he loved me and that he just couldn't bring himself to move in when I was paying the rent. 'It hurts my pride,' he told me.

I was so very, very happy.

That night we stayed up till dawn talking about our past and our hopes for the future. Muhammad said that he did not care what I might have done in the past as long as I told him everything there and then.

'If I find out later that there is something you haven't told me it will kill my love for you. Tell me everything and we will forget it and start again as if it hadn't happened.'

So I told him about the boyfriends and the engagements, the gropes in the dark and the doomed relationships.

Muhammad told me of an affair he had with a woman at university while he was still married to his other wife. He had not told the girl that he was married. 'It was not important,' he remarked. 'I will never hurt or betray anyone if they are fair to me, but if they betray me I will never forgive it,' he then said. 'Sepideh betrayed me by getting pregnant.'

Shortly before we had met, Muhammad had become close to the wife of a minor minister who had taken a younger, second wife. Muhammad said he had wanted to see if a blow like that would make a devout Muslim wife betray her principles and take a lover. She had taken him to her home on the night the husband was with the second wife. They had kissed and he had stroked her breasts. She had wanted more, had begged for more. But Muhammad had lost his nerve as she started to undress and had left, having proved to himself that any woman, however pious, could be had.

The story had excited my dear husband and he started to make overtures towards me. This was far too grubby for a wimp like the one I had turned into and my nervous stomach came to my rescue, churning up those acids until I had to rush to the loo. By the time I had stopped throwing up my loving husband was snoring his head off, his mouth open to reveal those blackened gums.

I would rather have died than have anyone discover that I was just a temporary wife, a concubine, a second-class woman who couldn't get a real husband so had to settle for what she could get. Which was how I began to see myself. I would wake up most mornings alone and in a panic. 'I'm not a real wife. Everyone will find out. I'll never have a proper husband. I'm not a real wife, I'm not a real wife.' But by the time my love came home, when he did come home, I had turned the argument to 'I'm a modern woman, I have the best of both worlds, I can leave without any fuss, whenever I want.'

Then things got worse.

Apparently Muhammad's parents had needed a new home, their old one having fallen down around their ears, so it had been decided that they should move into their late son's home in Shiraz and his widow and children move to Tehran to live with Muhammad. The Tehran house was paid for by another brother, Akbar, a refugee in Sweden who had fled after Muhammad's eldest brother (Sepideh's late husband) had reported him and other members of his family as 'enemies of the revolution'. The eldest brother had then had the top of his head shot away by the Iraqis.

In Shia Islam, the *seegheh* marriage is supposed to be devoid of all feeling and simply a means for men to satisfy their sexual needs while away from their real wives. The man is not obligated to support the woman beyond giving her the marriage price agreed at the beginning of their contract – two gold coins in my case. She has no rights and her children under the strict interpretation of the arrangement have no claim on their Father's estate, although truly pious men often leave something to their various offspring.

The last Friday prayers leader of Tehran before the revolution is reputed to have advised the Shah to spend 16 million dollars among the mullahs to keep then in line, saying: 'The mullahs cannot resist two things: money and women.' I was beginning to believe that he was right. Life in nineties Iran revolved around two things: money and sex. The more you had of the former the more you could afford of the latter. The mullahs were so preoccupied with sex that it sent all our minds in that direction. When you can apparently get turned on by feeling the warmth of a man's bum on a seat, then you can get turned on by anything. The media supplied answers to sexual questions no Western media would broadcast. One woman asked one of the many radio mullahs when it was correct for a man and woman to have sex again after the woman's period. She was told that bleeding must have ceased completely, but if she was in any doubt she should take her sanitary towel to the local mosque for the mullah to judge. I conjured up images of women in line with their bloody rags. This was not the sophisticated Iran we had all been a part of just fourteen years earlier.

The more spineless I got at home, the stroppier I grew at work, taking risks that I would never have been foolish enough to take in the past. I was again held by the authorities, this time only for an hour, after falling out with an uniquely unpleasant member of the security forces. It all started at a UN-sponsored conference at the Azadi Grand Hotel, on another of those pointless and boring subjects that I had to report on in Tehran in those days.

I arrived wearing my keffiyeh and had my way blocked by a tall, very hairy and gaunt SAVAMA toady. The head of whatever PR agency was running the Iranian side of the conference intervened to explain that I was improperly dressed and could therefore not sit in the row of black egg-headed sisters. So apologetically he showed me to a seat beside the men, out of sight of the television cameras. As luck would have it somebody apparently from the Hair Liberation Army was on the camera and the nation got a glimpse of yours truly happily chatting to the boys as my grim-faced sisters sat in rows of black.

The next day I decided to compromise and arrived in the mourning black complete with the *maghneh* wimple that I wore when not at work. This time the skinny SAVAMA man blocked my path as I entered the hotel and I was practically dragged out of sight of the visiting ministers from various Third World friendlies.

'Don't you know not to touch me?' I screamed. 'Call a Pasdar. I want this man arrested,' I instructed the assorted security people gathered round to watch the floor show.

'You cannot go in dressed like that – I told you yesterday,' Skinny screamed back.

'Firstly, take your hands off me. Secondly, yesterday you told me my scarf was wrong and today it is a nice black *maghneh*. So what is wrong?'

'What is wrong is that your coat is buckled, showing your figure, and it stops above your knees. Your trousers are tight and you are wearing make-up,' he said with a smirk.

'I have no desire to go to your stupid conference; it is you who need me, so I suggest you don't do anything that will give your country a bad press. I am not wearing make-up – I just happen to be more blessed by God. I wore these trousers to interview Mr Rafsanjani, so they should be good enough to get past your high standards,' I said, knowing before I had drawn breath that I had stepped over the line for no useful purpose. There was so much outrage and frustration in me that I just exploded.

'You may be a journalist, but you are an Iranian and I can do whatever I like with you. If anyone bothers to complain it will be too late. They didn't save Bazoft, did they?' he said, sending a shiver down my spine.

Bluff it out! ... Give in! ... Spit in his face! ... the voices raced through my head.

'I'll just sit here and we can call Mr Nategh Nouri [the parliamentary Speaker] to come and give his judgement after he has delivered his speech,' I said, sitting on the edge of a table decorated with a flower arrangement so loved by Raffers.

'You'll speak to who I say you can speak to,' Skinny replied.

'The people didn't die so that you could come and order us around,' I said.

'They died to make sure that people like you could never come out looking like this again,' he retorted.

By this time officials had been summoned from Interference, Intelligence, the Foreign Office, the Majlis Public Relations and other assorted broad-shouldered and black-suited servants of the republic.

'Phone Mr Mousavi, he will tell you what I can and cannot do,' I said to blank faces. Then I gave the telephone number. Boy, did I enjoy the slow look of recognition followed by panic that crossed their faces as they registered the significance of this number. They obviously knew a lot more about its home than I did, but I wasn't hanging around to find out why they all suddenly fell apart and ordered Skinny, the only one still stubbornly sticking to his guns, to let me go.

'She can go, but I won't let her into the conference,' he said.

'I would not cover it if you begged me,' I said, translating straight from English and thus making no sense whatsoever.

To make my point I arrived at a press conference given by the Interior Minister that afternoon in exactly the same outfit. The security and morals officials did not even notice me, let alone try to eject me from the building. However, I received a mild rebuke from Mousavi, who phoned the next day to warn me never to mention his name in public again. He also told me that he would be coming over to see my new flat.

A house visit? This was a new development. What was old Bright Eyes up to?

Muhammad panicked at the news that Mousavi was to come a-calling. 'We have to get married properly before we are discovered,' he said.

'But that was why we got married,' I said.

'No, darling. That only protects us in case we are stopped in the street or they raid the flat or something like that. Intelligence will never accept it as a real marriage. We have to do it properly. I'll ask around to find a mullah,' he said.

Mousavi arrived the next day more than an hour late and with a new side-kick: a truly Islamic body, with requisite stubble and prayer beads. This man was introduced just as 'my new colleague who is in charge of your affairs'. He was the new broom being brought in by a new minister and he was there to meet me and to 'offer me a very advantageous arrangement', Mousavi explained.

I went to fetch the tea and thus give them a chance to plant their bugs – I noticed the new man's briefcase had been moved in my absence.

'We have had a request from the *Financial Times* for them to open an office with a new correspondent,' the new man told me. (By this time I had left the *Independent* and was writing for the *Financial Times*, where I already worked for a year in London.)

'No that's not so, you must have misunderstood. We are doing a survey on Iran and my editor and a couple of reporters are coming to help write it,' I assured him.

'I'm afraid they are fooling you. Our London Embassy has had a request from another Iranian woman to come and be the paper's accredited correspondent in Iran,' he replied.

'This cannot be so. I am their correspondent. They wouldn't put in a request for someone else without telling me. It is true Sharri is coming for the survey, but she works in the London office.'

'She wants to stay on after the survey. We have her request here,' he said.

'But I have told our superiors that you are a very good correspondent and we don't see why we should allow another to replace you. You know there are a number of people who would be happy to see you gone,' Mousavi said.

'If you were to work more closely with us, then we would be willing to refuse her request,' the new man said.

'I told you a long time ago that you would have to be more co-operative to keep your press card. We won't ask you to say anything that is not true, but it is important for us to have a way of putting our side across to the world,' Mousavi said.

Mousavi suggested that the three of us meet in a week's time when we could discuss a feature I was writing on a series of bomb attacks in Tehran and other major cities over the last month.

Muhammad was very near hysteria when he came home that night. No matter how I tried to calm him, he insisted that we were in great danger unless we got married as soon as possible. I had hoped to wait till we went back to England before getting fully married – at least then I could get a divorce. But Muhammad insisted that we could not afford to wait, and he now claimed that he had lost his birth certificate, so we had to marry in Iran.

'Why?'

'Because we have a *seegheh* document and at a pinch any mullah would marry us with that, without insisting on the birth certificate. I'll apply for a new one, but it will take at least six months,' he told me. He said that the document had been stolen from his briefcase shortly after the *seegheh* marriage. I did not know then that a married man needed his first wife's permission to take a second wife but he could have as many *seeghehs* as he liked without telling her.

Finding a bent mullah to marry us was as easy as opening the Yellow Pages – if they had Yellow Pages, which they don't, so it makes it a touch more difficult. The really difficult part was trying to get the blood tests which were required for people getting married.

We were sent to a clinic in North Tehran, where a woman we accosted in one of the many empty rooms told us to come back on Wednesday, when they held their bride clinics. On Wednesday another 'nurse' told us that they had not done marriage blood tests for more than two years. But she knew a place that did – right the other side of town, way, way out on the Resalat Expressway.

We went straight there, wanting to get that certificate in our hands before 'they' attached handcuffs to our wrists. We arrived at a red-brick three-storey building down a side street of new buildings off the highway.

'It's too late for today,' an aged woman shrieked at us from behind a sparkling new reception station.

'But it's only 10 a.m. It says on the door that you are open until noon,' Muhammad argued.

'You have to be here by seven tomorrow morning if you want the tests,' she said, dismissing us.

Next morning we missed her deadline by fifteen minutes and were told to come back the next day.

'I'll go and talk to the doctors,' Muhammad said, leaving me at reception while he disappeared into the depths of the building in search of someone to bribe. I stood there and watched the prospective brides and grooms as they went about the business of getting tested. All the men were wearing those white socks, while their women held an assortment of bags with fake Chanel emblems plastered all over them. Not one was anything near any style that Chanel ever produced, but then they didn't know that. They all sported that upturned nose that Iranian plastic surgeons specialise in. It was strange, these women whose clothes showed they were from the lowest rung of that class-ridden society, and yet they had all spent good money on plastic surgery.

God, I was such a snob.

Ten minutes later Muhammad appeared, motioning me to follow him down a winding staircase that took us to the basement of the spanking new and antiseptically clean clinic. Inside a large reception room, men lined up against one wall and their women along the opposite wall. As I took my place among the women I saw the column of white-socked youths stare at me. Even the women turned to have a good look at me and then at Muhammad. We were being sized up and the obvious conclusion of most seemed to be disapproval. I must have looked out of place. In Iran more than anywhere else I have known the classes stand out by the different clothes and styles they wear. While I clutched my genuine Louis Vuitton bag the girls ahead of me delved into the plastic Chanel imitations much in vogue that year. Shoes, buttons, handbags and shopping bags all had the distinctive linked 'C' stuck on some-where. While I stared down at leather Bruno Magli court shoes, my sisters shuffled along in white cracked patent or fake Reebok trainers.

Sex was on all our minds and thus a subject for coy sniggers and modest blushes. Standing there I felt that everyone staring at me was thinking 'She's going to have sex'. I was embarrassed and I felt ever so slightly dirty.

There were three women to go before it came to my turn, but the man taking the urine samples from the women came out and announced that they had run out of the chemical necessary for the process and we would all have to come back next day. Men have a blood test, but women give only urine if it happens to be their first marriage. Most of these women were technically virgins, and could not have any sexually transmitted diseases – yet.

The next day, the sixth of our attempts to get married, I got as far as giving a urine sample before the nurse announced that I could not be tested because I had not attended the 'marriage class' which was held at 7 a.m. sharp.

Back we came the next day at the crack of dawn. Muhammad was taken to the basement for a blood test while I was shown to a room on the first floor where a young female doctor started to tell us the facts of life. The women with me in this class were aged from fifteen to twenty. My being older by a considerable margin made me the centre of attention, especially as I had turned bright red as the woman explained exactly what went in where and what the girls were to do to clean up after losing their virginity.

Then we were shown various methods of contraception and advised to use them 'until you are sure that the man you are married to will be the man you want to stay with'. Few of these girls had spoken more than a dozen words to the boys who were downstairs preparing to turn them into women. Most of the brides told me that their groom had been chosen by their parents or that they were cousins.

'I had the choice of saying no when my parents suggested someone, but I could never go and find someone for myself,' Marsieh, a seventeen-year-old virgin, confided.

After class we were taken to another room where we were given a tetanus jab – to protect us 'virgins' on the marriage night!

Finally I was led to a toilet where an attendant handed me a jam jar and instructed me to leave the toilet door open so that she could see that I wasn't filling it with anything other than my own urine.

Two days later we were pronounced fit to marry.

*   *   *

I hated him. Really, really hated him.

He sat there, spitting out of the car window. In unguarded moments, I still think of those lumps of 'gob' lying on the road, trailing our path. The path from 'exclusive North Tehran' to Tehran Pars, the other side of the tracks.

The Resalat Expressway was gridlocked, the cars steaming under heavy rains that had been belting down for three days. I was trapped. On that November day in 1992 everything about the man who was about to become my husband sickened me: his mud-caked shoes, those white socks, the rumpled trousers – and above all the spitting.

For six months I had been trying to change the way he dressed, and today, our wedding day, he was wearing *white socks*! To top it all, he had the nerve to call my outfit 'disgusting'.

'Listen!' I had screamed. 'This coat happens to be very smart. You know you have no taste. It's not my fault you can't tell what is stylish and chic . . . Only a very sick person would consider this split disgusting. For heaven's sake, it only goes up to my calves,' I had said in a pathetic effort not to surrender.

With that I-know-better voice he had replied: 'You women really think it's only the hole between your legs that you have to cover. You are going to be my wife now, and I want to be the only man to see you. I'm not unreasonable. No man would be any different,' he had argued. 'Get a pin and close it up now, or I'll do it for you,' Muhammad commanded as he got into the car.

If my Farsi had been better, I would have argued the point. I would have reminded him that I had only agreed to go under the veil because he had assured me that if I didn't most Iranian men would believe that I was inviting them to bed. I had let him persuade me that even those men I had known since childhood would be lusting after me if they could see my legs. 'In England you can go about in the nude,' he said. 'But in Iran you have to behave in ways that won't encourage men.'

I rummaged in my bag for a pin.

It struck me later that night that he had very neatly avoided having to explain why he was over two hours late. I hadn't even got round to asking him where he had acquired those love-bites on his neck.

So I settled for silently fuming as we crawled through the traffic. We had been down that road at least ten times in the last month, trying to persuade the mullah to marry us. You would think that two healthy, consenting adults would have no trouble in getting married. But things are different in Iran. Even before the arrival of the mullahs, a woman could not get married for the first time without her Father's permission – whether nineteen or ninety.

Not for a second had I thought that my Father, in exile somewhere in the West, would ever give his blessing to this union. There was very little chance of Muhammad ever being clasped to the family bosom. I only hoped he would not be turned away at the front door. So my only legal route to marriage was by getting the permission of the marital court, which would assign another man to be my guardian.

The first indignity in the marriage process had been the day we presented ourselves at the marital court. It was like one of those weird dreams when you are shouting at the top of your voice but no one can hear you. 'Come back in four years for the answer,' the magistrate had told Muhammad. My attempts to intervene were totally ignored until even I doubted that I was really there.

So back we had gone to Hadji Tabrizi, our tame mullah, at the poor end of Resalat. After much negotiation he had agreed to perform the ceremony. In turn we agreed to make a large donation to his favourite charity – the Children of Tabrizi Trust.

In the car on the way to the ceremony, Muhammad had begun to grumble. He was exhausted, and it was a pain going up and down this road. If Tabrizi didn't marry us today, Muhammad announced, he would not make the trip again. He failed to mention that on previous occasions he had turned up so late that the marriage had had to be postponed.

Hate was too soft a word for it. I really, really loathed him. But I was going to marry him even if it killed me. I had started this and I was going to finish it. No one would again look at me with pity as they told of how older women always gave birth to mutants. It did occur to me during that journey that the mutant was the man who would soon be my husband. Why had I never noticed his black teeth before, or those bulging purple lips? These surely were the ugliest ears in the world.

I had loved him, and would again persuade myself that I loved him. But on that road I faced the truth: I really, really detested him.

We finally reached the office from which our little mullah operated. This was a far cry from London's Dorchester Hotel where my sister, Pari, was married. Instead of the three ballrooms my Father had hired there was a basement room, divided into five sections by walls that appeared to be held up by dirt. Down fifteen steps from the road, I entered another world and felt lost for ever. The condemned woman was about to meet her executioner. On the other side of town there would be women getting married at the Hilton. The cost of their flowers alone could keep this part of town ticking over for a week. But here in a far-flung corner of Tehran, forgotten by all, it was among abject poverty that I was going to start my new life.

'Are you crying?' Muhammad asked, his manner suddenly mellowing.

'No, it's the smoke from the heater,' I lied.

Could I leave? Would I be able to find my way back to a part of town I recognised? Rain-soaked couples lined the walls of the reception room. On the left, those about to be married. Opposite them, those who were about to be split apart.

Families milled around between divorcing couples, involved in some last-minute mediation. A tiny girl came into that dark dungeon, her small hand in that of an old man I presumed was her grandfather. At the sight of her the Mother broke down and wailed in pain. The child was led in front of her Father. 'For her sake think again,' the grandfather begged. The Father stormed out into the makeshift kitchen on the right of the room. The men of the family followed him, their women turning to console his wife. The little girl was left standing in the middle of that stifling room – scared and abandoned. I felt like taking her into my arms and telling her: 'Don't worry, I am also lost.'

Hadji Tabrizi was ready for us at last. We shuffled into his squalid office where I was loath to sit on the stained settee. My reluctance made me feel like a rich bitch turning her nose up at the real people. Much ashamed at my natural inclination, I flopped down gritting my teeth and hoping that whatever had stained the seat wasn't wet. It was.

My grandmothers had both married in wedding dresses made of silk and covered with lace made out of 22-carat gold. All the newspapers had reported Mahshid's marriage to Donald in Oxford. Now I was sitting on a stain, coughing from fumes and waiting for an old man with scorched hands to join me to my 'master' out of the sight of everyone who was dear to me. I wanted to scream from the loneliness.

As the mullah joined us as man and wife, Muhammad slipped a small box into my hand.

Oh, joy! He had thought of getting me a wedding ring! I opened the box with expectation. Inside it was a wafer-thin heart the size of my thumbnail with the words 'Congratulation on your joining together' engraved on it.

When my cousins had married in Iran they were strewn with Cartier rings, Bulgari necklaces and gold Rolex watches. I had a heart a fraction of the size and value of the heart already on the chain round my neck. That bulging, solid-gold heart had been left on my desk at the *Hongkong Standard* one Valentine's Day a lifetime ago.

'I'm going to take you to the best restaurant in town to celebrate,' my new husband told me.

When we arrived at the Duck Restaurant a couple of Muhammad's closest friends, Reza and Said, were waiting. If this was the best restaurant in town then I was the Queen of Sheba. It was a Greasy Spoon with a difference: it specialised in roast duck. No sauce; just a whole roast duck with a salad on the side.

The boys were engrossed in a conversation about whether men and women could ever be friends without sex coming into it. Reza said yes but Muhammad and Said mocked him. I struggled with my overdone duck and wondered why I had done this. After the dishes were cleared away my loving husband lovingly whispered in my ear: 'Darling, I had to give the last of my money as a tip to the mullah's office staff. Slip me some cash under the table to pay the bill.'

I had already paid 30,000 tomans to the mullah before he would agree to marry us. Muhammad now took another 10,000 to settle a bill of less than 2,000. All in all it had been a much cheaper wedding than my sister's, especially for the groom.

'We should go to England as soon as possible,' Muhammad said as I lay in his arms one night less than a week after our latest marriage.

I just cuddled up, trying to dismiss the thought that I had been used as a way out of God's Republic.

'Don't you think so?' he continued.

'We'll go for the Persian New Year in March, if you can get away,' I replied. As soon as I said it I felt him tense up and he pushed me away.

'The more we stay the more the danger that Sepideh might get pregnant,' my husband said, fixing me with steel-cold eyes.

My entire body turned to ice.

'I'm sorry, I didn't want to tell you like this, but I am going through agony.'

'What are you talking about?' I managed to ask.

'She came to Tehran after she met you at the wedding, I told you that. She begged me not to divorce her. She swore that she would accept you and put up with sharing me,' he said.

This could not be happening to me. Nothing so bad could happen to me. Please, God, take those words away; let it not have happened.

'Son of a whore!' I screamed at him as I struggled to loosen his grip and get up from the bed.

But he clung on to me; his face showed sorrow and regret, but his fingers dug into my flesh until it ached.

'Get your filthy hands off me, you son of a whore,' I said, and I wriggled free, tripped over my own feet and lay flat on my back on the floor of my bedroom looking up at a monster.

'You are so selfish,' he was shouting at me. 'Sepideh is just an illiterate village girl but she is worth more than a hundred of you. You have taken her husband and her life and she has accepted it. She doesn't moan and demand that I don't sleep with you,' he spat at me.

'You said you were divorced. You lied to me. You tricked me into marriage,' I moaned.

'I never told you anything. You wanted to have me so you believed what you wanted. I was divorcing her, I intend to divorce her, but now I have you it wouldn't be fair,' he said, trying to hug me again.

I wriggled away on the ground like an animal desperate to avoid the claws of a predator.

What happened then I cannot tell you. I vaguely remember him getting dressed and my crawling into the kitchen. I kept thinking over and over that I had been contaminated, that every time he had entered me he had made me dirty, made me sick.

The sound of the dawn call to prayer woke me. I was on the floor of my kitchen, rammed into a corner behind the door. The flat was empty except for a pair of his dirty socks left in the middle of the floor where he had taken them off the night before.

It hadn't happened. There was no husband, no other wife.

In the bedroom I stuffed the bedclothes, the pillows and my nightdress into a black rubbish bag. I put on my coat and scarf and went out into the corridor, opened the rubbish shoot and cast away all memory of the previous night.

I was out when he returned to our flat that day. I was out most of the next day and the day after. I was out shopping. From early morning to late at night I shopped. I spent the evenings at Mrs Mo's or with my new neighbour Bibi and her family.

On the fourth day I woke up to find a note under the door. My husband thought he could speak English, but he certainly could not write it – not anything that made any sense anyway. I threw away the note.

He came home that night.

'Are you OK?' he asked sheepishly.

'Why shouldn't I be?'

'You were upset.'

'No. What I was is stupid. But I'm better now.'

He gave a sigh of relief.

'I am going to get a divorce and then I'm going to forget you ever existed,' I told him.

Instead of looking upset, he laughed.

'I'm so glad you agree,' I said.

He then sat me down and explained that he would never, ever give me a divorce. He explained that because we had married without my Father's permission we had been party to a crime. He reminded me that the marriage had not been entered into my birth certificate and so questions would be asked if I tried to get a divorce. 'They'll give you a divorce one day, after we have all spent many years in jail.'

'I hate you,' was all I could manage.

'You didn't let me explain. Everything will be find in the end. I love you and you are the only woman I want to be with. But Sepideh is going through a very bad time; she has to learn to depend upon herself, not me. You are a strong woman, you can look after yourself. But she has never had to live without being looked after. I can't just throw her out. Give her time to get used to the idea that she is no longer my wife and then I will bring up divorce again.'

He continued: 'Slowly, everything can be done slowly. Once we go to England she will be forced to cope on her own. She can't forbid me to go because she knows studying is more important to me than anything else. She knows if she stops me studying I will leave her. We will be together in England for years and while we are there I will divorce her.'

'Why did you say she might get pregnant?' I demanded. 'You are still having sex with her.'

'Don't be stupid. Do you really think I am an animal? I have not slept with Sepideh since I married you. But if I am with her . . . well, anything could happen. I am not planning anything, I am just saying that something might happen. I am a man after all,' the slime explained.

He left me to think it over, saying that he would respect any decision I made. I could live apart from him. 'But I married you for life, and I will be your husband until one of us dies,' he reminded me before leaving.

My feelings exactly.

That night he phoned to see how I was.

'I want a divorce,' I snapped. 'You'll give me one or I swear we will both spend the rest of our lives in an Islamic jail.'

'OK, OK, if that's what you want. I will never force someone to live with me. I will pick you up at ten in the morning,' he said.

I was so relieved. I could get out of this; he would give me a quick divorce and it would be as if I had never married someone else's husband.

What would I tell people in Tehran? What would Mrs Mo and my other neighbours think of a divorce so soon after the marriage? Did I really want to be alone again? This is Iran and we are Muslims. If it was wrong to marry someone who is already married then it would not have been allowed, I argued with myself. Sepideh is a devout, fundamentalist Muslim, so she must accept that a man can have four wives. I've done nothing wrong,' I told myself.

The next morning he arrived on the dot. Before our marriage he had either not turned up or been so late for the ceremony that we had to delay the great day four or five times. But now I wanted a divorce and his highness finally managed to turn up on time. I should have been furious then and joyous now. But a resentment, the like of which I had never known, welled up inside me, pushing my heart against my chest with a loathing so violent that it made me want to throw myself over the railings of my balcony.

That would teach the little bastard! He'd be sorry once he saw my guts spewed out on the pavement for all the world to see. Then he would be sorry, then he would hurt the way he had hurt me. Thus thought the madwoman of North Tehran as she watched her lover get out of his car, light a cigarette and slump against the dust-encrusted vehicle. He looked so smug, even from nineteen floors up. I was running a fever from the pain he had imposed on me. I could feel the hate working within me, eating away at the cells and spreading its disease of hatred and humiliation.

Not a single word was exchanged as we once again made our way along the highway to perdition. But the mullah was out and his henchman instructed us to come back in a couple of hours.

'Let's drive up into the hills,' Muhammad suggested. 'You like the snow, it might calm you.'

'Anywhere,' I replied. 'Just don't talk to me, OK?'

I stood on the side of a sheer mountain track, knee-deep in snow, and looked to heaven for help. I didn't want to live another second of the agony raging inside me.

'Please God, let me die,' I prayed over and over again until even I was sickened by the forsaken figure I must have cut on that ridge. 'Kill me, God, please, please kill me.'

'We should talk,' Muhammad said, trying to hold me.

'I said I didn't want to talk,' I replied, but as I pulled away I stumbled and fell. The tears rolled down my face while I lay there on the ground, cold, miserable and pathetic.

Next thing I knew I was in his arms and he was swearing that he would go straight back and tell Sepideh that it was over and they had to divorce. He went on and on about how I was his last chance, how he couldn't be happy without me. He asked if I could blame him for not wanting to destroy Sepideh just to ensure his own happiness.

No, I couldn't blame him. I couldn't demand that another person be made wretched just so that I could have something I no longer believed, deep in my heart, that I even wanted.

'Let's go home,' was all I could say. It was the easiest thing and I no longer had the strength to even care.

14

Mr Bean Goes to Tehran

The life of a young woman ended in a hospital halfway across the world from her home in poverty-stricken South Tehran. Three days earlier flames from a paraffin heater had engulfed her body. Her death was, in part, the consequence of a lifestyle her successful husband refused to abandon.

Muhammad had come back from the funeral of the wife of Mohsen Mahkmalbaf, one of Iran's most successful and controversial film directors, shaken and claiming he hated his own comfort and that we would have to move away from North Tehran.

At the funeral Mahkmalbaf had told of the plane journey to an English hospital in a last desperate attempt to save his young wife's life. He had explained to his wife that he might not be able to be with her all the time when they reached England and tried to teach her what to say if she needed a drink of water. She replied that all she could say was: 'Help me, oh my God.'

Such faith and such loyalty to the poor had made Muhammad ashamed of himself and of me, he told me. 'That man had lived in the place he was born despite all his success and the money he made from his films. She never blamed him but died thinking of God,' Muhammad said on the verge of tears.

'Can poor people afford to rush their wives to England?' I asked. 'What?'

'It seems to me to be a bit of an act, this living in poverty when he can afford to rush to England. It would have been better if he had created a safe home for his wife so she didn't have to struggle with paraffin lamps,' I replied rather coldly. I hated the pious hypocrisy in which those who wanted to keep in with this regime indulged.

Mahkmalbaf was a revolutionary who had been the darling of the Khomeini era. But as he strayed from strictly religious or revolutionary themes to exploring the relation of man to God and politics he fell foul of the censors. Perhaps it was the mass sympathy generated by the death of his wife that softened the hearts of these protectors of moral welfare and allowed them to release at least one of the films they had locked away. After a year on the banned list, *Nasseradin Shah, Movie Actor* went on general release in Iran. But his masterpiece, *A Time for Love*, which explored a woman's need for the love she could not get from her husband, stood no chance of ever being released.

Mahkmalbaf had been an idealistic student in the turbulent last days of the Shah, and he and a friend had attacked a police officer with a penknife. Instead of cheering this blow for freedom, the masses turned on the two youths, beating them to within an inch of their lives and handing them over to the police. Mahkmalbaf went to prison as South Tehran began to heave with the forces that a few years later ended in the overthrow of the Shah. He was released after the mullahs seized power and soon began a career as a screenwriter and director that saw him travel the road from favoured son to banned dissenter in fourteen years.

Muhammad now said he wanted us to move to that very suburb where Mrs Mahkmalbaf had lost her life. This was the last thing I wanted to do: all my background screamed out against the move and my guilt told me I had to go.

When he left me that night with the promise that he would find a new home for us the next day, I wanted to die. I loathed the idea of moving to a district where not even my family's servants would have accepted a home. All our staff had been housed, at my Father's expense, in newly developed middle-class enclaves around Tehran. And now I, the granddaughter of General Pessian, a former débutante and millionairess, the Tehran correspondent of so many prestigious publications, would have to move to the very slums I had so despised the Shah for creating. I would have to go and live in a house with one room, with no electricity and no gas.

There stood in that luxury flat two people forged into one. The first argued that it was shameful to live in a flat that cost seven times the average monthly wage. The other argued that I would never be able to look my family in the face again if I sank so low.

'*That's their problem,*' the first person said.

'*But I wasn't brought up to live like that – I'd die,*' the second said.

'*Don't be pathetic. You won't die any more than those poor wretched people living there now,*' the other replied.

'*I couldn't stand it – all the grime and the misery. I wouldn't know anyone and my family would never set foot in such a home,*' the rich girl whined. '*I'd have to wear the chador to fit in . . . I couldn't do that.*'

'*Clothes maketh not the woman. If your husband doesn't like you flaunting your body, you have to cover yourself. You chose him, you can't change him.*'

By the time Muhammad came round the next evening I had talked myself round to the nobility of poverty. This was the beginning of the process by which I was dying. The me that had grown and developed over the previous thirty-six years was disappearing, dissolving – but I had nothing to put in its place. There wasn't a single part of me that shared a single gene with the woman that should have been my husband's wife.

Friends and family started telling me how worried they were about me, how much I was suddenly changing. 'You are becoming a robot,' Minu told me over lunch – a lunch during which I felt I was paralysed. I had always dominated conversations; ideas and views fell over themselves to get out. But now I didn't have anything to say, I knew nothing. I wanted to hide away from everybody, to scream: 'Just leave me alone.'

I stopped seeing my family and all of my friends except for a handful of neighbours who were part of the nouveaux riches. They were good, pious people, who were trapped between the old and the modern. I was subjecting myself to a form of sensory and intellectual deprivation which was not helped by the total lack of any real recreation. I even began to wonder what was happening in *EastEnders*.

Entertainment was somewhat limited in Iran, to say the least. There was theatre, but only the most tame and orthodox of the plays ever made it to the stage. The cinema was thriving, and many Iranian films were beautifully made. But there were only just so many films dissecting marriages that one could stomach, and once you'd seen one group of pimply youths being slaughtered by the evil Saddam you'd seen them all. Raffers's promise to provide more entertainment for the young had inspired his brother at the television station to buy up yet more Japanese sagas of family life, and a handful of British TV series such as *Secret Army* and *Miss Marple* – all of which I had seen.

Going out to dinners or to parties was too much of a bother after a while. Who wanted to have one ear on the conversation and one on the doorbell in case of a raid?

That left the illegal film on video brought to your door at dead of night by the hire-man – who risked his freedom. Once you got your hands on these films it was a nightmare trying to make out the picture and sound. During an interview with one of these rebels I was taken to his home to view *Dances with Wolves*, but which one was Kevin Costner and which was the wolf? I saw *JFK* five times, but it wasn't until I saw it again in England that I finally heard the dialogue clearly. Videos of films often reached Tehran only days after being released in the cinema in the States, but the quality was so bad that sometimes I wondered why anyone bothered. The hire-man would explain that so many people had borrowed this 'excellent' video that the quality had deteriorated. I later discovered that they were illegally filmed in US cinemas by a man with a camcorder hidden inside his coat. Since video films of this kind were not dubbed into Farsi, I was much in demand for translation purposes. My broken Farsi was driving me mad, so could these people really be enjoying the films I translated for them?

'It is better than not knowing what is going on at all,' my neighbour Bibi explained.

My little video man started coming later and later as the soldiers at our door made life increasingly difficult. The man showed no surprise to see me wearing scarf and coat to greet him at 3 a.m. He did not ask why, after a year of choosing films from him without feeling the need to cover myself, I had suddenly imagined he might get the urge to rape me.

'You must have this – it is the most popular video I have had for years. Many of my clients have purchased their own copy. I can do one for you by next week if you want,' he enthused, as I read the name: *Agha Nokhod, or Mr Pea.*

'Is it Persian?'

'No, no. It is a very popular American comedian.'

I needed a good laugh so I took the film and eagerly sat down to watch it. This popular American comedy was none other than *Mr Bean*. And, sure enough, wherever I went after that people were enthusing about Mr Nokhod. Many a stifled spirit was raised by our very own Rowan Atkinson.

Another year, 1992, was coming to an end and I could see my life slipping away. I was soon to be saved from the deep boredom into which I was sinking by the arrival of two representatives of the *Financial Times*. For a month before the arrival of Roger Matthews, *FT* Middle East editor, and Raymond O'Donnell, survey supremo, I was running around like a headless chicken trying to organise visas, interviews and accommodation.

Meanwhile, Muhammad seemed to have lost the use of his hands and his desire to move south. At night he would arrive to flop on my settee. I would be instructed to remove his socks, put sugar in the tea I had prepared for him and stir it. As he lounged I put on a video for him, brought his house clothes to him in the sitting-room and put his work clothes away. Then I had to sit on the edge of the settee, by his feet, and translate the film.

'Get a book and make a note of the director and the actors in films we see,' Muhammad instructed.

'Why?'

'Intellectuals know about films, and we don't want to appear ignorant,' he explained.

Speak for yourself, my sensible voice said. *I already know more about films and directors than you or your so-called intellectual friends will ever know.*

I was in love and in hate all at once.

'I might be with you tonight,' he would tell me before leaving one morning. We had settled on two nights with me and five with Sepideh, but as I became busier I was put on twenty-four-hour alert for a visit by my dear husband and his band of friends.

If it had not been for Shirazi, however, we might never have got the visas for my visiting colleagues, and I was thus under an obligation to Muhammad. He used it as a weapon to silence me whenever I complained that I could not prepare food for him, keep the flat spotless in case of his bringing visitors and organise the survey on Iran planned by the *FT*, all at the same time. There was no Marks & Sparks ready-prepared food in Iran. Fruit and salad had to be disinfected for at least twenty minutes, chickens had to be beheaded and gutted, rice had to be separated from the bits and pieces mixed in with it.

'How come you can suddenly get away to come home to lunch so often anyway?' I asked Muhammad when he arrived on the stroke of noon for the third day running, just as I was leaving.

'I'm just up the road now,' he replied.

'Has Guidance opened a new office?'

'No, I've left Guidance. I took that job I was offered at the paper,' he told me casually. I knew he and his friends were involved with a radical newspaper, but I could remember nothing about a job.

'When? Why?' I spluttered.

'About a month ago,' he said.

'Did you tell me?' I asked. My husband had succeeded in making me doubt myself, and I was ready to believe that it was possible that I could have forgotten.

'What does it have to do with you?'

'I'm your wife.'

'And you can't even have a meal on the table in time for your husband. Sepideh has always put me first. She has never gone against my orders and she has never interfered in my business.'

'I put you first. I do more for you than any woman of my family has done for their men. I hand you your clothes, I put on your socks, I wash your clothes with my own hands. What more do you want of me?'

'Today you will stay at home. Don't step out of the front door until I come and tell you that you can,' he said, putting on his coat again. 'You'd better be here when I get back or it will be over for us,' he warned as he left.

For two hours I cried my heart out; then I started to shout at the walls – a futile attempt to lash out against someone who was on his way to his other wife. Then I started to beat myself. I pounded my head with my fists. I pounded that other woman who had taken over my body and my life – that other woman who had thrown away my freedom and who couldn't even get pregnant to make it all worthwhile.

Not that I had tried ever since the day I learnt that I was not the only wife. At school, in that other life, my house won the rhetoric cup with a rendition of *Under Milk Wood* in which I played Mrs Dai Bread Two, the number-two wife of the village baker. Now life was imitating art.

Now I wasn't really married, not in the way I felt a marriage should be, and I would never have a baby by this man who could take it away and give it to another wife whenever he wanted. A couple of nights after I discovered Mrs Dai Bread One, he had denied he had ever promised to let my family bring up our children. I was convinced that I would die; I already felt a little dead, living a life that was false and being in a relationship that made me lie and hide.

Then some days I would think: Have a baby anyway. Give yourself something to live for.

What was I going to do?

Go out. I was going to go out just to prove to myself that there was something of me left.

But what if he came back and found me gone? He would leave and we would get divorced and it would come out that he had another wife.

God! Oh God! My husband had another wife. I couldn't even get a man like him – a poverty-stricken, unattractive village boy – to myself.

I had to pay for him to be with me and even then he held on to that other woman. I felt so angry at her – but I was really ashamed of myself. He was her husband; so who was I?

I went out. I went as far as the next block. Mrs Mo was out, so I went to Bibi's upstairs, and I sat there like a lemon in my *hejab* to hide my body from her husband and her son – men who had seen me a thousand times when I was someone else.

'You are a wife in a million,' Bibi told me.

'Yes, she is,' her husband said.

'A girl brought up in the corruption of the West, who can come back to her homeland and become such a devoted wife . . . to do as your husband tells you without question. What remarkable loyalty and purity. They should make your statue in gold,' Bibi's eldest daughter, Mona, enthused as she wasted away waiting for someone to come and take her away to her very own kitchen.

They were right; I was a wife in a million. I was noble and self-sacrificing. And I was his last chance at happiness. I had brought him so far, disrupted his other life. None of us could ever go back.

I had better go home and wait for my husband.

He came round the next morning just long enough to apologise for being 'so angry'. Apparently he had left his job because of me, because he would get in trouble if he was still working for the government.

'But that's why we got married,' I protested, again.

'You don't understand how things work here,' he said, and started cuddling and kissing me.

All the loneliness of the night dissolved. He put his hand between my legs – I was still in the extra-large T-shirt in which I had slept. There was a sharp pain. He was pinching the flab on the inside of my leg, sending a stab of pain through my body. I was pushing him away, trying to wriggle loose.

He giggled. 'What's the matter, darling? It's just a sign of affection.'

I hated him, really, really hated him.

'I won't be hit!' I shrieked.

'Nobody hit you. I was just pinching my little angry wife,' he said, trying to pull me into his arms.

As I got away from the bed and his grasp, he said, 'Can you give me some money?'

'How much do you need?'

'Ten thousand tomans.'

'What?'

'I haven't paid the instalments on the other house for three months,' he explained. 'Akbar promised to send money from Sweden, but he hasn't sent anything.'

'I can't pay for your other life,' I protested.

'Your wardrobe is full of money. Money that "Mummy" sent you so you could buy all the things you don't seem to be able to live without. Money that you people stole from people like Sepideh. You have her life, her husband. Now do you want to see her lose her home as well?'

Put like that I could hardly refuse. He called me an angel and went off to his new job at the newspaper, although his exact role there was still not determined.

'My friends brought me in – they'll find a proper job for me. Then

I will have more money. I'll be able to pay you back and to keep you and her and the children,' Muhammad told me.

I went off to the airport to welcome Roger Matthews, my immediate boss at the *FT*, a teddy-bear of a man with twinkling eyes and a razor-sharp sense of humour. We were planning a twelve-page survey on Iran, only the second since the revolution. The last survey had been organised by one Roger Cooper, who had been invited to spend five years at Evin for his pains.

Not another Bad Omen, I hoped.

After ten days of sitting in the lobby of the Laleh Hotel waiting for the promised interviews to materialise, we had lift-off. The head of one of the new Duty-Free Trade Zones, set up to spearhead Raffers's thrust into the world of capitalism, granted us an audience. We arrived in an ultra-modern, open-plan office on the eleventh floor of one of the ministries. In a corner, behind a small screen, a man in an Andy Capp cloth cap was studying a file. Behind him porthole-like windows looked out over Tehran.

As Roger, this vast but fluffy, professional senior editor of one of the world's most influential papers, stepped forward to shake hands with Andy, the Iranian official looked out of the window over a cold December day and asked: 'How are you coping with the inversion?'

A look of puzzlement passed over Roger's face and was gone in a split second. He bowed his head and looked out of the window in the direction that Andy had indicated.

'Well?' Andy asked.

Roger was stuck for words. Was he supposed to be pleased or upset? Should he say it was great or regret its existence?

As these thoughts flashed across Roger's face, Andy said: 'You don't know what an inversion is, do you?'

Roger confessed his ignorance, so we sat round a pine table on pine chairs behind pine screens and Andy explained that an inversion occurred when cold air rises to meet hot air – or was it the other way round? – and a table of smog is trapped. I am afraid I was too busy trying to stifle a fit of giggles to fully absorb the details of the creation of inversions. Most comical of all was the effort Roger was making to keep a straight face and look as if this knowledge was invaluable and exactly what he had come all this way to discuss. You must remember that we had set a lot of store by this interview, for so far we had twelve blank pages and no interviews to fill them with.

Twenty minutes later, Roger managed to turn to conversation round to the subject of our interview by asking what the weather was like on Qeshm, the island free-trade area.

Ten minutes of weather report later and Roger was getting more than a little agitated. 'And do you have inversions on the island?'

Big mistake. Big, big, big mistake.

We were back to the explanation of the inversion, which we had obviously not understood or else we would have realised that they could not occur in warm areas such as the Persian Gulf. An hour had gone by before we got around to talking about the Free-Zones policy. In mid-sentence Andy suddenly dropped the names of a couple of 'famous' economists. In a vain attempt to avoid going off on another tangent, Roger ignored the reference.

'You do know who they are, don't you?' Andy asked.

'Can we go on to discuss . . .' Roger continued

'You don't, do you? You don't know who they are. How can you be an editor on the *Financial Times* if you don't know such famous economists?'

The rest of the interview was taken up with the life histories of John Maynard Keynes and his like. I contained my hysterics of laughter until we hit the street. Then I collapsed; I didn't care how many Pasdars were looking, I didn't care that the staff of the ministry we had just left had gathered at its glass door to watch this strange behaviour. And I really did not care that in God's Republic women should not be seen laughing.

The truth of the matter was that, despite hundreds of millions of hard-earned petro-dollars being ploughed into these trade zones, there were no solid examples of what had been done with the booty.

Now, I have no objection to the imposition of Islamic law and custom, if that is exactly what it is. But in Iran the hypocrisy was maddening. The revolution was supposed to have swept away corruption, to have put morals in the place of money and to have created a climate in which fraud was not tolerated. Instead nothing was done unless a bribe was forthcoming; money talked louder than morality. Government grants rarely reached the people they were meant for, and the law was subject to who you knew or how much you could pay to get round it.

The most immediately obvious, and least sinister, example of this hypocrisy was the stationing of men in hotel lobbies to enforce women's dress codes. The philosophy is that the only men who are permitted to see women are their husbands and close male blood relatives such as Fathers, brothers and sons. Some say a son- or brother-in-law are also allowed, or *mahram*. Women, we are told, have to hide themselves under the *hejab* to protect them from the stares of strange men, who would of course be aroused so much by the sight of the female body that they would take the woman. Then why, oh why, do the powers-that-be in Iran place a *man* in every hotel lobby, his sole task to study women closely to ensure that they are not improperly dressed?

Just such a man worked at the Laleh Hotel, and I was the only woman in Iran about whose appearance he seemed to give a damn. I could not walk into his domain without this man finding something to criticise, and if that wasn't bad enough he would follow me about as I struggled to arrange more interviews for myself and Roger and to contact potential advertisers for Raymond O'Donnell, whom I always thought of as Raymondo.

My life was lived in the Laleh that month, and it was tormented by this security pest. Other women came in and out of the hotel with hair piled high under sheer scarves, their faces caked in make-up, reeking of perfume. But would he lift a finger to discourage them? In a pig's eye he would. But should the tiniest tip of the smallest strand of hair suddenly creep out from under my wimple, he would spot it and materialise at my side to order me to cover it up. This was driving me crazy, this constant worry about what might be sneaking out for a glimpse of light from under the rag round my head.

Two weeks into their visit, I was sitting with my two colleagues waiting for Ali, Raymondo's kamikaze driver, to pick us up when I saw the bane of my month bearing down upon me. Now I am not accusing anyone of any wrong-doing, but there was a faint aroma of vodka emanating from our little corner and gently wafting over the early-morning coffee crowd at the Laleh and towards that little bit of space along which this man would have to pass to get to me. I immediately sprang into action, leading him back to where he had come from, and pretended to be standing guard for the errant driver. Sure enough he followed me to the door, and then to the telephones, while I feigned making an urgent call.

At first this man's persistence had been funny, but as I grew increasingly exhausted from being up all night either with Muhammad or worrying about our life together and then rushing round all day to balance work on the survey with cooking and cleaning, it began to make me feel degraded and disgusted. Just when I needed more peace and quiet Muhammad took to inviting all and sundry to eat, drink and make revolution in our sitting-room. In honour of the survey he had increased my share of him to three nights a week as well as lunch on Thursday – the start of the weekend.

A month earlier I would never have believed that I would be pleased to hear that my precious husband would be away for ten days. A group of French journalists were in Iran and they wanted a guide, so those friends who seemed to exist only to find work for Muhammad had arranged for him to accompany them.

Before he left, Muhammad brought an envelope full of hundred-dollar bills and asked me to keep it for him. He claimed it was a tip from the French, and that he had insisted on cash first, tour later.

It seemed so dirty, I had never been on the receiving end of 'tips', so I told Muhammad to put it where he wanted, but not to tell me about it. There are times in the career of a journalist when he or she has to oil the wheels of officialdom, and I admit that during that long autumn of 1992 I facilitated my fair share of 'tips' changing hands in order to get a story. But I had always despised those who took them and now my husband was the one on the take.

'I'm not going to keep it myself,' he told me. 'It's for the boys at Guidance. I'll give it to them when I get back.'

Later that night we sat in front of the video. Unusually I was given space to cuddle up beside my husband as he told me all the places he would be visiting. He complained that the French wanted to go by car and that since there had been a heavy snowfall along most of the northern part of the route they had agreed to pay extra 'danger money'. I was terrified, and begged him not to go. I argued that he didn't need the money and promised to give him the money myself rather than let him go. After an agonising night of pleading, Muhammad rang Reza to ask him to take his place. Muhammad stayed, as did the dollars hidden under my underwear.

But apparently Shirazi was very angry that Reza had been given this great chance to make money, so I was instructed to put some of our survey work Shirazi's way. What I suspect was the real motive was that Muhammad wanted someone to keep an eye on me.

Shirazi had taken us to the bazaar, because Roger had expressed interest in buying a carpet. As my editor looked at the goods on offer in the carpet bazaar in the midst of the labyrinth of covered streets that make up the greater Tehran bazaar, Shirazi asked me: 'Would they expect you to sleep with them?'

'What are you talking about?'

'We have often wondered, me and the boys at Guidance, when these journalists come here from England or America, do they expect the woman or man working here to provide them with sex?'

'Are you mad?' I said, turning away to look for a metal bar with which I could beat him about the head until what little brains he had oozed out. This frenzy, this feeling that there was no recourse but to lash out in anger, was common among many of the women I spoke to in Iran.

When I complained to Muhammad he just laughed: 'He told me he would ask. I didn't think he would have the nerve. I know you are not a bad girl, but the other women must sleep with their bosses. I am sure even the men go to bed when a woman comes over. There was a Japanese journalist over here last year, and she was dying for it. Every time she came to the office she smiled at me, looked straight into my eyes and told me how kind I was. She was asking me to fuck her,' he chortled as I choked back the rage.

I was tired of arguing, of trying to explain that people outside Iran did not think of sex all day and all night. I told Muhammad that most of my friends in England could get so much sex whenever they wanted that they were even weary of it in some cases. 'No one can ever have enough sex,' he would say. Had he cared to listen he would have heard me tell him time after time that I had had enough of him. But he didn't listen, he didn't even consider that I played any part in the process of sex other than to provide an instrument through which he could satisfy his lust.

It was a scene straight out of a caveman joke. I would be standing in, let's say, the bedroom, ironing a shirt or pairing his socks, when I'd suddenly find myself being pulled away from the ironing board. A slight lift and a massive toss and I'd be flying backwards on to the bed. Never mind that I missed the edge of the bed and caught my head on the bedside table as I went down. He-man was going to do whatever He-man married in order to do and I could just wait until he was finished before I attended to the gash in my leg and the bump on my head.

Did I hit back? Did I lash out? Did I lock him out?

No. I started cowering in corners. I started to make excuses – headaches, periods, anything. But nothing stopped him; he didn't even realise that no meant no. It was just a vote that he could override.

Never in my worst dreams had I ever imagined that I could end up in this situation. I was the woman who at the age of eighteen had walked out on the best-looking man in Oxford because he had driven off without waiting for me to get into the house after a date.

Now I jumped every time I heard my husband's footsteps. I cringed and hid in a corner sobbing as he ordered me to bring fruit so he could get his strength back. I felt even dirtier because we hid our marriage from everyone but our closest friends and family. As far as officials were concerned, I was still single. I felt I was some sort of criminal; I hid in my flat all weekend so that Bibi would not see me alone and realise that he was elsewhere at weekends. At night I stood alone and miserable on my balcony wondering if I dared flip over it, I was a caged animal, a dirty, pathetic, filthy, filthy animal.

'I love you, my darling, you are my life, my breath, my very soul,' I would tell this man as I tried to convince myself that I hadn't made a tragic mistake.

Mummy, Mahshid and Said had warned me not to get married, to wait until I returned to England and thought it through. But I had gone full steam ahead; I had said I knew better what was right for me and that I adored this man and nothing would keep me from him. We had been in danger of being arrested, I could have got him locked up for life, so I had bitten on the bullet and done it despite all the warnings. I would lose face, I would prove to my family that I was not capable of running my own life. I had made my own bed; now I had to lie back and think of Islam.

In fact what I used to think of was a very large knife. But I also depended on him for support, so I buried all those thoughts; I switched off my life, my mind, and put my beliefs and upbringing on the back burner. I was existing on automatic pilot.

Schizophrenia ruled my life. In the morning I was in love, happily cooking my husband's breakfast when he was there, or longing for him to return when he was at the other place. By the evening I wanted to kill him, either for being with his other wife or for treating me like a slave.

Getting dressed was becoming a nightmare – was this Islamic enough? How would this look if he turned up with guests? All my old clothes, mini-skirts, strapless dresses, and so on, went into a 'to get rid of' suitcase, as did my red nail varnish and lipstick, as only whores wore these.

It was one of those good nights that Muhammad brought up the question of England again. He started by giving me the good news that after he had seen Mr Shirazi get an invitation to England from a visiting journalist he and Reza had also tried it – with success. I was overjoyed; he could afford to come back to Oxford with me when I went back in March for the Persian New Year.

I told him all the things I wanted to show him and to teach him. Muhammad had been in a remote village for most of his early years and then he had lived at the heart of revolutionary Iran. He had no idea who the Rolling Stones were, he had never heard of Elvis Presley, he didn't know what happened to Jackie after that day in Dallas when a bullet put an end to her life as First Lady. He had never seen a James Bond film or heard about Woodstock. There was so much of modern culture he had no idea about.

Yes, he could roll off the names of the world's great philosophers, he could quote from Marx and Freud and Khomeini, but I wanted to take him to McDonalds or San Lorenzo's. It would be so wonderful, I would finally have someone all of my own to go to the pub with, to cuddle up to watch *Hill Street Blues* with, to enjoy the theatre and the ballet and opera. He would love it.

Muhammad had to go back to Shiraz to file for the divorce I now know he never had and, since it was coming up to Auntie Homa's birthday on New Year's Eve, I decided to go along. This time I was sent out to get plane tickets while his lordship sat around at Guidance 'making sure the boys do their best' to arrange the last few interviews we needed to complete the survey.

Tickets for internal flights are worth their weight in gold in God's Republic. Many people book seats as much as six months in advance to avoid the 'little extras' that travel agents charge to find an empty seat if you need a flight in a hurry. Knowing someone who works for Iran Air is a definite plus, because if they have not grabbed the seats themselves they will know a colleague who had invested in a couple of advance tickets that they could let you have at a 200 per cent premium. Like so much else in Iran, it took me two days of waiting around in travel agencies, getting friends to phone a friend who had a friend who knew a travel agent. Muhammad added the cost of the tickets to the rest of the money he owed me and I let my aunt know that we would be with her the following week.

I waved Raymondo and Roger off at Mehrabad with great sadness. I had felt safe in their company. Now I was again alone with strangers.

Maman Joon was in Shiraz when we arrived and I could tell from the moment she set eyes on Muhammad that she was appalled. Never one to mince her words, she spent the first evening making quite sure that the new addition to the family knew just how lucky he was to be where he was. Soon she was telling Muhammad how one of her many general brothers had put down a rebellion among the Qashqais of his clan to keep them in their place. She didn't tell him that her other brother had taken their first-born daughters hostage to ensure they never stepped out of line again. This did not exactly help to create the sort of atmosphere in which one could relax, and I couldn't really blame my new husband for spending the next week as far away from this home as he could. He 'allowed' me to spend the first two nights with my family, but the rest of the week we were to spend on his sister's floor.

Muhammad picked me up two hours after expected on the second day of our stay in Shiraz and took me to Motaram's home. My husband stayed long enough to have tea with us before leaving me to get to know the sister and her six lovely children. My sister-in-law was illiterate, having married at the tender age of thirteen. It amazed me to listen to her questions and comments about the behaviour of women in the West. She had been a child when she married a man she had never met before the wedding night, and yet she was appalled at the thought of unmarried couples sleeping with each other, even if they had socialised for months.

She asked why Western women were so shameless, how they could let a man other than their husband see their hair and bodies.

I had no answer for her. I could see how from this woman's single L-shaped room it must seem disgusting and immoral. There was no way of telling her that it was her brother who got turned on by the sight of a sliver of skin on my neck, it was his mind and the minds of men like him that created the filth. I could not tell her I had men friends with whom I had shared a bed without sharing my body, that there can be more between men and women than sex. She would never understand that the veil she wore around her body was the greatest aphrodisiac.

She may not have had a role outside that room, but you could eat off the stone floor. The place was spotless and although her children's clothes were old and frayed they were clean and fresh, as were the children inside them. This is one thing I had noticed in which the more religious homes outdid the 'modern' household – immaculate cleanliness. The entire country was a cleaner place on the whole if you managed to avoid private hospitals and expensive restaurants.

The three youngest children – a delightful girl called Mali, whom I would gladly have taken home with me, and two boys whose names I never managed to memorise – crouched over the books on the floor in their own little corner while their three elder sisters helped their Mother clean and cook and entertain the new in-law. Of all those I met in Iran I miss these children most; they were so innocent, still so pure and had so very little to look forward to.

A month after our visit the eldest girl turned fourteen and quickly became engaged to a cousin, despite opposition from Muhammad, who had taken on the role of head of the family, although his Father still lived.

That night Muhammad returned in time for supper, with several hairy and dusty men in tow. These, I was warned, were Sepideh's brother and cousins. They had not been told of Muhammad's marriage and so I had to sit apart and was introduced as a friend of the family.

How dare these people treat you like this, my arrogant voice told me. These people would never be allowed in your Father's house unless it was to wash the floors, so how dare they hide me like a dirty secret.

The good voice soon made me realise just how bad I was. *These are God's people with just as much right to pride and respect as you. Who are you to look down your nose at them?*

It was the strangest night of my life, being put in this sub-class whispering in one corner in order not to disturb the men who discussed the important matters of life. I bit my lip and tried to absorb myself in the conversation of the young girls. They knew nothing of the fashions and pop music that occupied their contemporaries in the West. The girls discussed who their young cousin would be married to, giggling as the six-year-old turned her nose up in disgust at the top candidate.

'He looks like a donkey,' she whispered in my ear, knowing that she would be reprimanded for such rudeness towards an adult if her Mother heard her.

'He will get all his Father's land now that the brothers have left to live in Tehran,' the eldest sister explained.

'I don't want to marry,' the little girl confided in me. 'I want to go to college and be on television.'

'Uncle Muhammad wants us all to study and to work,' the eldest daughter explained, much to my delight – only to continue: 'He says we should work to help our husbands and to be more interesting for them.'

Once the meal was over and the guests had gone, the girls spread mattresses across the floor while I made my way to the toilet at the far end of their small backyard. It was raining, and my long coat was already muddy as I tried to hoist it round my waist while I squatted over the toilet. I had had nightmares about toilets like this, where the water washed under your feet as you struggled to keep your balance and try to avoid spattering urine over yourself. As I peered down to make sure of my aim, something moist splashed on to my lip as the porcelain bowl filled. I washed and washed my face under the tap in the middle of the yard until my skin tingled with the rubbing.

Given the chance I would wipe that night from my memory. As six young children, my sister-in-law and her husband settled to sleep, Muhammad started to fondle my breasts. I froze in the silence of that dreaded night, I listened for the sounds of sleep but there were none. These people were wide awake and lying within three or four yards of where Muhammad was climbing on top of me.

I pushed him away, but he just whispered that no one would know.

'*I* know,' I replied. 'We can't do this, it is disgusting.'

'Don't be stupid. It's natural.'

My nails dug into his back, but he kept fumbling with my underwear. I struggled as much as I could without making too much noise in that feigned silence. The more I resisted the more he got excited and the more violent his clawing became. I ripped into his back, but, to my disgust, he just moaned with pleasure.

The only thing worse than what he was doing to me would be the rest of the family realising what was going on, so I gritted my teeth and stifled my sobs.

The next morning I couldn't look anyone in the face. This time I gave him the silent treatment and asked to go back to my aunt's. He said no. Muhammad spent more and more of that week with his family and friends while I was left to help his sister.

As we left after an agonising week, the children hugged and kissed me and wept as they begged me to come back soon. They were such lovely, kind and generous people and I could not wait to get away from them.

That last evening was Homa's birthday and we were to spend it with her. But instead of being happy and carefree my graceful and elegant aunt looked a hundred years old. She suffered from the family bone and back weaknesses and she was lying flat on her back, in a bright-green tracksuit, on a green-and-navy-checked mohair blanket on the floor of her sitting-room as she confirmed that her daughter Shirl, who had lived in LA for the last decade, had really married for the fourth time. And it was true, her new husband was that very same poet who had broken Bahar's heart and started the chain of events that had shattered the happiness of our family. Auntie had asked her not to go through with the marriage, but news had come that they were married.

Homa had known for some time but was obviously reluctant to admit that it had happened. Suddenly the pain and the horror of Bahar's death were renewed. All in all it was a miserable birthday for Auntie and an even worse New Year's Eve.

15

Falling Out with Rafsanjani

My flat – I still considered it mine, not ours – was turning into a bed and breakfast for assorted members of the Iranian Civil Service, students and members of Muhammad's family. I rarely had an evening with my husband without at least one other man coming round to eat and talk, and eat and talk, and talk and eat.

Very little of the talking was directed at me, which was just as well because I was having some difficulty hearing – what with having to wear a scarf to hide my hair and being in the kitchen for most of the evening surrounded by the sounds of cooking, kettles boiling and water running as I rushed back and forth serving my guests and washing the dishes ready for the next round. This was God's revenge for all those years I had avoided doing a stroke of housework.

My first house-guest had been Reza, who came to inspect our 'love-nest'. I remember him standing at the window in my sitting-room, staring out over the January snow all the way across to the southernmost tip of Tehran and on to the shrine of Imam Khomeini: 'It's easy to imagine you are in love from here. I'd like to see if your love would survive in my room and a half over there,' he said, motioning towards Shoush.

'Of course it would,' I said. 'I'd live with Muhammad anywhere.'

'Would he live with you anywhere?' Reza responded.

'Yes, of course he would. In fact Muhammad is looking for a place somewhere cheaper, somewhere near the real people,' I said, defending my loved one.

'Really! Where have you found?' Reza asked, turning to look at Muhammad.

'I have seen a few places, but everywhere is just about as expensive as this place. There is no point moving now, not until I decide whether we go to live in England or not,' Muhammad explained.

Reza warmed to the subject of England and education and spent the next hour trying to persuade my husband that he owed it to himself to make the great sacrifice and move to England. It was also my duty to support him while he studied. Muhammad held out, but Reza argued and argued in favour of flight.

As I prepared the dinner I started to wonder if I had just witnessed some kind of prearranged show. Was I being set up? And what was that burning smell?

My mind had wandered off, and the end of my scarf had strayed on to the open flame on the cooker, causing a minor fire. I screamed and tore off the rag as Muhammad came running into the kitchen

'Don't come in here, Reza,' he shouted, then stood and giggled at the sight of my headgear going up in flames in the sink. 'I'll go and get you another scarf,' he volunteered, once he had had his fill of laughing.

I had to admit it was funny, hilarious in fact if you weren't the one about to go up in flames. I had almost burned to a crisp, and all my love could think about was that Reza might catch a glimpse of my incinerated head and be turned on.

What was not so funny was the arrival of his two younger brothers, Pirouz and Firouz – not their original names but ones they had adopted in place of their rather old-fashioned, religious original names. This meant that I was now the prisoner of my *hejab* almost twenty-four hours a day. The two boys, in Tehran to take up places at the university reserved for the family of martyrs, camped in our small flat. They were very sweet, innocent and extremely polite boys, and I can forgive almost anything to someone with manners. It was their brother Muhammad who presented the problem. He had brought the boys without warning and demanded I acquire mattresses and so forth while his brothers assured me they would be fine on the floor without sheets.

This was quite normal in Iran. The extended family lives and thrives in God's Republic, and relatives are expected to drop in unannounced to stay for months and months. This is considered a favour, not an imposition, and I was happy to have the boys stay. But their arrival coincided with the run-up to the fourteenth anniversary of the revolution, to which the world's press were welcomed. This is normally the busiest time for Tehran correspondents as the powers-that-be vie to get their names in the Western media.

For me it was the end of my self-delusion, the fallacy that I had married a man who understood that I was someone in my own right, that I had a career and that it was as important to me as anything else. Perhaps I would have accepted Muhammad's attitudes if he had played the traditional husband. If I was expected to do the work in the home while he worked to pay the bills, I might have understood and respected him – I still would not have accepted it, but I would have understood. I might have respected his religious beliefs if he had not stopped saying his daily *namaz* the moment he had married me. I might have forgiven him a lot if he hadn't allowed me to pay for everything, including the wedding ring which I finally persuaded him I needed.

I was expected to cook and clean and entertain, I was expected to discard all my traditions and adopt his, and in my spare time I was expected to earn enough to support him, his other wife and children, and to feed and house his friends and family.

'Sepideh does it when it's her night,' he would tell me.

I thought it would be too cheap to bring up the subject of money, to say that Sepideh didn't have to earn his keep. So I ate my words, and the meal didn't agree with me. Inside I was burning up, my mind raced with fear and rage, while my body got weaker and weaker until there were nights I collapsed unable even to lift my arms.

On those nights Muhammad was lovely: he would pick me up from where I had fallen and carry me to my bed. He would rearrange his nights with me so he could be around to nurse me. He would make me sweet drinks to raise my blood sugar and he would rub my feet to try and get the circulation going again. And the next morning he would shake me awake, kiss me and say: 'Hurry, it's time to get up. I'm late – get my breakfast quickly while I have a shower. My shirt needs to be ironed.' It never bothered him that his shirts were crumpled before we were married.

I had seen the brothers off after a lavish breakfast at which they learnt the joys of cornflakes. There are things that divide man from man that are so trivial that you would not imagine they would make the slightest difference, but when things start to go wrong it's the trivial you notice first. My new family had never, never had cornflakes before. They had no idea what they should do with them. Neither had they ever had coffee, and as I brought out the eggs I found the cornflakes swimming in the hot milk and the coffee being added to the cold.

'Shouldn't we have some water to add to the coffee?' Muhammad asked.

'I'll just get it, darling,' I said, too embarrassed to tell them they had got it wrong, and ashamed at myself for minding so much.

By the time they were gone I was drained; I just wanted to sleep. I had been up for two hours after the men had retired the previous night, clearing the debris of dinner. I was up an hour before them to wash and iron Muhammad's clothes before starting the breakfast. As I lay down I switched on my radio to listen to the BBC news. It was Lyse Doucet reporting from Tehran – something about an air crash.

I sprang to life. I was on the phone to Interference, to Mousavi, the airport and the air force. An hour later I had finished an article for the *FT* on how an Iranian Air Force plane had crashed into a passenger flight taking pilgrims to Mahshad. There were no survivors and some fears that the planes might have gone down over the highly populated area of Karaj, just outside the city. I was about to go to the Hilton to fax the story when Sky TV phoned asking for a report. By three that afternoon I had done the story for the *FT*, a couple of US publications, Sky and a Swedish radio station. But Sky wanted more: they wanted me to go and see the crash site.

Muhammad and the clan were due back in half an hour, so I waited for them to arrive before I left. I was still waiting two hours later as the light faded. My nervous stomach was hysterical. I knew Muhammad would make a fuss if they came and there was no wife to greet them and no dinner. But I had to go; Sky were pressing me for more and I was not going to miss the story. So I left a message for Hubby with the man at reception and called a taxi to take me to find the debris.

The road out of Tehran to Karaj is an ultra-modern four-lane toll motorway that ploughs through the capital's industrial hinterland. To leave this very expensive motorway you turned off on to dirt-tracks. To cross it you had to drive through narrow viaducts roughly constructed under this super-highway. We finally tracked down the site of the crash – in the middle of a military base close to the airport. By now the official story was out. The passenger plane had been taking off from Mehrabad at the same time as a fighter plane left the base, which doubled as an arms depot. The two aircraft flew into each other, ending the lives of several hundred pilgrims, many of whom had been invited at the expense of the state to attend the celebrations.

The guards outside the base gave me and my over-enthusiastic driver the gory details. They had been separating limbs from fuselage all day.

'There are still bodies all over the place,' a fresh-faced conscript told us.

'Can you let us in to see?' my driver asked. My stomach sank.

'Sure. Just wait here,' the boy said, going to get his superior.

The officer refused to let us in – much to my relief. But this was not going to stop my driver, who was at that moment engaged in deep conversation with another officer. You could not miss the wad of money that the driver slipped into the soldier's pocket.

'Oh no, please God, no,' I prayed as we were ushered into the base. 'Please, dear God I'm not up to seeing any dismembered bodies.' This was one sight I did not want to see, but I wasn't going to let these men know that I was already feeling like retching just at the thought.

Just then a yet more senior officer rushed out of a hut deep within the base and barred our way. As my driver put his arm round this officer and started to negotiate, I turned on my heels and made my way out of that place while ranting at the top of my voice at the shame of corruption in this country.

It was well after eight when I got home to find the two brothers waiting for me. Muhammad was nowhere to be seen. The brothers told me that my husband and his friends had gone out to dinner and then to the cinema. The boys offered to cook, but I got up anyway and prepared dinner – three varieties of main meal followed by ice cream and fruit. *Couldn't they have got a pizza or burger for once?* my uncharitable and very tired voice asked me.

Then we put on a film, a western, and waited for Muhammad to return. I started to get worried when he was still not back at eleven that night; the film he had gone to see must have started by nine at the latest and should have been over long ago. At one o'clock the next morning I was stationed at the window looking down on to the street below, hoping that every set of lights coming up the road would turn out to be his. Ninety minutes later Muhammad arrived with Reza. 'We are hungry,' he instructed as he flopped into a chair.

I wanted to tell him to go to hell. I wanted to tell him to take his brothers and his friend and go to hell. Nevertheless they were my guests, I might be angry at Hubby, but it would have been the height of bad manners to show that I wasn't 100 per cent happy to have these people invade my world. I was so tired I didn't know what I was doing, but somehow I managed to cook yet another meal. The men sat about until four in the morning talking, smoking and devouring fruit. When they settled to sleep my flat was covered with plates piled high with orange skins and the remains of cigarettes. I tiptoed between them clearing and washing and wiping. They woke up to an immaculate home and a paralysed hostess, who nevertheless restarted the process of feeding and cleaning.

The night before Raffers was due to give his first press conference in twelve months, Hubby was all mine again. It was the first time we had spent an evening alone together for more than a month, but for me it was the wrong time of the month.

As I lay underneath my husband while he rubbed himself between my legs, pressing down on my bloated and painful stomach, I realised how little I had understood of Nahid's agony. Would I too turn to the love of strangers after twenty years of marriage to this reptile? Would I also one day take money and gifts from strangers I picked up in sandwich bars and tell myself that this was love? Would I one day forget what love really was?

He hadn't even heard my protests; he had not cared that I said no, that I said I was tired and just wanted to be left alone. After all I wasn't expected to do anything – just lie there like some erotic aid bought from a sex shop. He then slowly lifted his body, took aim and sent a massive lump of lubricating gob cascading down between my legs.

I lay there all night as he snored contentedly beside me. I could kill him, I could cut him into tiny little pieces. I nodded off at about seven, only to be shaken awake two hours later by my husband, who was saying: 'You've missed Rafsanjani's press conference.'

I was out of bed and gone before he could say 'breakfast'. At the presidential offices I was allowed through with only a cursory attempt at searching my belongings. This was strange to say the least; in the past you were stripped of even your jewellery before being allowed anywhere near the mighty.

By the time I was inside, the conference had already started, and much to my horror all the earphones through which the great man's words were translated into English had gone to the foreign press. Nor could I get close enough to put my tape recorder on the desk in front of the President. It was essential that I stay alert and take in every word. By my mind kept straying to that lump of gob between my legs, to the divorce I was powerless to demand.

Then, looking beyond my own circumstances, I saw the women sitting in that hall with their scarves firmly wrapped around their heads, while beside them sat their overseas colleagues in their temporary prison. My mind wandered to the fate of the millions outside that room who had been dragged back to the thirteenth century, screaming and shouting for someone to save them.

I stood at the end of the long line of journalists wanting to ask a question of the man. As I stood there I formulated a rather complicated question on Iran's medium- and long-term debt crisis. But I couldn't keep my mind on the politics, on the set replies that were coming out of our leader's lips. I wanted to echo the words of Peter Finch in the film *Network*: 'I'm mad as hell and I'm not going to take it any more.'

There were TV cameras from all over the world. There were journalists from the *New York Times, The Times, Der Spiegel, Figaro* and many, many more. And there were cameras, lots and lots of cameras; both local and foreign. I wanted to get up there on that podium beside Hojat-ol-Islam Ali Akbar Hashemi-Rafsanjani, and to rip the scarf from my head and tear the coat from my body. I wanted to scream: 'Let me free! Let my people be free!'

Of course it would have been useless: the photographers would have had their films confiscated, the cameras would have been impounded, and I would be lost in Evin before the news ever reached the outside world. Someone had asked a question about political prisoners and Raffers was inviting the assembled journalists to visit his prisons to see what wonderful, humane places they were.

It was my turn. The master of ceremonies said: 'Mrs Mosteshar of the *Financial Times*.'

I stepped up the microphone and opened my mouth, but only a squeak came out.

'Speak up!' someone from the crowd shouted in English.

As I pulled the mike closer my hand was shaking. Rafsanjani's eyes were boring into me, looking inside and already knowing the thoughts that raged inside my head. The scarf that was choking me told me that I was just a mass of hair, breasts and vagina and I had to be wrapped in a shroud that would hide the dirty traces of womanhood.

'Mr Rafsanjani, you have often encouraged women to take a greater part in public life,' I croaked in English. 'But how can a woman aspire to, say, becoming your Foreign Minister, when every time she needs to travel she has to get her husband's permission? There remain many things that women still find intolerable, and that does not mean the *hejab*, but many, many other things such as being half a man when giving evidence. Islam says that you must change with your time and your place. Is this the time and is this the place to finally give women their human rights?'

He smirked at me, but his eyes seemed to be saying: I'll see you behind bars, sweetheart.

The reply was pathetic. Women were respected; they were encouraged to study. There were more women at university than ever before. There remained some areas that needed change and those reforms would come in time.

As I walked back to my seat, assorted journalists and even the odd official or civil servant congratulated me on my question. I jokingly asked one of my male colleagues from a Murdoch paper if he would be accepting the offer to visit our prisons. 'Yes,' came the reply. 'What fruit would you like me to bring you?' Everyone thought I had been brave, if somewhat foolish. But I had just been angry. Very, very angry.

I was at breaking point, and I longed to get away. I longed to be back in Oxford walking down the Banbury Road without looking over my shoulder for the morals police. I wanted to stand in the lobby of the Old Parsonage Hotel and joke with the waiters without being told to leave. I longed to consume ribs at Brown's. I wanted to chat with a male colleague without one of the security men skulking in the background trying to hear what we were saying.

I had not thought twice about meeting people in the lobby of the

Tehran Hilton until the day one of the women in the telecommunications office disappeared. It was the previous summer and several members of the Hilton staff were going around scowling at the little chunky man who sat at a desk by the door, and whose exact role I had never realised until then. It appeared that the poor woman was only employed on a pittance and having been widowed with three children was desperate to get a more profitable job. The Cuban ambassador had been chatting with her while she sent a fax for him, and he had mentioned that he would soon be expanding his mission and would require more local staff. She had given him her telephone number – at work at the hotel – in case he had some work for her. The next day she was taken away by security and her colleagues told that she had been dismissed for immoral behaviour.

Knowing this, I was understandably concerned when the security man hovered behind me as I exchanged telephone numbers with a rather attractive young BBC journalist in town to cover the cap-in-hand visit of Eduard Shevarnadze, the Georgian leader. I was feeling slightly ashamed anyway because ever since Raffers's press conference I had rediscovered a world full of interesting and good looking men, and wondered why I had so desperately wanted to get married. I had been brought up to believe that one should give total loyalty once married, and that to find another man attractive was a betrayal. As the man from the BBC went about his business I felt a pang of yearning to be free again, to wake up every day with the expectation that I might meet Prince Charming that day. I was thinking this when the security man came up to me, stared into my face, smiled and said: 'You really had Mr Rafsanjani sweating.'

The great press conference had been televised the night before, a week after it took place, and I had suddenly become a superstar.

Muhammad had been really supportive and encouraging about my performance with Raffers; that is, until people started joking that he should be careful or Raffers would steal his wife. 'You got married too soon,' Mrs Mo told me. 'Did you see the way Rafsanjani looked at you? You certainly caught in his throat.' I had seen something much more villainous in those bulging eyes.

But now I had to put up with my husband's constant instructions on how to stand, sit and talk in order to avoid giving the impression that I was available. I was no longer allowed to say hello to the doorman or the receptionist at the flat. I was forbidden to sit in the same room as the men at Guidance – an opinion shared by the new head of department, who segregated the sexes into two rooms, making it rather difficult to tell the boys through a brick wall who one wanted to interview.

* * *

Iranians commemorate a death every year on the anniversary of the demise of a loved one, but the first year is the most important. Once again the immediate family have to open their doors to one and all. I have met people who never miss a mourning ceremony and set great store by the quality of the hospitality. It was at a ceremony to mourn one of the many great men who had died in the post-revolution upheavals that one of my fellow journalists whispered the best mourning joke I had heard:

'A woman and her daughter-in-law were going to pay their respects to the family of a deceased servant.

'The dead man had lived in the poorest and most disreputable part of Tehran and the two women were soon lost in the back streets. About to give up hope of ever finding the man's home, they finally noticed a house where a continuous stream of male visitors, among them several mullahs, came and went. Thinking this must be the house of the deceased they went in.

'What they had walked into was in fact the best little whorehouse in Tehran. Once they were in, the men set upon them and took their fill of them for six hours non-stop. When the two women finally got away the younger turned to her Mother-in-law and begged: "Please, please don't tell my husband what happened in there."

'The older woman replied: "I don't know about you, my dear, but I will back for all his funeral, his week and his *chehele* [forty days] ceremonies and I won't miss a single anniversary,"' my mischievous colleague said, chuckling as Ahmad Khomeini, the late Ayatollah's surviving son, honoured the martyr of the revolution.

* * *

It was the tenth time I had read his letter. I started sobbing on the third reading, but by the sixth I was determined that one day I would be free again. A second later I was disgusted with myself. *You can't keep running, girl. You chose Muhammad, now make the best of it*, I told myself.

I didn't even think to hide the letter. Gervase was a very good friend, not a lover. We had worked together on the *Independent* and had shared a low opinion of many of the same people. He was just one of half a dozen male friends I wrote to. There had been a special man back then on the *Indy*; I had been dotty about him, but it couldn't be, so we had settled for being friends. These friends were very precious to me because they were picked carefully and I gave them my complete loyalty. In my heart I knew that I would climb any mountain, cross any desert and fight any demon for my friends. But some days I was no longer sure if I would bother to cross the room to help Muhammad; while other days I thought I would die for him.

Gervase's letter was sitting on the dining table when Muhammad arrived that night – on a fleeting visit before going to 'the other side'.

'What's this?' he said, holding the letter.

'It's from a friend who has just been travelling through Africa. Do you want to read it?' I offered, knowing full well that he couldn't.

He made a pretence of reading the letter for a minute or so, then threw it back on the table and rounded on me. 'Is it a man?'

'A male friend, yes.'

'Did you sleep with him?'

Something flipped. I was enraged that he should presume to ask such a thing. I knew that he thought if it was a man it was bound to be about sex. 'Yes. I slept with him hundreds and hundreds of times. In the middle of the office, on the table in the canteen, under the table during editorial meetings,' I mocked.

I was just thinking that a year ago I would never have been able to say all that in Farsi when Muhammad rushed towards me and grabbed my arms.

'What are you doing?' I laughed. I always laugh when I am really and deeply frightened or unhappy.

He pushed me and I fell. I fell with an almighty thud. My spine throbbed from the pain. How had I fallen so far?

Muhammad was drawing his hand back and I realised it would slam into my face at any moment, so I scrambled out of reach. I scurried backwards on my aching backside.

'You hit me and you're finished!' I screamed in English. 'You hit me and I will pound you to a pulp!'

He may not have understood the words but he understood the look on my face and suddenly he was a puppy, nestling up to me and all but licking my hand.

'I am sorry, but you know how I feel,' my liberal husband explained. 'It is impossible for a man and a woman to be friends, sex always comes into their minds. Sooner or later friendship leads them into bed.'

'I've been friends with many men. I have known Gervase for several years and others such as John, Daniel and David for more than ten years, and it has never crossed our minds that we might go to bed together,' I told Muhammad.

Then I had to explain that John was a friend from my days on the *Hongkong Standard*, that we had been friends ever since, both having worked on the *Tehran Journal* when the Shah still sat on the Peacock Throne. We had ended up together again on the *Indy*. John knew all my secrets, but I didn't tell my husband this.

'I love many men as friends, and that is all,' I tried to explain.

'Impossible,' was my husband's rebuttal.

There was no point in arguing. He had an idea in his head bred of generations of indoctrination and segregation of the sexes. Eventually he would see the error of his ways and get used to the innocent mixing of the sexes.

'I don't want you to write to these men again,' he told me.

The next day I got a letter from another male friend, Fergus, a colleague on the *FT*. He was going to travel round Central Asia and wanted to know if he could come and see me. There is nothing I would have enjoyed more than a visit from what I was beginning to think of as 'real people', but there was nothing that was more impossible.

*　　*　　*

Finally things were moving on the bid to reclaim our property. The Oppressed had decided that they would return a sliver of what they had taken; just enough to allow us to buy somewhere to live. But to get the full grant my Mother was required to sign a few papers and show herself at a couple of ministries.

So Mummy was on her way back to Iran. I was terrified because I knew that she would be horrified by her new son-in-law and I feared that he would behave badly. We live by a very basic code of etiquette, one that many a past love had failed to live up to. I could overlook the way Muhammad ate, so never mind if people could hear him munching two blocks away. I had come to overlook the occasional lapse if he forgot to use a tissue when delving into a nostril. The gob still turned my stomach, though at least he wasn't spitting in the corridors any more. But Mummy was not going to be so forgiving.

Muhammad was thrilled at the prospect of his new Mother-in-law arriving. He was like a child about to get a new toy. He kept saying how he had always hated Sepideh's family – even though her Father was his uncle – and he was thrilled at the prospect of having a family he could actually love.

'Let me have a bit of money before she arrives. I want to take your Mother out to the best restaurants and show her Tehran. I'll look small if you have to pay when we go out,' he explained.

How sweet, I thought: he wants to play the perfect son-in-law. So I handed over 10,000 tomans. But what about the car, he argued; he had to fix the car so that it wouldn't fall apart in front of Mother. Some 30,000 tomans later we had covered all eventualities. In less than thirty minutes he had earned three times his monthly salary – but I didn't see it like that. I didn't mention that he still hadn't repaid the 50,000 tomans I had spent on repairs to his car before we had even started dating.

Before Mummy arrived, however, there was one more press conference that I really had to cover. The only handsome and smart minister in Raffers's cabinet, the debonair Ali Akbar Velayati, Foreign Minister, summoned the assembled world's press for a conference at the Foreign Office. This really was a bit of a pain, I had no time for press conferences, with Mummy on her way over, and Muhammad's deteriorating health – he had now lost all uses of his hands and had to be waited on hand and foot to the extent that I even put the food into his mouth on some nights.

It was in a foul mood that I arrived to see the man I had once hailed as the only decent person left in government. More than a year earlier my heart had missed a beat when while interviewing Boutros Boutros-Ghali, the UN Secretary-General, I realised that the shoulder caressing mine was that of the very same dashing minister whose job I lusted after. After the army, the Foreign Office had played the greatest part in my family history, and I had always thought that one day I might hold some office in the ministry – perhaps the top job itself. That looked impossible now, and I resented the man who had watched as Iran lost its international status. Now I despised Velayati, his first sin being that he was one of the 'they' whose existence had so affected my life. It was also obvious to me that he was a mere puppet for right-wing factions who would keep Iran in the dark ages. This was indefensible in a man, a paediatrician, who had the vision and intelligence to know better. The revolution had put the fear of Allah into the hearts of the world's leaders, but Velayati had turned out to be a paper tiger.

Again I waited, half my mind on the job while the rest was planning dinner and worrying about how we would manage the problem of the two wives once Mummy arrived. I would rather have died than let her know what a nightmare I had made of my life.

Someone called for the last question, and I was on my feet and speaking.

'Dr Velayati, during the revolution Iran promised to liberate the oppressed Muslims of the world. Fourteen years later not a single issue in the Muslim world has been resolved; the Palestinians are still oppressed; in Bosnia Muslims are being slaughtered. Would you not agree, in the light of these facts, that your foreign policy is a little tame?'

Silence. Everyone shuffled about uncomfortably. Dr Velayati spoke English so there was no excuse of waiting for the translation. He just sat there looking as if he didn't believe I had asked the question.

'I'm sorry, I don't understand the question. Please repeat it,' he said at last.

I repeated it, to astonished gasps from my Iranian colleagues and a 'Hear, hear!' from a visiting German journalist.

Velayati frowned as he looked at his head of public relations, who was staring at me with fury in his eyes. A half-hearted 'We never promised to liberate Muslims' was the only reply I was given. But as the others left the building, I was stopped by the PR supremo, who warned: 'Ask questions; don't make political statements.'

One of his lackeys lingered beside me as his boss moved out of earshot. Once safe he said: 'You may not mind getting into trouble, but you risk our position when you behave the way you have. This society is not like your world in England. Ministers are very sensitive here. Be careful – I tell you this as a friend.'

All I wanted to do was to put work and politics behind me. I was being beaten into the ground, sinking further and further into solid granite.

Who was I anyway?

At our marriage there had been some confusion over the actual certificate. Our little mullah had claimed that he had to use a document that had been specially flown in from Rashte, a northern province, where the inspectors were a little less vigilant. Now with the imminent arrival of my Mother Muhammad was pressing him to produce the document.

On the morning before Mummy's arrival we drove back down the Resalat Expressway to get our pieces of paper.

As Muhammad read out the document, I signed, not knowing if he was reading the genuine article or leaving out the bad bits. What he read was bad enough. I would be allowed a divorce under fourteen circumstances, but first Muhammad had to sign the document giving me permission to divorce if he became a drug addict; went to prison for more than six months; failed to pay for my upkeep; took another wife without my permission; was unable to fulfil his sexual duties; was unable to Father children; and a whole host of other minor failings. It was Muhammad who was giving me permission to do this; he had to sign every article of the conditions before they became valid. This was beginning to rankle.

There was no time to think about it, Muhammad had to go and get some witnesses, then I had all the shopping to do before the final dusting and hoovering in the flat in preparation for Mummy's early-morning arrival.

By the time we arrived at the airport at three the next morning, I was exhausted. Mummy would have a fit: I looked like an old woman; I had got fat, and my hair was frizzed and had gone the strangest colour after months of neglect. But worst of all was my right hand, which was deformed, the dry skin dangling from my fingers like rotted flesh off some discarded carcass. It could have doubled as sandpaper, it had grown so rough through unaccustomed housework.

The moment I saw Mummy's elegant figure pass through customs

I lost all hope of her ever accepting the ape-like man standing at my side. Beside my Mother he looked cheap, stupid and sinister. From the moment they set eyes on each other the two people I loved so dearly were at war. They were from two different worlds, and both of them realised on that first meeting that each would never be able to live in the other's world.

Muhammad was convinced that I had to become like him, while Mummy knew that after thirty-six years of being one thing I could never be the wife of a man who would one day call me by the name of our first son, as Sepideh was called 'Ahmad's Mother'.

Looking at my Mother I began to realise – to feel rather than understand – just how far my world and my values were from that of my husband. When we had been alone I had followed his instructions, his orders, rather than rock our precarious boat. But I was so embarrassed in front of my Mother.

For three weeks I went between the two trying to keep the peace and to please both parties. Muhammad spent most of that time sprawled out on his back in front of the television. Occasionally he pretended to go out to work just so that he could come home unexpectedly at lunch-time, stand in the middle of the room staring out of the picture window and say: 'Woman, where is my lunch?' Had my Mother not been there he would have gone straight out of the window, but instead I scurried about trying to keep the peace, while he debated the roles of men and women with my Mother.

'A man has certain jobs in the home and a woman has others,' he would say. 'A man does things like lift heavy objects, and a woman cooks and cleans and looks after the home.'

'Not in this world. When a woman works, then both sides have to do their share of the work in the house. Chehreh hasn't been brought up to do housework. She has been brought up to be free and independent for thirty-six years. It is impossible that she will change,' Mummy tried to explain to him, without losing her temper.

'She is a good girl – she will learn,' he responded.

In a pig's eye I will, I thought as I washed the dishes.

For months I had longed to have my husband to myself, to wave him off to work in the morning and to welcome him home at night with a foot-bath. Now I just wanted him to stay away, I prayed he wouldn't come home till late, and my heart sank as I heard the key turn and saw his purple lips come through the door.

But at least he was leaving the flat early in the morning. Or should I say he was making a show of leaving.

Mummy had been in Tehran for just one day. It was our second morning and I was fast asleep in the bedroom while my husband slept on the floor in the sitting-room. On a good day Muhammad would get up at 10.30 and be off to what he maintained was work by noon. But that day he was up at dawn. I only realised he was up when I heard the door slam and then open again as he made a show of coming back for a book before storming out again. As I stood in the corridor with my scarf over dishevelled hair and my coat draped over a large T-shirt, he complained that I was neglecting him, that I had not bothered to get up and have his food ready for him. He said that if I didn't do better he would have to stay with Sepideh, where at least he was the most important person in the home.

'It is your duty to be alert, to be awake before me and ready to send me off to work with a full stomach,' he told me.

I apologised and begged him to come back and let me make him breakfast. 'OK, OK. Please just come back,' I begged, terrified that my Mother would hear, or that it would develop into a row.

Muhammad refused to attend most of the family parties thrown in Mummy's honour. The ones he did attend he did so with such bad grace that I wanted to die. One night we were invited to dinner by Hamzeh. When Muhammad didn't arrive to take us, we called a taxi and left a message for him. Mummy thought he might have had an accident, but I knew him too well by then. Sure enough we were sitting down to eat when he phoned to say he couldn't come. Hamzeh urged him until he reluctantly agreed – quite disgraceful in terms of Iranian etiquette. On another evening he turned up at my uncle's home more than seventy minutes late, then got drunk and disagreed with everything Mummy said – again very bad form for an Iranian son-in-law. I wanted him dead, but Mummy put him in his place with the subtlety and charm that her upbringing had trained her to use. This made him froth at the mouth and I was dragged into a war of wills. I was fighting to convince myself that I still loved this man, and yet I could not fault Mummy on her behaviour or her objections.

How could I defend his behaviour? Perhaps I would have been ready to respect his wishes if he had shown devotion and piety. However, while during our courtship he would stop whatever he was doing to perform his ritual prayers, these had come to a stop the moment we were wed. He drank, he refused to fast during Ramadan and, I was beginning to realise, he lived off bribery and corruption. None of the constraints of Islam for him. On the other hand, I was expected not to drink, not to smoke in public, to give up my male friends, to cover my hair and to perform all the other duties of the good Muslim wife. Worst of all, I was expected to grit my teeth and allow him to take me where and when he wanted me. Then I was supposed to leap out of bed and bring him fruit and sweets so that he could regain his strength.

There had been a horrific night, just after our return from Shiraz, when I had stood over him with a plate of fruit and the large carving knife he liked to use to quarter his oranges. I was tempted, and it worried me as I stood there wanting to take the blade and thrust it into the parts that made him a man. It was not a moment of madness; I was no Loretta Bobbitt. It was cold, furious hatred and loathing.

16

Waking Up

Where is home?

I had had this idea that there was a place where I actually belonged. But where was it? How did I get there and would they have me once I arrived?

Home is where your Mother is.

And home was exactly where Mummy stayed night after night, unless we had a family party to go to. Her new son-in-law seemed to have lost all interest in entertaining his new relative despite the money he had 'borrowed' to do just this. Mummy had been in Tehran for less than a week and Muhammad's constant attempts to order me around had ensured that she thought very little of him.

There were moments when I hated him and others when I pitied him and almost loved him again as he looked like a fish out of his social water. Perhaps his reluctance to join us at family gatherings was due to this mismatch of cultures and incomes. Next to my cousins, their wives and husbands and aunts and uncles, he looked like the cook or the waiter. His twenty-years-out-of-date suit stuck out next to the Paris fashions and the LA casuals.

Yes, I felt sorry for him – until that afternoon when he arrived with a wad of notes in his hand.

'Here, this is for you,' Hubby told me as he handed over the 50-toman notes. Large-denomination notes were almost impossible to get hold of in Iran if you didn't have a friend in a bank.

'What's this for?' I asked.

'It's ten thousand tomans. Our share of the commission from the lawyers' fee,' he said.

'What lawyers?' I asked, genuinely puzzled.

'Your lawyers. This is our share of the commission they pay Reza and Said for introducing you to them.'

I really did not understand.

'The lawyers give us ten per cent,' Muhammad explained.

'Who is "us"?'

'Reza, Said, and me and you.'

'Oh, I see,' I said as the fury welled up inside with understanding. 'I get ten per cent commission on the money I gave them in the first place.'

'Yes,' he said sheepishly.

I wanted to scream at him, to hit him, to stab and bite and scratch him. But Mummy was lying down in the bedroom and I didn't want her to see us having a row. She was already having difficulty recognising me as her daughter.

'Why shouldn't we get a little back? It's our own money,' he argued. 'Reza said I shouldn't take my cut this time, not now we are married.'

'This isn't the first time?'

'Well, no. They gave me a bit every time, but we were not married then. I don't think it was wrong to take it, really. Why not? Why let them have it all?'

'You watched me crying with the panic of whether I could pay them or not, you watched as I went out and sold my rings to cover their bill, and all the time you were getting a percentage? You son of a whore.' Death was too good for him.

'I spent it on us – I didn't take it for myself. Now that we are married I'm letting you have the money. What is the problem?'

'Oh, thank you, my generous husband, my darling lover. Thank you so very, very much for giving me my own money.'

'I suppose I didn't deserve something for introducing you to the lawyers, for helping you get back your money when you had given up hope?'

'You're filth, and you don't even know the difference between right and wrong, good and bad. There is more to morality than not getting into bed with a stranger.'

Mummy came out of the bedroom at that point and I held my tongue. It was five days before we spoke again.

Sleep. I needed lots and lots of sleep. I needed to be in bed where I would be safe. The night before, Muhammad had insisted that I sleep beside him in the sitting-room. His hands had started travelling over my breasts and delving between my legs.

'Stop it,' I had implored, feeling like a prostitute being taken by a client. I was body, not soul, I had frame but it was without essence. I wanted to scream: 'Mummy, help me, save me, stop him! Please, dear God, stop him.' But I couldn't, I felt ashamed at being there underneath this man who now felt like a stranger, this man who had lied to me and who had terrified me into marriage and to whom I had handed power over my future.

'You're my wife, my wife, my wife,' he had murmured.

He hadn't done this, I thought, as he fumbled and fondled; this is *my* fault, this is because of my own stupidity. What had I been thinking of? How had I walked into this situation? It would be better in England; I would have rights in England and he would learn to abide by them.

* * *

Two years earlier I had set out on a journey of discovery; I had explored my history, searched for my roots. I had thought that they would find 'Iran' carved across my heart and I had gone to reclaim my heritage, to discover Me. Now as I stood with Mummy at Mehrabad airport I had not only failed to find my place but I had somehow lost myself somewhere along the way.

Muhammad stood at the airport waving goodbye, and suddenly I realised how very relieved I was not to have to see him again, not to have to talk to him and to listen to what seemed like nonsense to me now. I had been fascinated by what he had taught me about the way Iranians observed Islam. He had been my teacher and I had thought he was all-knowing. Now, deep down, I never wanted to set eyes on him again.

He had cheated me, he had stolen money every time I gave him sterling to change for me, he had betrayed me by taking bribes from my money and worst of all he had lied to me. He had lied about his wife and he had lied about his beliefs. I was married to a stranger and all I wanted to do was to get away.

There had been a moment of panic the week before our departure, when he volunteered to go and book our tickets. He came back with a booking for Mummy, but nothing for himself or me.

'I don't think I can get on with your family. Your Mother is very unreasonable,' he complained. 'So I have decided not to go to England yet, and you will stay here until I am ready to go to university.'

I was shaking, I was crying and all I wanted to do was die, to be rid of the life I had created through my own stupidity. Mummy would kill me, and then she she would kill him.

My nightmare was going to come true: I would have to be smuggled out over the mountains, and even when I got to England I would be caught in this Islamic trap.

I had been crying every day since my Mother arrived, from exhaustion – physical and mental – and from total inability to control my life. I was a broken woman, sometimes angry and determined, then a second later whimpering and pathetic. I was pathetic as I cried in my Mother's arms, as I blubbered and whined and told her how he would not let me go.

It took just over two minutes. Mummy told me to stay in the bedroom when Muhammad came home that afternoon, and after a very short conversation he left to book my passage to England.

'What happened?' I asked amazed.

'Nothing,' Mummy replied.

I never did find out what she said to him and I probably never will, but from that day he looked ever so slightly frightened whenever he was around Mummy.

One of the advantages of our marriage not having been entered into my birth certificate was that I didn't need to produce written permission from my husband to get my exit visa. He could have stopped me leaving by writing to the passport office and banning me from travelling, he could have had my passport taken away by withdrawing his permission for me to hold one. But to his credit he did at least realise just which side his bread was buttered. He too wanted to get out of Iran; and I was his passport.

It was Ramadan, the month when all fit and sane Muslims are obliged to fast from dawn to dusk or risk losing their ticket to heaven. This is a time when tempers flare and mouths smell of hunger. It is not a good time to be out and about, especially if like myself you have a slight tendency to hypoglycaemia and have to eat regularly. As it was early March, the days were already getting longer, but at least it was still mild. When Ramadan falls in one of the summer months, things can get nasty; tempers flare as hunger and thirst set in, and smokers climb the wall.

We, groom and bride, had been out all day doing the little chores that you have to go through to get out of God's Republic. All that was left was to pay my 5,000-toman exit tax at the bank. By the time we got there it was what would normally have been lunch-time and the masses had swooped down on this particular branch of Bank Melli, the national bank, for what was in short supply that year – money.

I went through the glass doors of the bank on the corner of Vali-e-Asr and what used to be Takhte Tavous Avenue in the old days, to find a couple of hundred people in the bank climbing over each other and waving bits of paper in the air, trying to get one of the singularly uninterested staff to serve them. I stood there for two hours, politely queuing to be served at the foreign payments and exit charges desk, while a drowsy teller went through the motions of serving the fifty or so people clamouring for his attention.

In front of me a privileged woman paid for whatever tax or penalty she had incurred with brand-new, crisp and very red 1,000-toman notes – a thing unseen in this bank's recent history. Instead of popping the notes, about forty of them, in the counting machines that had become essential in a country where the shortage of banknotes meant that you had to buy even your house with 50-toman notes, the teller examined each one laboriously and thoroughly. I could have wrung his neck.

By the time I had handed over my fee and had yet another teller enter it into his ledgers and then finally into my passport, my nerves were a little the worse for wear. As soon as we got back into the car, which as is the norm in Tehran had been parked illegally on a convenient piece of pavement, I lit a stale Silk Cut to ease my tattered nerves. We were halfway up Vali-e-Asr when a patrol jeep waved us over and a green-clad defender of the faith got out to order me into his vehicle.

'What's wrong now?'

'You were smoking. Don't you know it's Ramadan, Hadji Khanoum?'

'I am not Hadji Khanoum, and I am sick so I don't have to fast,' came my rather rash riposte.

'Well, we will just go along to your doctor and find out what is wrong with you,' the sly fox replied.

Before I could call his bluff, my husband was grovelling and asking the man to 'forgive' me. 'She didn't realise what she was doing,' he explained.

'Control your wife. It's up to you to make sure that she obeys the law,' the man told Muhammad. I was ignored and discounted as man talked to man, equals in their power over me. Muhammad promised not to allow me to smoke again, and we were off.

Call me stupid, but I was always getting caught eating or smoking or chewing on the streets during Ramadan. I just couldn't help myself; something inside me drove me to sin. Every time I set foot outside the house I had this compulsion to nibble something, and I would go about laden down with crisps, biscuits and sweets.

*   *   *

'Are you happy?' Mummy asked me when we were safely airborne.

'Of course I am,' I lied, far too ashamed and too stubborn to admit that I had been a total and utter idiot. It was wonderful to be going home to freedom, but even then I realised I would never be free while I was married. I wouldn't admit that I had been warned of all the dangers and yet I had gone ahead and married this man and in so doing had broken my Mother's heart. If nothing else she had been deprived of seeing her daughter get married; instead she had to hide her pain at the thought of a hurried ceremony in some hovel. She had to accept that her daughter had been married like a nobody, like an orphan with no one to say: 'This is the daughter of a great woman and an honourable family.'

Sitting there with my hair at long last flowing free for all the other British Airways passengers to see, sipping refreshments and watching the seeds of Western decadence on the screen, inexplicably I felt guilty. I was off to my nice, comfortable life and had no need for Muhammad any more. The love that had been denied me among those strangers was now being piled on by my protective and devoted

Mother, and I was on my way to my friends. I would be safe in a world I understood, and I wouldn't need my guide who had helped me through the maze of Islam and God's Republic. But I knew that I had done wrong and I was determined to create the life of comfort and ease for my husband.

I loved him. Really, I did love him. Couples always have their problems, ours were small ones and we will get over them once he gets out of the atmosphere of Iran, my naïve voice told me.

I was so tired of being serious, of having Marx and Engels quoted at me every ten seconds. It had come as a shock after our marriage to discover that Muhammad had never read these great men's work, but he had simply memorised extracts from 'The Reza Guide to Being an Intellectual', for which my husband's best friend charged 1,000 tomans.

Heathrow was a nightmare. I could have been an alien just landed from Mars, not the woman who had left this very airport two years earlier. Although I had come to hate the veil and would have risked my life to oppose it, suddenly being among so many unveiled women was making me very nervous and physically ill. It was a miracle that I got through without throwing up. Even my sisters struck me as strange, their clothes revealing to an eye that was used to the *hejab*. I hadn't been out in public without my *hejab* for a year; I had even worn it in my own home. I felt naked, I felt cheap and I felt guilty.

So how come I also felt liberated, released and unfettered? The thongs that had tied me had burst as the five-hour flight took me to another world, a world I could at least understand. Being back in England was at once thrilling and terrifying.

Once safely back in Oxford I sat myself down in front of the video and watched a year's worth of *Knots' Landing, LA Law* and best of all *M.A.S.H.*

Muhammad phoned that first night, and I realised I did not miss him. My heart leapt with joy when he said he couldn't come over after all, and then it plummeted when he chuckled and confessed that it was another of his jokes. He promised that he would be in my arms again within two weeks. In the meantime I was to pick Shirazi up form the airport and take him to relatives in Manchester. 'Give him a little money,' Muhammad said. 'He has been very helpful to you and will be again.'

I had already acted as a courier for the particular newspaper that was paying for Shirazi's trip and they had not reimbursed me yet, so I had not planned to throw more money at him. But Shirazi was really very helpful and comparatively honest – he did the occasional favour without financial encouragement. We had been friends, and in the normal course of things I would have arrived at the airport without the veil. But I didn't want to give Muhammad cause to be ashamed in front of his friends, so I donned the *hejab* again, in the car park at Heathrow, and I threw it off as Shirazi's train pulled out.

I was turning into a maniac. I had hated and despised those wrappings that I was forced to swathe around myself, but without them something deep within me made me feel as if I was walking around wearing somebody else's head and in a stranger's body.

I finally made it to tea at the Old Parsonage Hotel, but I felt on edge. My mind was racing, searching for signs that someone was about to appear and catch me doing something illegal. The walls were covered with paintings and prints, there was a wonderful flower display in the lobby and the people were colourful and happy. The women had hair – yes, real live honest-to-goodness hair. It had been a whole year since I had seen hair on women other than those few I socialised with in the privacy of their homes. Now everybody had it, lots of it in all different styles and colours: long hair, short hair, permed hair and dyed hair. I just couldn't take in all this variety in people and inside the buildings, and above all the clothes around me. There are only so many looks you can create with a coat and scarf. I had been used to everyone looking the same. Now everyone was different. I was going mad.

Even today I sometimes have this horrific dream that I am back on the streets of Tehran. As the ghosts of the martyrs march towards me, I suddenly realise that I have come out with bare legs, or sometimes it is the scarf I have forgotten, and other times the coat is missing. I wake up in a cold sweat.

I was like a hunted animal, so used to looking over its shoulder that it was unable to accept that 'they' could no longer hurt it.

Everyone was telling me that I had changed. I expected this from my family; after all it was in their interest to show Muhammad's negative effect on me. But when Corol, a friend from way back, pointed out that I was not the woman she had known, I was shocked and deeply depressed.

'How have I changed?' I asked defiantly.

'Well, you look like you're under the thumb,' she said.

Was I? No, not me – I was famed for my strength of character; I could never be under anybody's thumb.

Could I?

Reluctant to have me accuse them of not letting me live my own life, Mummy and Mahshid offered no opinion on my marriage. However, Said was not so delicate. My brother was not at all convinced that I had done the right thing.

'You're not like yourself,' he told me about a week after my return. 'I have never seen you sit by and not have an opinion on something. You have never been able to hold your tongue. The sister I knew wasn't happy unless she was dominating the conversation. She didn't sit in a corner in a daze.'

He was right: I was quiet, scared of expressing myself.

'Really, sweetie, I want you to be happy. I wish you were, but you are not,' he insisted. 'You think you can live like this now, but you have just suspended all your beliefs. One day you will see that you are still that someone who left here.'

I half-heartedly denied that I had made a disastrous match.

'For heaven's sake, whatever you do, don't have any children yet, dear,' Said urged. He dismissed my objections and my contention that I could look after a child and work while my husband studied. 'Having children isn't a game; it's a serious and very difficult business. You think you can work and bring them up while he studies, but you can't,' my brother argued.

Two weeks after my liberation in March 1993 a very confused me was driving to Heathrow to collect my husband. To be honest I already felt like driving straight past the airport and into a new and husbandless life. It had been an effort convincing myself and those around me that I was missing this man. Would it look strange if we had separate bedrooms?

On that journey I started to understand my dilemma – why I could not reject this man and yet couldn't be as one with him.

When you grow up in another country with another culture, it becomes a matter of loyalty and pride to maintain your individuality, your own Persian – or whatever – identity. But you also grow up with your new society, you absorb parts of your new culture. You cannot help but become a hybrid. Then there comes a day when you are faced with the pure form of your first culture – in my case it was Muhammad – and you see things in your adopted home that conflict with it in the most fundamental of ways. Yet to accept the latter is to betray the former. Before you realise it you are tearing yourself apart trying to be all things to all men, and most difficult of all to yourself.

Somewhere in the middle is a world that we should be proud of being a part of, neither East nor West. We who live between two worlds are a unique people and new culture, and one day we must forge a new identity for ourselves instead of clinging to one culture for fear of betraying it for the other.

I was clinging to Muhammad for fear of losing my Iranian self, for fear of betraying my Muslim identity. In doing so I was killing the medley of worlds that was really me.

He was a vision of vileness, standing there – short, stupid, ugly and tatty. I saw him before he saw me, and I wanted to run, to turn round and run for my life. I had most definitely gone off the poor fool.

Let them tell him I've gone mad. Tell him anything, but don't make me have to be with this stranger again. My voices were at it again.

But you love him, he is your husband, and he is the world's most handsome man, one of my voices tried to convince me while I tried to stifle a cringe as he leapt on me and hugged me to his bosom.

As he stood with that half-wit grin, watching me pay for the car park, I wanted to leave him, his suitcase and his cardboard box and to bolt. We had nothing to talk about while I loaded the cardboard box he used as an extra suitcase into the back of Mahshid's Volvo and made my way through the traffic parked on the M25.

'It's nothing special, is it?' this idiot said as we started to drive through the countryside.

'Look at those lovely trees and the fields – isn't it beautiful, that luscious green?' I said, like a rather bad salesman trying desperately to interest a doubtful customer.

'You should know by now that I don't concern myself with such pleasures. Who cares if something is beautiful of not? I can't tell anyway. Books are all that matter to me, the gaining of knowledge and intellectual growth,' he pontificated.

Surprise, Buster, this is knowledge. This is the world, so have a good look, I thought, as I put on a Springsteen tape. Heaven only knows what he was thinking when he turned off the music again. Was this really the man who had driven me around Tehran with Ian Dury blasting from the stereo? Ironically, Shirazi had been given the tape by the very spy-master so beloved by the minions at Interference. After all he was from the BBC, he had run the British Council in the old days of the Shah and was therefore a bona-fide intellectual, and thus what he liked the boys liked. Me, I was just a woman who obviously listened to music only for its carnal content.

This was not a good start to the rest of our life together.

Once in Oxford it was so obvious that Muhammad would never fit into our way of life that everyone walked around as if on glass, afraid that the odd word or gesture would cause the collapse of this paper world I had created and was trying to hold together with very fragile glue.

'You don't have to take off your shoes,' I told my husband as he passed over my Mother's threshold for the first time.

But he took them off anyway, much to the disgust of my Mother. She had, after all, been brought up with men of a military bearing who took pride in being immaculate at all times. Mummy often told me that when she got married she imagined that my Father would come to bed in his pristine navy suit and starched white shirt. It had taken her some years to reconcile herself to the sight of a man in pyjamas.

That first evening went relatively well. Mahshid was away on a birthday treat at a health farm, which puzzled Muhammad. 'A married woman should not go away on her own. What is she doing there?' he asked. There was no way I could even start to explain how ludicrous his attitude seemed to me.

Thankfully all Muhammad wanted on that first night was to sleep off the flight. We had been put in the spare room on the second floor as far away as you can get from Mummy's room. But he was up at the crack of dawn and trying to pull me out of my nice warm bed. There was a rare glimpse of enthusiasm when he put on this revolting, sky-blue nerd's tracksuit. The navy go-faster stipes down the sides were bobbing up and down as he urged me to join him for an early-morning jog.

The moment we got out of the door he began to bug me. This man who never left for work before 11 a.m. was expressing surprise that there were so few cars around at 7 a.m.

'In Iran people would be at work by now. It is true that people in the West are lazy and decadent. Probably can't get up after their nights of getting drunk and having sex with any girl they can get their hands on,' he announced as we joined the joggers in the glorious University Parks.

I was at home in this green and lovely land. At last I had understood what I was and what I could never be. Those fields, those trees I had climbed as a child, that river I had fallen into on countless occasions – this was me, this was my world, and I didn't want to leave it again.

Things didn't start going really wrong until lunch. Mummy had cooked something delicious and Iranian. But as I walked into the dining-room carrying two dishes while my husband followed empty-handed behind me Mummy asked: 'Is there something wrong with Muhammad's hands?'

Suddenly all hell broke loose, with Mummy saying she had not brought me up to be a servant and she would much rather not watch me act like one, and my husband storming upstairs to get his ticket to book himself on the next flight back to Iran.

What did I do? I went into my room, crawled into a corner and cried and cried and cried. I had been crying for one reason or another ever since I became this man's wife. The day wouldn't be complete without a little outburst. There was nothing else I could do. Somehow my life had taken on a momentum of its own and I was powerless to control it.

Late that evening my husband finally decided to see what had become of me. As a great favour to me, because he loved me so deeply and did not want to see me upset, he agreed to give us another chance. My misery turned to rage.

Day two and we were jogging again, but this time I was treated to the accumulated wisdom on the West as seen by Muhammad after a day and half of intellectual quest. The English were lazy because they did not start work at 7 a.m. as they did in Iran, he announced, passing the glories of Balliol College without so much as a glance.

Should I remind him that his pals at Interference could not be found before 10 a.m., and then only half of them ever bothered to turn up? Should I remind him that in England they worked until six or seven in the evening while he was rarely to be found at work after three? Perhaps better to say nothing; he was my guest after all, and I didn't want to spoil his first visit to the West. I wanted him to enjoy this heaven that we had escaped to.

'It's not as grandiose a home as I had imagined. We will have to find somewhere newly built to live,' this man, brought up in half a room with fifteen other people, said as he jogged around the acre of garden that surrounded Mummy's six-bedroom home just five minutes from the centre of Oxford.

Not wanting to be uncharitable, the new me thought that I must start looking for our own house as soon as we had settled.

It was strange: I was two people. One thought she had to go through with this charade to the bitter end. I had all but given up hope of finding my knight in white armour, and so this man was in my muddled brain also my last chance. Reject him and I had to settle for that other life, the life where my career was my mate and my articles my babies. But articles don't get up and hug you when you are feeling lonely, articles don't keep you company in your old age when your contemporaries are gone.

I had grown tired of all those evenings waiting for the latest object of desire to phone. All those false starts – mainly my own doing – had left me drained and cynical. I just wanted someone to be there to share all the things I enjoyed, and to share my fears and my demons of self-doubt. Someone with whom I didn't have to be strong. There was also a me who did not share a single feeling or opinion with the man who sweated next to me throughout the night. There was a me who wanted to put a pillow over his head just so that I wouldn't have to wake up to his demands for breakfast 'and be quick about it' another time. Instead I had ended up with a man who had been brought up to believe that sex was purely for the boys and that compatibility between man and woman is only measured by the size of their respective genitals.

It wasn't his fault, I kept telling myself; he was after all just the product of our culture. But this caused its own pain as I cringed at the words 'our culture'. I was clinging to a world that my parents didn't even recognise, for fear of losing that difference that made me special. Persia was dead, and I was faced with being part of Iran or being nothing.

'Darling, it's Saturday night. I thought we could go out and I could show you the clubs and discos,' I ventured one evening.

'What for?'

'To see people having fun, have a few drinks, do a little bit of dancing.'

'You want to go dancing? Are you mad?'

'What's so wrong with dancing?' I asked.

He gave me that incredulous look of his, the one that said I was stupid beyond belief. 'It is sinful. People dance so that they can touch one another. It is wrong and disgusting.'

'But we are married.'

'So that makes it all right to make love in front of hundreds of drunk, drugged people? I don't want some man to watch you wiggle your bottom.'

What did my husband do on his first trip abroad? What did this intellectual want to see first? Nothing. Muhammad didn't want to do anything, he wanted to sit at home and read the magazines that he had brought with him from Iran, and he wanted his breakfast, lunch and dinner put before him where he sat. As the days went by the morning jog got later and later and was accompanied with yet more of my husband's accumulated wisdom on the morals of the Western world, of which he assured me people had none. 'Look at her, just look, I can see her pussy through those trousers,' he said as an anorexic jogger passed us in her Lycra leggings and Pembroke College sweatshirt.

Should I have said that in Oxford people's minds are aimed a bit higher than between the legs? No, I really shouldn't have – but I did. For the rest of the day I lived with a deaf-mute. He ignored me; he refused to even acknowledge my existence.

I was also saddled with someone whose arms had not recovered their powers of movement on one side and a family from whom I had to hide the terminal condition of my massive mistake on the other. No one noticed how quickly the sherry was disappearing.

'Let's make up,' he said in bed that night and started climbing over me.

For the first two weeks of his stay I managed to avoid sex. A week of 'that business' was followed by another week of my claiming to have burnt myself. When Iranians go to the loo they do not just wipe themselves with paper; this is a disgusting and filthy Western habit. Iranians, and I imagine all Muslims, have to wash themselves with water, each and every time. Thus reluctant wives can from time to time claim to have got the mix of hot and cold wrong and thus avoid molestation. But now I had no more excuses.

Never in my wildest dreams had I imagined that there would

come a day when I prayed not to have to have sex. Nice Muslim girls were not supposed to do that sort of thing until married, and from the age of sixteen I had longed to marry so I could have regular, legitimate sex. Now I wanted to be sealed up so this man could never enter me again.

'Did I tell you they just released a woman after she killed her husband?' I squeaked desperately in the dark.

'You're joking,' he replied, and started doing unspeakable things to my ear.

'It's true. He had raped and abused her for years, so she killed him in self-defence,' I explained as I slipped out of bed.

'A man can't rape his wife. Where are you going?'

'You can here. If a husband makes love to his wife without her consent she can phone the police and they will arrest him and take him away. I'm just going to the loo.'

I went back up half an hour later to find the room filled with the smell of more cigarettes and the gentle snore of my husband. I don't know if it was the smoke or the man but I rushed back to the loo where I emptied the contents of my stomach. Since then I haven't been able to have a cigarette without feeling all the horror of that night. Overnight Muhammad had cured a fifteen-year, forty-a-day smoking habit. I guess it wasn't all bad.

17

Money Rears its Ugly Head

There was a fair in town and I was yearning to mingle with ordinary people with ordinary smiles having ordinary fun.

'You'll just love it. There'll be lots of rides and yummy things to eat. I want at least ten hot dogs, twenty candy-floss sticks and as many toffee apples as I can manage,' I enthused.

It was late April; spring had come at last, despite the early-morning showers. Our bedroom was becoming like a cage even worse than the bigger cage that had been Tehran. I wanted to go out and feel the wind in my hair and the sun on my face.

After much begging, Muhammad reluctantly gave in. He didn't show the smallest sign of enthusiasm, but he did manage to get dressed and drag himself down the stairs and into my car. Here he remained, refusing to get out even after I had pulled something vital in my neck trying to squeeze into a tiny parking space.

'What is the point?' he asked. 'Look at them, pathetic, thoughtless people only out to enjoy themselves. Look at those women with their bottoms showing for any man to see and their breasts and arms displayed for any man to take. It's a whores' place and I will not allow you to get out.'

Perhaps he was experiencing that fear of freedom that I had felt when I first arrived.

Don't be angry. Just keep calm; try to understand him.

We drove around Oxford, my husband's eyes firmly fixed on the dashboard just in case he saw something that was beautiful or that would fill this tiny, stupid and backward brain with any thoughts other than what lurked between his legs.

I really, really hated him.

Then it happened, in the car park of the Trout Inn just outside Oxford. We were parked looking at the river and he was insisting that he would not get out to have a quick drink. I was in tears, and he suddenly pulled down the car window and hawked a large blob of gob on to that precious earth.

I was livid; I felt personally insulted that this man should pollute the ground which had played such a part in my youth. I couldn't tell him that I had been to this inn with my very first love, Peter, and that it always reminded me of that happy time. OK, I felt a little guilty that I had been more than the mere friends with Peter that my parents had believed me to be.

I had loved those days when we got rid of the 'chaperon' that my Mother always sent out with me and had fled to the Trout. Peter was the most handsome of all men in Oxford – everybody said so – and I lost more than one friend because of their efforts to snatch him away. But Peter had been mine; he had been a Wadham scholar and he had been beautiful with it, and witty, and everything else any woman would want in a man. It had been like a fairy-tale, until my parents realised that there was more going on than friendship and had conjured up a French course at the Sorbonne overnight, sending me away without a word of warning to the man I was head over heels in love with.

It was exactly twenty years later and I was there with this gob-spitting, sex-obsessed idiot whose claims to have gone to university I was beginning to question as I realised the limitations of his intellect.

The handful of people at the Trout that lunch-time were shocked by the sight of a frenzied, not-so-young-any-more woman storming down the stairs of the garden in tears of despair with a white-socked man in hot and now worried pursuit. He was worried and all of a sudden concerned and loving. And, unfortunately, still alive. I emptied the drink he bought me into the river and went back to the car. It occurred to me to leave him there, but I was still not that far gone and he got in beside me as I drove up.

Then I was hit by guilt again. I was being cruel and nasty and I was ruining his last chance of happiness. He wanted to talk and

I agreed, pulling into a picnic area by the river a few yards down the road. We were walking hand in hand and I summoned up the courage to broach the question of fun.

'Please, darling, don't be so stubborn. We are on honeymoon, we are finally free of all the restraints of Iran, let's have some fun,' I argued.

'Fun! That's you all over, isn't it? All you think of is having a bit of fun, while the poor of the world are suffering. How can I have fun while there is suffering, while there are still people who are poor? I feel it is my duty not to have fun, to always think of the plight of those who are oppressed and desperate,' he said.

A family were passing by on a boat along the river. 'What do you see when you look at those people?' Muhammad asked.

'A happy family having fun together,' I replied.

'You don't see the poor little girl, do you? You rich are so selfish that you close your eyes to suffering,' he said.

'What suffering?'

'Look! Use your eyes!' he almost shouted.

'All I see is a Mother, a Father and four very happy children,' I said, knowing full well what it was he thought he saw that I had missed.

'The little girl has no right arm,' he growled at me.

'So? She looks happy enough,' I replied.

'How can she ever be happy? She is a mutant . . . her life can be nothing but worthless. She will have nothing but pain,' he told me.

'Rubbish. So she has lost her arm, that doesn't mean her life has ended. People here don't look down on you or write you off because you have a disability. She has as much chance of a full and happy life as you and I,' I said.

Despite the increase in the numbers of disabled brought about by the war with Iran and the efforts of the regime to integrate them back into society, the 'Life-Sacrificers' were still seen as people to be pitied.

'That's very easy, isn't it? Justify your own indifference by dismissing her pain,' he said, beginning to get on my nerves.

'Unlike you I have not sat around feeling sorry for them. I have spent my life trying to actually do things to make the world better. That's why I became a journalist, to try and change the way condescending people like you get a kick out of feeling virtuous by pitying people,' I said with a calm that belied the fury within me.

'What have you ever done?'

'Lots of things, but I don't shout about it.'

'I've never seen you do anything. You don't even read the papers. You are just like those ignorant village women who know nothing of the world and can't open their mouths without putting their husbands to shame,' Muhammad said.

Could this bumpkin really be saying these things to me?

Muhammad was very, very lucky to survive the day. My fury had no bounds. I was angry but too tired to try and defend myself. How did I come to be married to someone who thought so little of me?

That night he had the nerve to suggest that we start on the making of a baby. My explanation that Said had persuaded me that it was too soon for us to start a family didn't go down too well, and the honeymoon now entered two days of total silence.

'I am going back to Iran,' Muhammad announced the next morning.

Glory be! was my first reaction. But no sooner had he given me his ticket to book his flight than I was overcome with a dreadful feeling of failure and of guilt. He had come over with so much hope, he had so much to see and so much to experience, and all I had done was to snap at him and treat him like an idiot – which he was; which made me even more responsible for him. So I begged for forgiveness; I promised to do better, to never snap at him again, to listen to him and to act like the wife he wanted me to be.

At last he agreed to some fun. He had, reluctantly at first, been persuaded to come out for lunch and a tour of the Oxford colleges. I was like a child, the smallest thing suddenly bringing happiness where moments before there had been only despair. Pathetic as it may seem, I did actually fear the end of this nightmare. This intelligent woman whom many considered determined and wise, and to whom others came with their problems, had given up hoping for anything better. She was defeated and unable to perceive anything in her future but to see out this relationship till one of us killed the other.

Oh joy! We were going out to lunch. I could show off my new status as wife.

'You're not coming out like that?' Muhammad asked.

I was wearing blue leggings and a baggy, long-sleeved, thigh-length Laura Ashley shirt.

'The whole world can see everything you've got,' he laughed.

'But this is England, it won't make any difference,' I pleaded.

'You still don't understand, do you? You are my wife and I am a Muslim man and I say what you wear and what you don't. Now go up and change,' he commanded.

I was dumbfounded. What had happened to the man who had asked me to wear the veil because 'these Iranian men are uncivilised', because it was the custom and it could affect his promotion prospects if his wife were seen without her proper *hejab*. There had been no talk of a lifelong commitment to the veil.

'I didn't say you had to wear your coat and scarf,' he said in justification. 'But there is a limit of decency and you have crossed it.'

'Why are you two still here?' Mummy asked.

'We are just going, but I have something to do,' I said. Then I went upstairs, and dragged on an ankle-length skirt and a long-sleeved, thick, button-up blouse.

'Do all the buttons up,' the monster commanded as we left the house. I had only left the top button undone and the rage was sending spasms of pain through my ever more nervous stomach.

I could not eat much as we sat in Brown's so I just watched Muhammad stuffing his face eyeing the lovely blonde who served us.

'See, there is nothing sexual here. Our waitress is in leggings but she isn't inviting you to sleep with her,' I pleaded.

He cast me a glance that said: Oh yes, she is.

I should have told him not to flatter himself, but I just picked at my tuna sandwich.

It was quite obvious that he had no interest in anything I showed him that day, only getting animated when it came to taking photographs that he could show people when he got back.

'Open a few of those buttons,' he instructed as I posed for a picture next to the lake at Worcester College. 'I must remember to separate this when I show them to my Mother.'

'Oh, you're going back now, are you?'

'We have to go back to get your money and to sort out Sepideh and the boys,' he explained. 'I want to make sure they have enough for at least three years while I am away getting my doctorate.'

'Didn't we just decide that we would stay here?' I protested.

'Only while I study, darling. I've always told you that I wanted to become a minister. That means that we have to go back, and you have to learn to behave like the wife of a minister in the Islamic Republic of Iran.'

I said nothing, but something inside me died as I contemplated a lifetime under the veil. I fought hard to accept the idea, but I just couldn't do it. I didn't believe in it and I felt insulted by it. The last few years had been a long and hard slog of work, work and more work with nothing in my private life but death and sorrow. There could be no life for me without pleasure, beauty or personal freedom.

'Let the men wear the veil and I'll accept it gladly,' I had told Goli a lifetime ago when I had still been that other woman. Despite all the arguments that men also have to dress decently in Islam, they still went about as much as ever. Imam Khomeini had even issued one of his famous *fatwas* to allow football players to wear shorts, but no such *fatwas* were forthcoming for female athletes. Women still played tennis at the former Imperial Country Club wearing their scarves and long coats and swam in the Caspian fully dressed with *chador* and trousers. We had turned ourselves into a laughing stock. Purity is within your heart and in your mind, and not dependent on how wrapped up you are. Let the men avert their eyes if they can't look at a woman without getting an erection.

I told my husband how I felt as we strolled by the lake. I told him that those restrictions were due to the smallness of the minds of those who impose them.

'I suppose you would say that to Dr Shariati,' he said. Dr Shariati was the guru of resurgent fundamentalist Islam.

'Yes, if he spoke such rubbish,' I replied.

Muhammad was struck dumb. He stared at me and shook his head.

'What?'

'Dr Shariati was a great scholar. What he said is beyond question,' my intellectual husband argued.

'Rubbish is rubbish no matter who spouts it,' I responded.

'It's not your place to question the great men of philosophy,' he enlightened me.

There was no use; we were not even on the same planet let alone the same wavelength. When there are no common parameters there is no structure within which to argue one's case. There is nothing more restricting to intellect than acceptance of norms, but there was no way I could persuade Muhammad of this. He had been brought up in an education system where you are taught to memorise and regurgitate, not to read and evaluate.

We had been walking for less than an hour and Muhammad started to moan and groan, claiming he was exhausted and wanted to go home. On the walk back I took the full weight of his body on my shoulders as his arm squeezed round my throat and he gave up all real effort to walk, allowing me to drag him the two miles back.

Now when I see lovers with their arms round each other my heart sinks and I feel so sorry for the poor woman having to tolerate the yoke of love.

I was cured of smoking, of sexual desire and of romance.

*   *   *

I was getting more and more exhausted by the strain of being with Muhammad twenty-four hours a day. He clung to me like a child terrified of being parted from his Mother. When I cooked he stood next to me – shoulder to shoulder – until I wanted to scream for him to get away. He had been talking to me all day. My mind was tired beyond any exhaustion I had ever known, but he had shirts he needed to have ironed and thus I was at my station.

How would he react to a request to go back from whence he came? Wasn't he telling me day and night that he wanted to return to Iran, that his factory was going bust and he needed to be in Shiraz to raise some money?

I had made two mistakes during those early days of our 'honeymoon'. First I had allowed him to let me persuade him to send his passport to immigration to extend his three-week visa. I am still curious to find out why, of all the Iranians who have come to visit us since the revolution, my husband was the only one not to get leave to stay for six months. Did they know something about him that I didn't? Then, exhausted by a night of tossing and turning and worrying that his factory would go down the drain, I had promised to give him the money – just as soon as a certain paper paid me back for the money I had spent on Shirazi's ticket and spending money. In exchange Muhammad had promised that I would be his only wife, that he would finally end the farce we had been living for the last six months. I had not asked for this, but it was my only chance for at least some shot at happiness. Or at least less misery than would otherwise await me.

Now as I slaved over a hot iron I was getting worked up over the amount of money he had managed to make out of our relationship. At least if I was paying then I shouldn't have to do all the work. On the way home from Heathrow we had stopped off at the cash machine for £200 – so that Mother wouldn't think he was living off me. This had been the last I had seen of this cash, since I paid for everything we did; for every meal, for the new Marks & Sparks shirts and suits and shoes, for the train tickets for him to go and see friends in London and in Manchester, and for presents for Mummy and the rest of the family. It would have been rude for me to ask what he had done with the money he had been supposed to have spent on entertaining Mummy when she was in Iran. It would have been un-Iranian to suggest that he pay the bill when we went for tea or lunch or dinner. It would have been expensive – for me – to suggest he return the hospitality of my sisters and brother by taking them out for a meal.

Even then, as I fumed with the thoughts of how much he had used me and how stupid I had been to be used, he wouldn't leave me in peace. He followed me and sat there delivering his lecture on the corruption in the West.

'We can't bring up our children here,' Muhammad finally pronounced.

'I was brought up here and I didn't turn out so bad,' I countered.

He laughed. 'You watch that trash on television and don't even realise it is muck, and then you say you have turned out OK. To think I almost gave up Sepideh for your sake!'

'Almost?'

'There is no way I am making her – a woman who has never shown a strand of hair to another man – unhappy just because you are too unreasonable to accept your place.'

'Why, you promised,' I gasped.

'That was when I thought you were worth it. But your behaviour so far has proved me wrong. I know now that you are not worthy of my sacrifice,' he said without a glimmer of emotion. 'You'll only make me hate you more if you cry,' he snapped as I started to weep.

He was pure ice: there was not an ounce of warmth or love in the face that stared at me as I crumbled in front of him, rolled up in a ball, sobbing. It was never going to end. He meant it when he now declared that England was out of the question and that he planned to take both his wives and his children to India, where he would study, Sepideh would look after the house and children, and I would teach English to make money.

'Don't cry,' he said, his voice suddenly soft and repentant.

I flew into his arms and sobbed and sobbed till his shirt was soaking with tears and stained with mascara.

'You'll have to wash this tonight,' he said, looking at the stain.

'Of course, darling.'

We had a fairly good week after this. I was meek and respectful and he strutted and pontificated on his overwhelming urge to study. I rang around the country and got quite a little collection of university prospectuses. But Muhammad paid them no attention; he did not even open one – not what you would expect from a fanatical academic.

Thus we came to another row, as the mouse that was me gave way to the woman who said 'Hogwash' when she heard it.

Why hadn't he shown any interest? Simple, really: choosing a course is nothing to make a fuss about; he would just pick something when the time came to apply.

'But you have to look at the courses, see what you want to do and where you can find the course that suits you best,' I spluttered.

'That's not how academics do things. We just want to study and it doesn't matter what we study, all knowledge is good,' he announced.

'I've lived in a city where the world's greatest academics have come and gone and I'm not exactly an illiterate myself. You really have to take this more seriously if you want to get anywhere,' I pleaded.

'Who cares about the course? I will do anything that I can get a place to do. International relations, politics or something else like that. Anyway, we have to go back to Iran first, so what is the point of looking now? I'll read them all when the time comes.'

What was the use? We were a million miles away from each other.

*   *   *

During the last few months in Tehran I had taken on some consultancy work for one of the world's leading caviar distributors. In the old days the entire supply of Iranian caviar was under the control of my second cousin. She was a wonderfully eccentric lady who lived in an elegant North Tehran home with a hundred or so cats who were fed primarily on caviar.

Now, back in England, the managing directors of the caviar firm and its parent company arranged for me to meet them in Paris to discuss future tactics. It was not the sort of work I liked to do but with a husband and several of his kith and kin to support there were few other options. It had not occurred to even the new me to check with anyone before agreeing to the meeting in Paris. Why should I refuse when I was charging by the hour and had a couple of French meals to look forward to? Muhammad didn't quite see it that way; he was furious that I had agreed to go without his say-so.

'You can't go, and that's final,' he told me. 'Go and tell them you are not coming.'

'But why not? I don't understand. We need the money,' I protested, while he stood in our attic room looking at me as if I had committed some unmentionable sin.

'My wife is not going to Paris to meet some strange men on her own. Don't you have any idea of what is proper and what is indecent? You'd do anything for money, wouldn't you?' he asked.

'I have a very good idea of right and wrong and I still don't see anything in what I am doing that is wrong,' I protested.

He got up from the bed, where he had been studying some Oxford University Press English-language books that Mahshid's husband, Donald, had brought home for him. My husband, in his go-faster tracksuit, made his way round the bed to where I was standing beside the door. He stared into my face and leered as he said:

'How many times do I have to tell you before you learn, you stupid woman? When men and women go together it is for sex and only sex. If you go there alone you are asking them to fuck you.'

My jaw dropped. 'Are you completely mad?' I asked.

'*Me* mad? You and your rich family and your disgusting corrupt English friends are the mad ones,' he shouted.

'Don't you dare call my family mad,' I screamed. 'I told you the first day I met you that I would excuse anything but I would not allow anyone to insult my family.'

Muhammad grabbed my arm and jerked me towards him. Before I could react he was shoving me towards the bed. He was on top of me and tearing at my clothes. I lay there struggling without much success. I saw his throat within reach of my teeth and longed to sink them into his flesh and rip and tear until it came away and the veins spewed out. I imagined him lying below me twitching for life as the blood spurted out. Funnily I began to enjoy this fantasy so much that I quite forgot about what was happening to me.

He was smoking again and I wondered if they would really put me in prison for beating this jerk to a pulp. It was good to feel the aggressor rather than victim and I believe this was a turning point in my road to escape.

Suddenly I heard my Mother at the door. We both panicked as she called my name over and over again. Had she heard something? Once again I began to feel ashamed and dirty.

'Chehreh!' Mummy called from just outside the door.

'Yes,' I replied.

'Phone call. Couldn't you hear me calling?'

'No, sorry. Who is it?'

The last thing I wanted at that moment was to talk to anyone.

'Your Father,' Mummy said, and made her way downstairs again. MY FATHER!!!

I hadn't heard from my Father in almost ten years. He still lived in Oxford, but we had fallen out after my parents' divorce. I suppose he blamed us children for not stopping her getting a divorce, but he knew better than anyone that there is no stopping Mummy from doing what she considers to be right.

What was I going to say to him? 'Hello, Baba, my husband has just forced himself on me. Can you please come and sort out my life?' How could I say anything; how could I ask him to save me from this man after ten years of silence?

Save me, Daddy, come and get me out of this mess like you always used to is what my secret voice said.

'Hello, Baba,' is all I could manage without crying.

'How are you?' he asked.

'I don't know,' I murmured.

'Better come and see Baba, don't you think?'

'Yes.'

'Tomorrow at two o'clock, and alone, Cherry dear, please?'

'Yes, Daddy.'

The visit the next day was the most traumatic meeting of my life. All the emotions of the little girl who had lost her Father welled up as Baba met me at the door of his house and led me in to hear the Persian song 'Kiss Daddy, for you are my life' on the stereo. It was our song, and all of a sudden I just wanted to be free of the husband I now knew I could never make a life with.

*　　*　　*

When your wife refuses to co-operate, best to show her who's boss. Muhammad demanded his marital rights yet again.

'It's the middle of the day. Everyone is up,' I argued.

'Never mind. What do you think they imagine we are doing up here anyway?' Muhammad asked.

The thought was sickening. 'It's been a really hard day for me. Just let me have a little rest,' I pleaded, to no avail.

Never before, despite the many times he had taken me against my will, had I felt quite so sick, so naked. I had just seen my Father for the first time in ten years, for heaven's sake. This was a small girl who had found her lost Daddy.

I really, really wished Muhammad dead.

Daddy had asked me to take Muhammad to see him a week after our own meeting. Ever since we first met, Muhammad had expressed a desire to meet my Father and had constantly asked for his address so that he could write or go there himself, even if I didn't want to go.

As Salman Rushdie learnt later, there are some people whose address you never give, no matter to whom. For fourteen years many members of my family had lived with the fear of the death squads. The world recoiled with horror at what Rushdie had to endure, but many Iranians were already quite used to flying halfway across Europe and back, changing planes, trains and trams before going to see a relative in hiding for fear of leading the mullahs to their targets.

Muhammad wanted to see all my family, he had told me. The exiled sons of a former Minister of War and his cousin and successor were top of his list. I may have been stupid, but not that stupid. It was painful to realise that although I had loved this man I was so suspicious of my fellow Iranian that I felt I had to hide these people from him.

For three days before the appointed meeting of new groom and Father-in-law, Muhammad demanded that I make an appointment for him to have his hair cut. My inclination was to have his head cut off so I ignored the request. After all he was a grown-up, he could find his own hairdresser. Finally, the morning of the meeting arrived, and as Muhammad stood washing his teeth at the sink in our room I asked what he wanted me to lay out for him to wear.

'I'm not coming,' he snapped through a mouthful of suds.

'What?'

'I'm not coming. I asked you to get me a haircut and you didn't, so now you have to be punished,' he said.

'This is another joke, isn't it?'

'It's no joke. Now shut up and leave me alone.'

'But my Father is expecting you – he'll go mad. It's an inexcusable insult, one that will mean we will never be able to live as husband and wife within my family again. Please don't be so silly. Get dressed and let's go, darling,' I begged.

'I told you that you have to be punished,' came the stubborn reply.

My patience snapped. 'To hell with you. I'm not your servant. Get your own appointment,' I said.

Who would have imagined he could look so violent and evil? 'I tell you day and night that I want to be your slave, that I long to serve you. It isn't ever my duty or place to be *your* slave. Why can't you do what it is your place to do?' he fumed.

'I have no time for your ignorance,' I said, leaving the room.

Downstairs I told Mummy and Mahshid what had happened.

'Leave him, Mummy, he isn't good enough to be in the same room as my Father,' I protested, fearing a massive row if Mummy told him to go and he still refused.

But to my surprise no sooner had Mummy called for him not to be so foolish and to come along than he was downstairs with his tail between his legs. 'I'm ready,' he said.

Muhammad was wearing an old pair of once beige but now threadbare greyish-yellow cord trousers that his other wife had massacred by putting in the washing machine. His shirt was unwashed and un-ironed, and he wore green mud-caked shoes – he must have brought them that way from Tehran, for I had not set eyes on them before. Over this fashion statement he wore a black leather jacket – a present from Mummy.

The Rolls was gleaming as we drove into the drive at Father's. Daddy came to the door, his security system alerting him to intruders before the car even came to a stop. He was immaculate; his suit, shirt and tie screamed quality. I just wanted the ground to open and swallow me up. How could I have brought this ruffian into his family, as his son-in-law?

Muhammad – thankfully – had lost the use of his tongue and merely nodded and grunted in response to Daddy's conversation. For most of the visit he stared at a spot on the Persian carpet.

As Daddy showed us out, an hour later, he looked into my eyes with a look that said: Get rid of him.

Back home it was more of the silent treatment, which came as a relief. The night I went up to get ready for bed and something stuck to my foot. It was a massive lump of gob; the bastard had been spitting on the floor in the bedroom. For the next couple of days I felt too disgusted to eat.

*   *   *

It's not the sort of thing a girl likes to advertise, but for some years I have had rather an embarrassing problem. In the normal course of events I would rather have died than to have alluded to my twenty-year battle with haemorrhoids. But it so happened that they became the part of my anatomy that eventually gave me the breathing space in which to make one of the most difficult decisions of my life: to swallow my pride and admit that I had made a real mess of my life and needed the help of all those who had told me not to do it.

I had gone to Dr Finnigan, my GP since I was a child, with a list of ailments from crippling pains in the general area of my ovaries to my lack of energy and chronic listlessness. He sent me to Mr Gilmere, a gynaecologist in a totally different class from the troll that had examined me in Tehran. Dear, clean, polite, charming and professional Mr Gilmere was happy to inform me that there was no massive tumour, but that I had an infection which I had acquired either by sleeping with someone other than my husband or by his sleeping with another woman. At no time did he put his arm round my shoulders nor make cutting movements against my groin to illustrate the point. I had escaped the world of the troll.

Had Muhammad been lying? Was he still sleeping with Sepideh?

Of course he was; there could be no other explanation. But I didn't really care. He was something from that alien world that I had escaped. I was safe and free and nothing would be that bad again. Nevertheless I confronted Muhammad with this revelation. But he swore, on his children's lives, that he had no sexual contact with his other wife. Secretly I began to wonder if Reza had been telling the truth when he claimed my husband also had another *seegheh*.

Blood tests showed not only infection but anaemia, which was due, it was concluded, to constant bleeding from the piles. Surgery was called for and yet another charming specialist, a certain Mr Mortensen, concluded that a little banding was called for.

The day I was to go in to have this excrutiatingly painful treatment, my husband took pity on me and started talking to me again as if we had not been daggers drawn for the last week or so. Muhammad had griped at my being treated by a *man*, but by this time I had very little time for him and spent most of the day snapping at him. He finally came to terms with Mr Mortensen coming into unholy contact with my posterior.

Whatever you're told, don't believe them when they tell you banding does not hurt. I have never, ever gone through such overwhelming pain. A quick in-and-out and it was done and I was sent home. Not one to bear pain well at the best of times, I took to my own bed, a bag of ice strategically placed to ease the anguish.

Muhammad removed himself to our new room to 'learn English' as Mummy and Mahshid ran hither and thither. That night I slept downstairs within shouting distance of my Mother, but the second day Muhammad popped his head round the door of my old bedroom to inform me that I was expected in his bed that night.

Two days of popping mega-powerful painkillers had left me slightly dizzy and more gaga than normal. As Muhammad and Mummy watched TV that second night I lay dozing on the chesterfield. That night my husband woke me to tell me it was time for bed. He was kind and very gentle as he took my arm and led me upstairs; I could hardly keep my eyes open. Once upstairs my understanding mate started pawing me and talking, talking, talking.

'Please let me sleep,' was all I could manage, while he carried on talking and pawing.

Finally sleep won the day and I passed out, regardless of the muttering going on beside me. The next morning I was once again married to a Trappist monk. Muhammad refused to leave his room, did not want anything to eat – although he consumed the eggs, bacon (forbidden to Muslims) and toast breakfast and the rice-dish lunch I took up to him.

No matter what I did he refused to talk to me or to give any indication as to what I had done wrong. Was he ill, Mummy wanted to know. Yes, I lied, too embarrassed to tell her that this creep was playing the hurt Pasha. I was quite unable to work out what had happened to cause this rift. I thought and I thought but couldn't come up with a reason. We had been fine the night before, he was talking at me when I went to sleep, so why was he doing his deaf-and-dumb act now? In bed again that night he regained his powers of speech long enough to inform me that he had expected sex the previous night and blamed me for falling asleep on him.

'Sex!' I gasped in genuine surprise. 'How could you have expected sex? I was dying of pain and half asleep all day.'

'You had a day to recover. You should have thought of my needs,' Muhammad informed me.

'It had not occurred to me that you would be so insensitive as to expect me to do anything in my state, let alone that. I can't sit, I can't go to the toilet; I can't even cough without pain. How do you imagine we could have sex?'

'Like this,' he said.

The pain was beyond anything I had ever known and it stayed with me for months after he had finished.

I look back on that anguish as the pain of rebirth. That night he killed any love that still lingered, and any pretence of passion. From that night he rarely got close enough to touch me. Not only did I start to plan how to separate myself from this monster that night, but I also started on the road to becoming a Born-Again Virgin.

Just let me get rid of him and I will never ever let another man touch me again, I bargained with God.

This was not a marriage arranged for me by my parents. On the contrary, I had chosen this man, and yet lying beside him night after night I knew that it would take a miracle for me to be able to have a normal, physical relationship again. Then what of many of my sisters in Islam back in Iran and other countries where millions of women are married to men they hardly know? How must they feel when they wake in the middle of the night and find their bodies covered in the sweat of a husband they had accepted in deference to their culture and in respect for their parents, but for whom they feel only a deep loathing?

18

Farwell, My Darling

Walking had become a major problem and so the next couple of weeks were spent at home in front of the television. Muhammad liked few of the films I tried to introduce him to, dismissing popular classics such as *Brief Encounter, Farewell, My Lovely, Some Like It Hot* and *The Maltese Falcon* as inferior to those produced by the Iranian film industry. *West Side Story* was a waste of time and Elvis couldn't sing. *The Godfather* and *Goldfinger* went down a little better, and westerns were much appreciated.

The entire family had gathered one Sunday towards the end of April when I foolishly decided to introduce Muhammad to *The Rocky Horror Picture Show*, a film I know backwards and to which I turn in moments of depression for a little boost. Even my ultra-conservative brother-in-law, Donald, had come to appreciate this splendid cult film. But Muhammad was appalled; he cringed and winced in his seat and finally got up and stormed out, saying he could not stand any more of this filth.

No amount of trying to explain the importance of exploring sexuality could convince Muhammad that the film wasn't just an excuse to promote homosexuality. He claimed that if men were exposed to acts of bisexuality they might try it and then come to like it and become homosexuals. He made some unrepeatable comments about the sort of people such as my family who would sit around and watch such filth.

The wrath he inspired in me had me actually worried that I might do him a physical injury. Talking was no good. Perhaps a clout round the head would make him see sense. Sense was something he could not see, but he saw sex everywhere – places where your average full-blooded male would be hard pressed to find sex.

We were watching a rather fine performance of *Swan Lake* when Mummy asked Muhammad if he still contended that he saw no beauty in art.

'It is very nice – if only they hadn't spoilt it by putting in the sex.'

'Sex? Where was the sex?' I asked in astonishment.

'Look at the way the men are dressed – you can see their penis and balls bulging through. Don't tell me that isn't because they want you to see their sex,' he said.

'Their sex?'

'It is just an excuse to look at parts of the body that should not be seen. They are half naked and they have their hands all over those women, feeling their breasts, fondling their bottoms. Men and women should not touch unless they are married, you know that.'

'I suppose that next you are going to say people cannot go dancing together,' I said, having quite forgotten that he had banned outings to debauched discos.

'You haven't danced with a strange man, have you?'

'Lots,' I giggled.

'Well, you will never do it again. I won't allow my wife to behave like a whore,' he said, the colour rising in his cheeks.

He must have been joking; no one could object to just dancing. But he wasn't. I learnt this when, while flicking through a photo album, he discovered a picture of me dancing round the garden with Charlie, a boy I had known since I was twenty and he was a seven-year-old at the Dragon School with my eldest nephew, Nader. I was obviously having an affair with Charlie, Muhammad told me. There was no telling him any different.

Things did not get better when Charlie turned up to our first family dinner. Mummy and Mahshid could not understand Muhammad's foul mood during the party. Nor could they understand my unease around Charlie, who, having spent most of his childhood with our family, was being as affectionate as ever. I was in such a state of confusion that it didn't even occur to me that my husband couldn't understand a word Charlie said, as my friend reminisced about our wild days of summer frolicking in my MG Midget. We were a team in those days, Nader, Charlie, Nick, Mike, Fergus, Dom, Sally, Sarah and me; and a handful of other boys from St Edward's. I loved them all, every single one of them, but they were just boys thirteen years younger than me.

Muhammad could not see this, they were men now, and I had the opportunity, so something must have happened. Why had we made such a fuss over Charlie's as yet unpublished book on his years in Japan if he wasn't my lover, Muhammad wanted to know. 'No one mentioned the six books Said has written, but you all went on about this boy's book.'

'Exactly!' I screeched at him later in our bedroom. '*This boy!* This *young boy* at the threshold of his career! That is why we made so much fuss – to encourage him and to show our support.'

'Why would you want to show your support to a strange man?'

'Forget it,' I said, resigned to never being able to explain to him that friendship can occur without sex.

We saw Charlie again at Mahshid's home. This time Muhammad was looking for signs and I was backing away from any possible contact with him, which was not easy as he was in a nostalgic mood and spent the evening recalling stories of how we had painted the town red. I even felt uncomfortable kissing Nader and my other nephew, Cyrus. Dear, sweet Charlie went on and on about the gold Lurex leggings and sparkling, skin-tight tube-tops. What fun we had, and what a nightmare I was having as Muhammad watched our every move. Nader and Cy looked on in amusement as the story got more and more exaggerated.

A few stiff brandies, a new discovery for Muhammad, and he was mellowing and getting into the mood of the party, abandoning me to sit and listen to Corol's teenage daughters tell stories and fall about with laughter. They were all a wee bit tipsy. The danger seemed to have passed, Muhammad had not turned the furniture upside-down over my talking to Charlie, and by the time we got home he was swaying happily.

'We are never going to go to any more parties,' he announced as he staggered into bed.

'Why, sweetie? Is your head hurting?' I joked.

'I feel sick,' he responded.

'Shall I get you something? A bucket to throw up in or something to ease your stomach?'

'I am sick at the behaviour of the people at the party and ashamed that I was a part of it,' he explained.

'What behaviour?' I asked, growing more puzzled.

'It is warped – men and women together getting drunk and slobbering over each other. We must never go anywhere where there is drinking. From now on we will only drink when we are alone together.'

'We must have been at different parties. I saw no bad behaviour,' I snapped.

'I had to kiss those girls goodbye; it's not proper. Before I met you I had never even touched a strange woman. Now I am forced to shake hands and kiss them.'

'Who forced you?' I asked, but he was already in dreamland.

The next morning I made a joke of his comments, putting them down to his being drunk.

'I was serious. That, my darling, was your last party.'

I had been holding on like grim death to this relationship, afraid of losing my last chance at being part of a couple, but it had lost its appeal. I no longer much liked this being part of anything; I wanted to be free to come and go as I wished. We were jogging when Muhammad told me he had decided that we should go back to Iran to live. He claimed that he could not stand being so far away from his children and that he could see no way of supporting the family in Iran and us in England. My husband explained that he could not bear to live at my home; he wanted a home where his word was the law.

'I want to go now. What am I going to do about the money for my factory? I can't raise if from here. I've already been away from my job for too long. They only gave me two weeks holiday. If I lose the job, then I will never make up the money I need,' he lied.

I had suspected that he had not gone to work for more than two months before we left Iran. Either he had been sacked or he had left to live off me; or his work was to be with me.

Suspicion is a terrible thing: never being able to trust and to confide and to depend on even your nearest and dearest. Perhaps it was a legacy of the double life Iranians had led when conquered by Islam – Zoroastrian in private but Muslim in public. We evolved into a race that hides its real self. The Shah had encouraged this double life by turning the nation into either spy or spied upon.

Here I was, not knowing if this man who shared my bed was my husband and lover or an informer who would one day betray me and my family. Was he here to make a life with me or to track down the minister, the general and many others in hiding to whom I could have led him? There was no love as I understood it, this I now realised. There was no desire to share and no respect for me as a person. The only thing we shared was my bank account.

'Will you stay if I promise to pay all the bills, if I buy you a nice private house and if I buy and cook the food? Will you be satisfied if I send money to Sepideh every day? How much does she need, tell me. Will one hundred pounds a week be enough? What about three hundred to make sure she wants for nothing?' I screamed at Muhammad as he made his way round the duck pond in the University Parks.

'I have never, never taken a penny from you!' he shouted back as a woman and her dog hurried past the foreign lunatics screaming at each other in the park.

'When did you ever pay a penny towards those meals I cooked for you and your friends? When did you pay back what I spent on your car? Where did you get those clothes you wear every day and the money to come to England? When did you last pay for anything?' I had fallen as low as I could get.

'You make me sick. All you ever think about is *your* money,' Muhammad spat out, turning on his heels and making for home.

He was right: I had behaved badly. My Mother would be shocked to hear me mention money; it was unladylike, and it had been cheap.

That night we slept apart and in the morning I woke to find that his lordship had gone off to the May Day celebrations on his own. I was bitterly disappointed, and offended. This was my home, my celebrations, what I understood and what I had looked forward to. And here I was left at home while he went off and enjoyed himself.

Could he possibly be having fun?

It was a very furious wife he found later that morning sipping her coffee among the revellers who were rounding off the festivities in Brown's restaurant. Going to Brown's on May Day had become a family tradition, but it had been a couple of years since I had been able to join in, and I had thought about that morning with longing on those lonely nights in Tehran when my husband was doing heaven knows what with his other wife.

331

On the walk home we fell into step beside each other. Muhammad turned and smiled that 'you-are-forgiven' smile.

'All I want from you is a divorce,' I snapped.

We were not to speak again until bedtime, when he whispered in my ear that if I slept alone again he would never let me go, but if I played the game in front of my family I could have the divorce I had asked for.

The next few days passed in a series of reconciliations and new arguments. First he couldn't live without me, then he didn't like the way I spoke to him. One minute I was his only hope and his last chance at happiness, the next I was some sort of ignorant woman who would put him to shame in front of his family. In truth I was nothing, reeling between hope and despair – a puppet who danced to whatever tune was playing at the time. I had no time and no patience to play the good wife any more, but nor did I have the willpower to stick to my guns and resist Muhammad's manipulative style.

I needed some firm, quiet ground on which to sleep and to think and to find who I was and what I wanted to become.

Most of our rows centred on his version of Islam and its role in the modern world. We spent three early-morning hours arguing about covering oneself during the *namaz*. I have no idea how we came upon this subject but I do remember being infuriated when Muhammad said no woman could be saved if she did not say her *namaz* properly covered, so that nothing but her face was in view.

'But why should she cover herself if she is alone? You can't argue that she has to be protected from the danger of rape when she is praying in the privacy of her own room,' I argued.

'When she is at prayer a woman is vulnerable – a man might sneak into her room and see her and take while her she is praying,' he told me.

'You really have a filthy mind,' I retorted. 'Does everything have to centre around the possibility of sex?'

'It is your world that is filthy. The women are all whores available for anyone to take,' he said.

I really did not have the energy to argue that old chestnut again, so I turned back to the question of prayer.

'Let's say no one can get into the room, then why must a woman cover herself up?'

'Because she is in the sight of God. Her sex must be covered.'

'God made her. He is not going to be turned on because he has seen her body, is he? For heaven's sake do something about this small mind of yours. Try and look beyond your stupid and limited world. Use your brain. You say you want to learn and to improve . . . Well, start doing that, start thinking for yourself,' I said in exasperation.

'It's not just me who says this. Dr Shariati wrote . . .'

'Then he was as big an idiot as you are.' I turned to leave him to sleep on his own.

There was a vast gulf between me and this man who now represented the culture I had wanted to return to. He had nothing to do with the Persia that I loved and respected, nor did he have anything to do with the world in which we were living and in which our children had to live. There had to be a new way, a way that the people of the East could be themselves to honour their culture and still be part of the world of humanity, and to grow and thrive in contemporary society. I could not even begin to understand a world where I had to hide my nakedness from God. It made no sense: these were the prejudices of men, not the words of the true God in whatever form you might choose to worship.

On one of the rare days when we were talking, Muhammad said he wanted to see London – well, he wanted to see the Iranian opposition groups at Speakers' Corner and he wanted to look at the Iranian Embassy. It was Saturday, but he insisted we went anyway, even though Mahshid assured him there was nothing to be seen in the park until Sunday.

Muhammad was like a child on a day out at the funfair. He wanted to sit next to the window on the train. It was sweet.

We were walking down Kensington High Street – or Little Tehran as we Persians call it – when the man in front of us was hailed by a couple standing outside Bakers.

'Abbas Agha,' the woman called in Farsi. 'Abbas Agha, how wonderful to see you again.' Soon the three were exchanging greetings and pleasantries. Muhammad stopped to read the banner the couple had put across the ground.

'They are opposition. Let's talk to them,' he said.

As we waited, the pleasantries turned to insults and the miniature woman, in a very grubby white jacket and with the worst dental work

I had ever seen, started to shout at the very Abbas Agha that she had greeted with such respect only moments earlier.

'You people have betrayed us, you are the servants of the British,' she screamed.

'We have actually done something for our nation, unlike you, madam. You are just a cause of embarrassment,' Abbas Agha screamed back.

The woman's companion, a six-foot stick insect with a three-foot moustache and a ton of grease smeared on his long spider-like fingers and under his long nails, now joined the shouting match, accusing Abbas Agha of being a British lackey.

'We have fought the British all the way. We brought down the Thatcher government and it was us that plunged Britain into this recession,' the woman claimed. 'We have destroyed England while you eat from its backside.'

'Leave me alone, you madwoman. I have no time for imbeciles like you,' Abbas Agha said. As he walked away into the department store, the woman continued to harangue him.

'Who do you support?' Muhammad asked the woman.

'We have no leaders. We support only a free Aryan Persia,' the man said.

The woman introduced herself as Gity and the man was Hamid. They were Zoroastrians and were working towards removing the 'stigma of Islam from the sacred Aryan soil of Iran'. In other words they were complete nutters. According to Gity, the British were behind all the world's ills and she had single-handedly destroyed Britain's power. There was just one trick left up Britain's sleeve.

'They have brought this Rafsanjani to fool us, to make us think that things are better so we go back,' she said, baring her ill-fitting capped teeth and waving two stubby hands in the air. 'Once we are all back in Iran they will drop an atom bomb and wipe us all out. Why else do you think they have kept Saddam in power? They are doing all this to destroy us,' she ranted, her yellow-grey eyes bulging.

'So why are you here?' I asked, remembering Abbas Agha's parting comment that she was not too proud to take sanctuary here.

'Twenty years ago the Shah gave England twenty billion dollars to take care of Iranian refugees. We are just getting back the money that is ours,' she explained.

'Who do you support?' Muhammad repeated time and time again. 'Where are your headquarters? How many members do you have?' he continued.

I started to get irritated. What did that matter? He should be talking to them about what they said, not getting details to add to the Intellectuals' File of Facts and Figures. Or perhaps he wanted to pass on the information – but surely there were enough spies here at the embassy already; they didn't need to send someone from Tehran who didn't even know the language.

Muhammad soon tired of his quest for Iranians and we made our way to Leicester Square for a Mexican lunch and then on to Madame Tussaud's. He loved the waxworks and had his photo taken next to President Clinton and Yasser Arafat.

Next we went to Covent Garden, a place he could not see the point of. A magician-cum-comedian busker was starting his act and we joined the crowd that had gathered around him. I really thought Muhammad was learning to enjoy himself. He was smiling at the man's antics and gasping at his tricks. Then the hapless performer called for help from the audience and grabbed the arm of a rather attractive young woman in a mini-skirt. As she joined him in the centre of the crowd, he kissed her on the cheek, and all at once I was sitting next to the masked avenger.

'Let's get out of here – it is a whorehouse,' my spouse said as I persuaded him that he would land in prison if he rushed to avenge the maiden.

Then my devout Muslim husband found a bar and spent the rest of the day downing Mexican beer to ease his irritation. It was a very merry Muslim that I guided back to Oxford in the evening.

That night I warned him that if he so much as touched me I would call the police. The next day he said he wanted to go to Iran. I repulsed his attempt to kiss and make up that night, and the following day we went to the Home Office in Croydon to get his passport back.

As we sat on the train on our way back to Oxford, Muhammad told me that I had been a great help in Croydon and he was grateful. In return he would continue to act on my behalf in Iran by dealing with the lawyers working to get my money back.

'Thank you, but I can manage my own financial affairs from now on.' I may be stupid, but I was not quite that stupid.

Our marriage was over, I knew it. All I wanted was for him to be gone and for me to have some time to recover before I thought what to do next. But he was still here, still breathing and grunting next to me.

Then next day Muhammad spoke to me just once, to ask that I go shopping with him for presents to take back to Iran. We shopped in silence as he bought well over £150-worth of gifts – mostly women's clothing – on my credit card.

He could have anything, just as long as he went and went quickly. By the end of his shopping spree I was so angry that I put him in a taxi; after more than two months in Oxford he still could not work out the five-minute route from the town centre to Mummy's home. Then I started doing some anger shopping of my own. As a result I am the proud owner of some pink pyjamas – one size too small – three pairs of M&S shoes, twenty pairs of underpants from the above and more brassières than there are days in the week.

Muhammad was booked on a flight a week later. But as the date of his departure approached he started to make affectionate overtures and I began once again to panic at the prospect of the day I would have to go back to Iran and be alone once again.

'Come with me,' he said, with tears in his eyes. 'I won't go without you, you know that, don't you? Tell your Mother that you are coming back with me,' he pleaded, and my blood turned to ice. For the first time in my life I was scared about my future.

'You know I can't come. I have to go for the last check-up for my piles,' I argued. 'We have already paid for the operation and it's not right yet.'

Reluctantly he agreed to leave without me. 'I'll have the money from the lawyers for you when you return,' he assured me.

The day he left I cried all the way back from Heathrow to Oxford. I wept tears of relief.

I knew that I would never get back into Muhammad's bed, but I could not face the upheaval and scandal that a divorce would cause. But to my surprise it was with even greater relief than mine that my family heard my decision to leave my husband. Said did not mince his words in giving his opinion of the match I had made and Mummy told me not to give a moment's thought to what people would say. But it wasn't easy, this splitting up. One day I was bloody, bold and resolute, and the next I was unset jelly.

Muhammad phoned every other day to find out when I might return, and I fobbed him off with the excuse of my aching piles, which I reminded him would have been all right if not for him.

'I hate to ask, but can you send me some money?' Muhammad asked. 'I haven't paid the instalments on the Tehran house for ten months and I'll lose it if I don't pay up. If it goes, Sepideh will have to live with me.'

'Never mind, you said yourself we would go to India and live together anyway,' I replied, no longer caring how many wives he slept with.

The next phone call brought a new tack. This time he needed £500 to save the factory, without which he would never be able to support me. 'You will have to spend the rest of your life paying for me,' he oozed.

'It will be my pleasure and my duty, darling,' I replied.

I should have told him I wanted to end our marriage, but it's not that easy, even when you wish your husband nothing but harm and pain. What an evil person I had become, to contemplate with pleasure the possibility of Muhammad being caught in, oh bliss, a sausage-making machine. Anything that would damage his body the way he had damaged my mind.

Only now I realised how wonderful it was not to brace yourself every time someone put his hand on you, just in case he was in pinching mood. How glorious it was not to be afraid of your husband walking in behind you and giving you a shove on to the floor – just as an affectionate joke.

'I still haven't seen the specialist,' I lied to Muhammad.

Then he started to click. 'The lawyers said they couldn't tell me anything about your money. Phone them and tell them I am handling things. They said they were instructed to talk to no one but you and your Mother. Do you realise how insulting and degrading that is for me in front of my friends and my family?'

Finally the Oppressed found a little cash, and coughed up a fraction of what they had taken. When the money was safely out of Muhammad's reach I told him that it had been paid.

The next day Reza phoned. 'Muhammad promised to pay ten per cent to our friend who introduced you to the the lawyers,' he told me.

'This is the first I have heard of it,' I replied, very angry but no longer surprised.

'Didn't he tell you? I told him to get it in writing but he said he would pay up, that he was our friend and you were his wife, so we did not need anything in writing,' Reza said.

'I am really sorry, but he never told me. Anyway he was just a friend from work when we first went to the lawyers, he had no right to make any promises,' I said, using his excuse for having taken his share of the backhander from my legal fees. 'If your friend wanted a cut he should have come straight to me. He should have mentioned it when he took me to negotiate the lawyers' percentage,' I insisted.

'But he trusted Muhammad,' Reza argued.

'Well, he will know better next time,' I said, calmly, although I was on fire inside. 'Furthermore, who in their right mind would agree to pay ten per cent in return for negotiations to reduce the bill by eight per cent? I would have been better of paying the full bill to the lawyers.' They really did think that I was stupid.

The next day it was Muhammad again – from my flat on the phone I had to pay for.

'I promised them ten per cent,' he insisted.

'Tough, you should have asked me,' I replied.

'You were my wife; I could speak for you,' he argued.

'Well then, you pay them the ten per cent,' I countered. 'Look, I may have been stupid, but I am not dumb. You all got your cut out of the money I paid to the lawyers. If I had known you and your friends were getting a percentage of the fee I would never have let you negotiate it for me.'

My darling husband and my so-called new Islamic friends were trying to rip me off; all their support and help had been to get a cut of the action. It was really disillusioning. No wonder so few Iranians trusted each other.

I, for one, will think twice the next time I have any dealings with my countrymen, even though I know many very good and honest Iranians and more than a few non-Iranian crooks. It was this betrayal by people who had shared bread with me that hurt. Did I blame them? How could I imagine what one would do if one were poor and had no prospect of getting any richer?

I was tempted to send them something, but first I wanted my divorce, so the next time Muhammad called I bit the bullet and asked for my freedom.

'Never,' was all he had to say on the subject. But he had plenty to say on how he had destroyed himself financially in order to be with me in England and how I now owed him money to live on.

'Let me see if I can get some money together,' I told him, still feeling guilty for no good reason.

My feelings of guilt soon turned to rage when Mrs Mo phoned to say that the management committee at my flat had given her my phone bill. When I left Iran I had settled my bill, which had come to 20,000 tomans for six months of use – mostly for work. Since Muhammad had returned he had created a bill of 48,000 tomans in calls not only to me in England but to his brother in Sweden, and heaven-knows-who in the States and in France. Mrs Mo also told me that my video was missing from the flat.

Muhammad had asked if he could lend the video to Shirazi over the Muslim New Year holiday, but he had said that Shirazi had returned the video and the twenty films he had hired for over ten weeks on my account. Mrs Mo had also been landed with the bill for the hire of the films – 250 tomans a week for each film, making it a massive and unbelievable bill of 50,000 tomans, five months' salary for Shirazi. And, at the prevailing rate of exchange at the time, an equally massive £200 for me to clear up, not to mention the embarrassment to me in front of Mrs Mo. Add the cost of the missing video (illegal but available in Iran) – the equivalent of £400.

I had been taught to be generous and that it was cheap to ever mention what you had spent on anyone, but I was so angry and hurt by Muhammad's demands that I constantly thought about the money he had made off me day and night, and he still wanted more.

*   *   *

The one thing of which I was certain was that I could not afford to go back to Iran until I was free. Some nights I lay in my safe and warm bed in Oxford and longed for the excitement of dicing with death on the streets every time I took a taxi.

I was even willing to go back under the *hejab* just to be able to walk down the tree-lined avenues of North Tehran one more time and to smell the smells and see the sights of the Middle East. More than ever I wanted to help this country find its place in the new world, to balance the values of the past with the pro-gress of the twentieth century.

But I could never hand over control of my private life and my actions to another person again. Neither husband nor state would tell me how to dress and how to speak and especially how to make love. I could no longer even try to accept a morality where I could be rewarded for killing Salman Rushdie but would be given seventy lashes of the whip for shaking his hand.

It was clear that Muhammad was not about to give me a divorce, so I turned for help to the Iranian Embassy in London. Yes, they agreed that I had been tricked. Yes, it was an illegal marriage because I had not had my Father's permission and Muhammad had not told me or the mullah that he was already married. Yes, it was illegal for the mullah not to register the marriage in my birth certificate. Yes, I was, nevertheless, legally married and, yes, he had grounds for refusing to give me a divorce. Yes, if I got a British divorce they would register it. But, no, they would not certify my marriage – which I needed to prove I was married before I could file for a British divorce.

Why not?

Because it was not in my birth certificate and I had not had my Father's permission.

So was I married at all?

Oh yes, I was definitely married.

How could I get a divorce, then?

'Get your husband to divorce you. But I advise you to return to your husband,' the man told me over the phone.

If I managed to get a British divorce and it was registered by the embassy, would I be free?

Yes and no. Under international law I would be divorced and free to marry again anywhere in the world but in Iran, where the divorce would not count under the divorce laws of Islam and so although I would be free of his control I would not be free to remarry.

Perhaps a bit of coercion in Iran would do the trick. I sent my wedding certificate to Minu and asked if she would please talk to the mullah and persuade him to annul the marriage. Of course I wanted this to stay between the two of us.

Before you could say D.I.V.O.R.C.E. half of Tehran knew the details of my disastrous marriage, but nothing was happening to end it.

Homa sounded ever more depressed during our frequent calls as she tried to be all things to all men. Her own pain was increased as she tried to deal with Maman Joon, who was in Damavand but constantly phoning to complain about the gardener's wife, who Maman Joon said had tried to poison her. Auntie was going to Tehran to sort it out and also agreed to pack up my flat for me.

'I am terrified of Tehran,' she told Mummy. 'Every time I phone I pray that Mother isn't constipated and that she hasn't frightened off another maid. I pray that Nastaran hasn't been rude to anyone and there isn't a new family feud.'

It was early in October 1993 when the phone rang out in Oxford at seven in the morning.

'What's happened to my Mother?' Shirl's hysterical voice came over the line as Mummy blinked awake.

'What?' Mummy asked.

'Something has happened to her, but no one will tell me what it is,' she screamed.

'No, it can't be Homa. Perhaps it's *my* Mother. Is my Mother dead?' Mummy asked.

'No, it's *my* Mother,' the wretched woman groaned.

'Perhaps it's Ghodsi; perhaps she has tried to kill herself again.'

'It's not Ghodsi. My husband said something terrible has happened to my Mother, but he could not bring himself to tell me what. You know, Auntie. I know you know. Please tell me what has happened,' she cried.

'Honestly, I have heard nothing. If something had happened to Homa I would have been told. Don't worry, nothing is wrong; perhaps she has gone into hospital to have the tests for her heart murmur,' Mummy said in desperation.

By this time both Minu (who was out of Iran by now and staying with us) and I were in the bedroom. As Mummy put the phone down she collapsed. She was limp and shaking. I called Mahshid and started to ring Tehran to see what had happened, while Minu tried to reassure Mummy.

'Don't,' Mummy instructed. 'I cannot take any more. I don't want to know.'

Shirl phoned an hour later to confirm that her Mother was dead. She had taken her own life. That very night, as Auntie Homa died in Shiraz, a terrible explosion had destroyed the home in which my grandfather had spent his last years.

341

It took several weeks to piece the story of Homa's last hours together – well, to piece some kind of story together.

Somehow I imagined that, if we could find out what had happened and why, we could change it or stop it. Homa dead was something that I could not comprehend; it had to be a lie or mistake that could be put right.

That dreadful October morning Homa was back in her southern home and Dada Jan had gone to collect Maman Joon from Damavand, who was going to Shiraz a little late that year. Homa was due to join her in Tehran, where they had an appointment for a visa at the British Embassy. But by the time Dada Jan and Maman Joon arrived back in Tehran, Homa and his house were gone.

Uncle had inherited the family home on the death of my grandfather more than forty years earlier. This was not the home that had been known as the Pessian Palace, a home that Reza Shah had demanded be given as a gift.

The Pessian family had moved into the new house, a few years before Grandfather's death. They had not moved far, just a few yards further along Pahlavi Avenue. When Dada Jan took very early retirement – at thirty-two – he built on the prime land along the avenue. These buildings he rented out at a pittance to anyone with a sob story. At the time of the fire the shop next to the house was occupied by a kebab restaurant and takeaway. There was no mains gas, so the owner, who paid a mere 3,000 tomans a month for a site worth twenty times that, prevailed on Uncle to let him store the restaurant's gas tank in his garden.

The day Homa died, piped gas had come to that stretch of what was now Vali-e-Asr Avenue and the restaurateur wanted to remove the tank from his landlord's garden. This he tried to do by putting a rope round the tank and then running the rope over the branch of a giant tree at the top of eight stone stairs that led up from the lower garden and servants' quarters to the front drive. He then proceeded to pull the tank up the stairs, step by step. The rubbing of metal against stone created first a hole in the tank and then a spark that ignited the gas still in the massive tank.

The fire raged through the house, destroying everything in its path.

Three days earlier, in Shiraz, Homa had spent the day preparing for her trip to Tehran, a trip she dreaded. She had a bath and had given herself a manicure and pedicure. Then she had phoned her youngest daughter in the States to wish her granddaughter a happy birthday. The child was still at school and Homa had promised to phone back. She had then gone to collect a dress she had had made to wear on her trip and then gone on to the hairdresser's.

There had been a party that night and it had gone well until the Fat Man starting mocking Homa's intended trip to England.

'You wipe your Mother's bottom here and you will do exactly the same thing in Europe,' he had taunted her.

That night, when Homa and her husband got home, they had fought, according to a friend who had spent the week at their home. What about is unclear: some say Homa wanted to move to somewhere better and blamed her husband for having squandered her fortune; some say she had asked for a divorce and he had laughed and told her he would never give her one and that he would stop her travelling to the US to see their children; others claim that she had discovered that he had fathered a child by a young, married woman who had been brought up in their home.

Before she went to bed, Homa had a call from Maman Joon, who had become worried at her daughter's cracked voice. Homa had claimed to have a cold and said she was going to bed with a couple of pills. Her husband had stormed out as she had tried to continue their row and she had gone to bed.

When the Fat Man returned he slept on the settee in the sitting-room, according to Badri, Auntie's lady-in-waiting and an all-round bitch. The next morning Homa was not up as usual at six, but no one bothered to check on her. By ten the maid was worried and went to wake her mistress. She found my magnificent aunt in a coma, surrounded by empty pill bottles and a half-empty bottle of vodka. But she was still alive.

Instead of rushing her to hospital the Fat Man called a doctor who was a family friend, an ear, nose and throat specialist, to treat her at home. He had wanted to 'save face' and avoid the shame of a suicide. This was a bit strong coming from a man who had already been in an Islamic prison for debauchery; a man whose young wife had discovered him in bed with a maid renowned for her repulsive looks; a husband who took every chance to slip his hands under the skirts of guests, who was so lecherous that Homa's friends and family feared staying with them in case he should try something.

Three days later Homa was dead. The last entry in her diary read: 'I have taken some pills. No one is to blame. I am just tired of being good.'

My sorrow at the news of Homa's death soon turned to anger. Life had become almost unbearable since we lost Bahar. How could Auntie have done this evil, horrific thing? How could she have added another tragedy to the catalogue of disasters that had befallen us? I was so angry with her, so incredibly angry. It is strange to feel rage against a dead person, a person you had loved. But with suicide sometimes anger is the only way of surviving the loss. Someone I loved very much had been murdered, but the killer was the very person that I had loved so much.

Homa's death made me realise the fate that had awaited me at the end of a life with Muhammad. I knew that I had done the right thing and been saved just in time. I had escaped before I was so worn down and exhausted that I took refuge in drugs, booze and possibly the ultimate refuge from the misery of life – suicide. I had made my bid for freedom before I was so far in that I could not get out and before every door closed in my face and all hope had gone.

19

Beyond the Republic

The question remains in the air: 'Why?'

Why did a beautiful, intelligent woman who could have rid herself of her husband and gone to live with her daughters in the States choose suicide instead?

Why did another intelligent and successful woman, Homa Darabi, a psychiatrist and a leading member of the Iranian Nation Party, set herself alight on a busy North Tehran road in a desperate attempt to highlight the plight of her countrywomen?

Why did six young women burn themselves to death in just one week in the tiny mountain town of Damavand?

Why have so many other women chosen death by their own hands? Why have they chosen to crush the spirits of their kin, the break the hearts of their Mothers and to leave their children alone to meet their fate?

Some of us take pills to end the agony, while a mere five hours' flight away some of us can get our due, some of us can walk away with more than the clothes on our backs.

Raffers did try to introduce a law giving women the right to half their husband's assets after divorce, but it still has to see the light of day.

When the Majlis debated the question of greater rights to divorce for women they concentrated on expanding the list of circumstances under which a woman can have a divorce. One of the main points of these debates was the question of when a man can be judged not to be able to provide his wife with adequate sex. A great step forward, finally acknowledging that women have some say in sexual satisfaction. The law even lays down the size of the man's penis smaller than which he is considered inadequate.

You have to feel sorry for men; for, after all, they are no more than the size of their penis. They are their Mothers' 'Golden Cocks' and if they fail on that front they are also nothing: 'worth less even than a woman,' my Mother-in-law explained to me once.

We stay and we suffer because we have no option, because we are trapped by the laws and the culture that expect us to be women and to be wife and Mother. And also because women such as Maman Joon still believe that if a man hits his wife she must have done something to provoke him. Because young women with Western educations still tell me that a woman who disobeys her husband is no woman at all.

Iranian men are not the only men who think they have the right to hit their wives; they are not the only men who cheat on their wives or lie to them. It is not only in Iran that women are put into hospital by the fists of their mates.

Several years ago I worked with a lovely young woman at an advice centre in Oxford's Rose Hill council estate. She walked with the help of crutches and would do so for the rest of her life. She still could not understand why her husband had started beating her when he got home from the pub that night. She only remembers waking up after the operation and hearing that he had crushed her hip and both legs and broken her jaw. He had gone to prison and she called herself 'the amazing plastic woman'.

Muslims will say: 'Aha! You see the evils of drink.'

Yes, there are many evils; anything can be evil in the wrong hands if you are not taught right from wrong. Not all drunks hit their wives and not all sober men are saints.

When some men read in the Koran that they may hit their wives they don't read on to see that they must not leave a mark nor hit her on the face or about the head. They read that they can have four wives and forget that they must treat them equally.

There is an old man who is a legend in Shiraz. He has four wives who live in separate houses in a large enclosure in the village he owns. Every day they get together to help prepare the home of the wife whose turn it is to have him that night. They help to bring up each other's children and to make clothes, to cook and to carry out all those duties of a Muslim wife. A male friend of mine was so impressed that he visited the man and asked him what his secret was. How did he manage to maintain so much harmony between these women?

'It is not difficult,' the man said. 'If one of them displeases me I beat them all.'

What, then, of the poor and the oppressed, for all this was about them – wasn't it?

Mullahs now drive around in the cars that were part of my Father's fleet of 'toys'. I heard with my own ears the leader of the revolution, the Fragrance of Khomeini, explain that they did not enjoy going round in the latest Mercedes or BMW. He explained that they had to do so because there were so many enemies of Islam who would destroy the revolution by killing its leaders. So these leaders had to be protected in bullet-proof cars and these only came in luxury models.

*   *   *

I couldn't stop thinking that somehow I had contributed to my aunt's death. She had been very worried that the failure of my marriage would plunge me back into the world of depression and gloom. Every time she phoned she would remind me to be careful not to give up on life. Was she telling me that she had given up?

Sometimes it all becomes like a dream and I can almost imagine Auntie Homa whistling like a canary as she arranges flowers or helps the cook with lunch. Then I remember how much I hate her, because that is the only way I can cope with the fact that she is not there.

On a good day Bahar is in her Caspian studio painting to her heart's content.

There is chaos in Iran. These people, my nearest and dearest, seem to have been driven mad by the madness of the nation around them. No laws of behaviour or decency seem to count any more, and families, once solid in support of each other, turn on each other.

In the middle of this mess Dada Jan's second wife has had another stroke which left her face lopsided. Four years earlier she had suffered a massive brain haemorrhage that almost killed her. She might have been saved two months of intensive care and partial paralysis if someone had believed her when she said she had a headache that was 'killing' her. If they had not dismissed her as a hysterical woman, she might not have partially lost her power of speech.

If his Mother had not found him a 'suitable wife from a noble family' my uncle might have married the woman he loved and not had a life of misery which ended in his first wife, Soraya, dying a 'failure' who only managed to produce a girl. Perhaps his house would not have been a dark and lifeless place for more than thirty years. As a child I could not understand the deep sorrow behind Soraya's hazel eyes. She was of that class that bore their pain in silence. Her fragile body turned on itself as she became the victim of a rare disease. It took her ten years to die. She died in God's Republic, her exit visa refused because the state did not recognise her disease. Now Uncle's second wife is going the same way, but her stroke had left her a little loopy and she is blissfully unaware of her pain.

*　　*　　*

There is a mountain road into Shiraz where weary travellers get their first glimpse of the city. Over the road there is a monument containing the Koran under which the visitor passes before going down to what was once the most stunning and prosperous city in the East, the city that was the heart of the great Persian empire which spanned the known universe. Today those entering the remains of that empire should be faced with a sign warning: 'Abandon hope all you who enter here'.

There was a day when I believed the words sung by Janis Joplin: 'Freedom's just another word for nothing left to lose.' But life has taught me that there is much more to it than that.

Freedom is something I found again the day Muhammad got on that plane and went back to Iran. It is the right to talk to another human being without fear, to walk in the streets without dread and to love whom you like, when you like, without terror.

Freedom is getting up in the morning and not wishing that you were dead. It is looking at the man beside you without wanting to scream. Freedom is the day they open the ballot box and the paper that is taken out corresponds to what went in.

I am free. I can paint my nails any colour that my heart desires without being called a whore. I can look through pictures of my punk stage without fear of being judged. Freedom is being with someone who can understand that you shaved your head or dyed your hair bright red because it was fun. And being with someone who realises that goodness is what is within and what you do to other people, not what you wear and how you speak.

There are days when I remember and I want to explode. I think of the man who lied to me and his first wife and who then told us to like it or lump it. I know that he still thinks he is good and headed for heaven, while some woman will burn in hell just because she went out of the house without her husband's permission.

But my freedom has a price: I am an exile from my beloved homeland; I am trapped as the wife of a man who says he will not consider divorce, who urges me to return to Iran to talk. Or if I am 'afraid' to meet him there then we could meet in a neutral country to talk over our problems.

I am free but I am also a prisoner: a prisoner of fear. The fear that imagines I am coshed over the head in some Delhi hotel and smuggled back to Iran to spend the rest of my days imprisoned in some nomadic tent with some man that I now detest taking me whenever he gets the urge.

I can see his family sitting there outraged at the suggestion that they would make me do anything against my will. A lifetime ago I would have spoken up for them. But can I risk it?

When the system is such that women are seen as the property of men and are advised to stay in their kitchens and obey their husband, who would save me if I trusted them and was wrong?

'Women can see men without getting excited but men can't see women without wanting to have sex with them,' Muhammad would explain to his dim-witted 'Westernised' wife when she argued that she would wear the *hejab* if men also wore it. For men such as Muhammad the word 'Westernised' was synonymous with 'prostitution', not only culturally but morally. I could have told him that women get just as excited at the sight of a nicely formed bum or a winning smile, and even a good haircut could make the heart leap. I could also have told him that there is such a thing as self-control and discipline, that morality is not avoiding temptation but being able to resist it.

Before I had left Oxford in 1991 I had felt a pang of comradeship as I saw the growing number of women wearing the Islamic *hejab* on the streets of England. Now it raises my blood pressure; I want to drag their scarves off their heads and shake them till they see what a disservice their choice is doing, not only to their fellow women but ultimately to their faith.

The very religion they wish to glorify is dying under the weight of hypocrisy and ignorance. It is withering in the thirteenth century and if we don't help to drag it into the twenty-first it could die. If we don't start to love rather than to hate, if we don't start to show the merciful and compassionate God instead of the avenger, we could damage our religion beyond repair.

Very early in my time in Tehran, President Rafsanjani made a speech that gave us all a faint hope. Addressing leaders of the Friday prayers from throughout Iran, he urged them to look to the modern world in their sermons. He argued that the youth of the nation needed more than prayers and threats, they needed entertainment and they needed hope, and above all they needed to embrace science and the modern world. He argued that if the regime went on as it was 'our youth will turn on us and they will turn us out as they did the regime before us, and we will be left with nothing'.

The next day Ali Khamenei, the Vali-e-Faghih, the omnipotent jurist of Islam, reintroduced the lapsed Muslim Duty of *Ambre-be Marouf va Nahyeh az Monkar*. Strictly speaking this just meant that every Muslim had the duty to point out the sins and mistakes of others and to show them the right path, but everything was bigger and better in the Islamic Republic and the instruction was interpreted by Muslim commentators as the go-ahead to inform on each other. The boys at Interference were instructed to grass on their colleagues if they failed to say their ritual prayers during the day, or did not observe their fast during Ramadan and so forth. Women were once again stopped in the street, but this time it was by their fellow women rather than the morals police.

Surely no one can ever have questioned the principles behind these morals police, or they would have scrapped them on the first day. I remember on that first post-revolution visit to Iran the son of a former cook had joined up as a Pasdar and been put on what he called 'pussy patrol'. In the days of the Shah the boy had prided himself on looking like Alain Delon and boasted at the number of women who threw themselves at him – so why on earth had he turned Islamic?

'Can you imagine a better job for a hot-blooded man?' he had asked me in reply to that very question. 'I get to dress up in this really neat uniform and carry any gun I fancy. All day I get to drive round in a powerful four-wheel-drive jeep with a bunch of my friends, and if we see a woman who looks particularly attractive we get to pick her up with the blessing of the state. The dowdy ones always get taken in, but the savvy ones know there are ways of avoiding being banged up for the night,' he said with a wink and a nudge.

Even when these all male patrols were followed by a carful of the Sisters of Zahra, the boys managed to have their fun.

'We send the crows out to round up the women and then we sit them in the jeep and give them guidance. If they accept our guidance and hand over a little incentive they get to go free and we tell the crows that they saw the error of their ways,' the boy had boasted.

He had been most put out when they had transferred him to the 'Michael Jackson' patrol. These rounded up the lads who were copying the style of their American hero – so it was not all bad I guess. From time to time these patrols rounded up men wearing short-sleeved shirts as the sight of bare arms was supposed to incite women to sexual frenzy, but on the whole men are safe.

*   *   *

Muhammad has realised that he will get nowhere by talking to me, so he has turned to phoning and writing to my Mother. Every few weeks or so he calls or writes to 'say hello' and to thank her for all her kindness.

Ten months after our separation his youngest sister and brother phoned me. I could not face prolonging my association and they were fobbed off by Mahshid. They had phoned to ask me to come back and be with my husband – where every good woman belongs no matter how he has betrayed her.

All I want now is to leave behind the memories of life with Muhammad, to go on with my life and try to get beyond the pain and despair that I felt at his hands.

There are rotten men all over the world, and to a certain extent I have only myself to blame because I went into his world and found that I could not be part of it. Along the way I hurt a lot of people, Sepideh perhaps most of all, and by so doing hurt the children who just wanted to be part of a normal and happy family. My only justification is that I knew not what I did until it was too late and then I justified myself by arguing that I was acting morally under the laws that Sepideh adhered to so strongly.

You cannot have it both ways: if you accept uncompromising Islam when it suits you, then you have to accept it all. Islam says a man can have four wives, I told myself, so if they accept the rest they have to accept that. I was wrong; there is no justification for hurting others and there are practices that made sense centuries earlier that no longer have any place in our world.

In the days when I blindly defended the practices of my fellow Muslims I had explained to a doctor friend that all the laws of Islam made sense from the point of view of health. In the days when alcohol was made in unsupervised desert stills, and when people went blind or died from bad booze, it made a great deal of sense to ban it. But today we can educate and control so it is not so important. I told him that even with modern refrigeration people have been known to die after eating bad pork, so anyone legislating for a desert people would forbid it.

He had turned on me truly angry and pointed out that most of the infections he found in his female patients were caused by husbands sleeping around. He explained that when a man had four wives he could not avoid infecting them all; he claimed that healthy bacteria from one womb could cause disease in another. He laughed off my argument that men were ordered to wash after sex and thus could avoid infection. 'Do you, an educated woman, really believe that a bit of soap and water can kill bacteria?' I guess not, for several years later I was myself in agony from that very cross-contamination.

The Fat Man is in an Iranian jail for heaven alone knows what.

Nastaran is sitting at home looking after her Father; she tried to go to work but instead of encouragement she was told that a girl in her position and who didn't need the money should not go out and work. Her sister Nasrin is well on her way to getting a university degree and has grown from still being a child at twenty-four to being a woman of twenty-six.

Homa is finally free in her grave, but her children bear the scars of her life. Their tears will not stop. It is too late to help those who have gone, but we can save ourselves and those women to come after us by changing the system, by being strong and independent and by making our own lives beside our men instead of under their thumbs.

When we have sons we must stop telling them they have a 'golden penis'. We can treat our sons and daughters equally and we can refuse to keep reproducing in the quest for a son.

For myself, I doubt that I will marry again and I fear I may never risk loving a new man. But I hope that one day I will be able to go out bareheaded in the street without feeling somewhere in the back of my mind that I am wicked.

I hope that one day I will stop having dreams that I am being pressed to death under the body of a husband who is stitched to me, or that I am out with bare legs or arms and that the martyrs are about to come and stone me to death.

I long to sit under an Iranian tree and to listen to the sounds and smell the smells of Iran. I want to be woken one more time by the sound of a street vendor trying to drum up business.

Most of all I want to stand on Vali-e-Asr one day and take a deep, free breath of Iranian air. I hope one day the dreams of the past will disappear and the dreams and hopes for the future will become reality.

I pray that one day I will stand side by side with my sisters and brothers in Islam in a country that remembers that the Koran was written in the Name of God the Merciful and the Compassionate. The Prophet Mohammad (AS) was centuries ahead of his time and the Koran a miracle of enlightenment. If we, the Muslims of today, insist in living centuries behind our time then we betray our faith and our souls.

The Beginning